殲鬼戦記

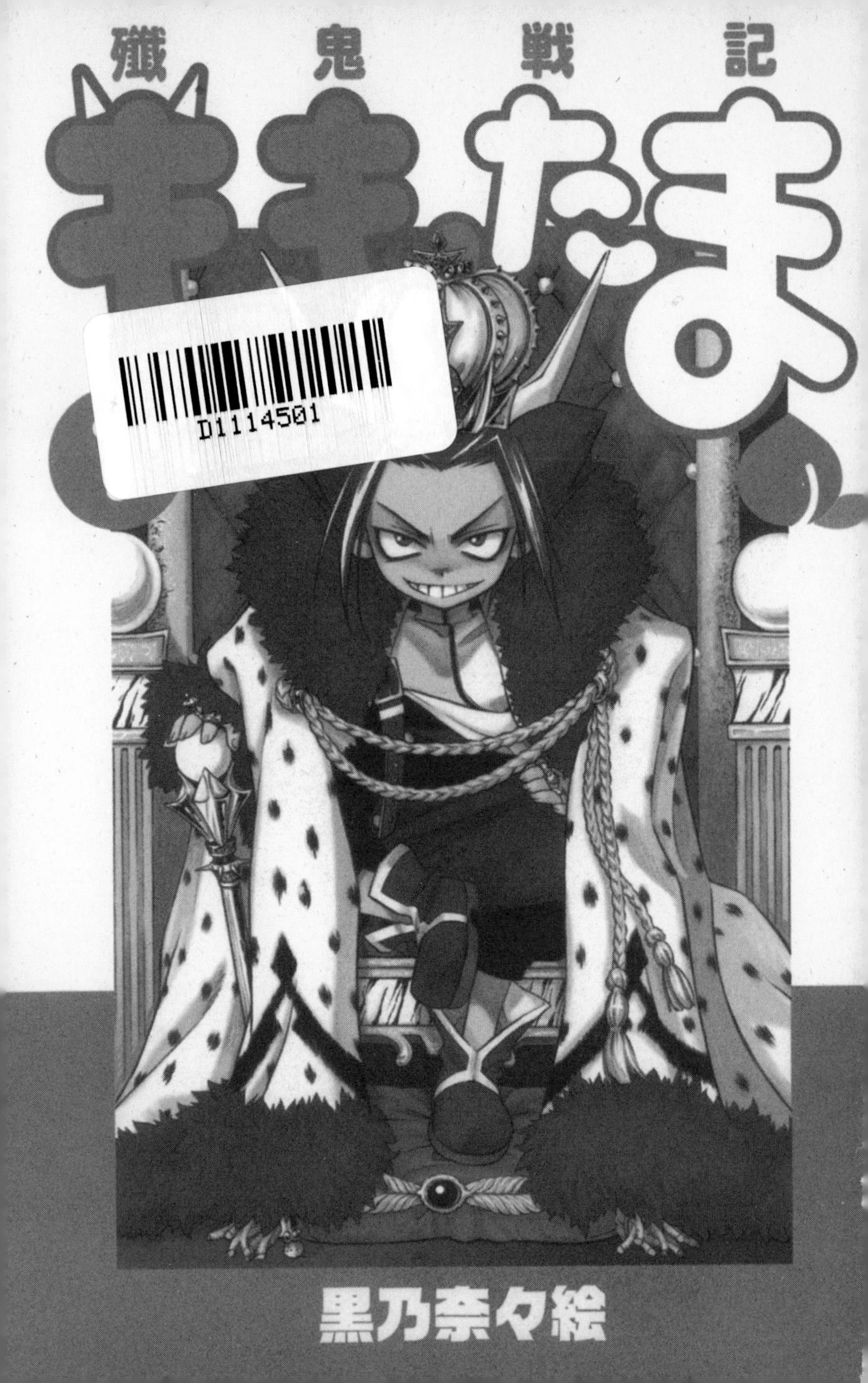

黒乃奈々絵

Momo Tama Vol. 1
Story and Art by NANAE CHRONO

Translation - Beni Axia Conrad
English Adaptation - Lorelei Laird
Retouch and Lettering - Star Print Brokers
Production Artist - Vicente Rivera, Jr.
Graphic Designer - Erika Terriquez

Editor - Hyun Joo Kim
Pre-Production Supervisor - Vicente Rivera, Jr.
Print-Production Specialist - Lucas Rivera
Managing Editor - Vy Nguyen
Senior Designer - Louis Csontos
Senior Designer - James Lee
Senior Editor - Bryce P. Coleman
Senior Editor - Jenna Winterberg
Associate Publisher - Marco F. Pavia
President and C.O.O. - John Parker
C.E.O. and Chief Creative Officer - Stu Levy

A **TOKYOPOP** Manga

TOKYOPOP and 🐢 are trademarks or registered trademarks of TOKYOPOP Inc.

TOKYOPOP Inc.
5900 Wilshire Blvd. Suite 2000
Los Angeles, CA 90036

E-mail: info@TOKYOPOP.com
Come visit us online at www.TOKYOPOP.com

ISBN: 978-1-4278-1109-7

First TOKYOPOP printing: January 2009
10 9 8 7 6 5 4 3 2 1
Printed in the USA

Volume 1

Story and Art by
NANAE CHRONO

HAMBURG // LONDON // LOS ANGELES // TOKYO

MOMOTAMA

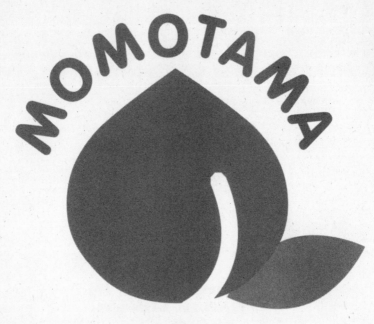

CONTENTS

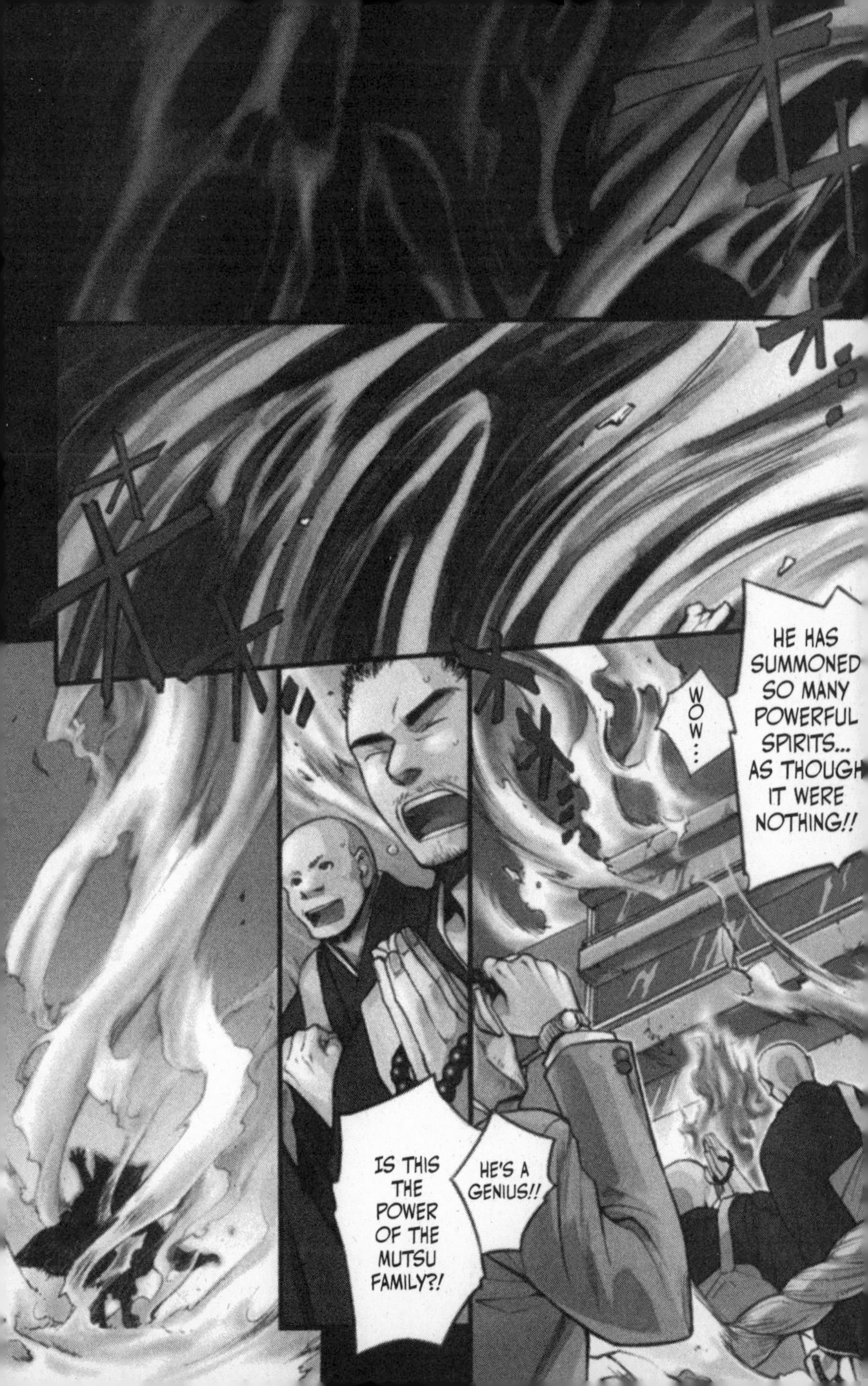
HE HAS SUMMONED SO MANY POWERFUL SPIRITS... AS THOUGH IT WERE NOTHING!!
WOW...
HE'S A GENIUS!!
IS THIS THE POWER OF THE MUTSU FAMILY?!

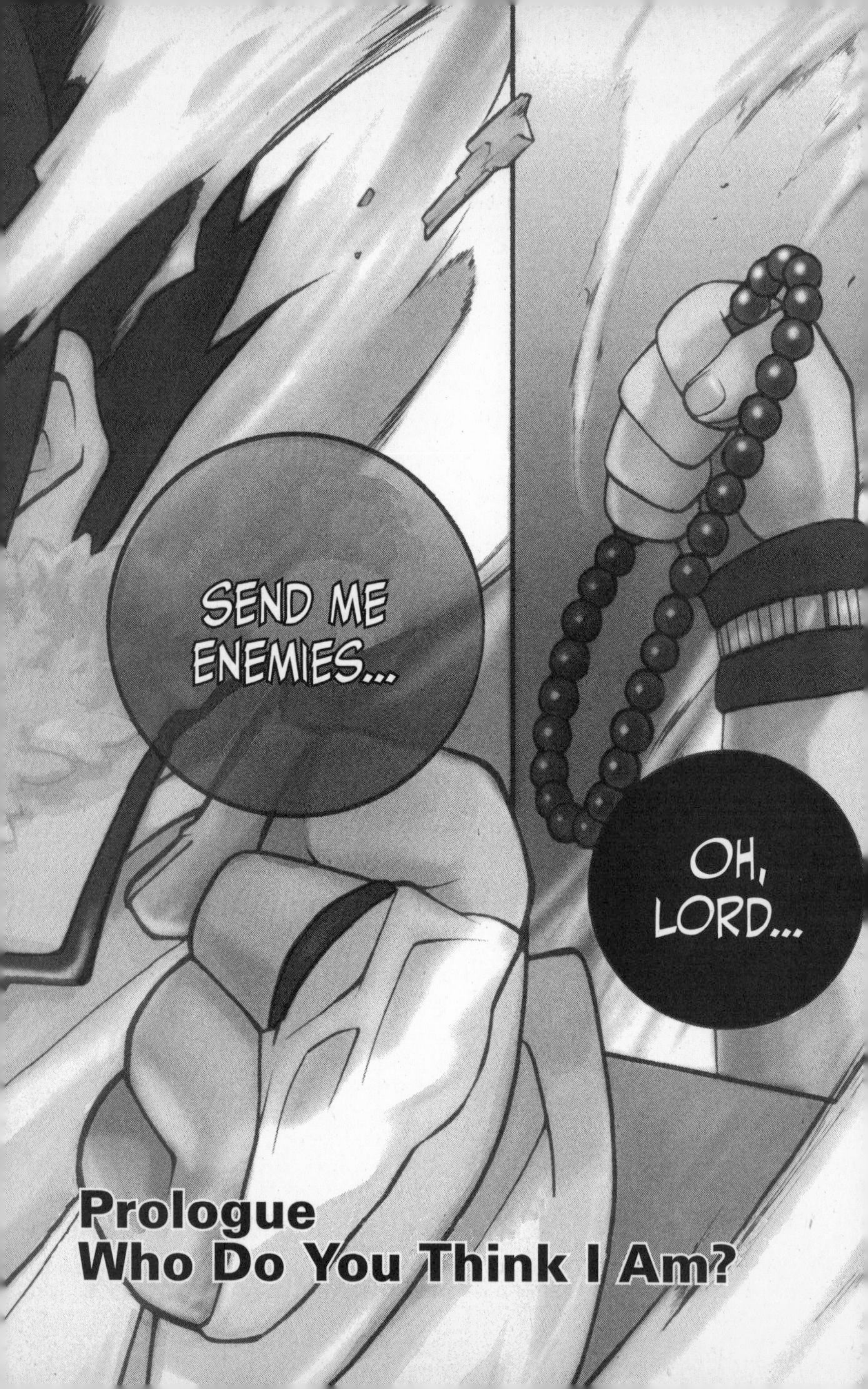
OH, LORD...
SEND ME ENEMIES...

Prologue
Who Do You Think I Am?

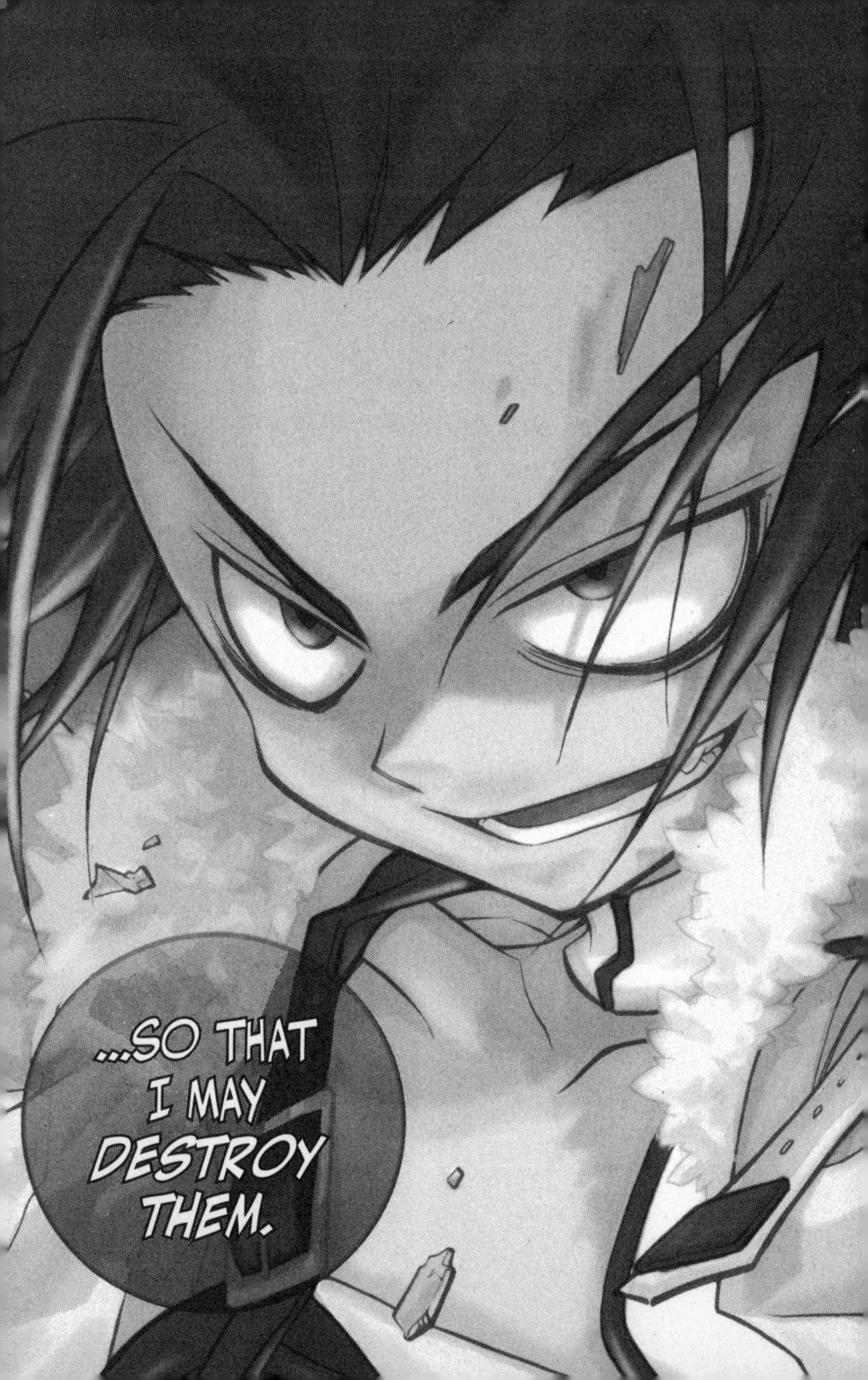
...SO THAT I MAY DESTROY THEM.

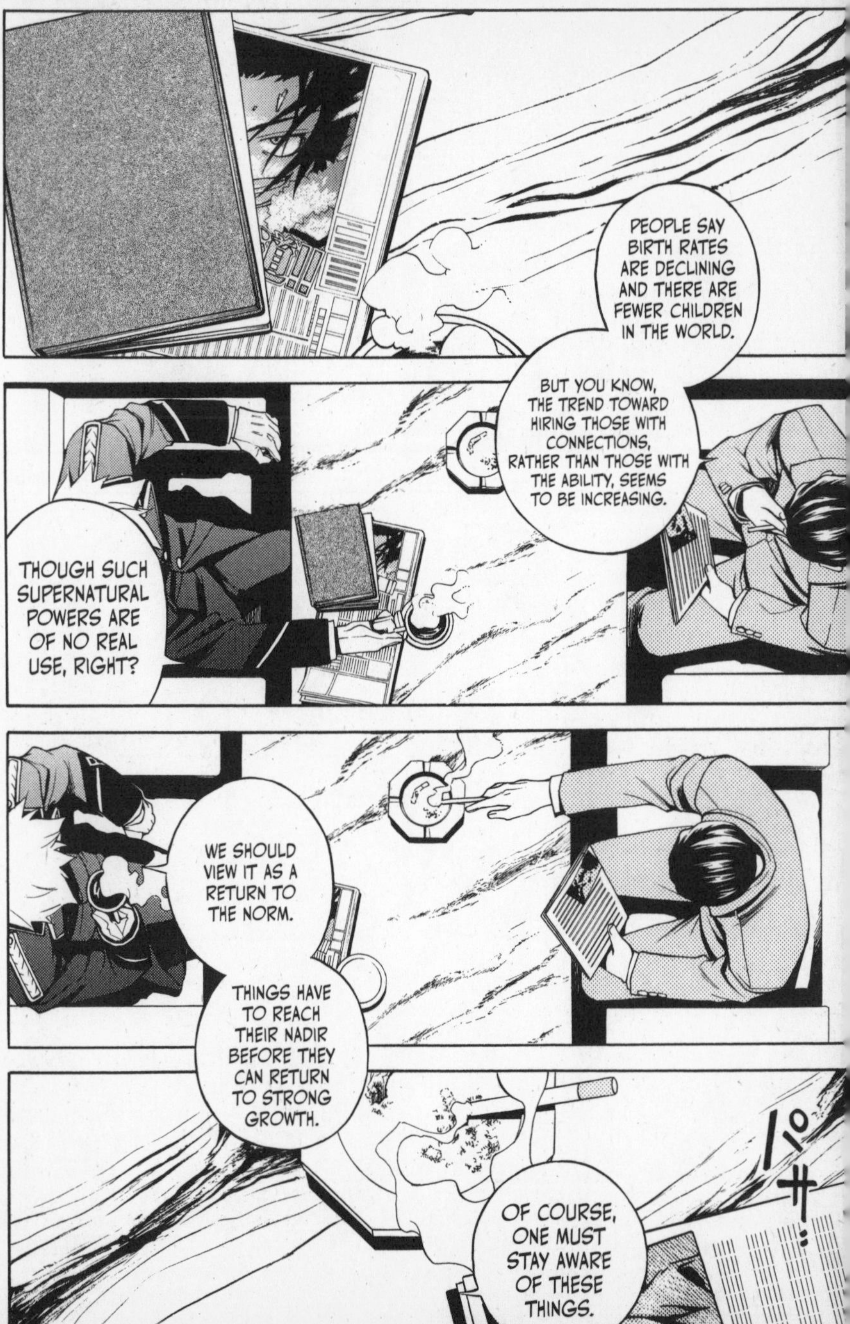
PEOPLE SAY BIRTH RATES ARE DECLINING AND THERE ARE FEWER CHILDREN IN THE WORLD.
BUT YOU KNOW, THE TREND TOWARD HIRING THOSE WITH CONNECTIONS, RATHER THAN THOSE WITH THE ABILITY, SEEMS TO BE INCREASING.
THOUGH SUCH SUPERNATURAL POWERS ARE OF NO REAL USE, RIGHT?
WE SHOULD VIEW IT AS A RETURN TO THE NORM.
THINGS HAVE TO REACH THEIR NADIR BEFORE THEY CAN RETURN TO STRONG GROWTH.
OF COURSE, ONE MUST STAY AWARE OF THESE THINGS.

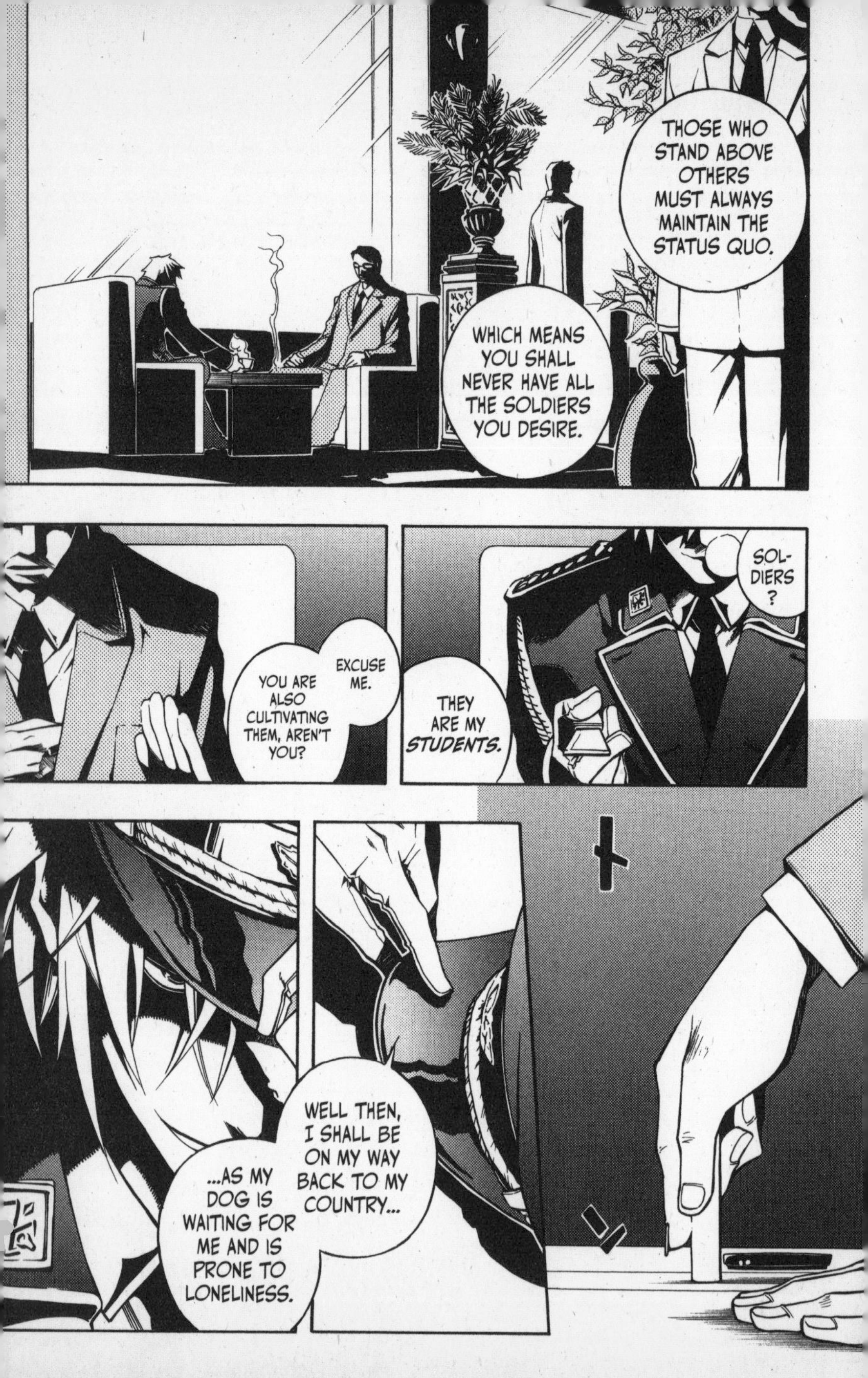
THOSE WHO STAND ABOVE OTHERS MUST ALWAYS MAINTAIN THE STATUS QUO.
WHICH MEANS YOU SHALL NEVER HAVE ALL THE SOLDIERS YOU DESIRE.
SOL-DIERS?
THEY ARE MY *STUDENTS*.
EXCUSE ME.
YOU ARE ALSO CULTIVATING THEM, AREN'T YOU?
WELL THEN, I SHALL BE ON MY WAY BACK TO MY COUNTRY...
...AS MY DOG IS WAITING FOR ME AND IS PRONE TO LONELINESS.

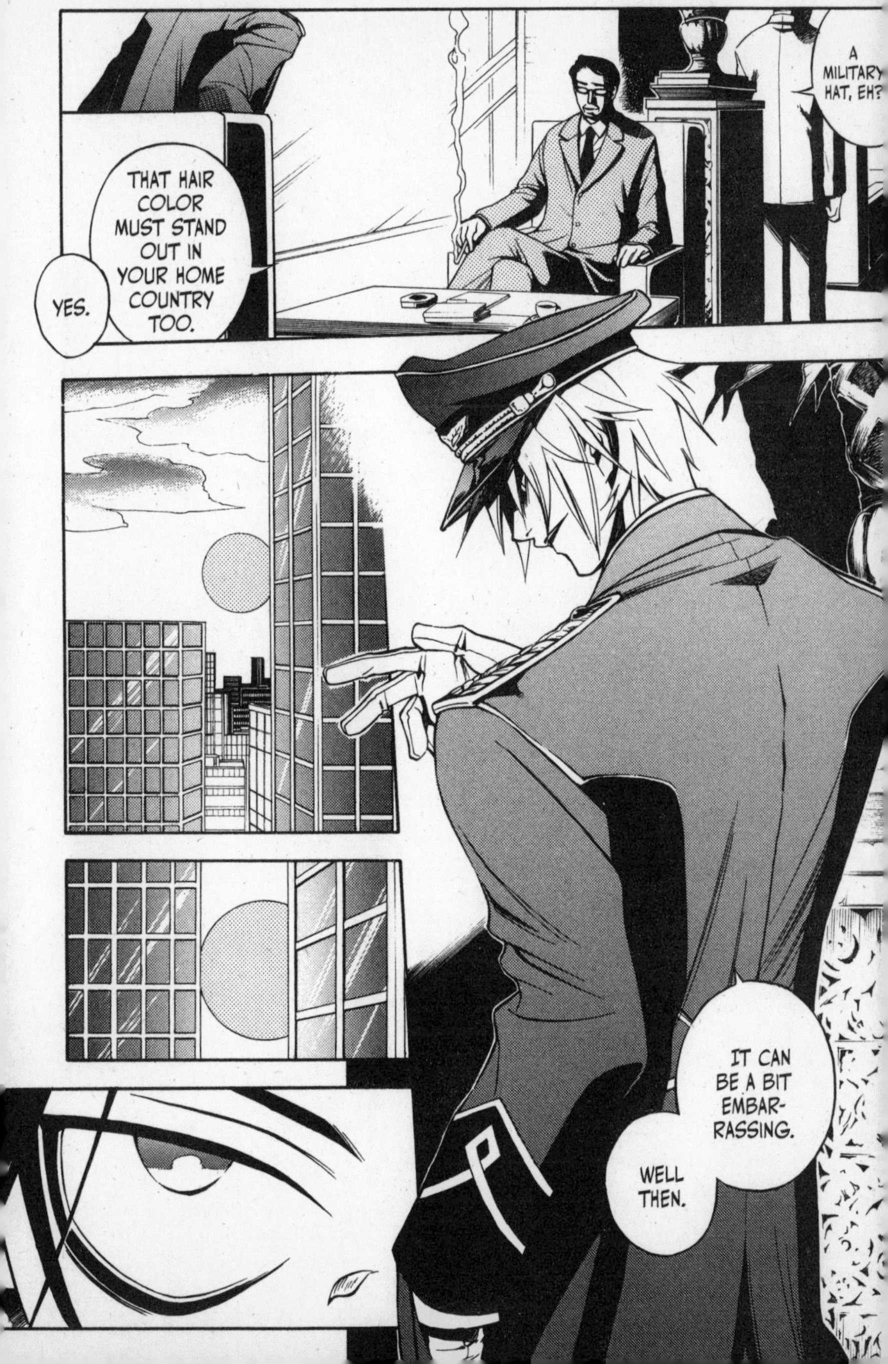
A MILITARY HAT, EH?
THAT HAIR COLOR MUST STAND OUT IN YOUR HOME COUNTRY TOO.
YES.
IT CAN BE A BIT EMBAR-RASSING.
WELL THEN.

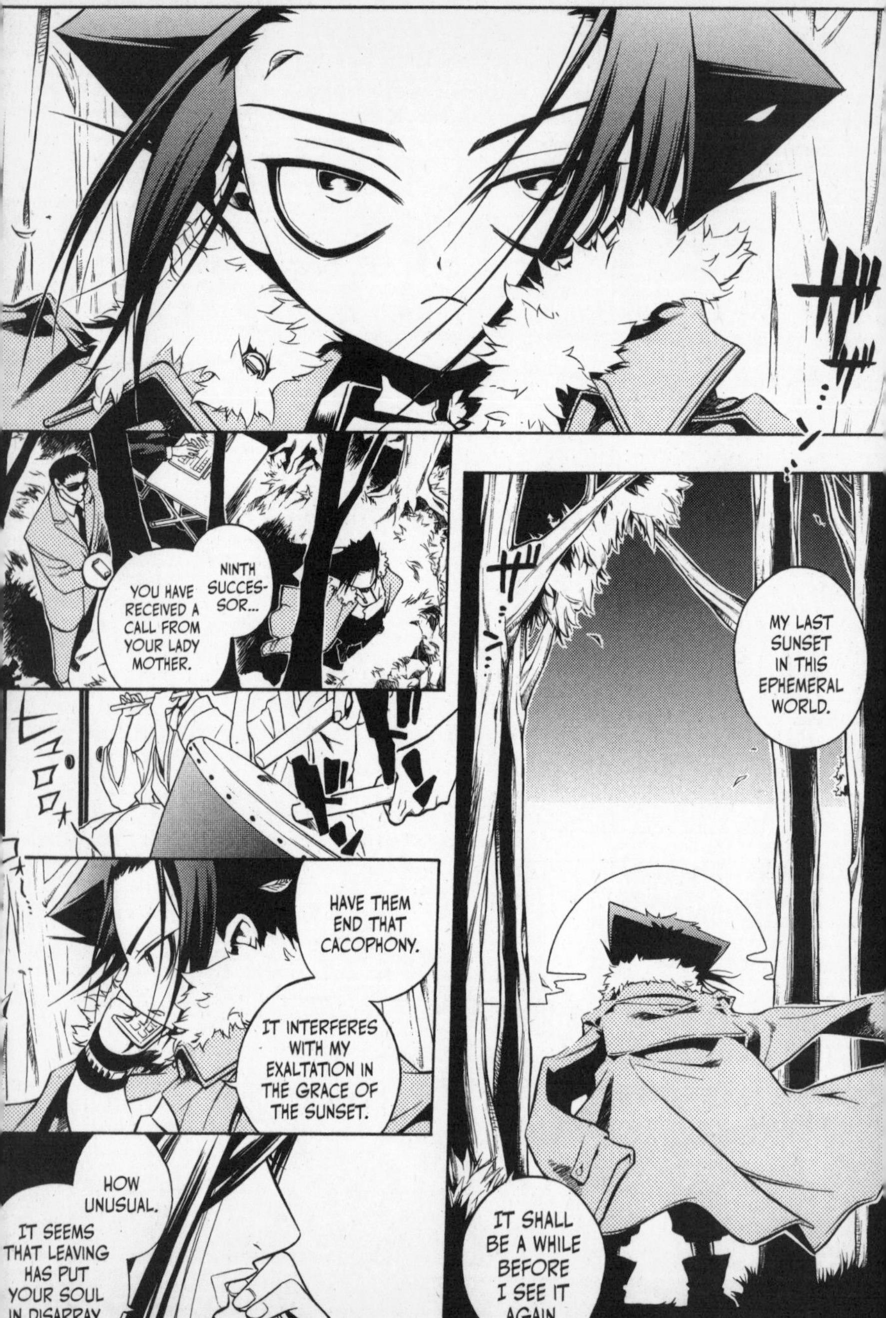
MY LAST SUNSET IN THIS EPHEMERAL WORLD.
IT SHALL BE A WHILE BEFORE I SEE IT AGAIN.
NINTH SUCCES-SOR...
YOU HAVE RECEIVED A CALL FROM YOUR LADY MOTHER.
HAVE THEM END THAT CACOPHONY.
IT INTERFERES WITH MY EXALTATION IN THE GRACE OF THE SUNSET.
HOW UNUSUAL.
IT SEEMS THAT LEAVING HAS PUT YOUR SOUL IN DISARRAY.

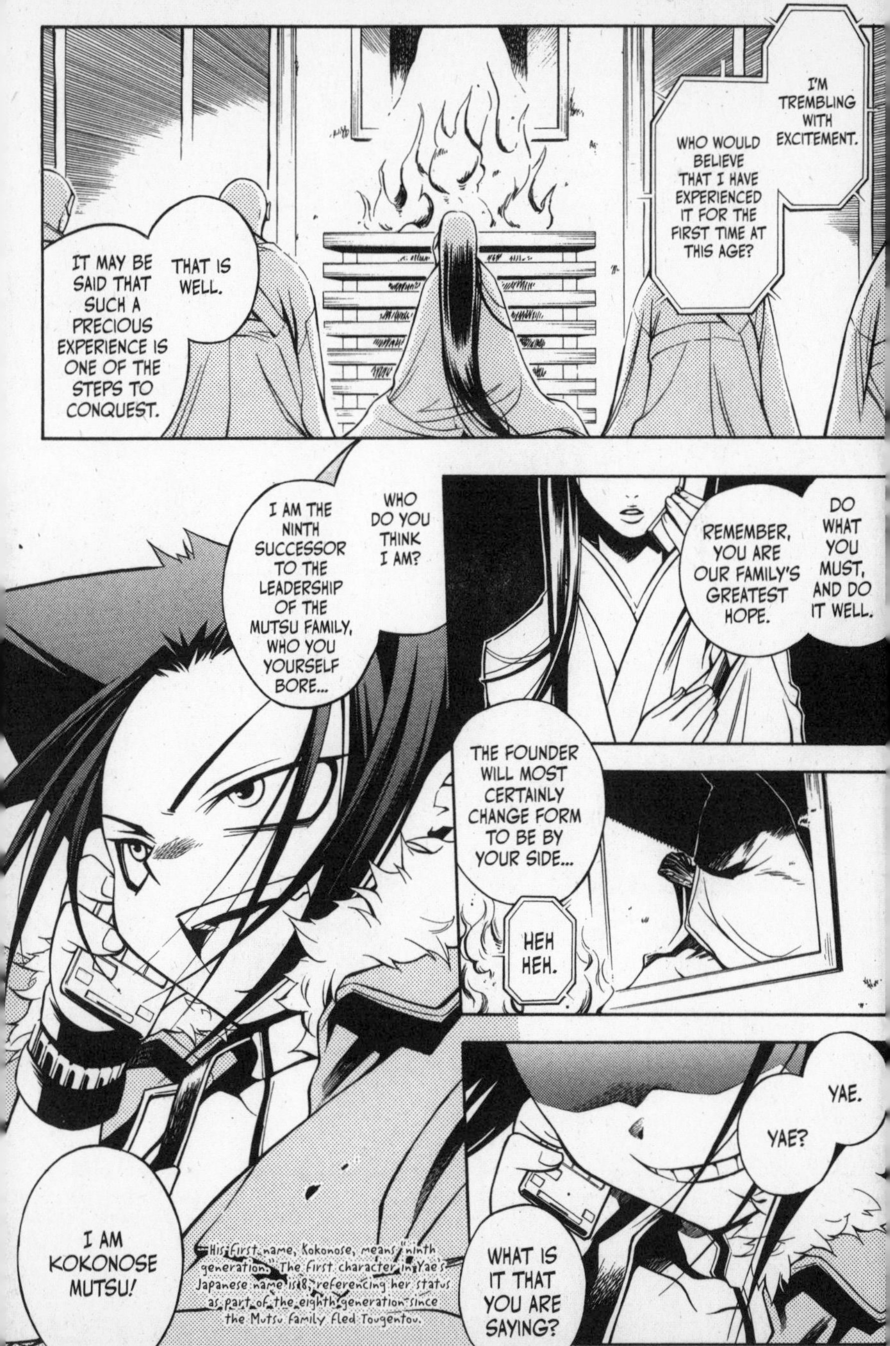
I'M TREMBLING WITH EXCITEMENT.
WHO WOULD BELIEVE THAT I HAVE EXPERIENCED IT FOR THE FIRST TIME AT THIS AGE?
THAT IS WELL.
IT MAY BE SAID THAT SUCH A PRECIOUS EXPERIENCE IS ONE OF THE STEPS TO CONQUEST.
DO WHAT YOU MUST, AND DO IT WELL.
REMEMBER, YOU ARE OUR FAMILY'S GREATEST HOPE.
THE FOUNDER WILL MOST CERTAINLY CHANGE FORM TO BE BY YOUR SIDE...
HEH HEH.
YAE.
YAE?
WHAT IS IT THAT YOU ARE SAYING?
WHO DO YOU THINK I AM?
I AM THE NINTH SUCCESSOR TO THE LEADERSHIP OF THE MUTSU FAMILY, WHO YOU YOURSELF BORE...
I AM KOKONOSE MUTSU!
His first name, Kokonose, means "ninth generation." The first character in Yae's Japanese name is 8, referencing her status as part of the eighth generation since the Mutsu family fled Tougentou.

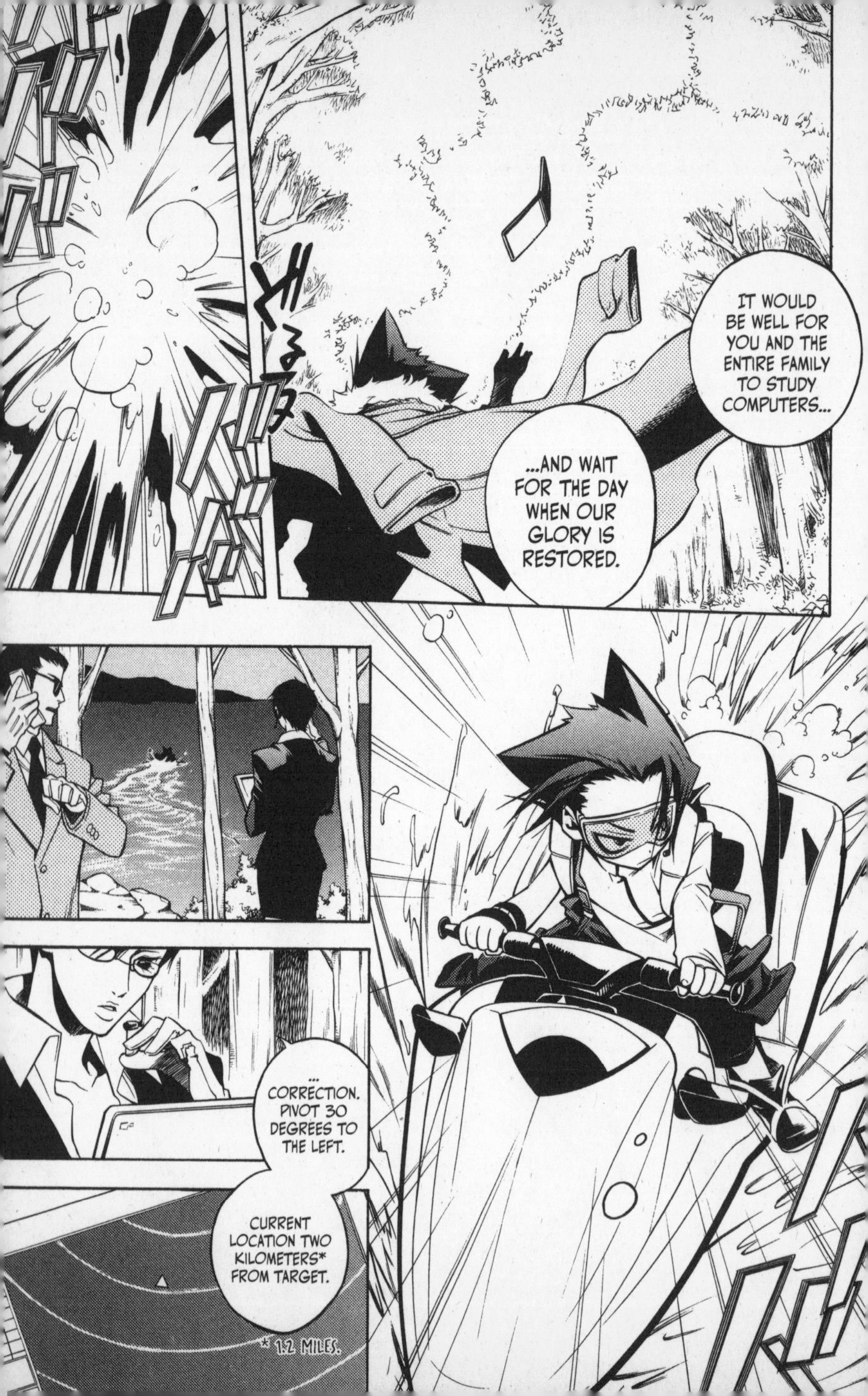
IT WOULD BE WELL FOR YOU AND THE ENTIRE FAMILY TO STUDY COMPUTERS...
...AND WAIT FOR THE DAY WHEN OUR GLORY IS RESTORED.
... CORRECTION. PIVOT 30 DEGREES TO THE LEFT.
CURRENT LOCATION TWO KILOMETERS* FROM TARGET.
* 1.2 MILES.

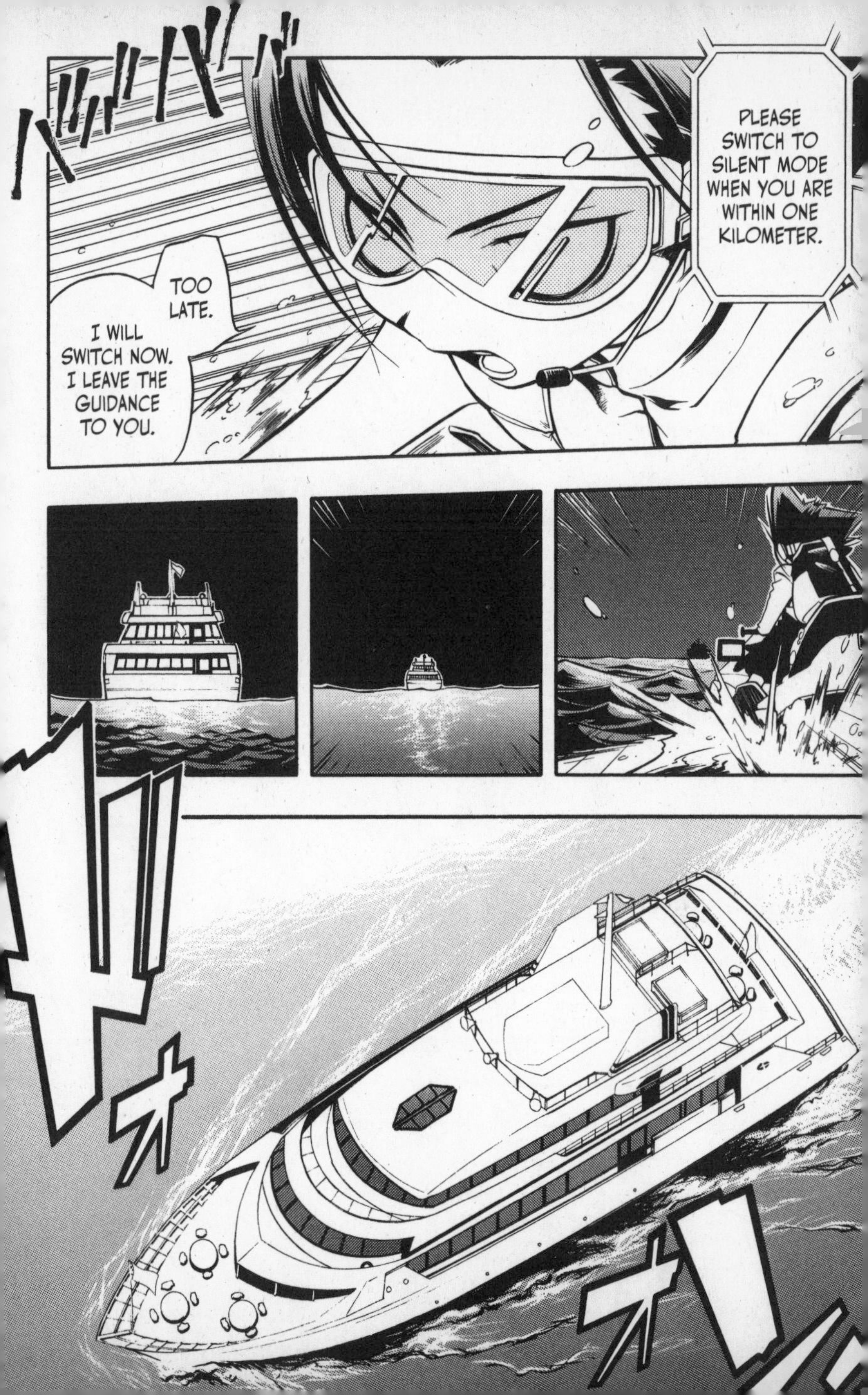
PLEASE SWITCH TO SILENT MODE WHEN YOU ARE WITHIN ONE KILOMETER.
TOO LATE.
I WILL SWITCH NOW. I LEAVE THE GUIDANCE TO YOU.

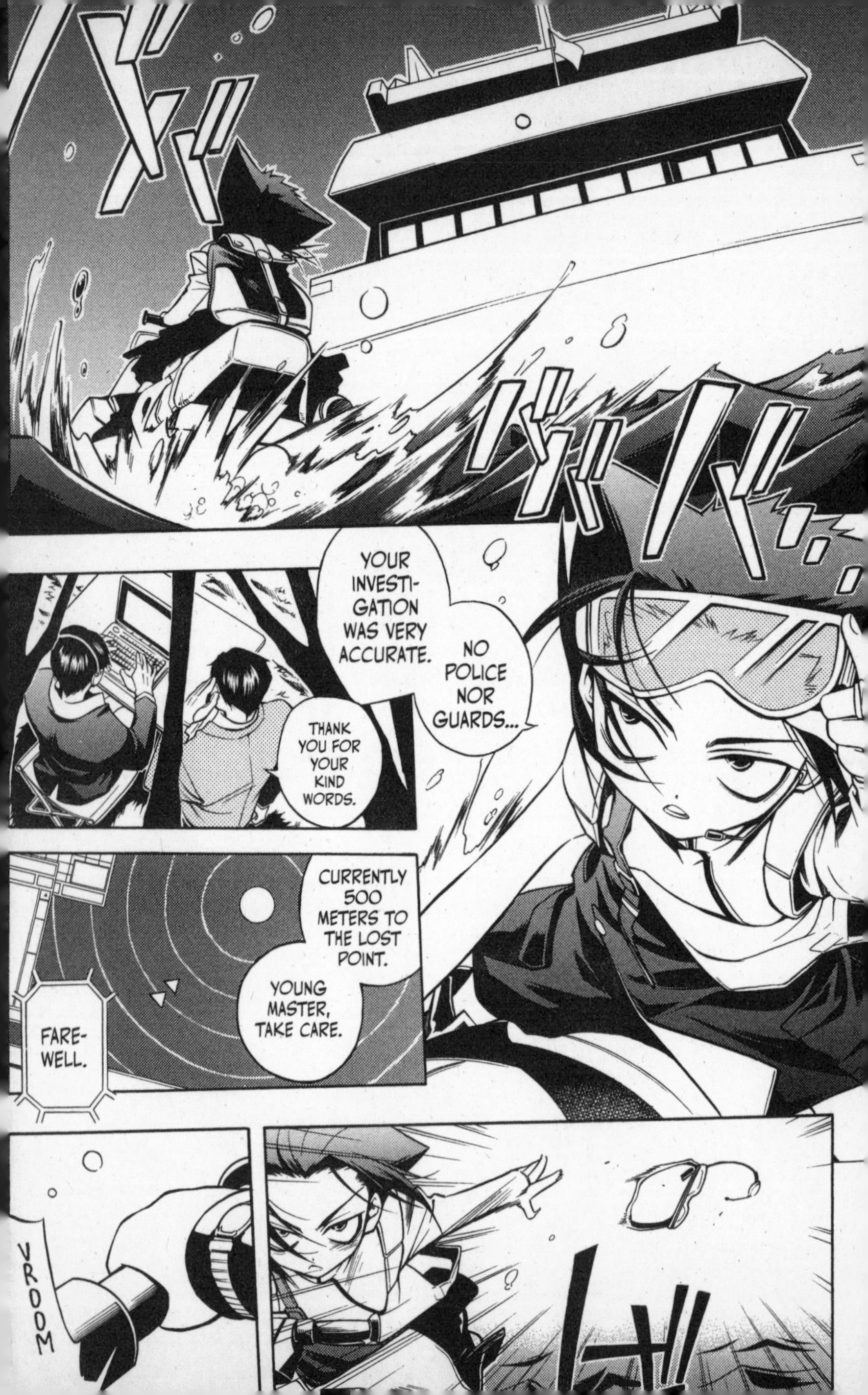
YOUR INVESTI-GATION WAS VERY ACCURATE.
NO POLICE NOR GUARDS...
THANK YOU FOR YOUR KIND WORDS.
CURRENTLY 500 METERS TO THE LOST POINT.
YOUNG MASTER, TAKE CARE.
FARE-WELL.
VROOOM

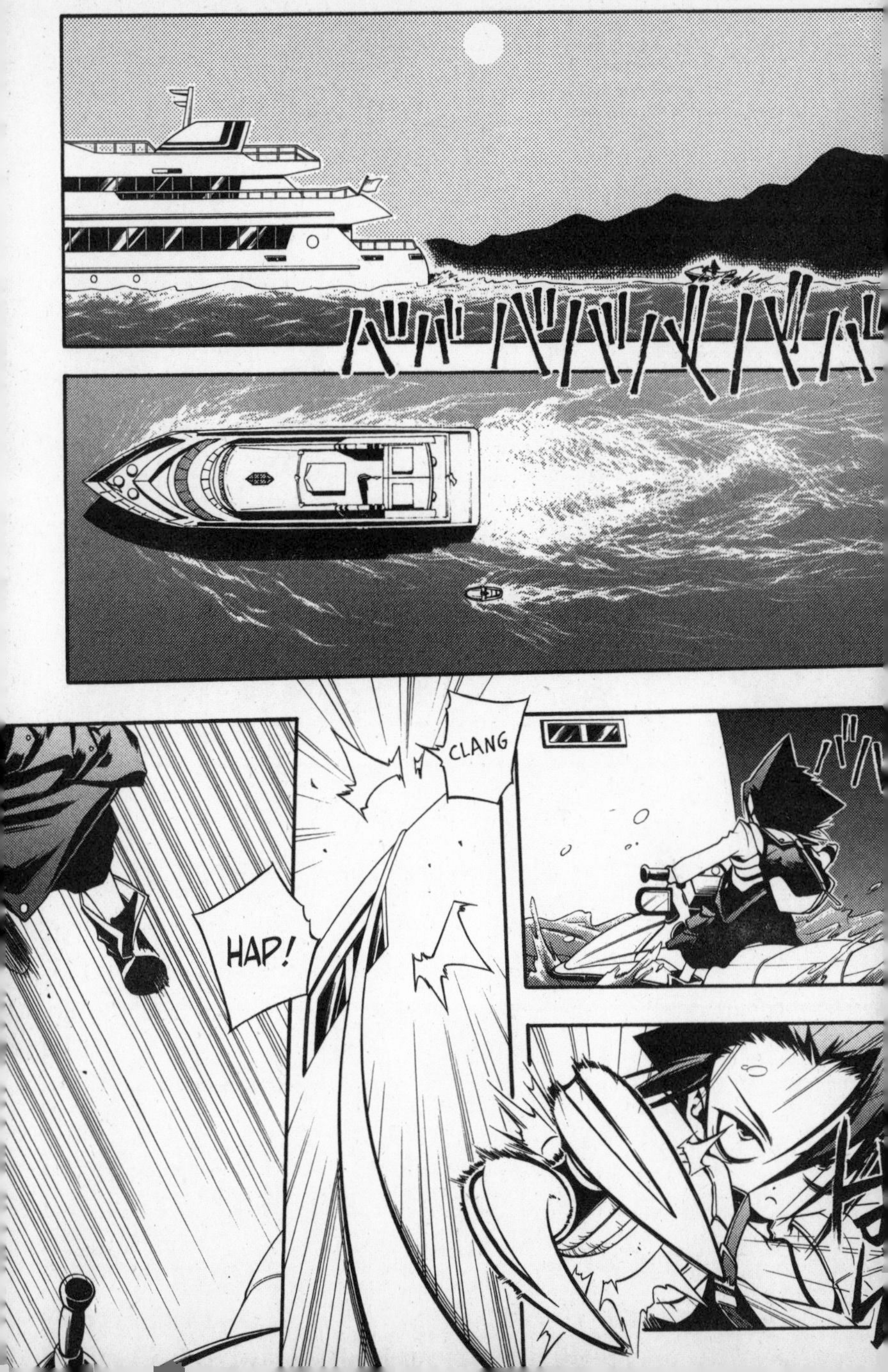
CLANG
HAP!

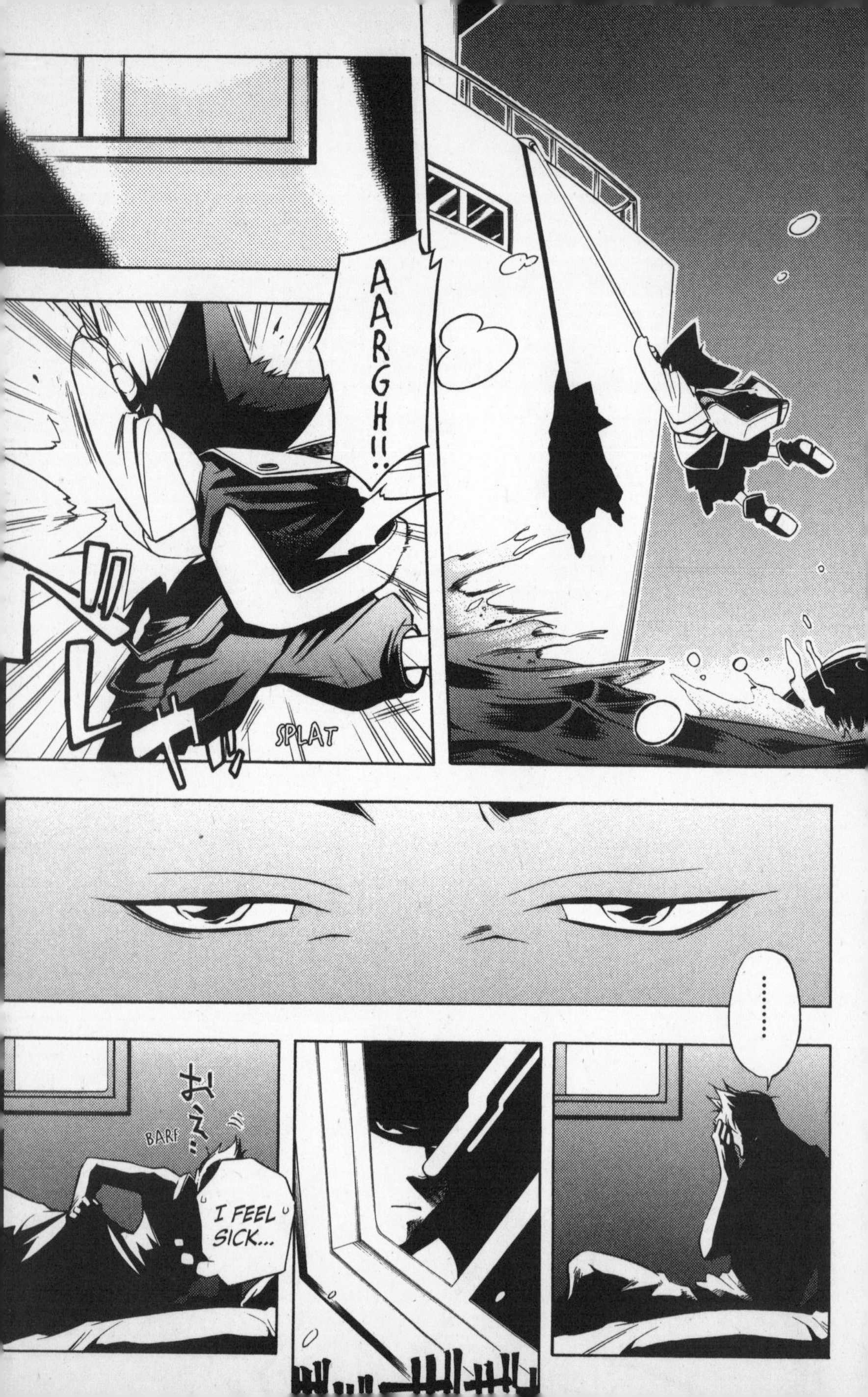
AARGH!!
SPLAT
......
おえ
BARF
I FEEL SICK...

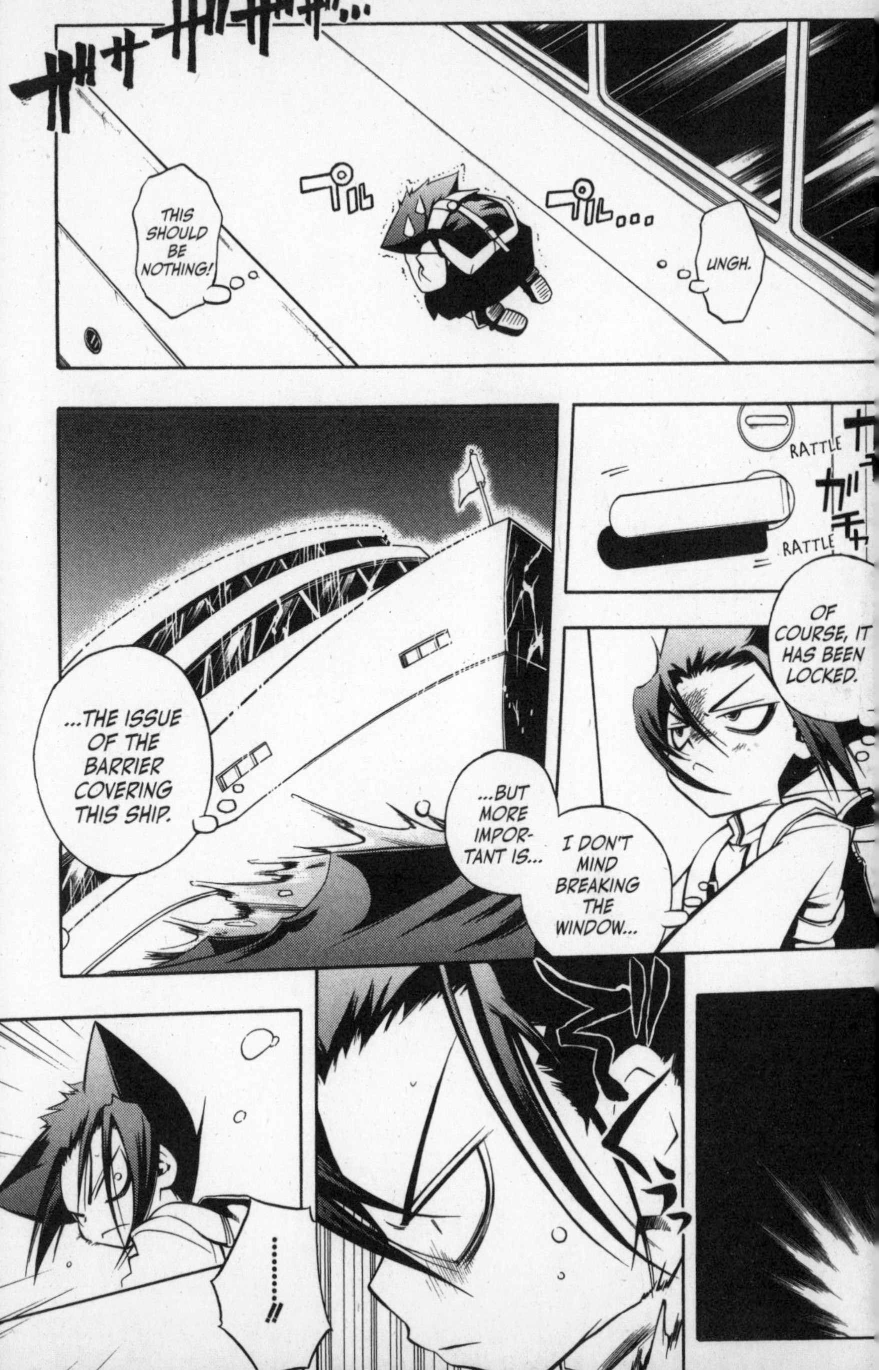
UNGH.
THIS SHOULD BE NOTHING!
RATTLE
RATTLE
OF COURSE, IT HAS BEEN LOCKED.
I DON'T MIND BREAKING THE WINDOW...
...BUT MORE IMPORTANT IS...
...THE ISSUE OF THE BARRIER COVERING THIS SHIP.

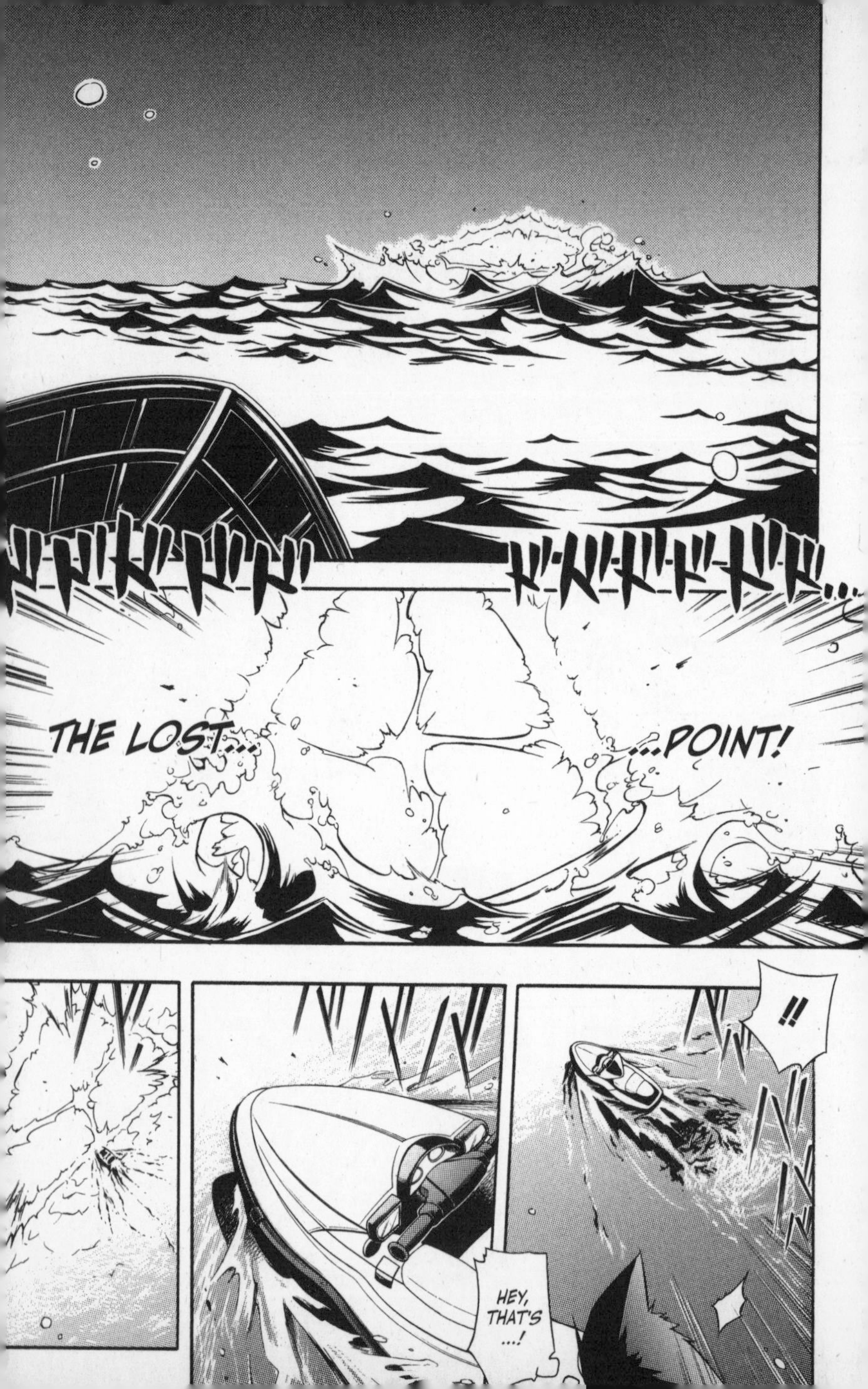
THE LOST...
...POINT!
!!
HEY, THAT'S ...!

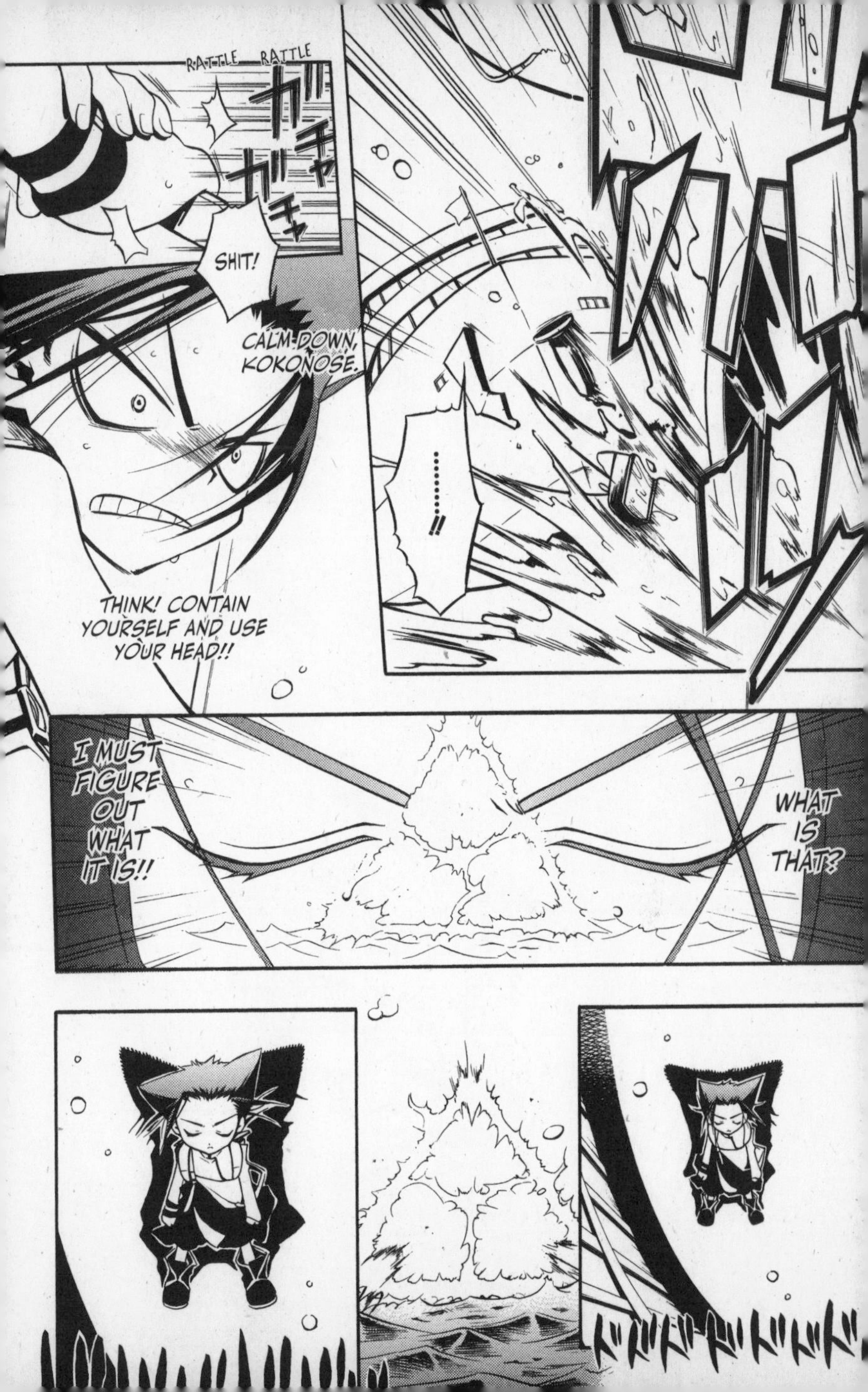
........!!
RATTLE RATTLE
SHIT!
CALM DOWN, KOKONOSE.
THINK! CONTAIN YOURSELF AND USE YOUR HEAD!!
WHAT IS THAT?
I MUST FIGURE OUT WHAT IT IS!!

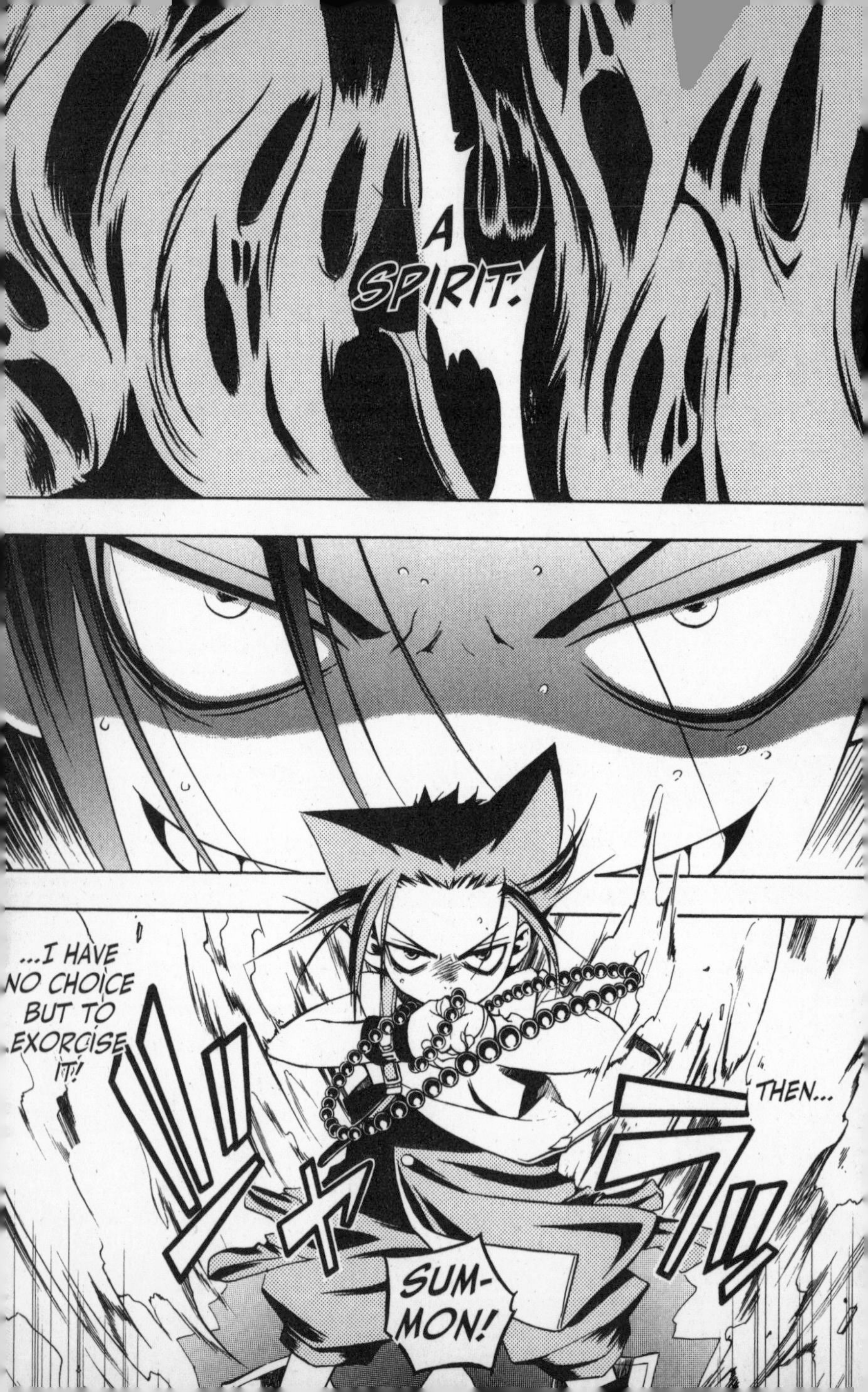
A SPIRIT.
THEN...
...I HAVE NO CHOICE BUT TO EXORCISE IT!
SUM-MON!

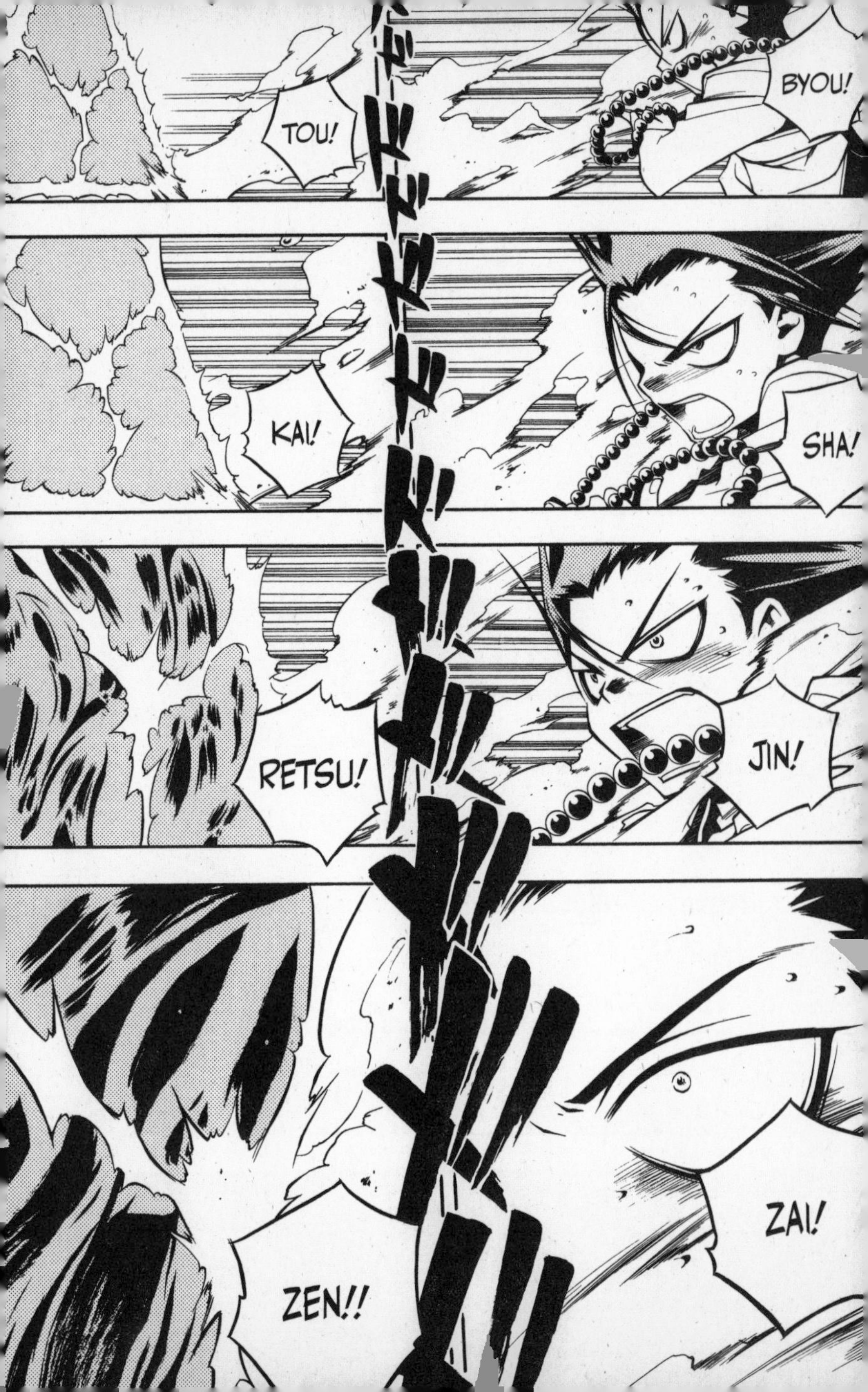

BYOU!
TOU!
SHA!
KAI!
JIN!
RETSU!
ZAI!
ZEN!!

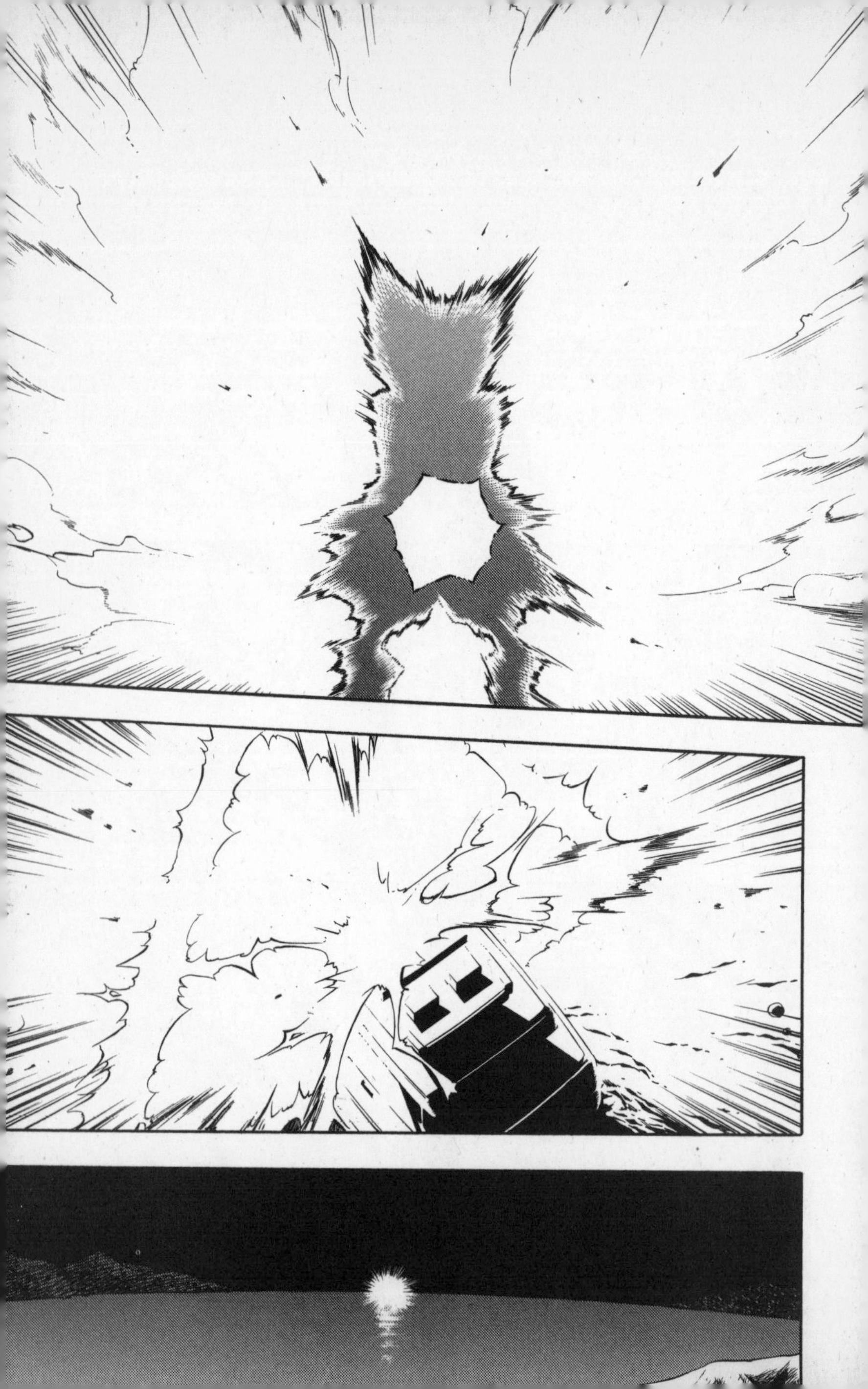

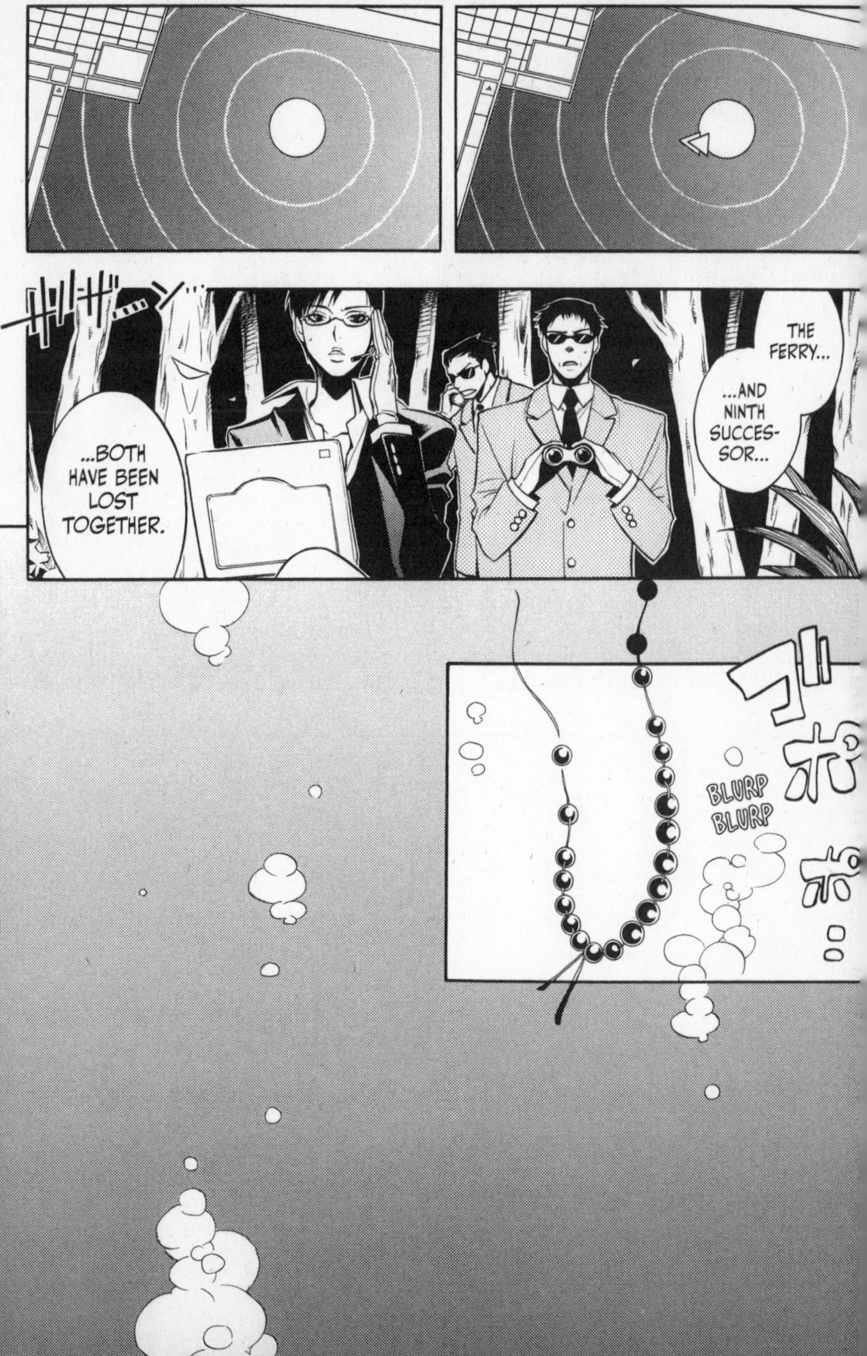
THE FERRY...
...AND NINTH SUCCESSOR...
...BOTH HAVE BEEN LOST TOGETHER.
BLURP BLURP

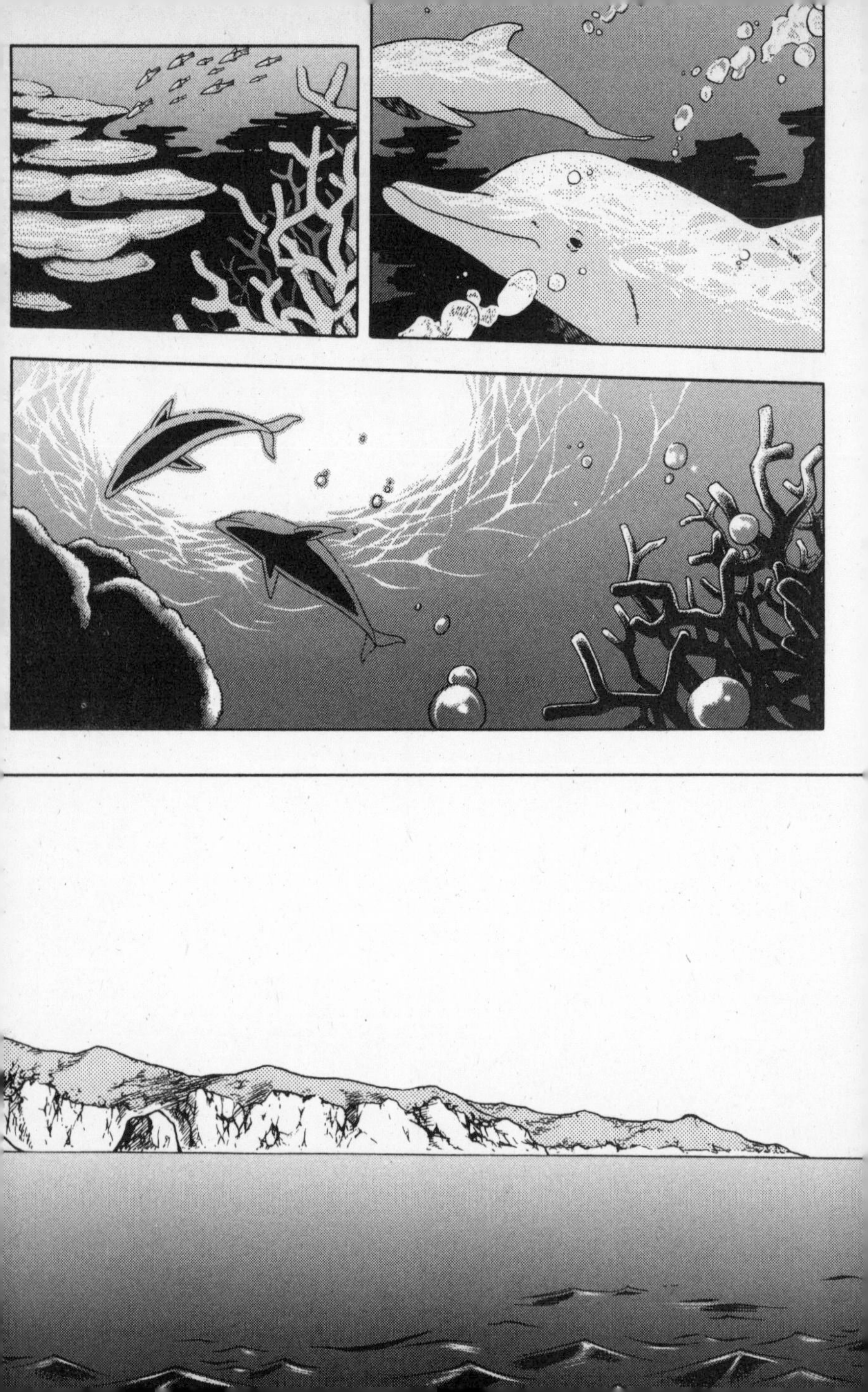

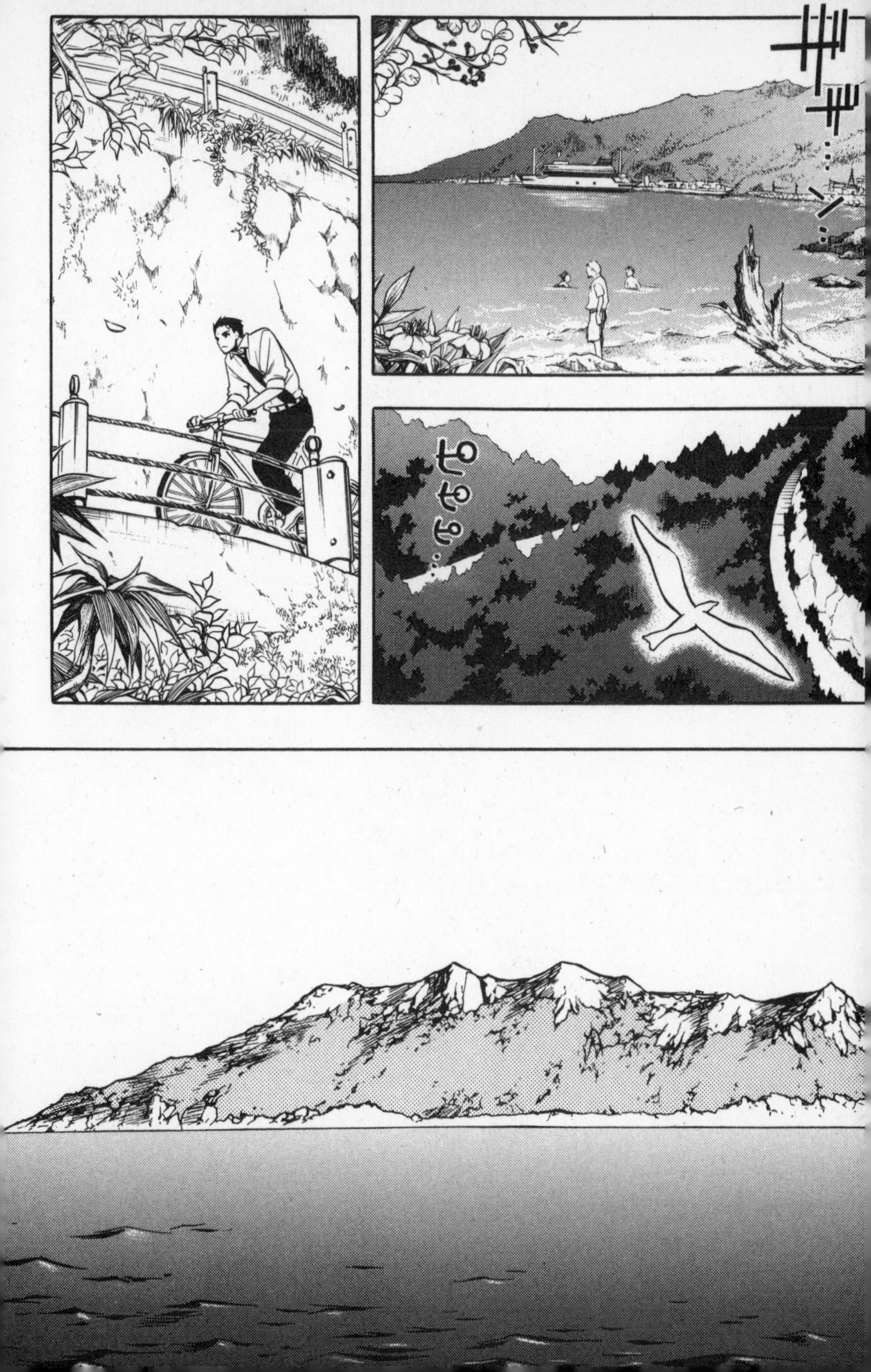
ザザ…ン…

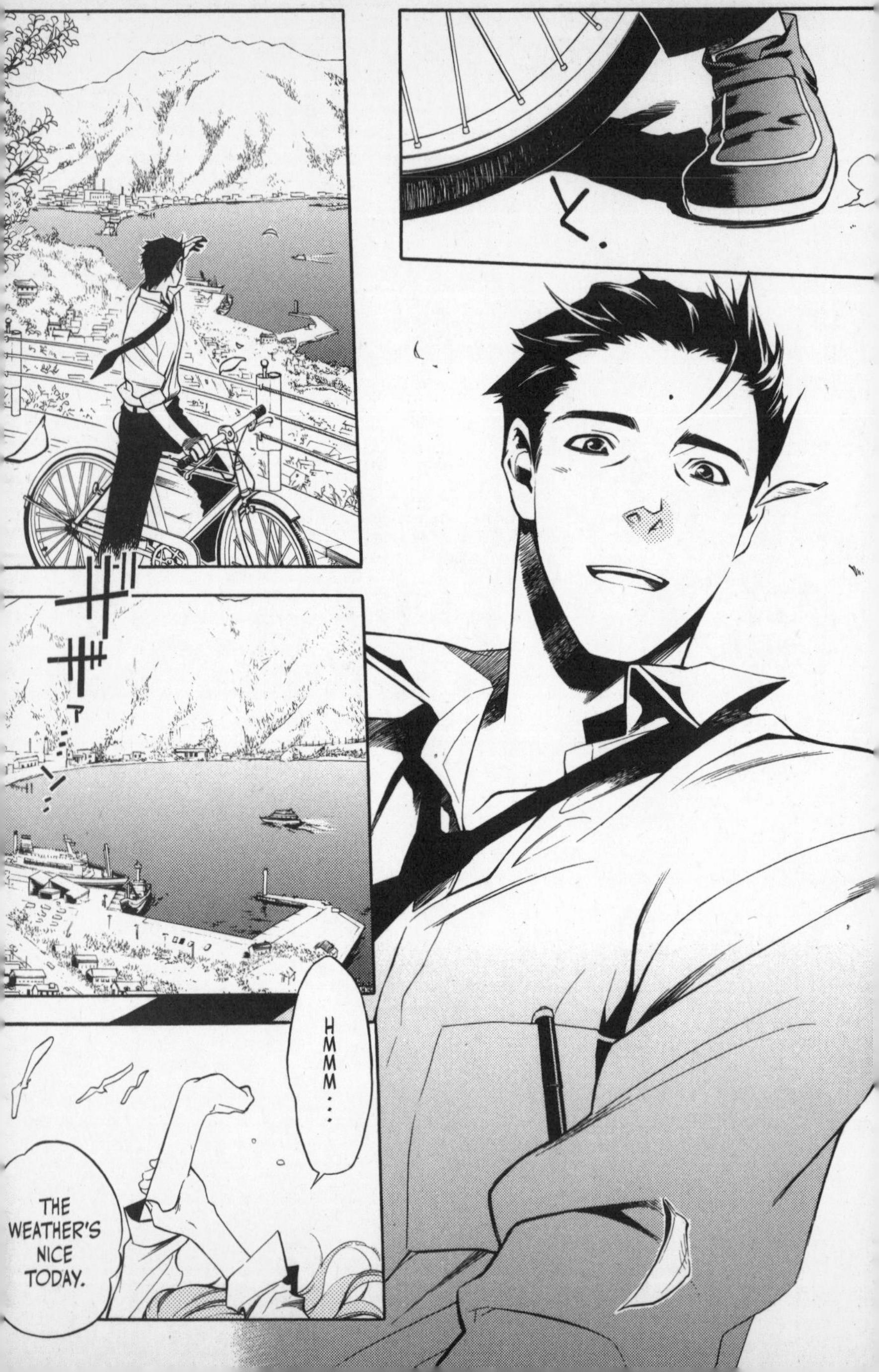
と.
ザザァ
HMMM...
THE WEATHER'S NICE TODAY.

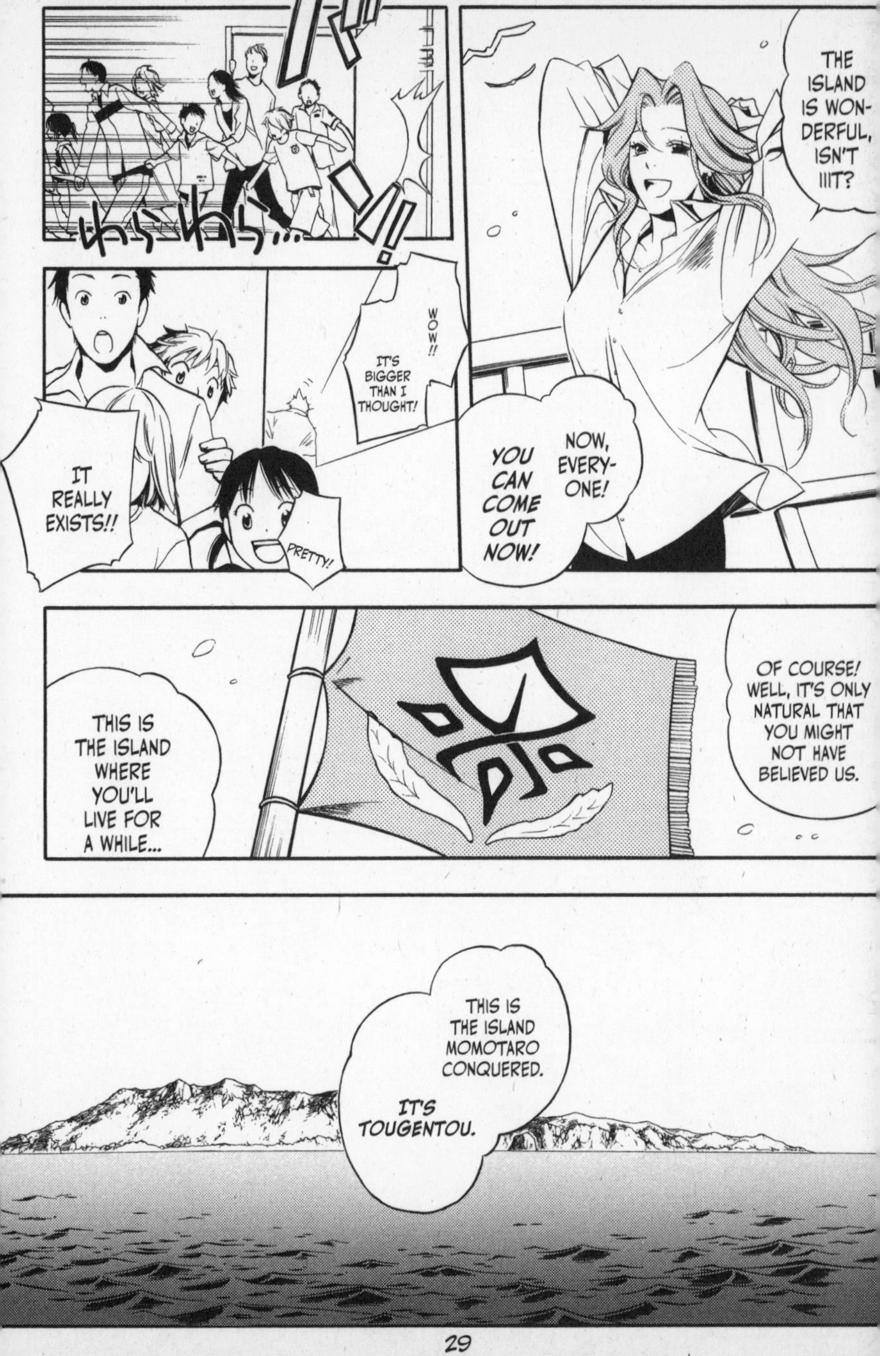
THE ISLAND IS WONDERFUL, ISN'T IIIT?
NOW, EVERYONE!
YOU CAN COME OUT NOW!
わらわら…
WOW!!
IT'S BIGGER THAN I THOUGHT!
PRETTY!
IT REALLY EXISTS!!
OF COURSE! WELL, IT'S ONLY NATURAL THAT YOU MIGHT NOT HAVE BELIEVED US.
THIS IS THE ISLAND WHERE YOU'LL LIVE FOR A WHILE...
THIS IS THE ISLAND MOMOTARO CONQUERED.
IT'S TOUGENTOU.

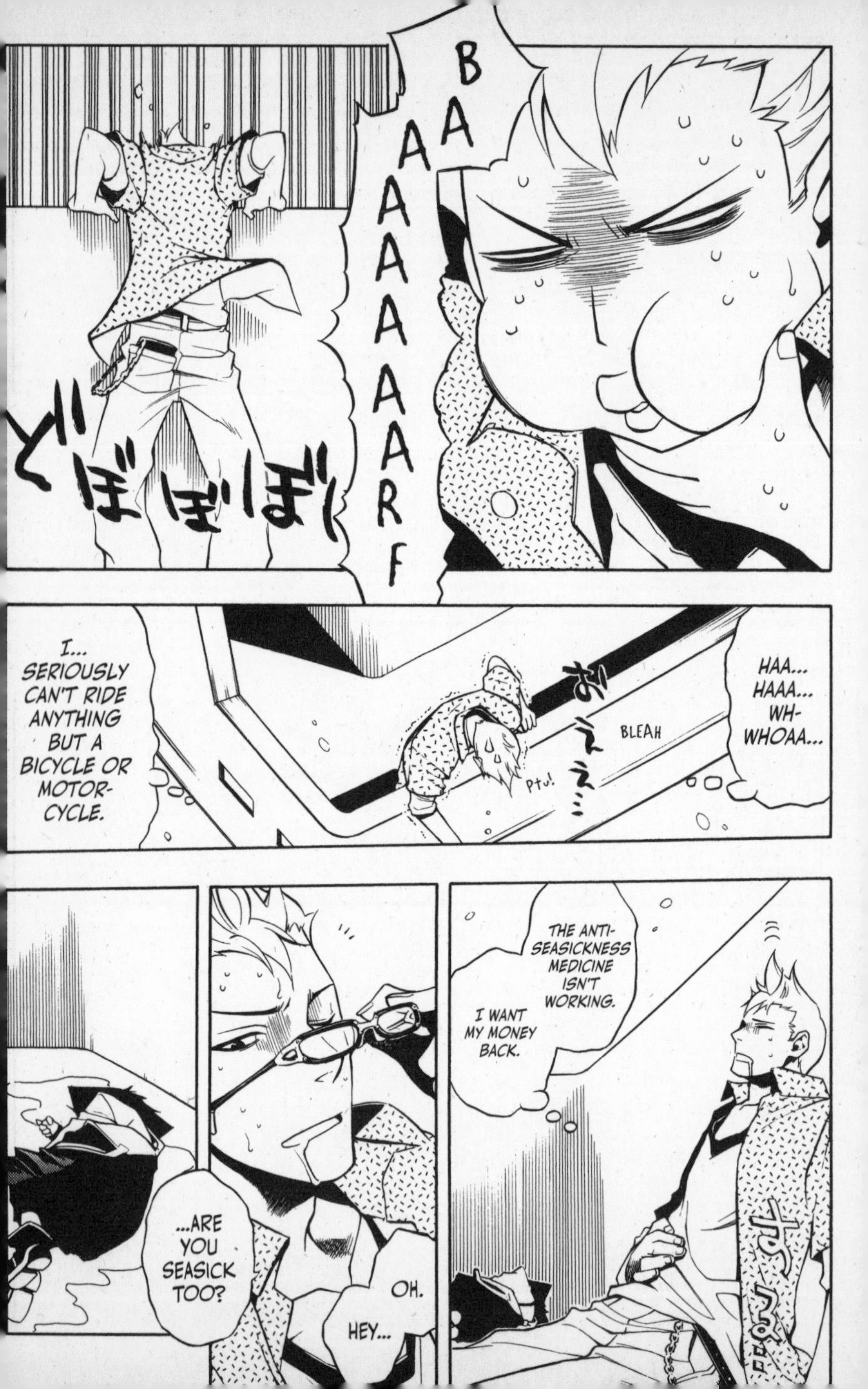
BAAAAAAAARF
どぼぼぼ
HAA... HAAA... WH- WHOAA...
おえぇ…
BLEAH
Ptu!
I... SERIOUSLY CAN'T RIDE ANYTHING BUT A BICYCLE OR MOTOR-CYCLE.
THE ANTI-SEASICKNESS MEDICINE ISN'T WORKING.
I WANT MY MONEY BACK.
OH.
HEY...
...ARE YOU SEASICK TOO?

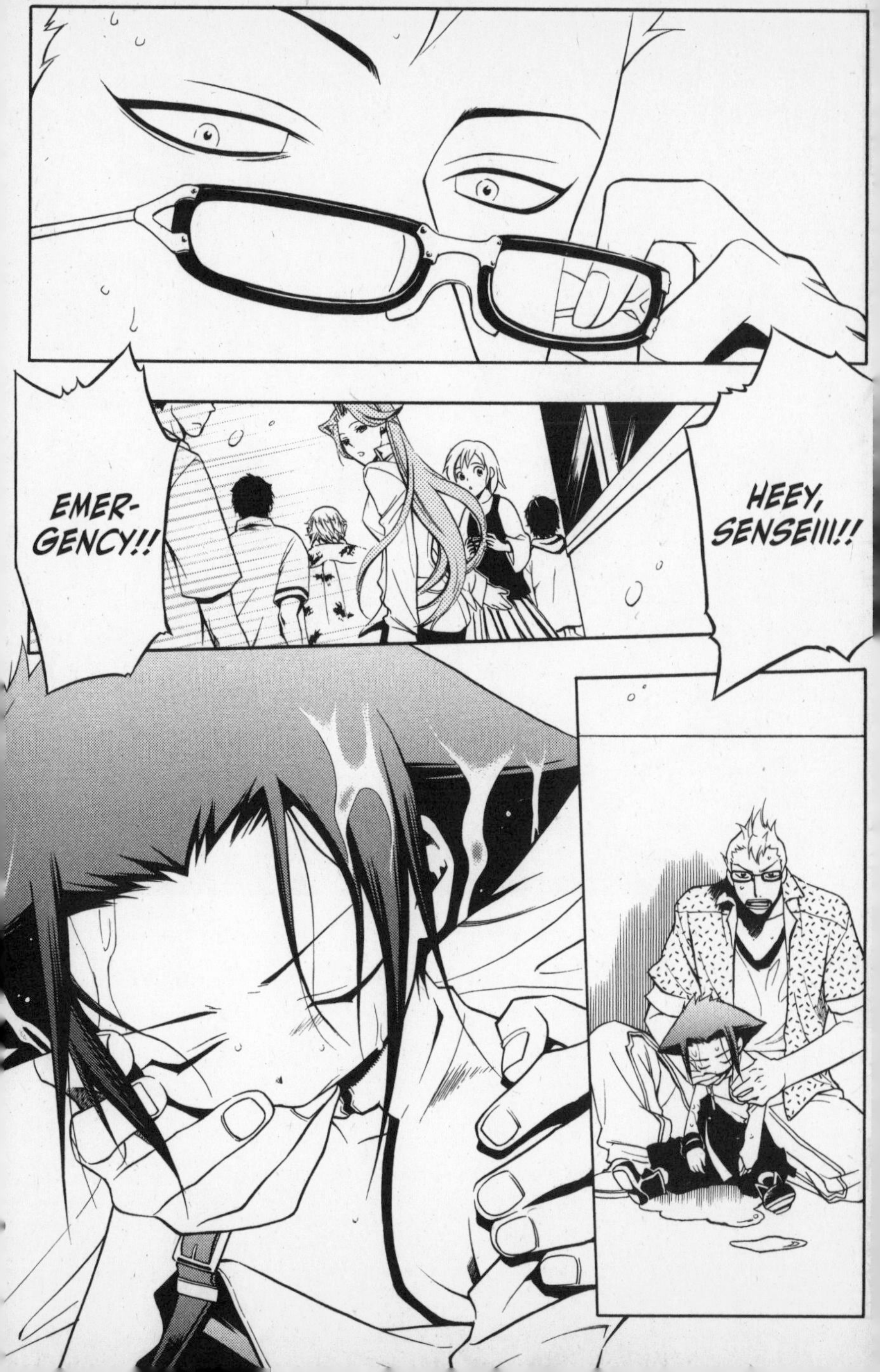
HEEY, SENSEIII!!
EMER-GENCY!!

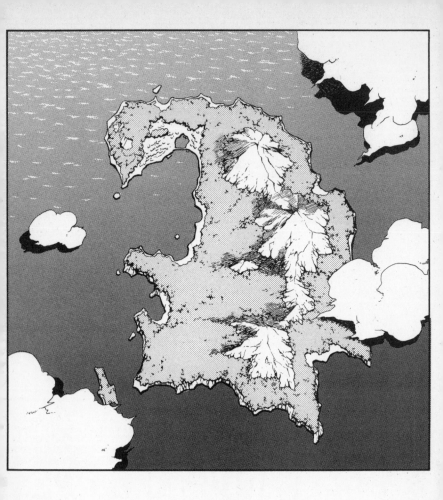

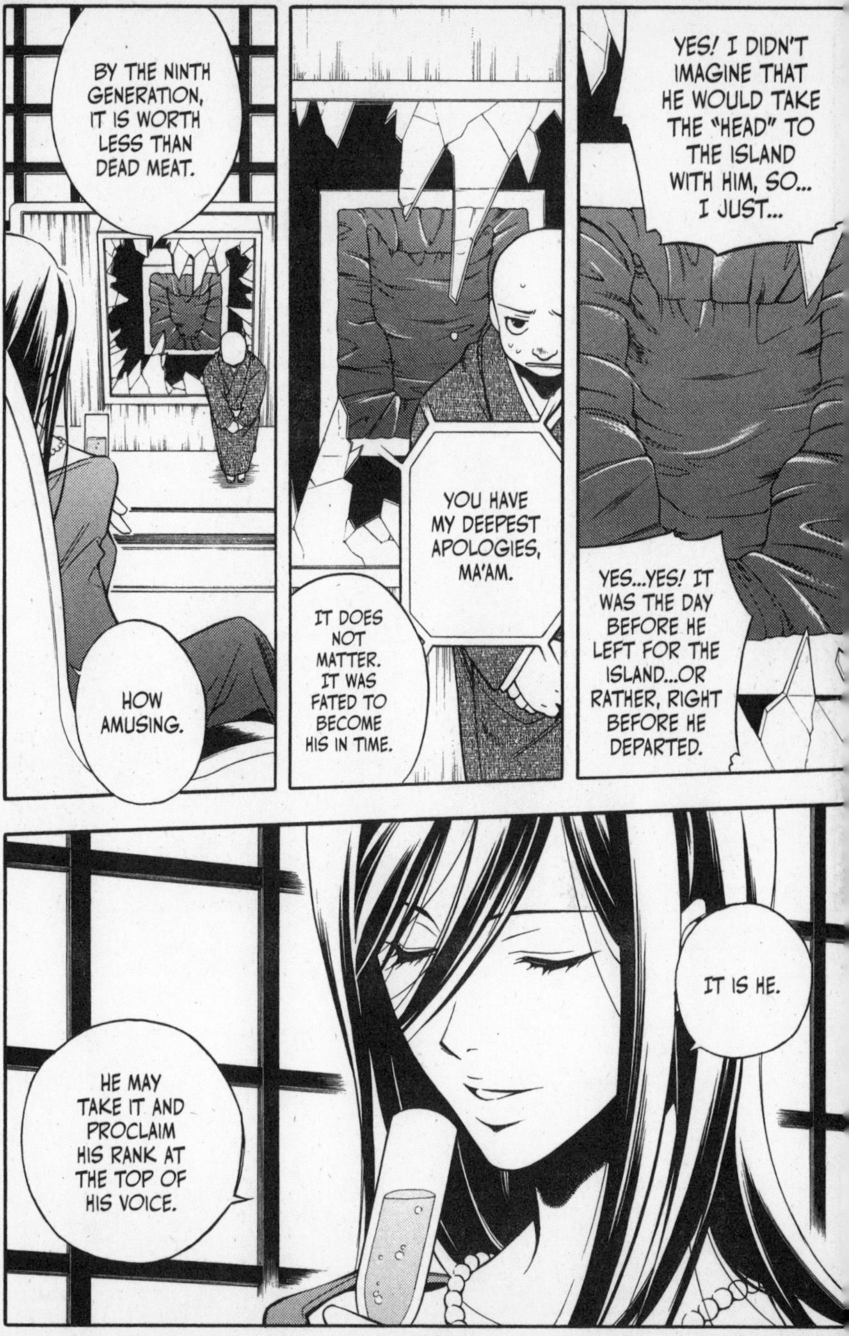
YES! I DIDN'T IMAGINE THAT HE WOULD TAKE THE "HEAD" TO THE ISLAND WITH HIM, SO... I JUST...
YES...YES! IT WAS THE DAY BEFORE HE LEFT FOR THE ISLAND...OR RATHER, RIGHT BEFORE HE DEPARTED.
YOU HAVE MY DEEPEST APOLOGIES, MA'AM.
IT DOES NOT MATTER. IT WAS FATED TO BECOME HIS IN TIME.
BY THE NINTH GENERATION, IT IS WORTH LESS THAN DEAD MEAT.
HOW AMUSING.
IT IS HE.
HE MAY TAKE IT AND PROCLAIM HIS RANK AT THE TOP OF HIS VOICE.

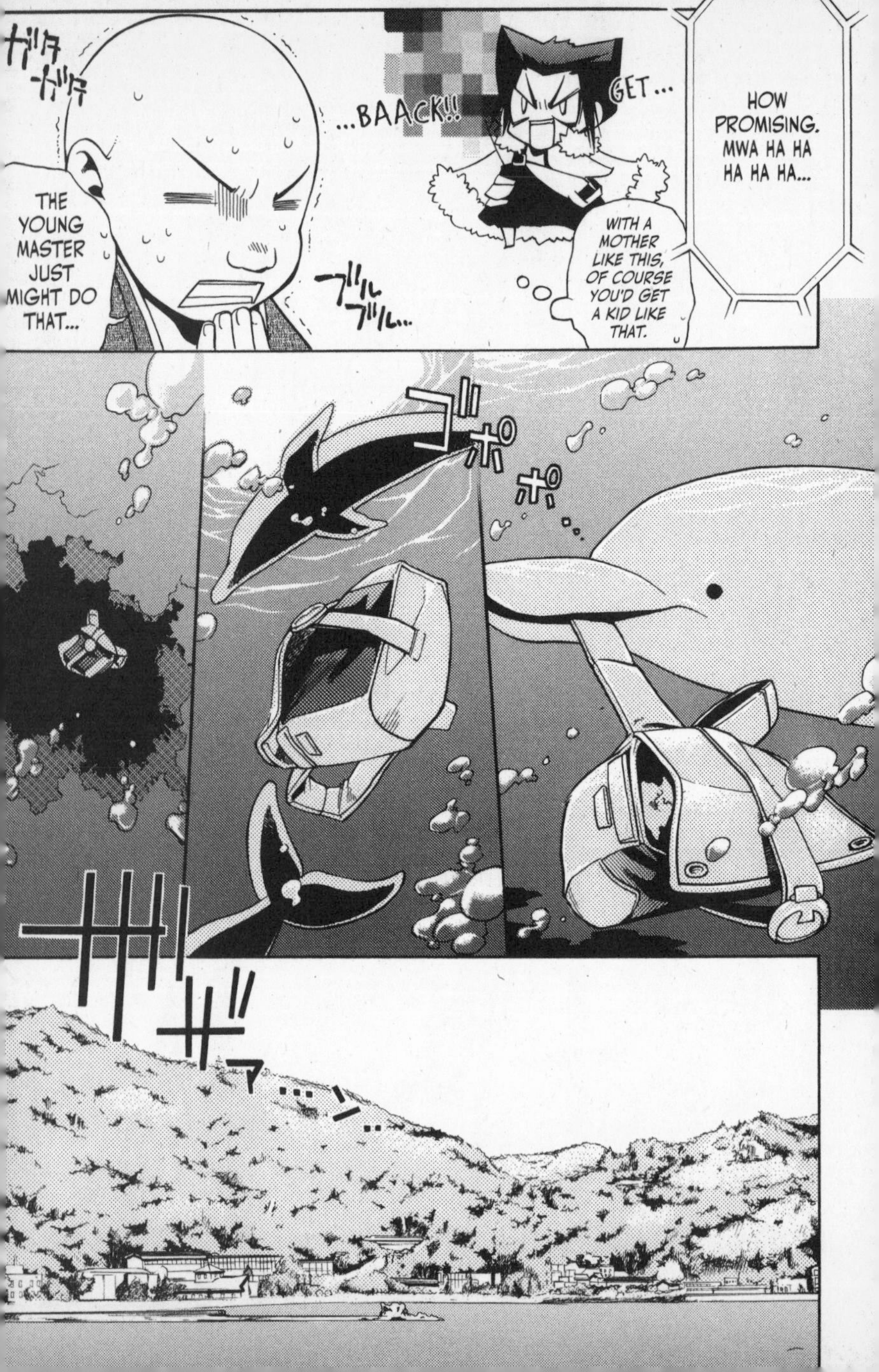
HOW PROMISING. MWA HA HA HA HA HA...
GET...
...BAACK!!
WITH A MOTHER LIKE THIS, OF COURSE YOU'D GET A KID LIKE THAT.
ガタガタ
THE YOUNG MASTER JUST MIGHT DO THAT...
ブルブル...
ゴポ
ポ
ザザァ...ン...

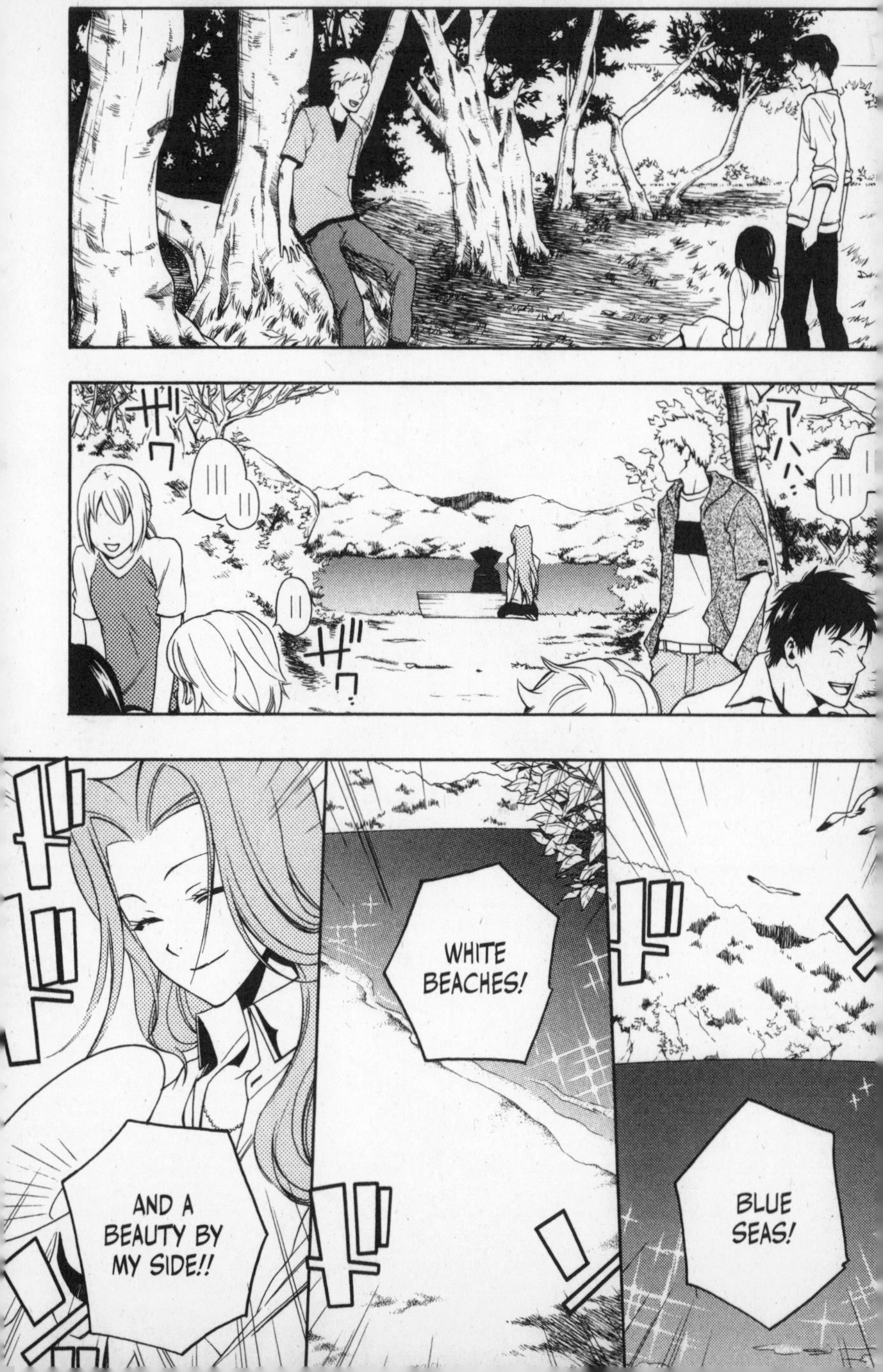
アハハ
ザワ
ザワ
BLUE SEAS!
WHITE BEACHES!
AND A BEAUTY BY MY SIDE!!

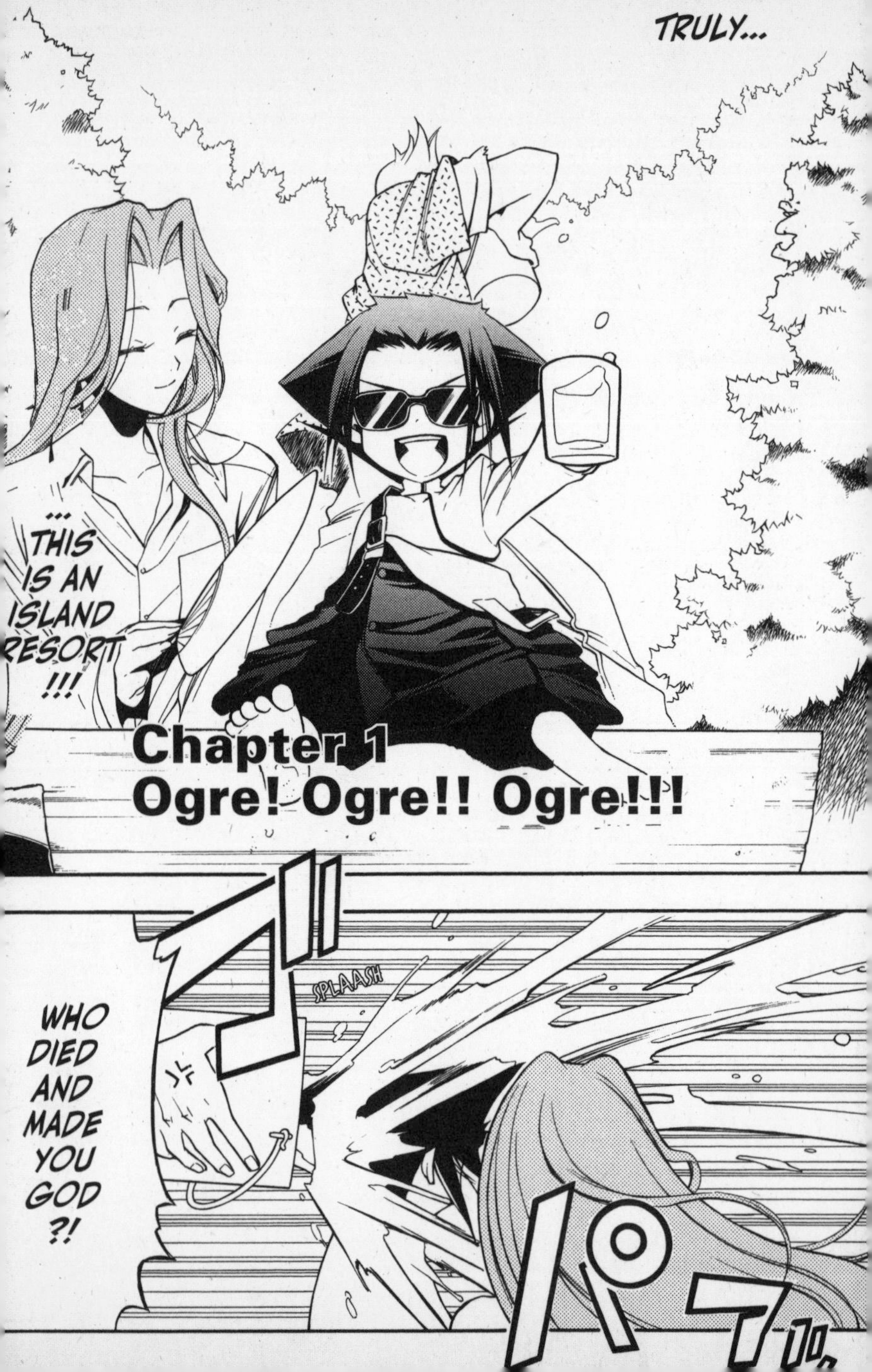
TRULY...
...THIS IS AN ISLAND RESORT!!!
Chapter 1
Ogre! Ogre!! Ogre!!!
SPLAASH
WHO DIED AND MADE YOU GOD?!

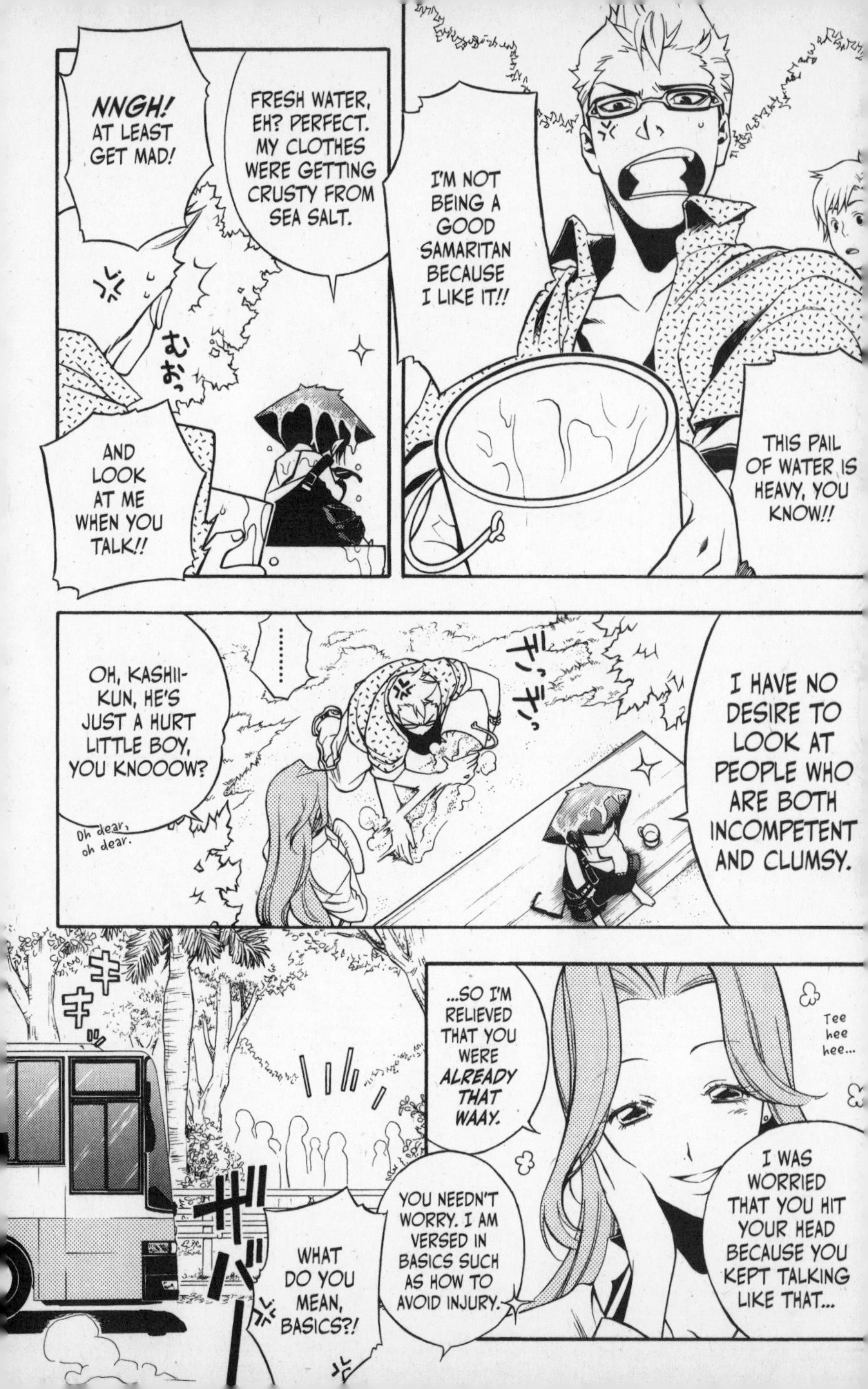
I'M NOT BEING A GOOD SAMARITAN BECAUSE I LIKE IT!!
THIS PAIL OF WATER IS HEAVY, YOU KNOW!!
FRESH WATER, EH? PERFECT. MY CLOTHES WERE GETTING CRUSTY FROM SEA SALT.
NNGH! AT LEAST GET MAD!
AND LOOK AT ME WHEN YOU TALK!!
I HAVE NO DESIRE TO LOOK AT PEOPLE WHO ARE BOTH INCOMPETENT AND CLUMSY.
......
OH, KASHII-KUN, HE'S JUST A HURT LITTLE BOY, YOU KNOOOW?
Oh dear, oh dear.
I WAS WORRIED THAT YOU HIT YOUR HEAD BECAUSE YOU KEPT TALKING LIKE THAT...
Tee hee hee...
...SO I'M RELIEVED THAT YOU WERE *ALREADY THAT WAAY.*
YOU NEEDN'T WORRY. I AM VERSED IN BASICS SUCH AS HOW TO AVOID INJURY.
WHAT DO YOU MEAN, BASICS?!

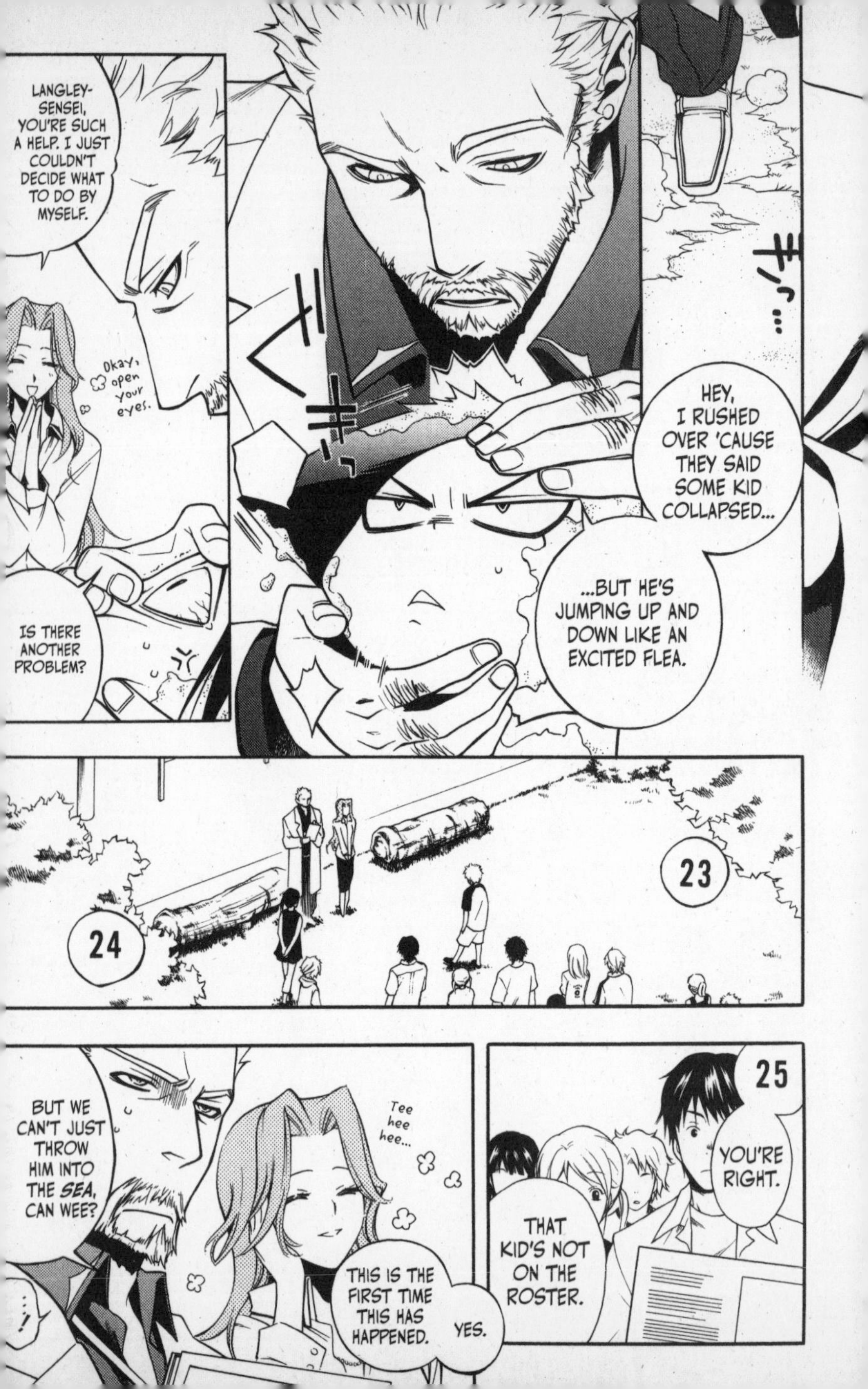
HEY, I RUSHED OVER 'CAUSE THEY SAID SOME KID COLLAPSED...
...BUT HE'S JUMPING UP AND DOWN LIKE AN EXCITED FLEA.
LANGLEY-SENSEI, YOU'RE SUCH A HELP. I JUST COULDN'T DECIDE WHAT TO DO BY MYSELF.
Okay, open your eyes.
IS THERE ANOTHER PROBLEM?
23
24
25
YOU'RE RIGHT.
THAT KID'S NOT ON THE ROSTER.
BUT WE CAN'T JUST THROW HIM INTO THE SEA, CAN WEE?
Tee hee hee...
THIS IS THE FIRST TIME THIS HAS HAPPENED.
YES.
...!

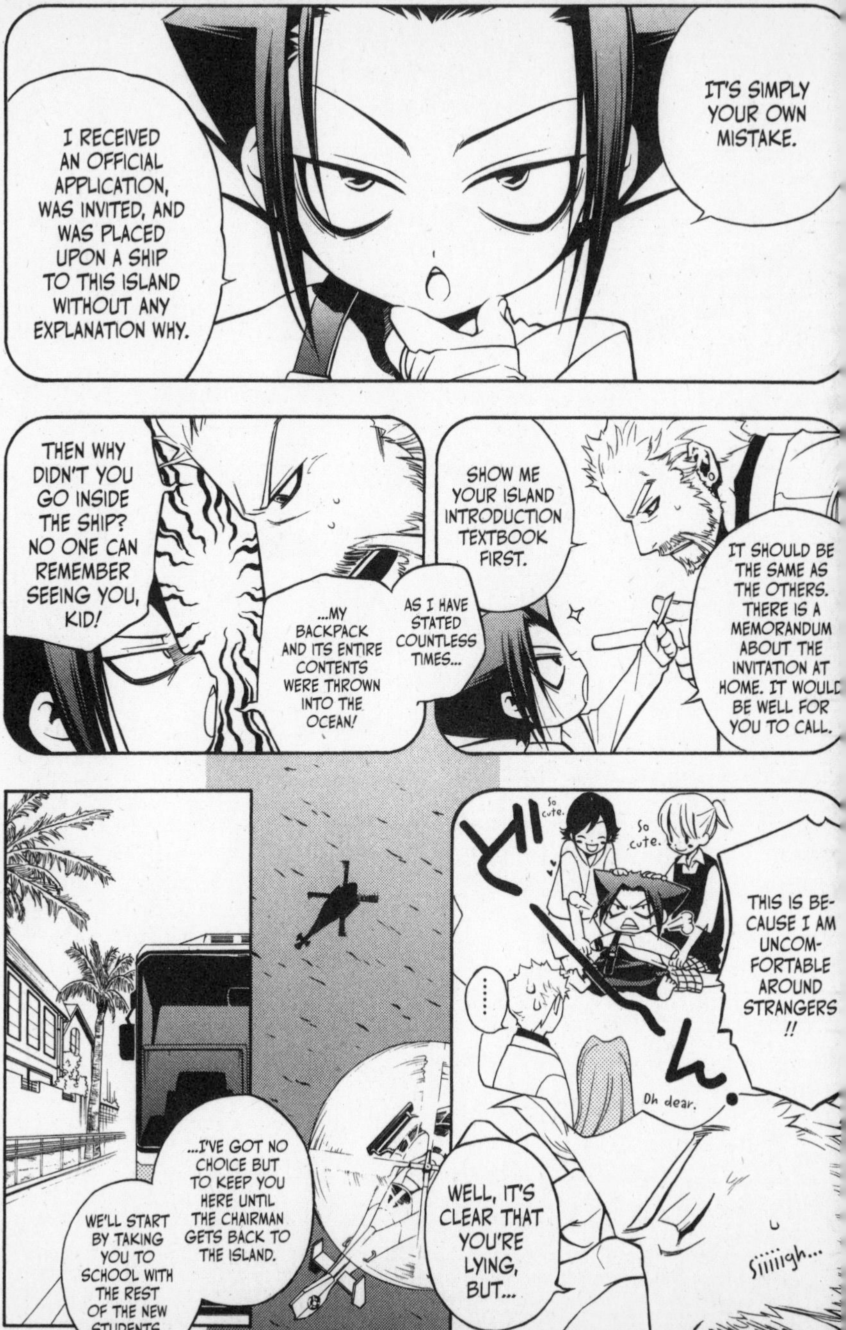
IT'S SIMPLY YOUR OWN MISTAKE.
I RECEIVED AN OFFICIAL APPLICATION, WAS INVITED, AND WAS PLACED UPON A SHIP TO THIS ISLAND WITHOUT ANY EXPLANATION WHY.
SHOW ME YOUR ISLAND INTRODUCTION TEXTBOOK FIRST.
IT SHOULD BE THE SAME AS THE OTHERS. THERE IS A MEMORANDUM ABOUT THE INVITATION AT HOME. IT WOULD BE WELL FOR YOU TO CALL.
AS I HAVE STATED COUNTLESS TIMES...
...MY BACKPACK AND ITS ENTIRE CONTENTS WERE THROWN INTO THE OCEAN!
THEN WHY DIDN'T YOU GO INSIDE THE SHIP? NO ONE CAN REMEMBER SEEING YOU, KID!
THIS IS BE-CAUSE I AM UNCOM-FORTABLE AROUND STRANGERS!!
So cute.
So cute.
......
Oh dear.
Siiiiigh...
WELL, IT'S CLEAR THAT YOU'RE LYING, BUT...
...I'VE GOT NO CHOICE BUT TO KEEP YOU HERE UNTIL THE CHAIRMAN GETS BACK TO THE ISLAND.
WE'LL START BY TAKING YOU TO SCHOOL WITH THE REST OF THE NEW STUDENTS.

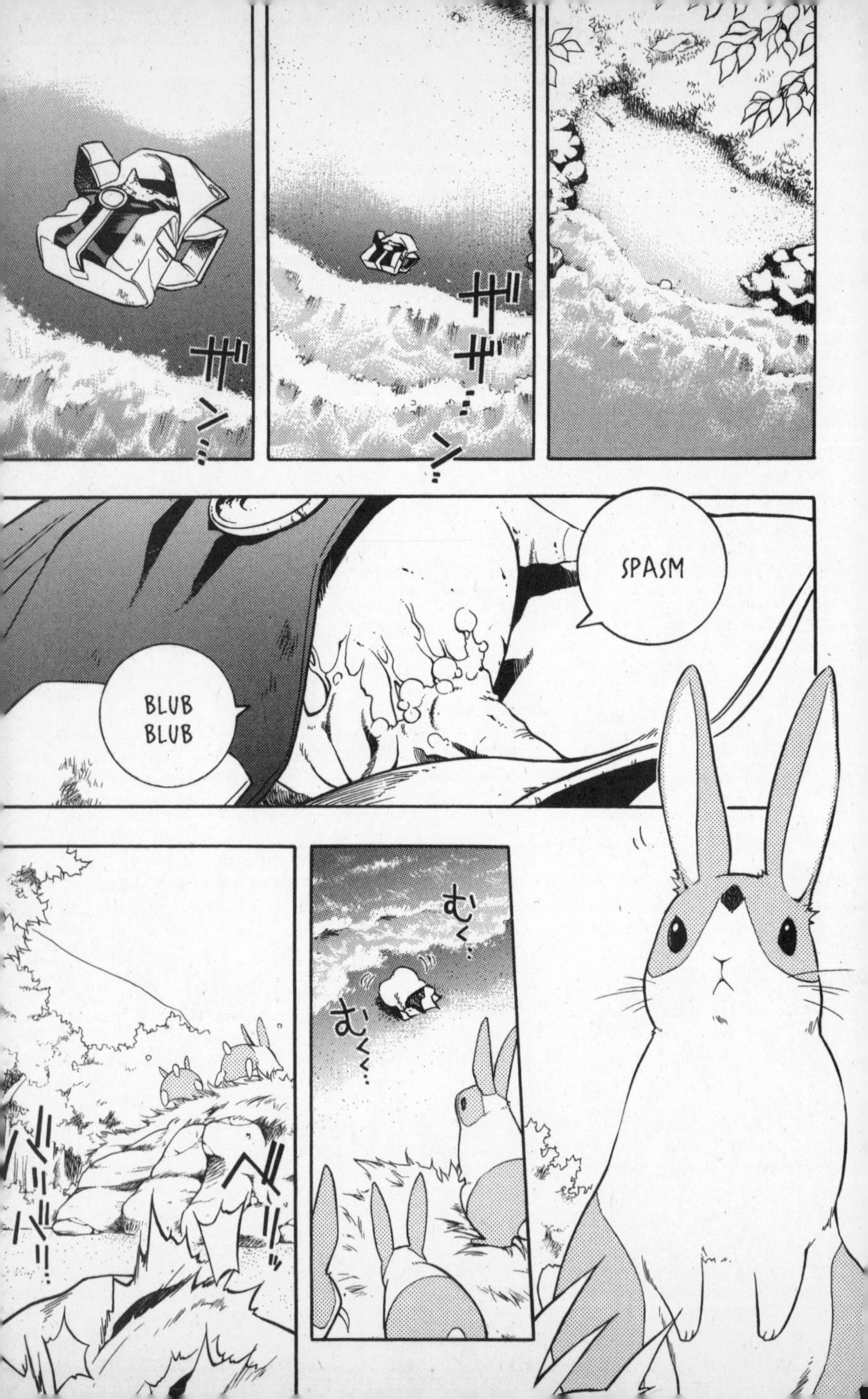
ザザ…ン…
ザン…
SPASM
BLUB BLUB
むく…
むくく…

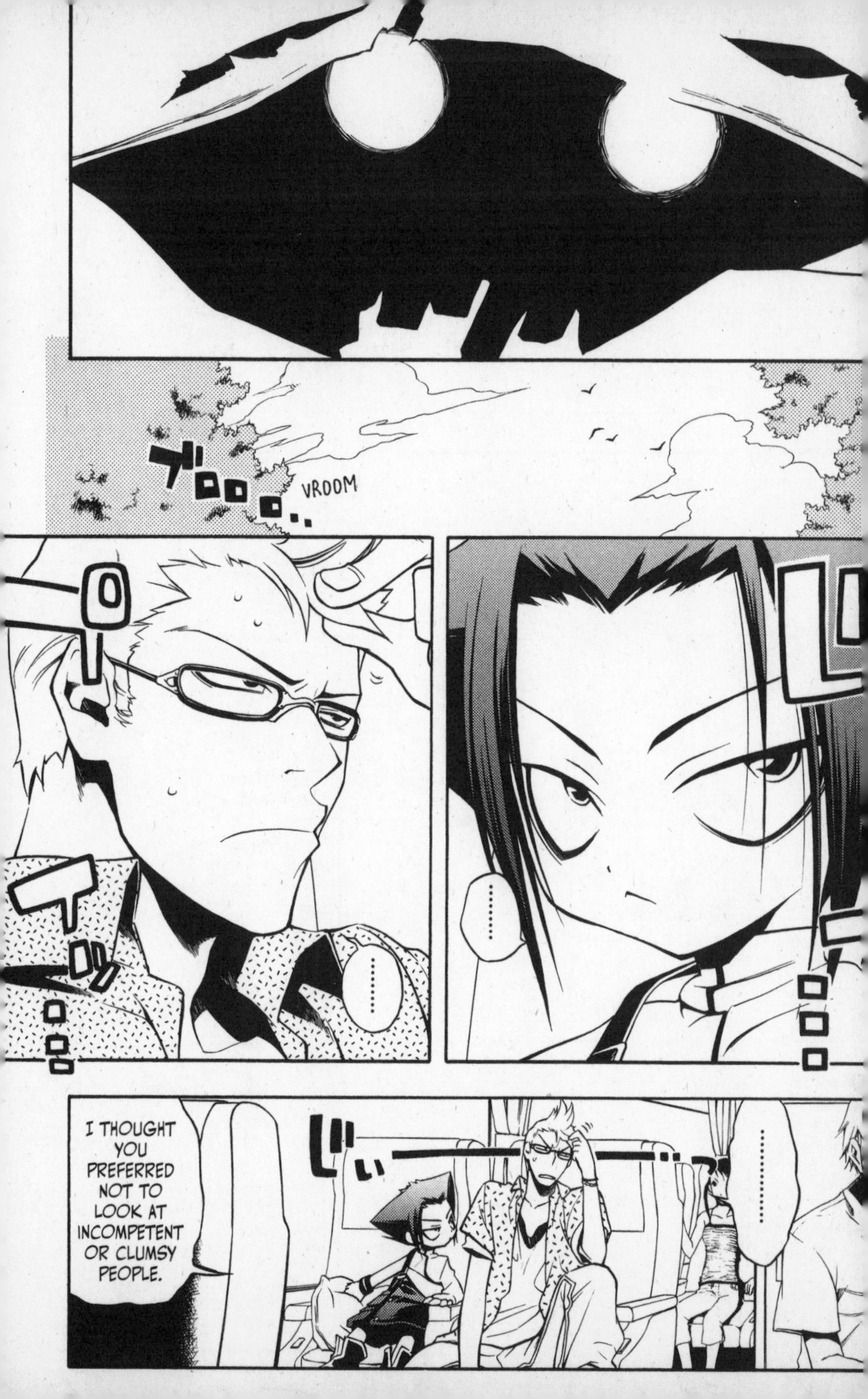
VROOM
......
......
......
I THOUGHT YOU PREFERRED NOT TO LOOK AT INCOMPETENT OR CLUMSY PEOPLE.

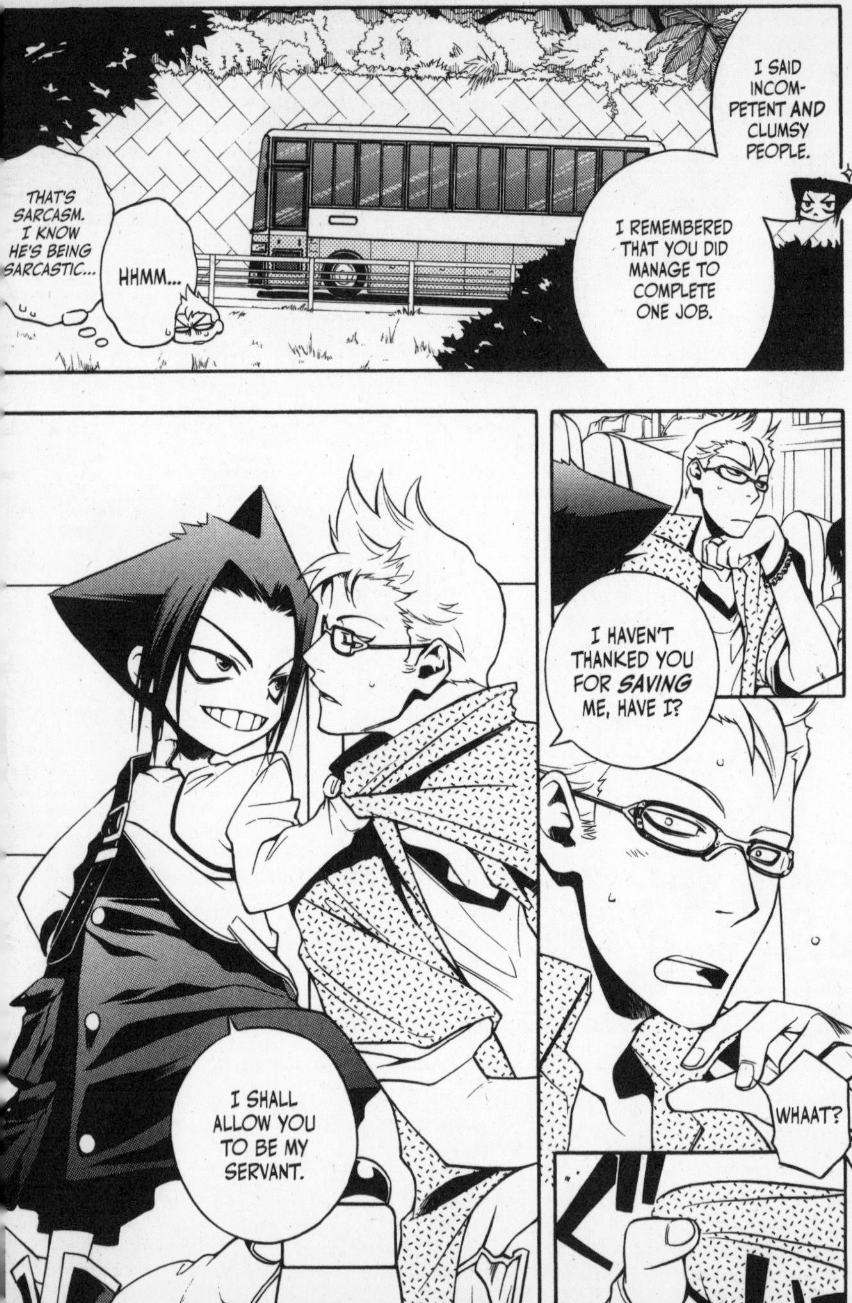
I SAID INCOM-PETENT AND CLUMSY PEOPLE.
I REMEMBERED THAT YOU DID MANAGE TO COMPLETE ONE JOB.
HHMM...
THAT'S SARCASM. I KNOW HE'S BEING SARCASTIC...
I HAVEN'T THANKED YOU FOR *SAVING* ME, HAVE I?
WHAAT?
I SHALL ALLOW YOU TO BE MY SERVANT.

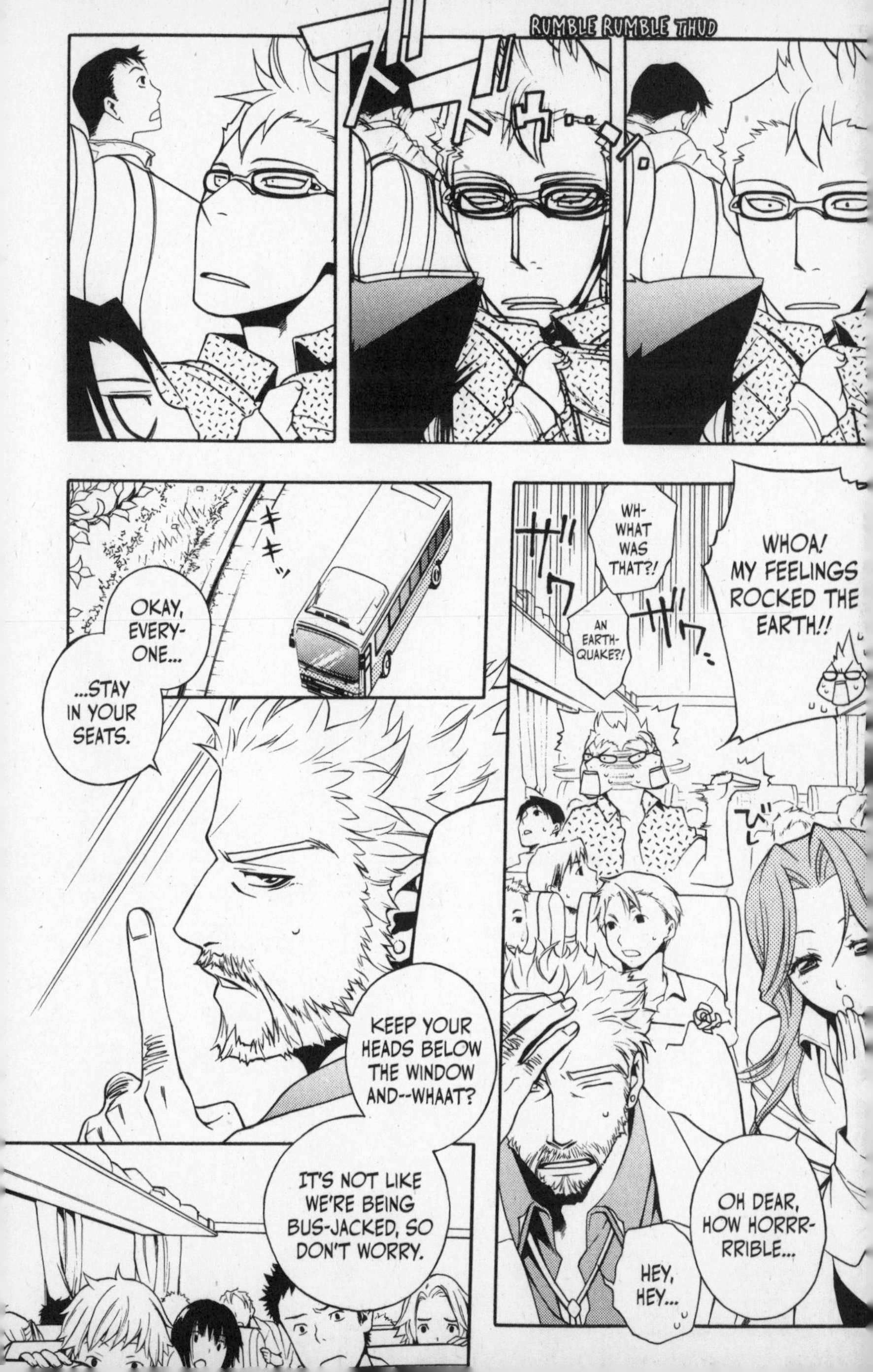
RUMBLE RUMBLE THUD
WHOA! MY FEELINGS ROCKED THE EARTH!!
WH- WHAT WAS THAT?!
AN EARTH- QUAKE?!
OKAY, EVERY- ONE...
...STAY IN YOUR SEATS.
KEEP YOUR HEADS BELOW THE WINDOW AND--WHAAT?
OH DEAR, HOW HORRR- RRIBLE...
HEY, HEY...
IT'S NOT LIKE WE'RE BEING BUS-JACKED, SO DON'T WORRY.

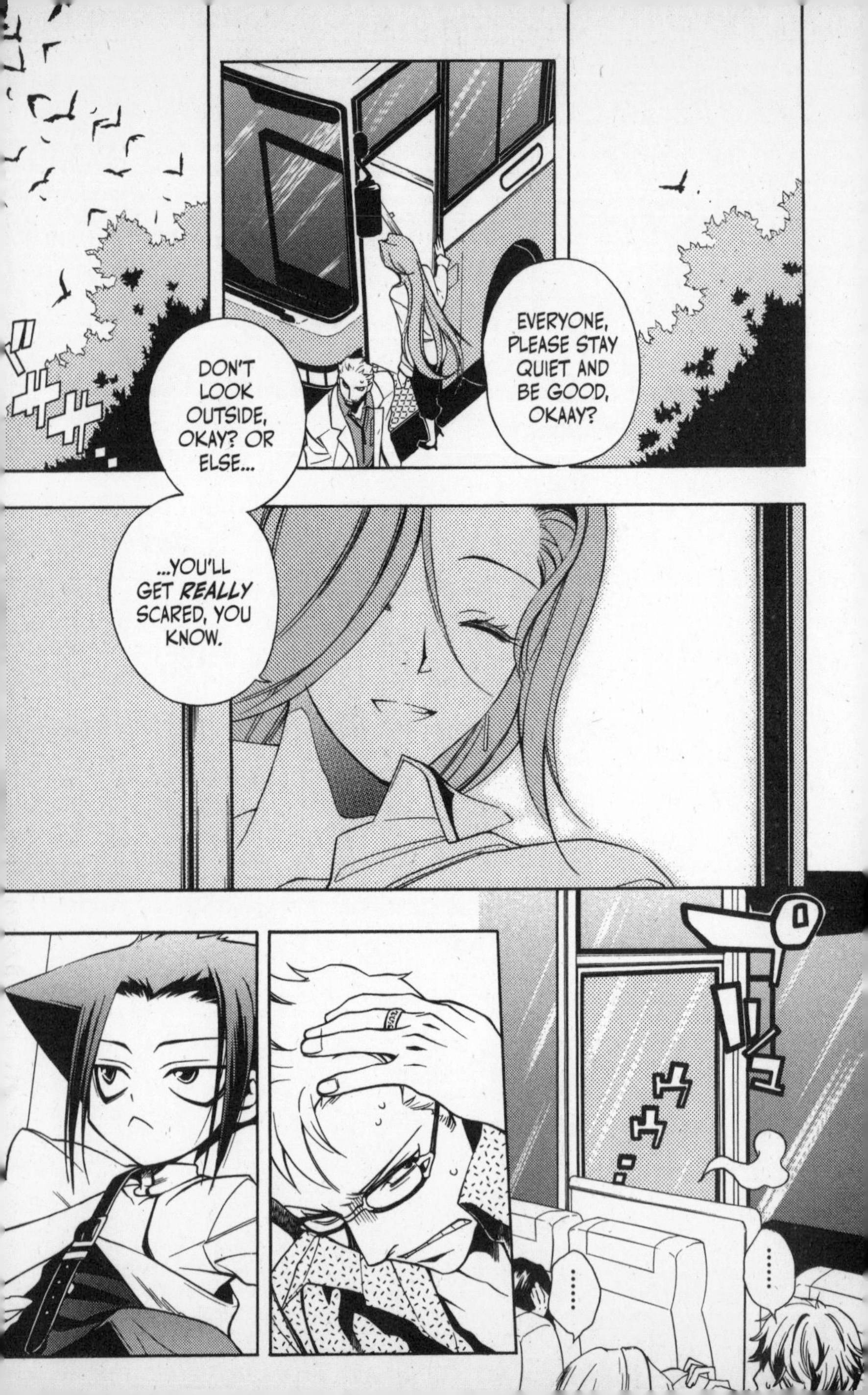
EVERYONE, PLEASE STAY QUIET AND BE GOOD, OKAAY?
DON'T LOOK OUTSIDE, OKAY? OR ELSE...
...YOU'LL GET *REALLY* SCARED, YOU KNOW.
......
......

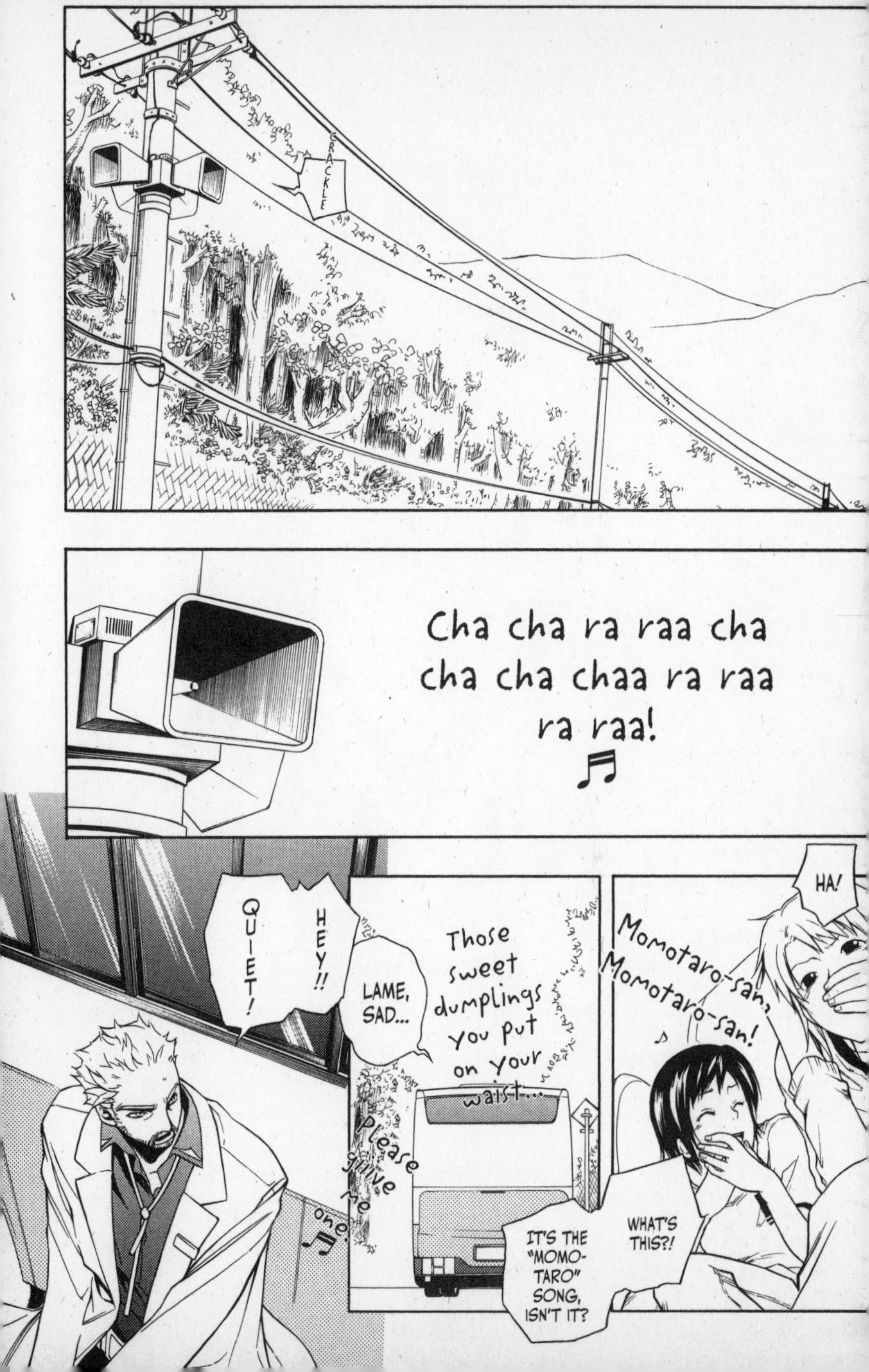

CRACKLE
Cha cha ra raa cha cha cha chaa ra raa ra raa!
HA!
Momotaro-san, Momotaro-san!
WHAT'S THIS?!
IT'S THE "MOMO-TARO" SONG, ISN'T IT?
Those sweet dumplings you put on your waist...
Please giiive me one.
LAME, SAD...
HEY!!
QUIET!

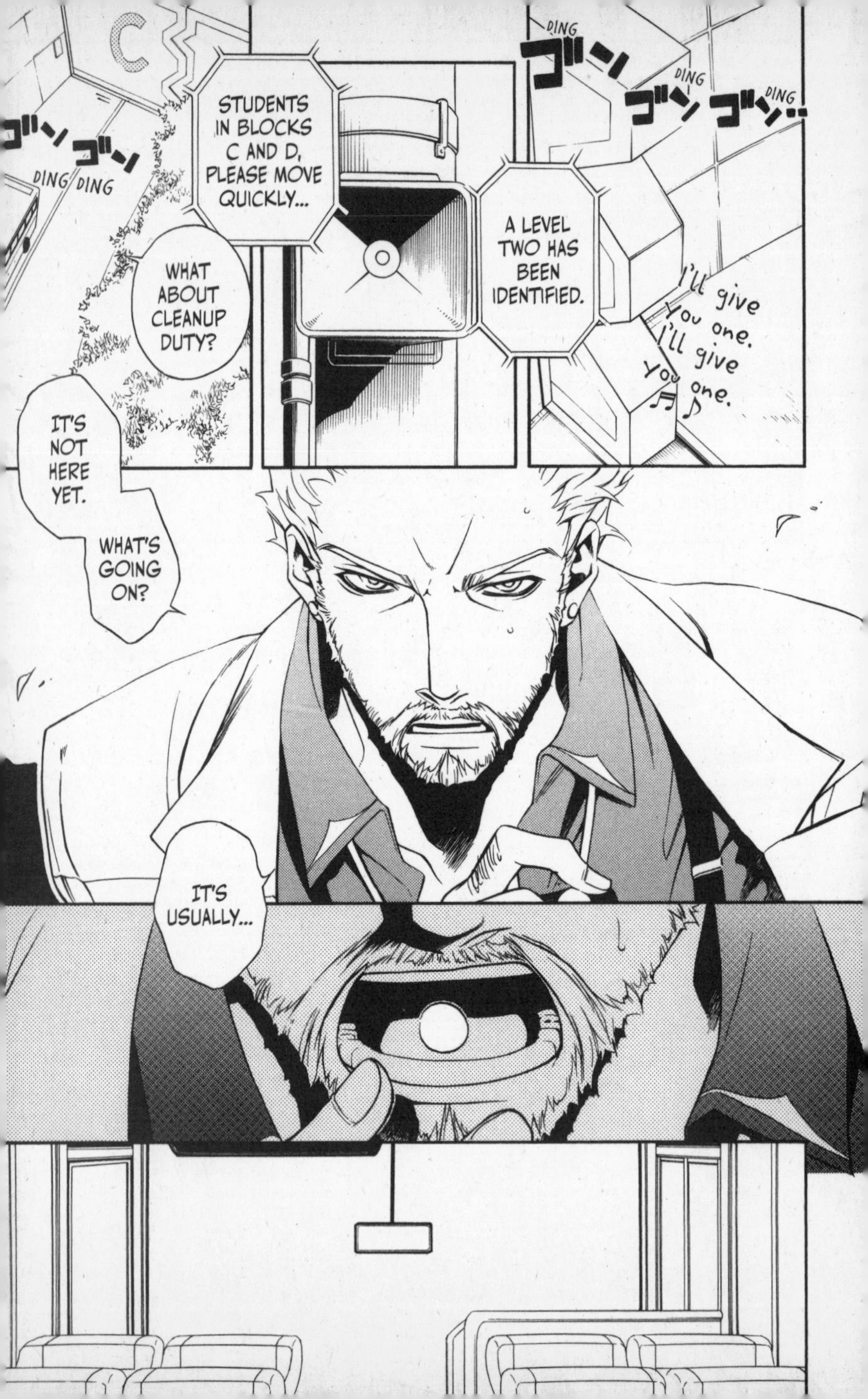
ゴーン DING
ゴーン DING
ゴーン DING
A LEVEL TWO HAS BEEN IDENTIFIED.
I'll give you one. I'll give you one. ♫ ♪
STUDENTS IN BLOCKS C AND D, PLEASE MOVE QUICKLY...
ゴーン ゴーン DING DING
WHAT ABOUT CLEANUP DUTY?
IT'S NOT HERE YET.
WHAT'S GOING ON?
IT'S USUALLY...

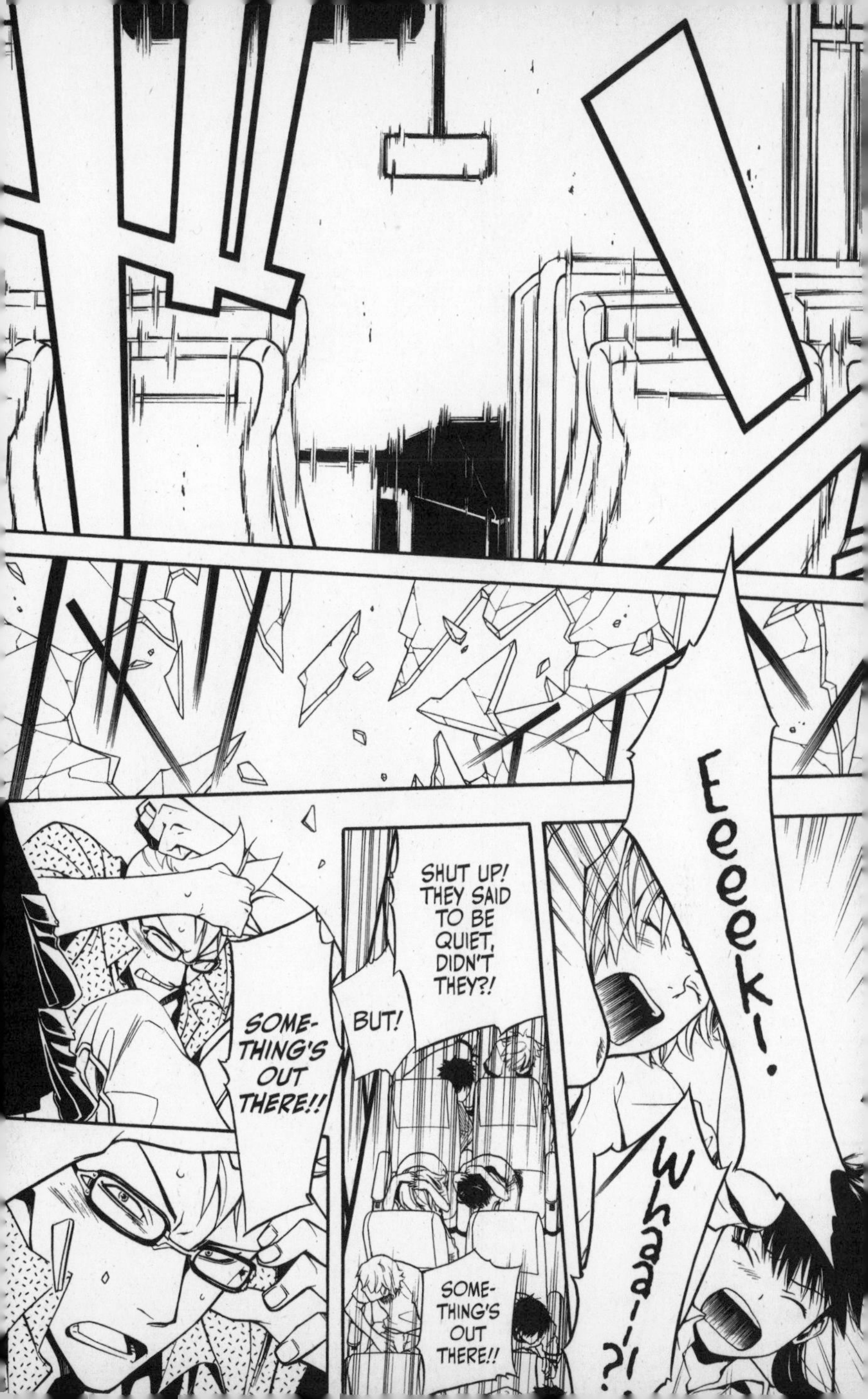
Eeeek!
Whaa--?!
SHUT UP! THEY SAID TO BE QUIET, DIDN'T THEY?!
BUT!
SOME-THING'S OUT THERE!!
SOME-THING'S OUT THERE!!

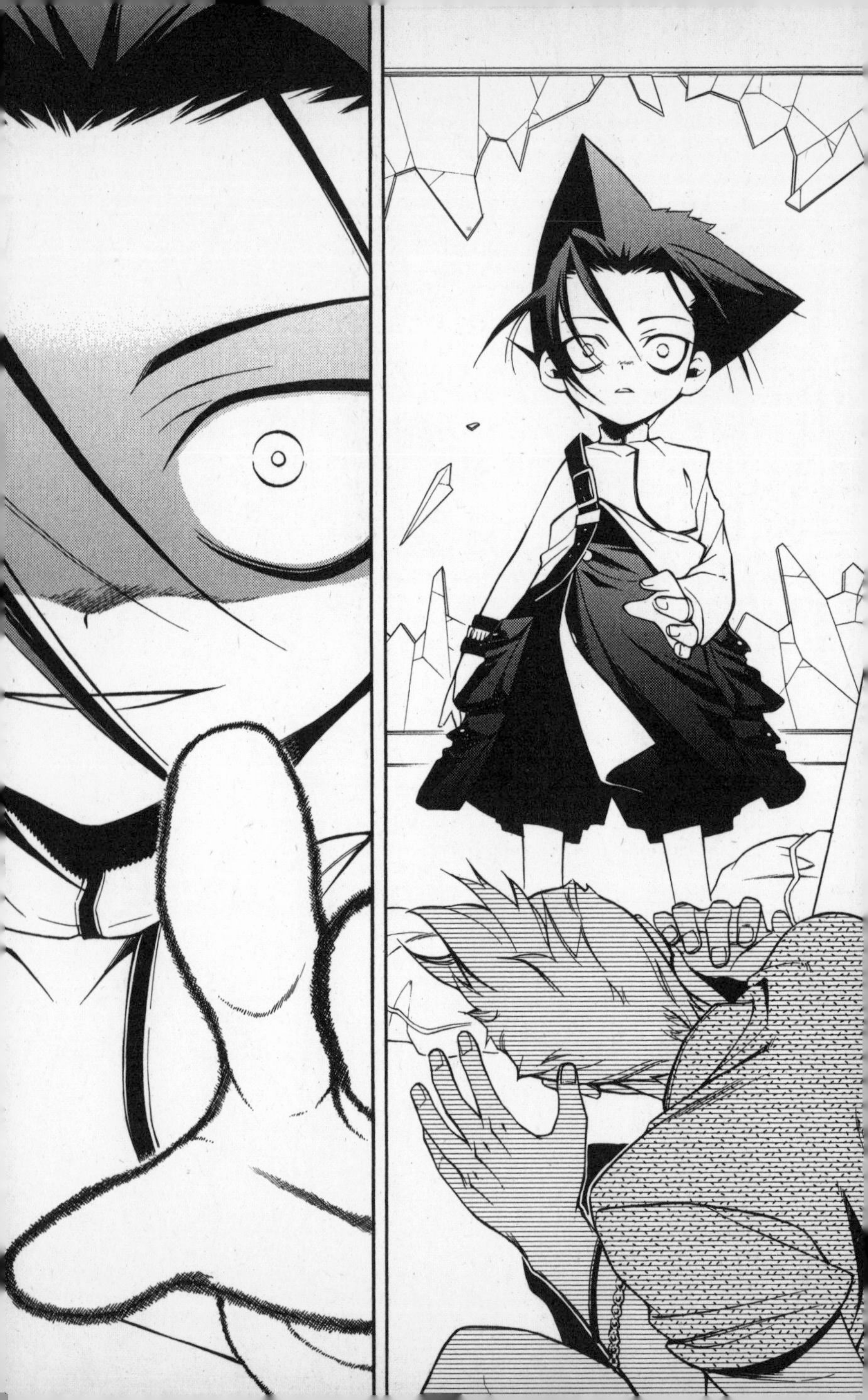

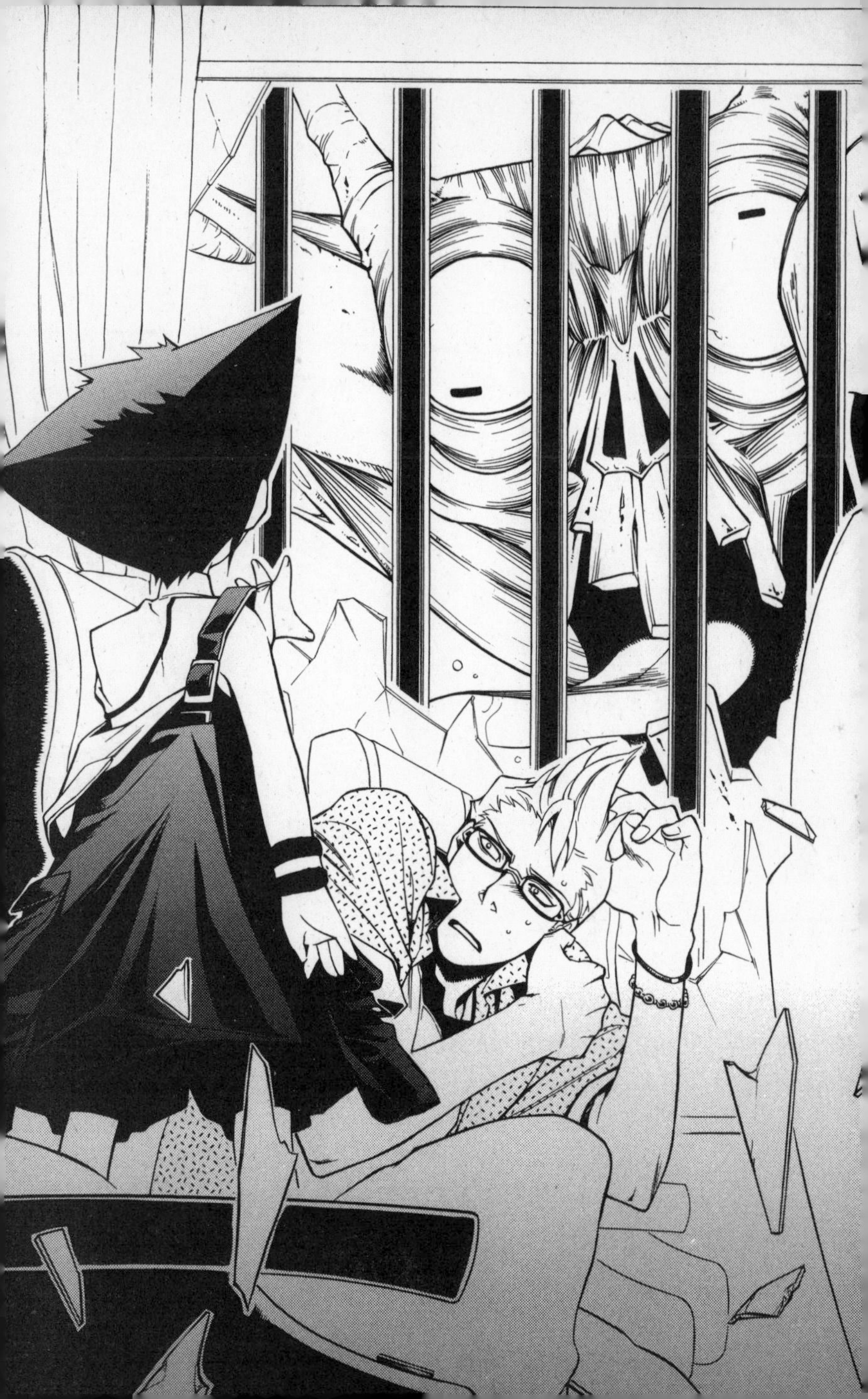

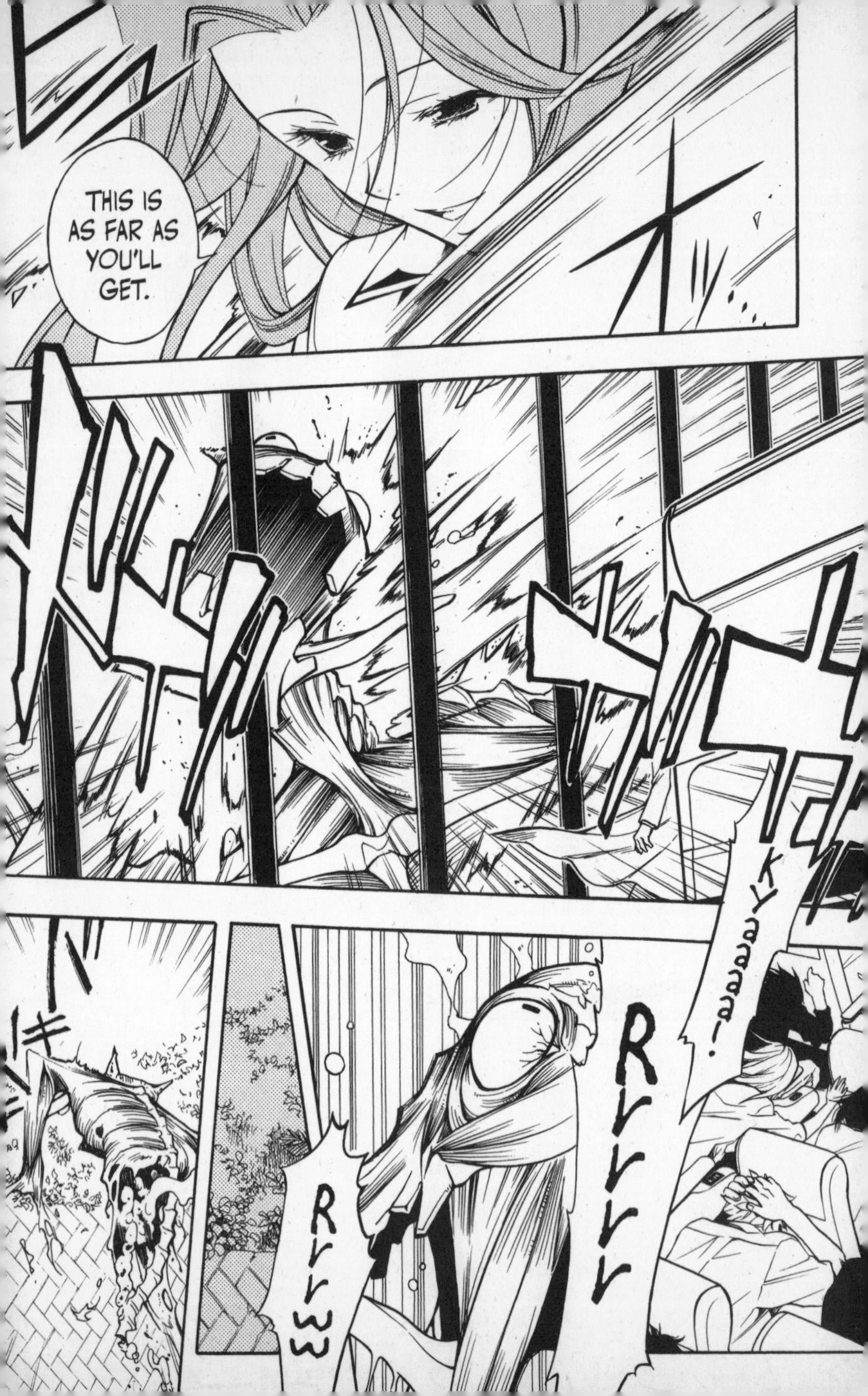
THIS IS AS FAR AS YOU'LL GET.
KYAAAAAA!
RRRRRR
RRRRW

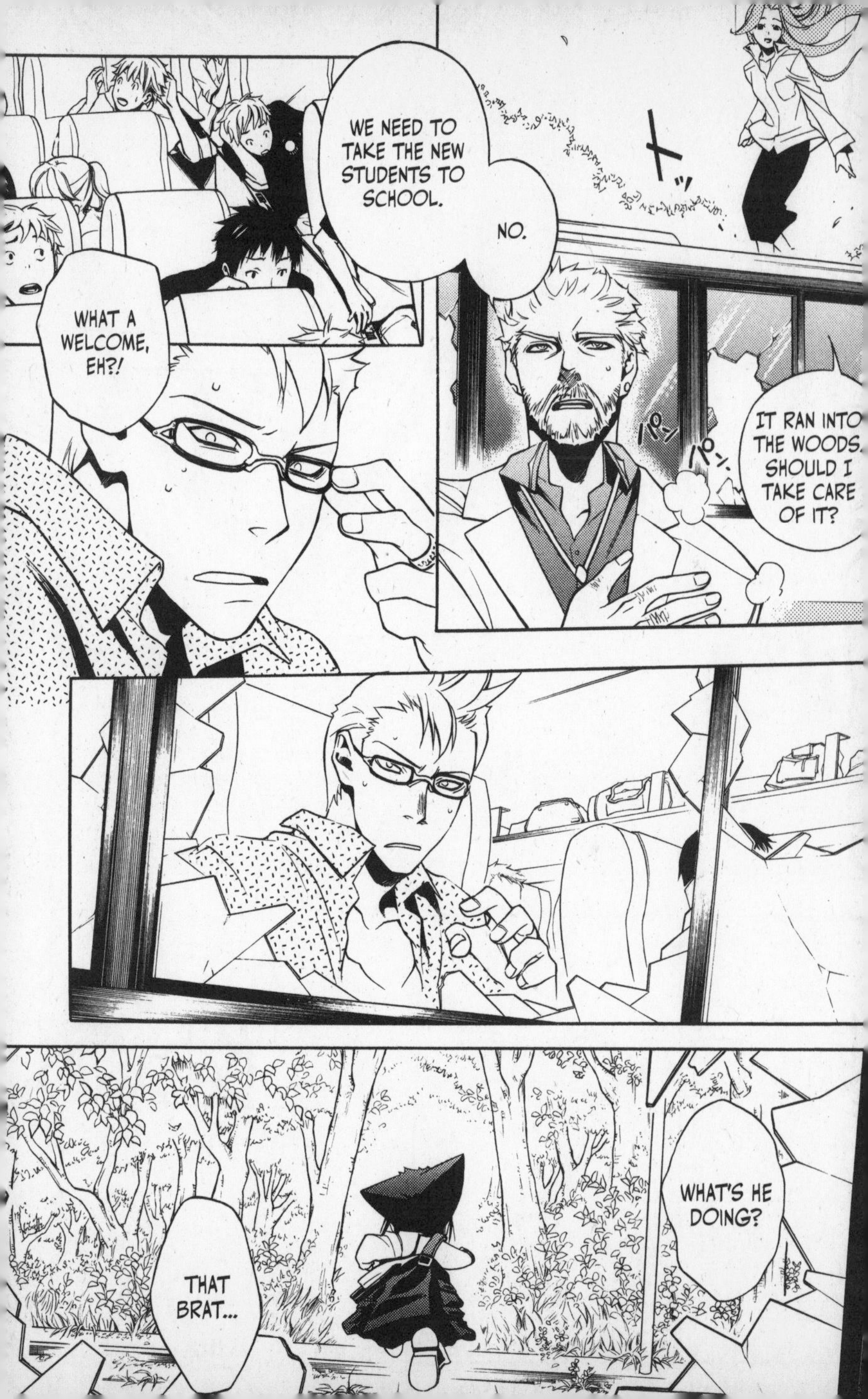
トッ
IT RAN INTO THE WOODS. SHOULD I TAKE CARE OF IT?
NO.
WE NEED TO TAKE THE NEW STUDENTS TO SCHOOL.
WHAT A WELCOME, EH?!
WHAT'S HE DOING?
THAT BRAT...

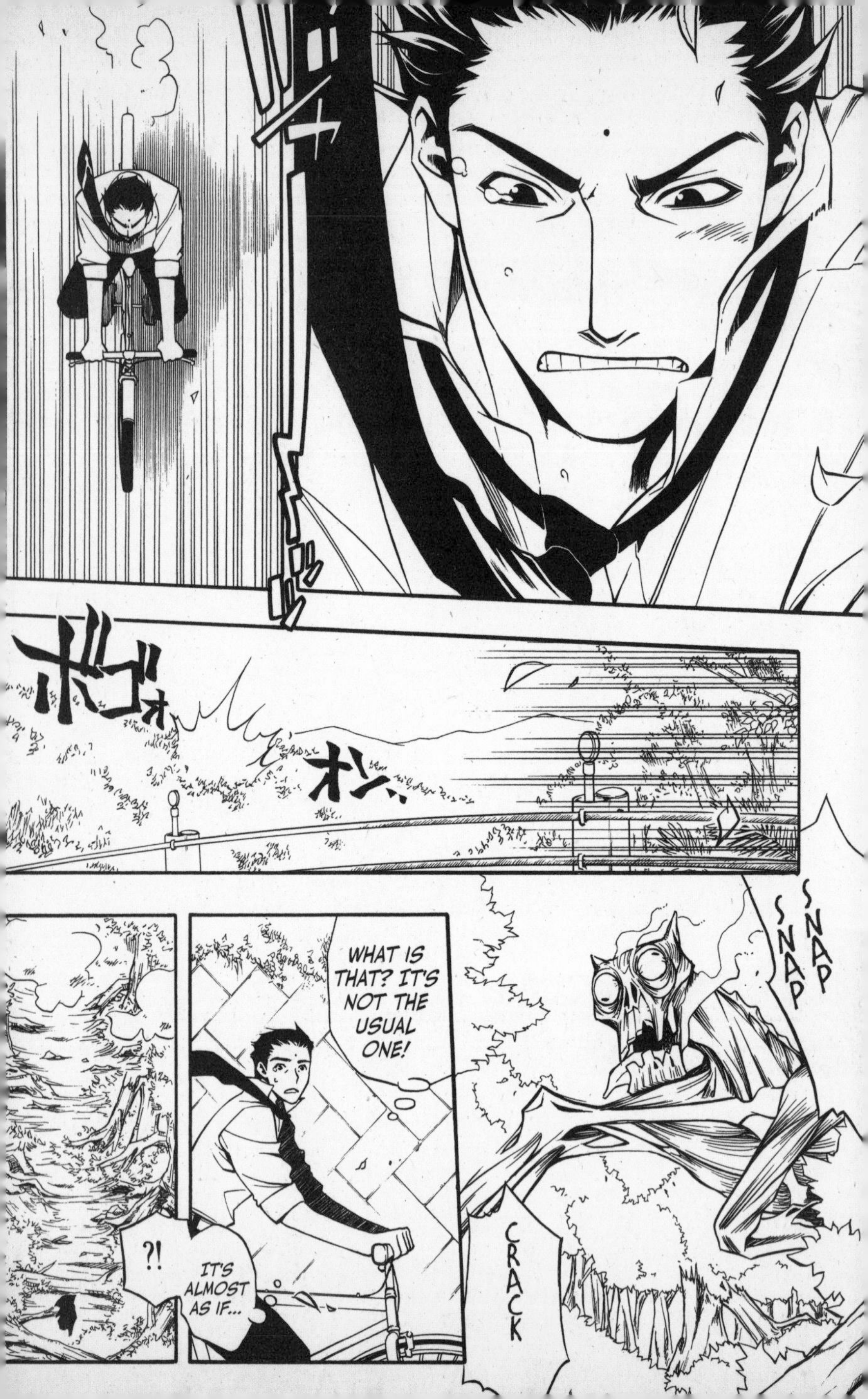
ボゴォ
オン
SNAP SNAP
CRACK
WHAT IS THAT? IT'S NOT THE USUAL ONE!
?!
IT'S ALMOST AS IF...

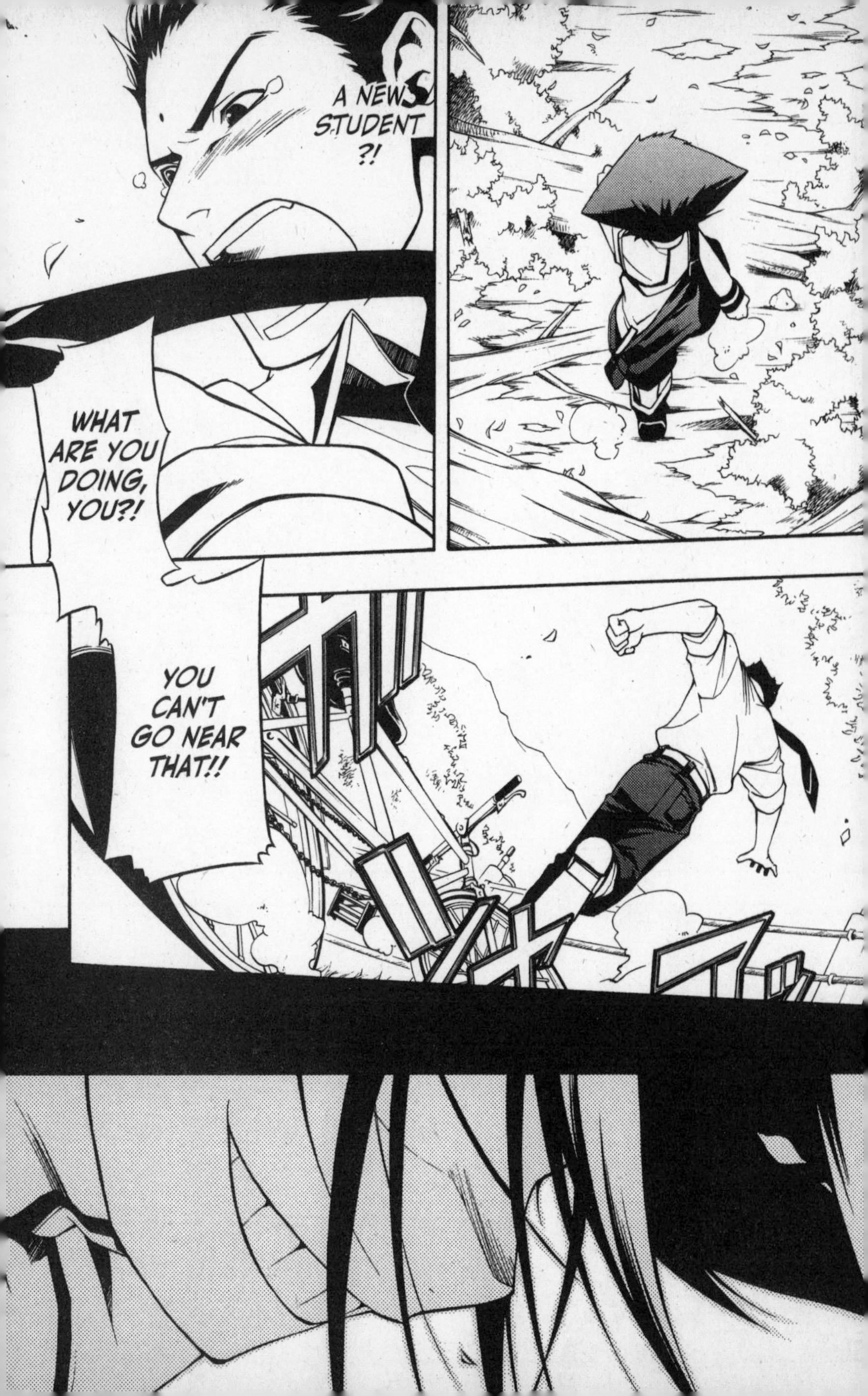

A NEWS STUDENT ?!
WHAT ARE YOU DOING, YOU?!
YOU CAN'T GO NEAR THAT!!

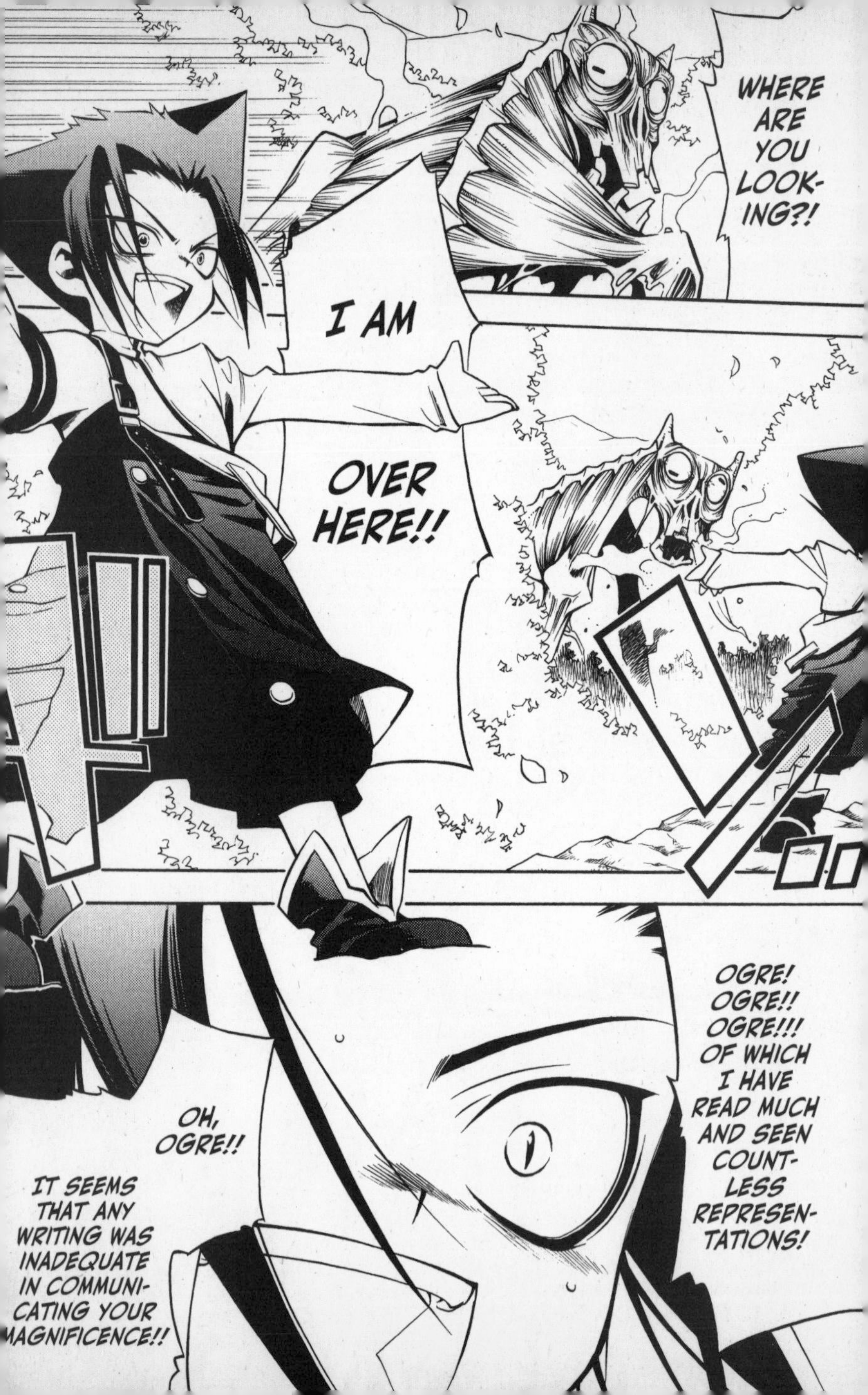
WHERE ARE YOU LOOK-ING?!
I AM
OVER HERE!!
OGRE! OGRE!! OGRE!!! OF WHICH I HAVE READ MUCH AND SEEN COUNT-LESS REPRESEN-TATIONS!
OH, OGRE!!
IT SEEMS THAT ANY WRITING WAS INADEQUATE IN COMMUNI-CATING YOUR MAGNIFICENCE!!

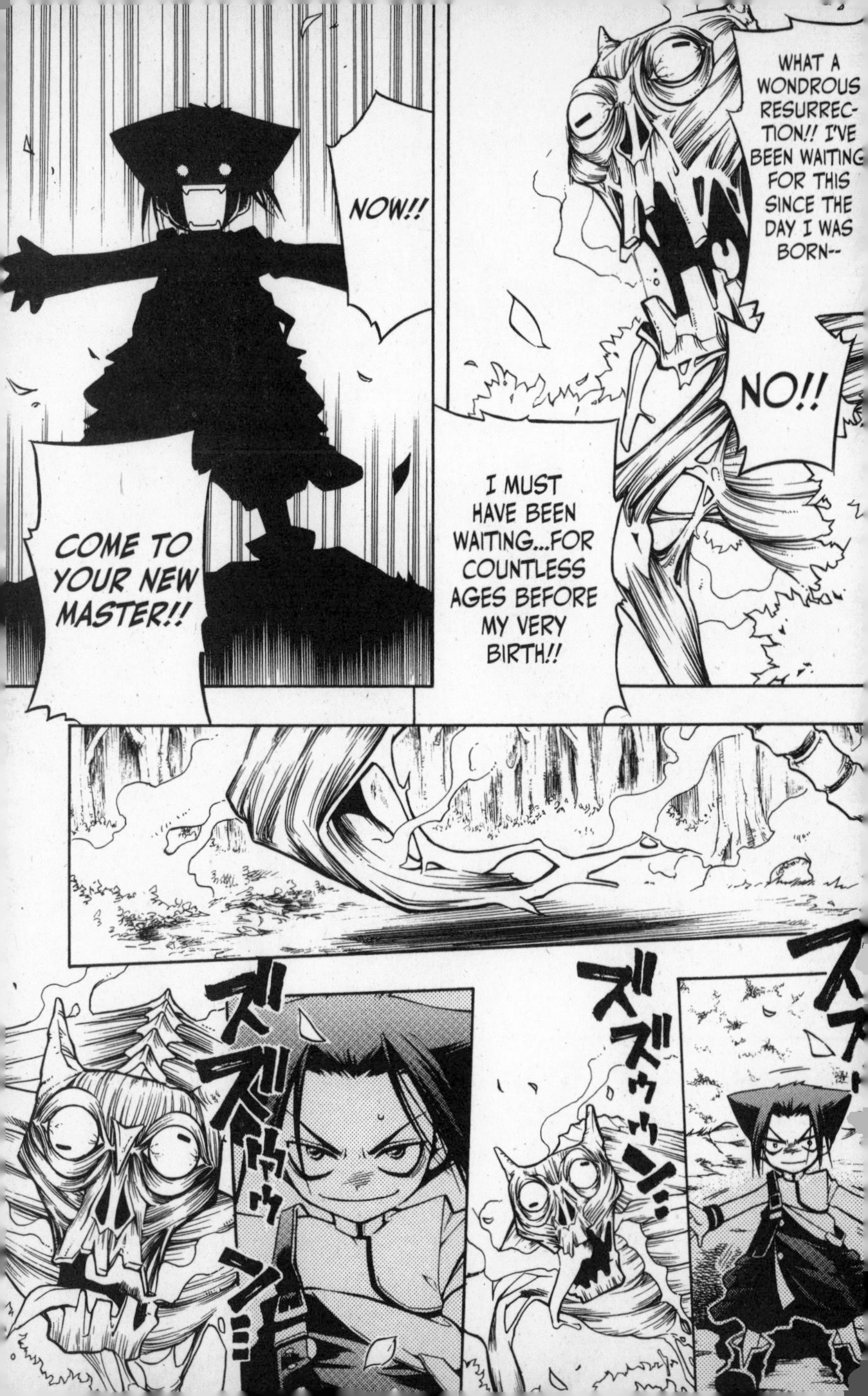

WHAT A WONDROUS RESURREC-TION!! I'VE BEEN WAITING FOR THIS SINCE THE DAY I WAS BORN--
NO!!
I MUST HAVE BEEN WAITING...FOR COUNTLESS AGES BEFORE MY VERY BIRTH!!
NOW!!
COME TO YOUR NEW MASTER!!

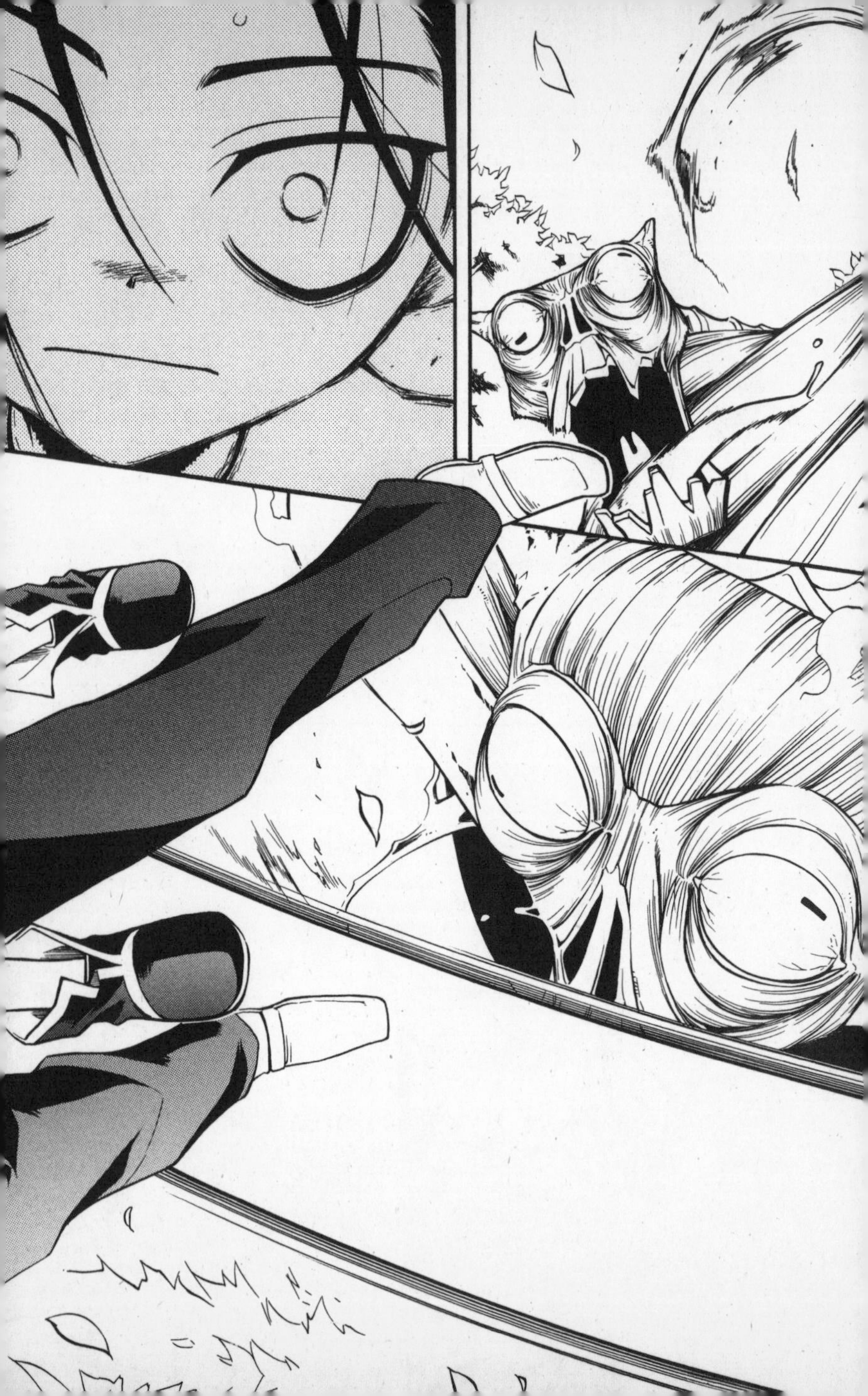

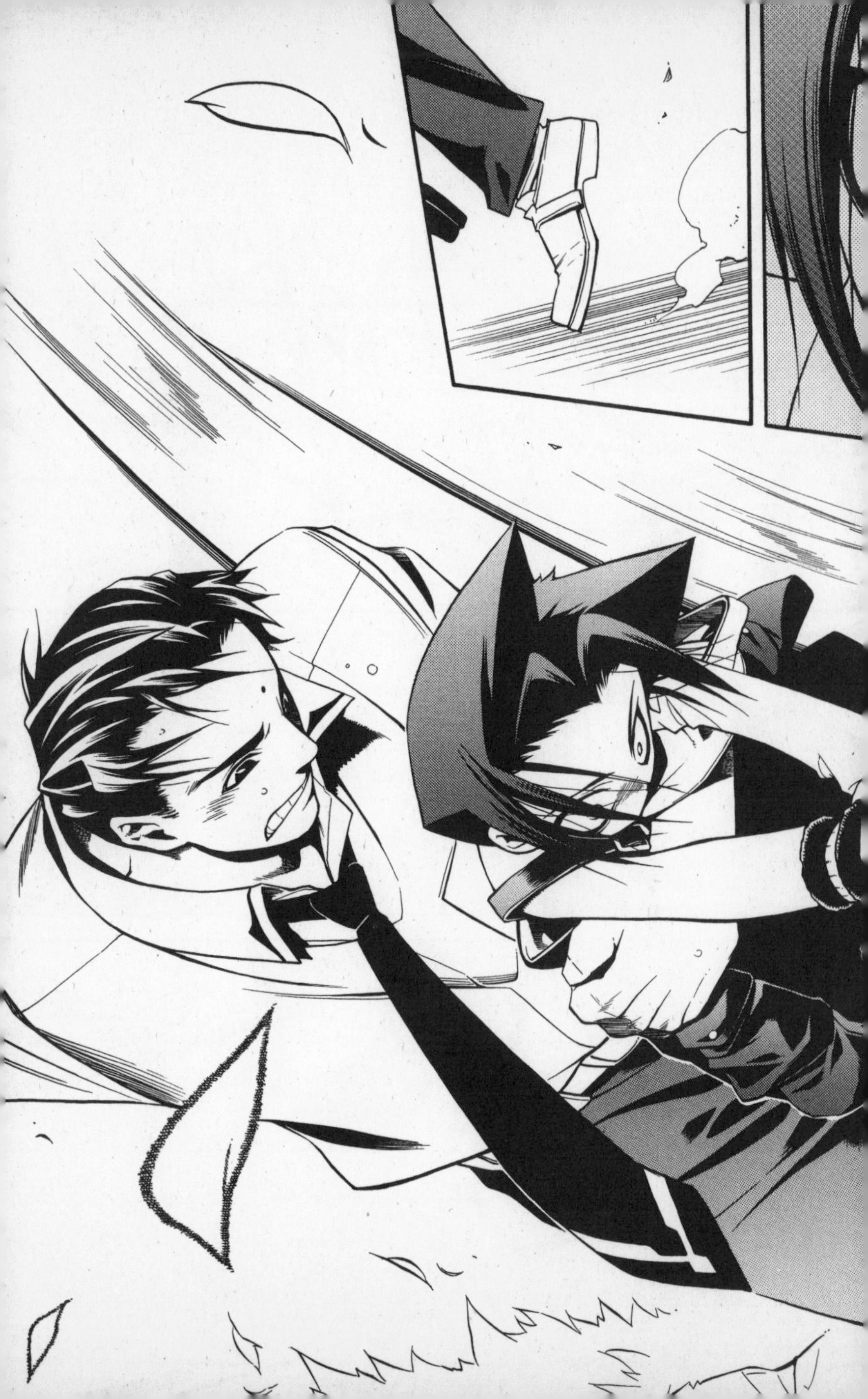

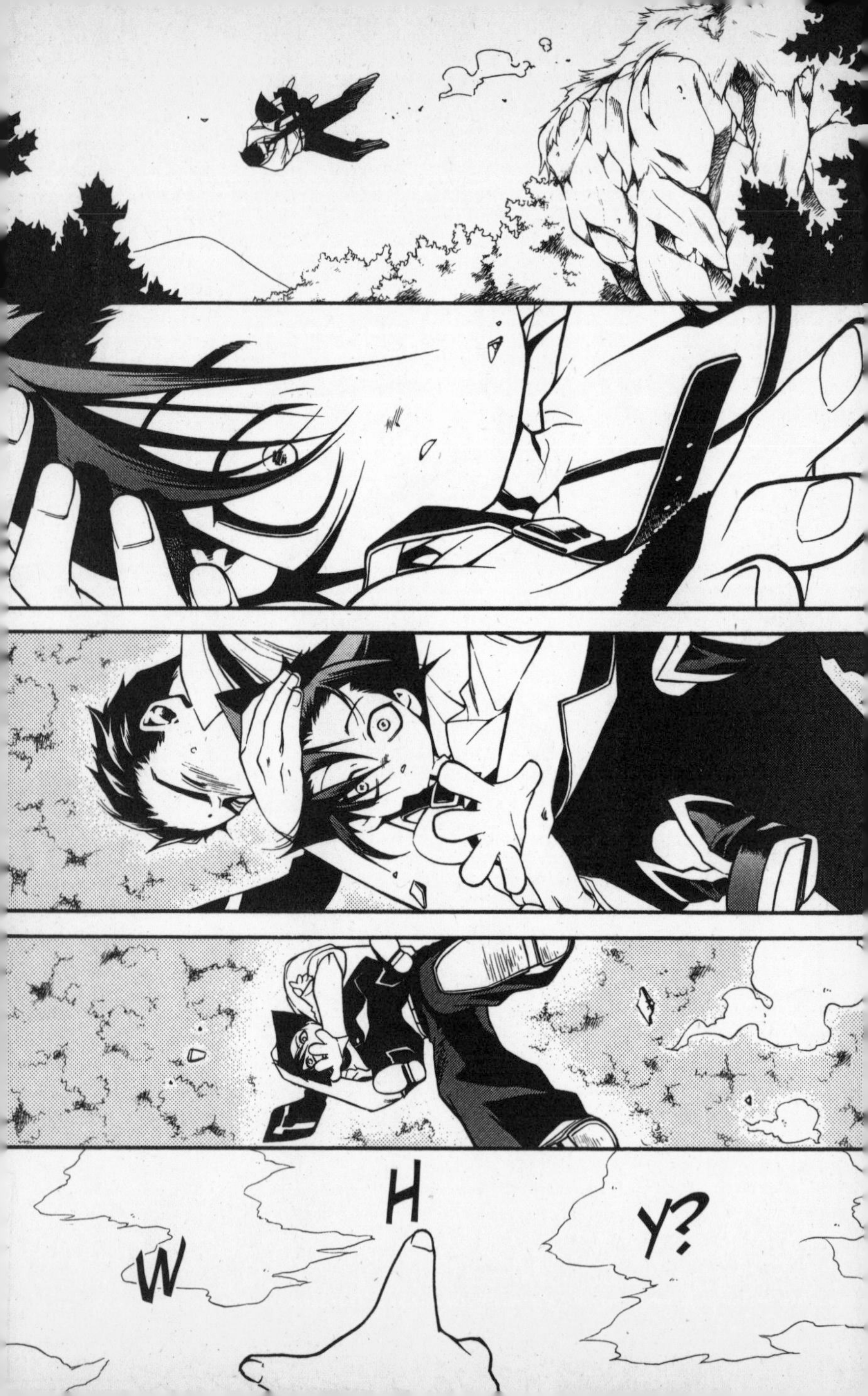
W H Y?

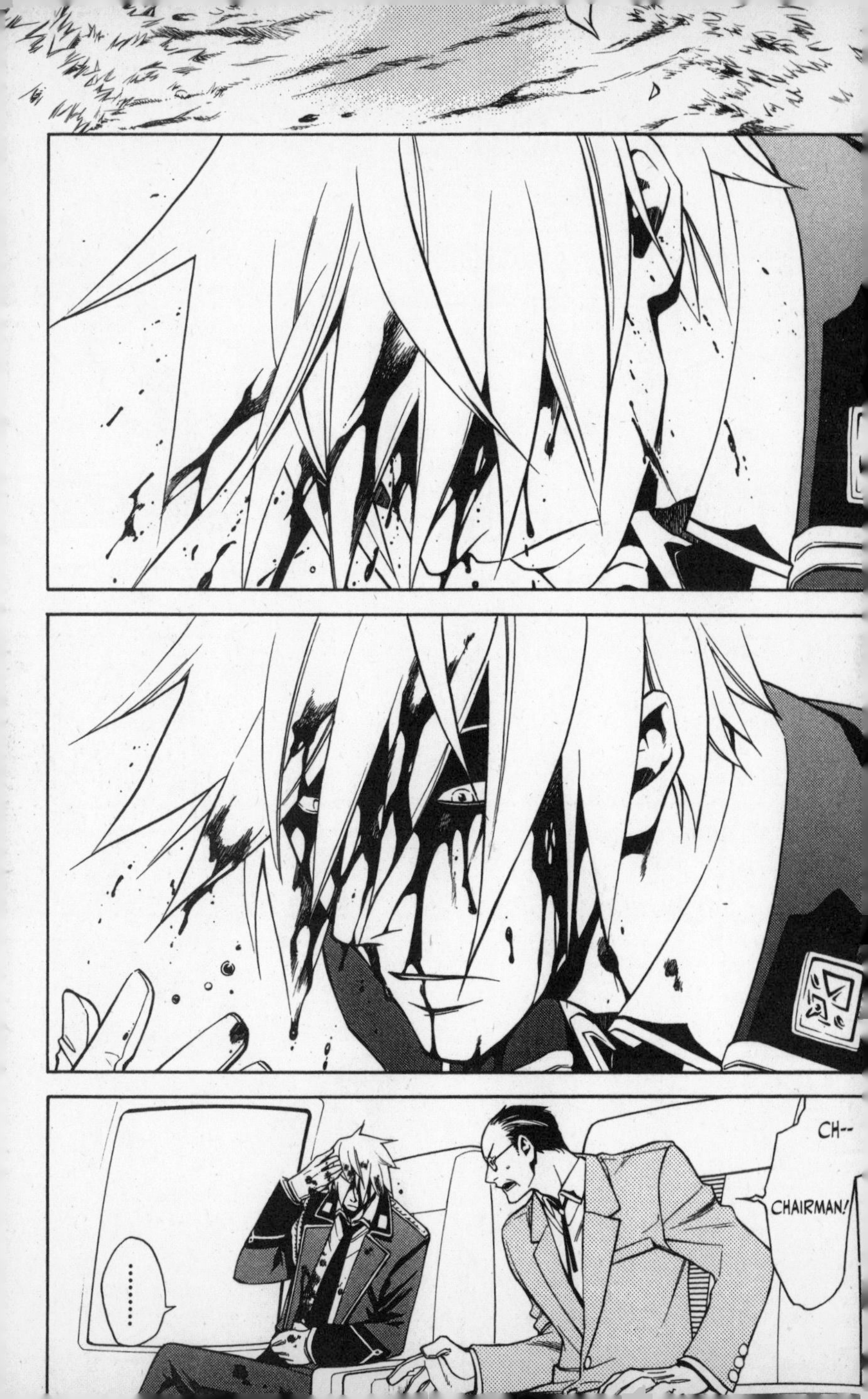
CH--
CHAIRMAN!
....

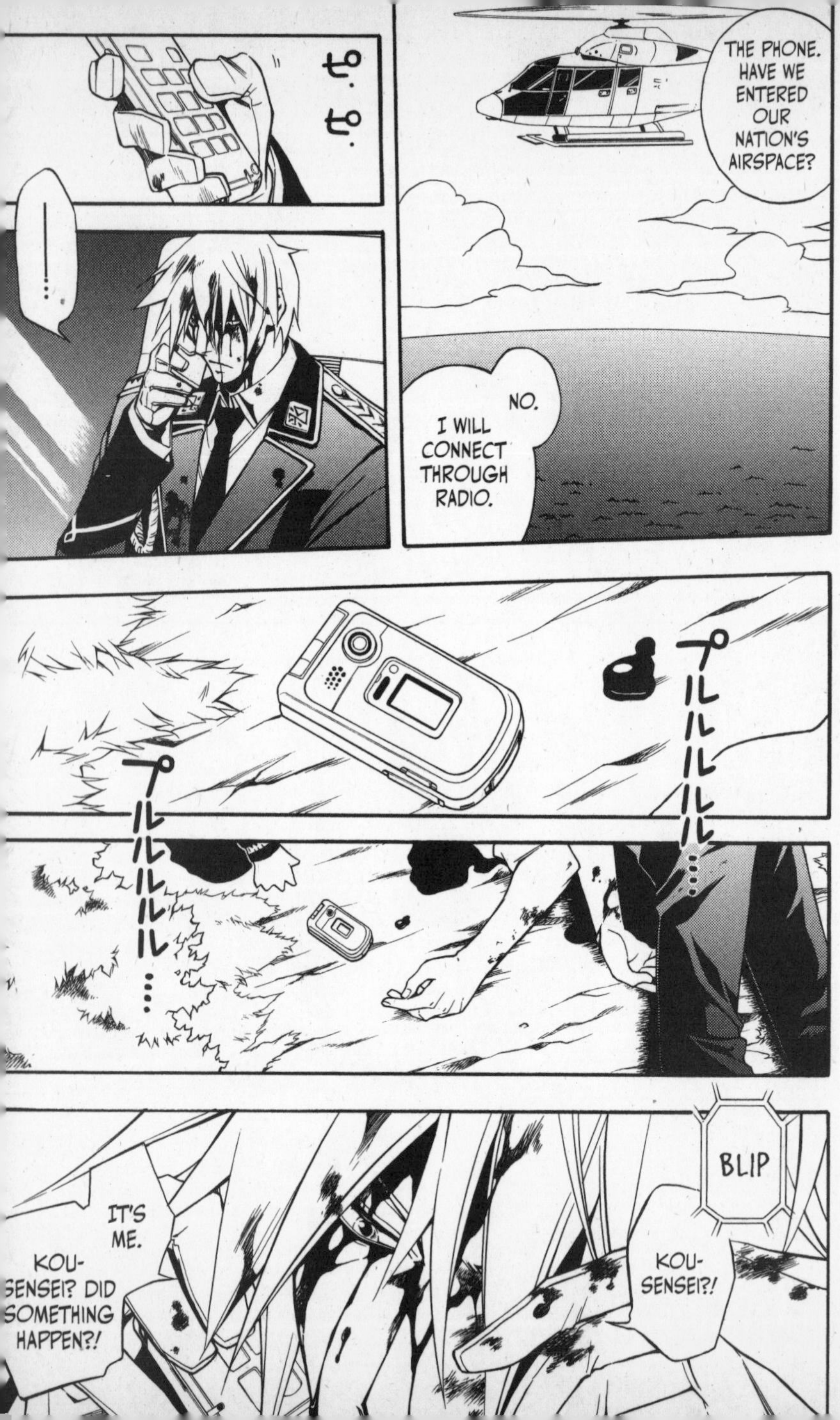
THE PHONE. HAVE WE ENTERED OUR NATION'S AIRSPACE?
NO. I WILL CONNECT THROUGH RADIO.
ピ. ピ.
......!
プルルルル....
プルルルル....
BLIP
KOU-SENSEI?!
IT'S ME.
KOU-SENSEI? DID SOMETHING HAPPEN?!

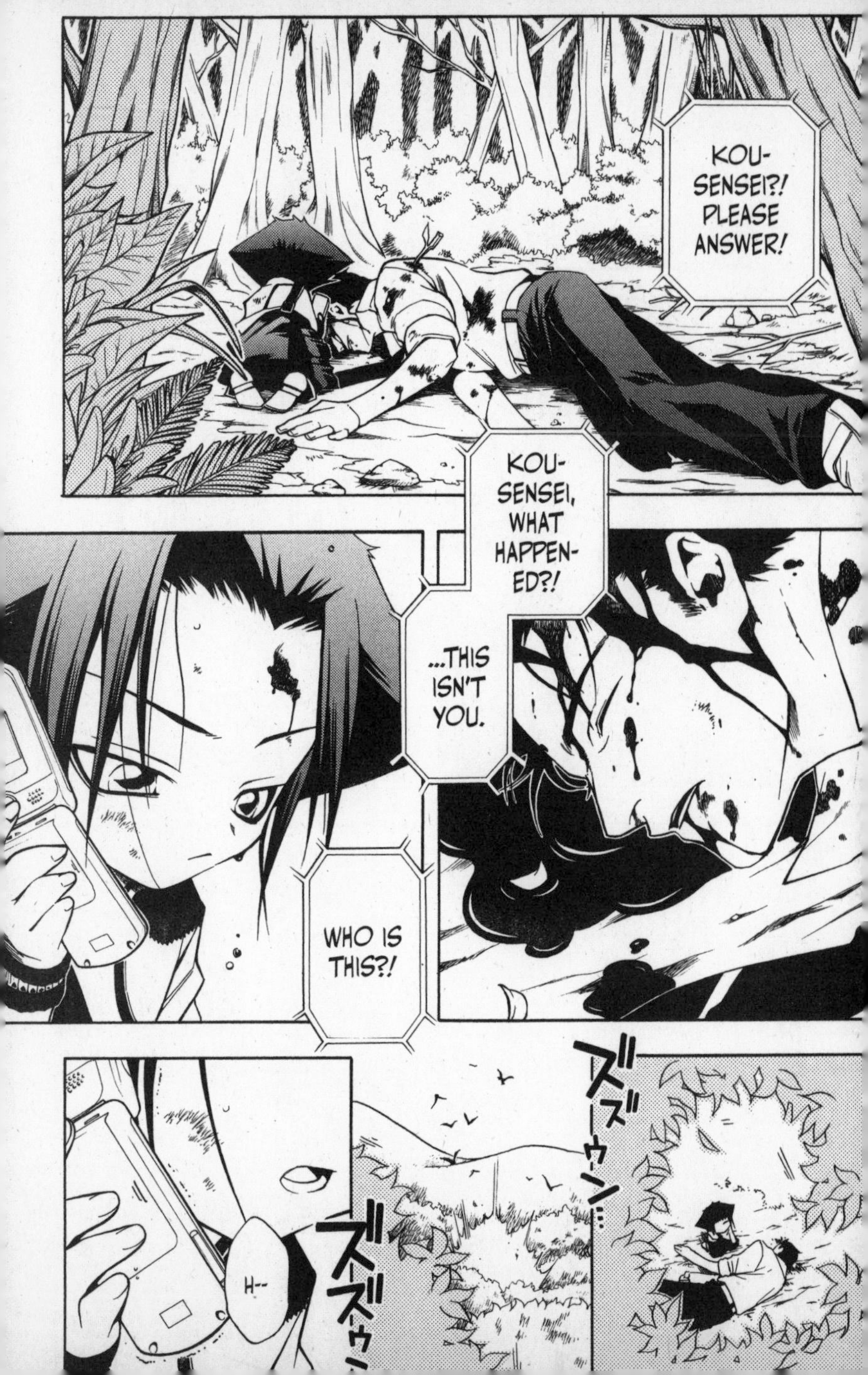
KOU-SENSEI?! PLEASE ANSWER!
KOU-SENSEI, WHAT HAPPEN-ED?!
...THIS ISN'T YOU.
WHO IS THIS?!
ズズーウン…
H--
ズーズーウ

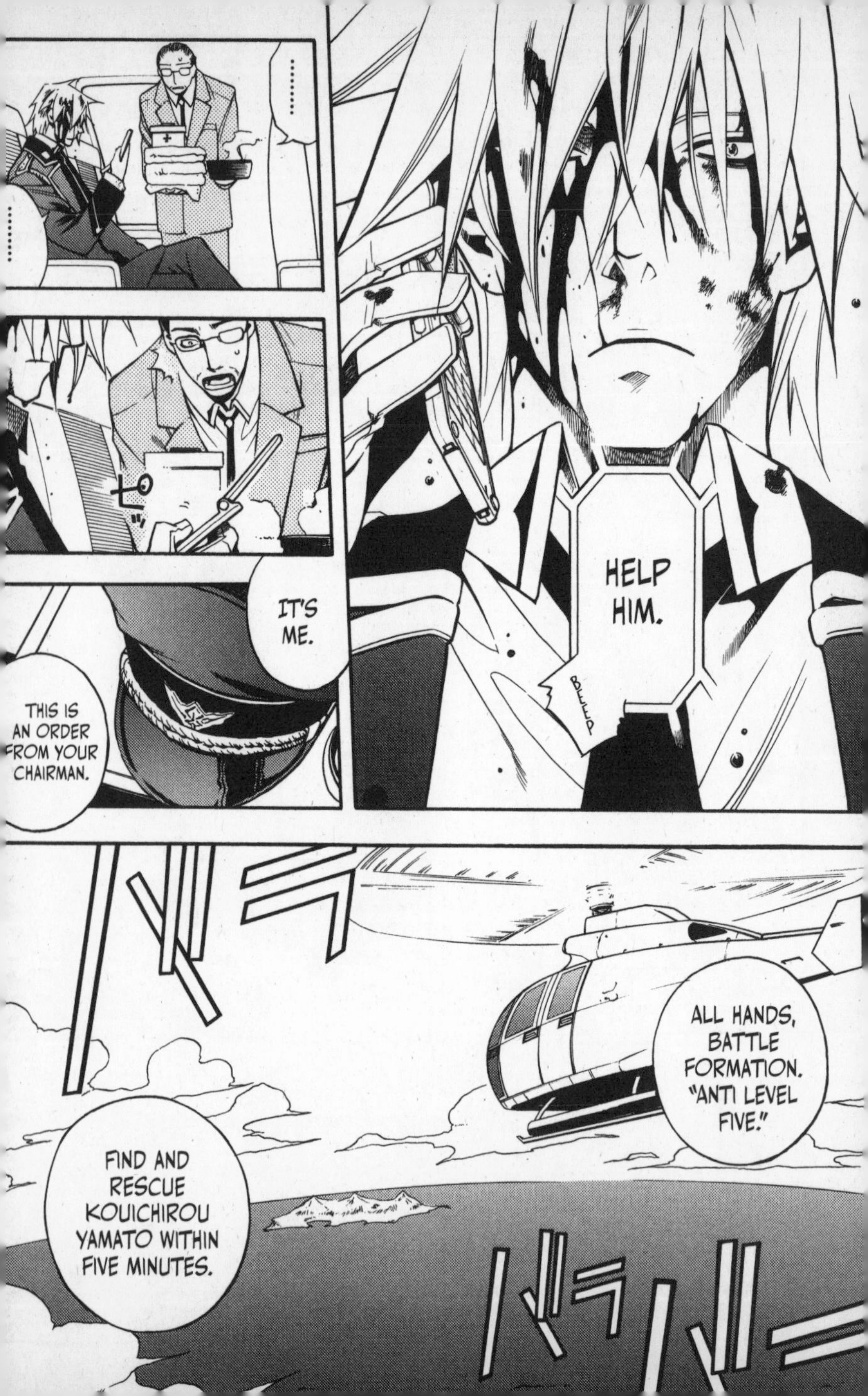
HELP HIM.
BEEP
......
......
IT'S ME.
THIS IS AN ORDER FROM YOUR CHAIRMAN.
ALL HANDS, BATTLE FORMATION. "ANTI LEVEL FIVE."
FIND AND RESCUE KOUICHIROU YAMATO WITHIN FIVE MINUTES.

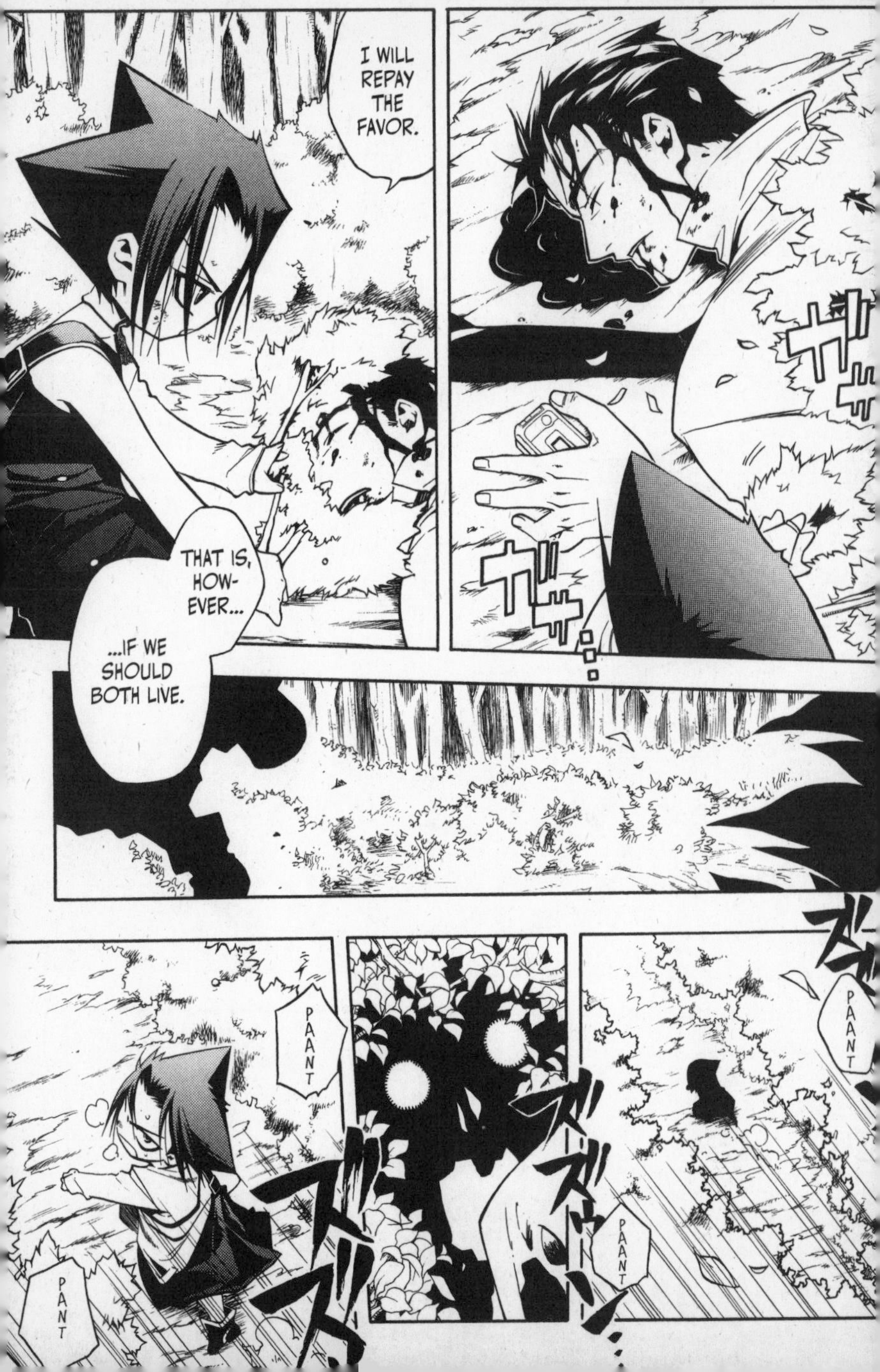
I WILL REPAY THE FAVOR.
THAT IS, HOW-EVER...
...IF WE SHOULD BOTH LIVE.
PAANT
PAANT
PAANT
PANT

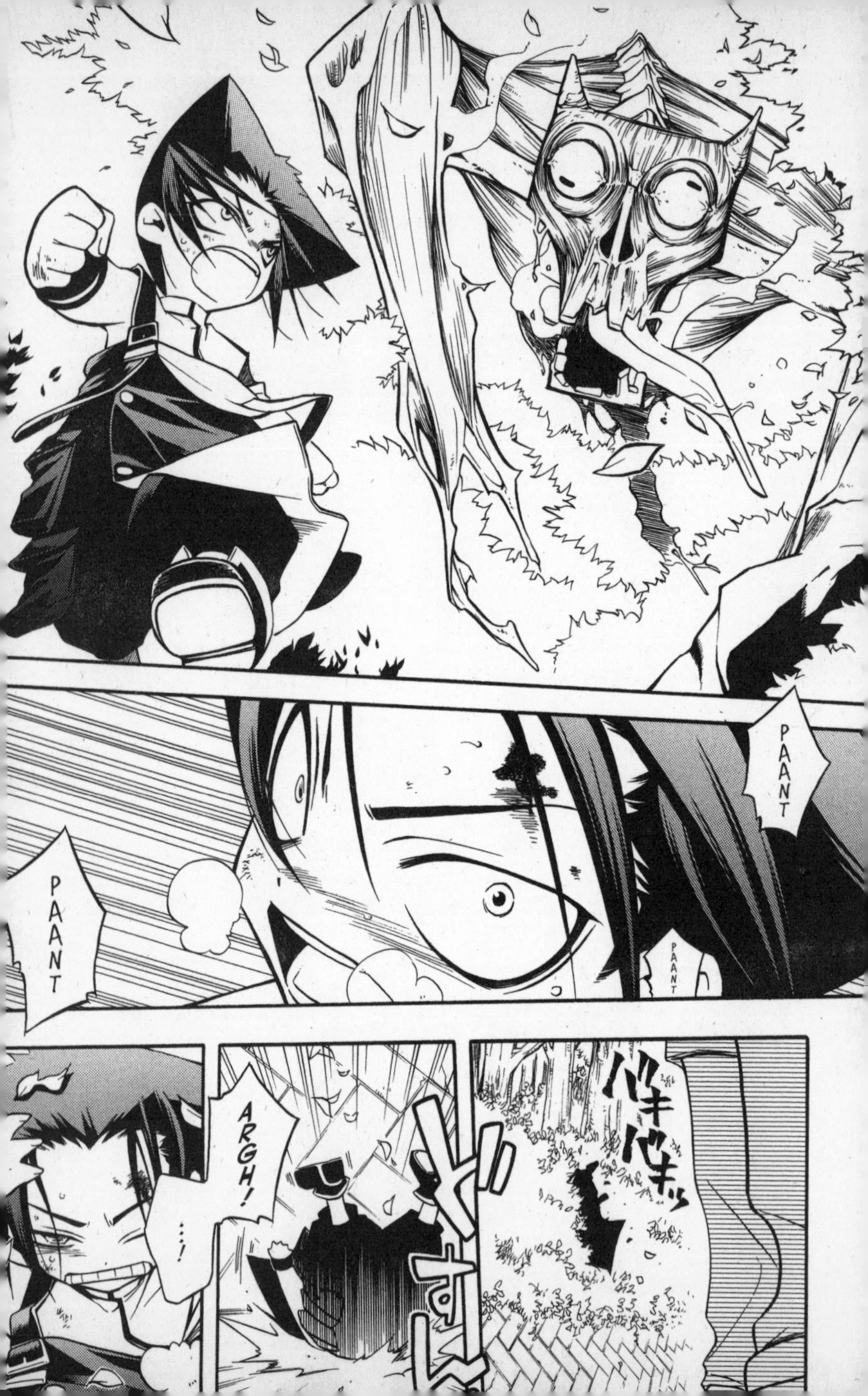
PAANT
PAANT
PAANT
バキバキッ
ドすん
ARGH!
...!

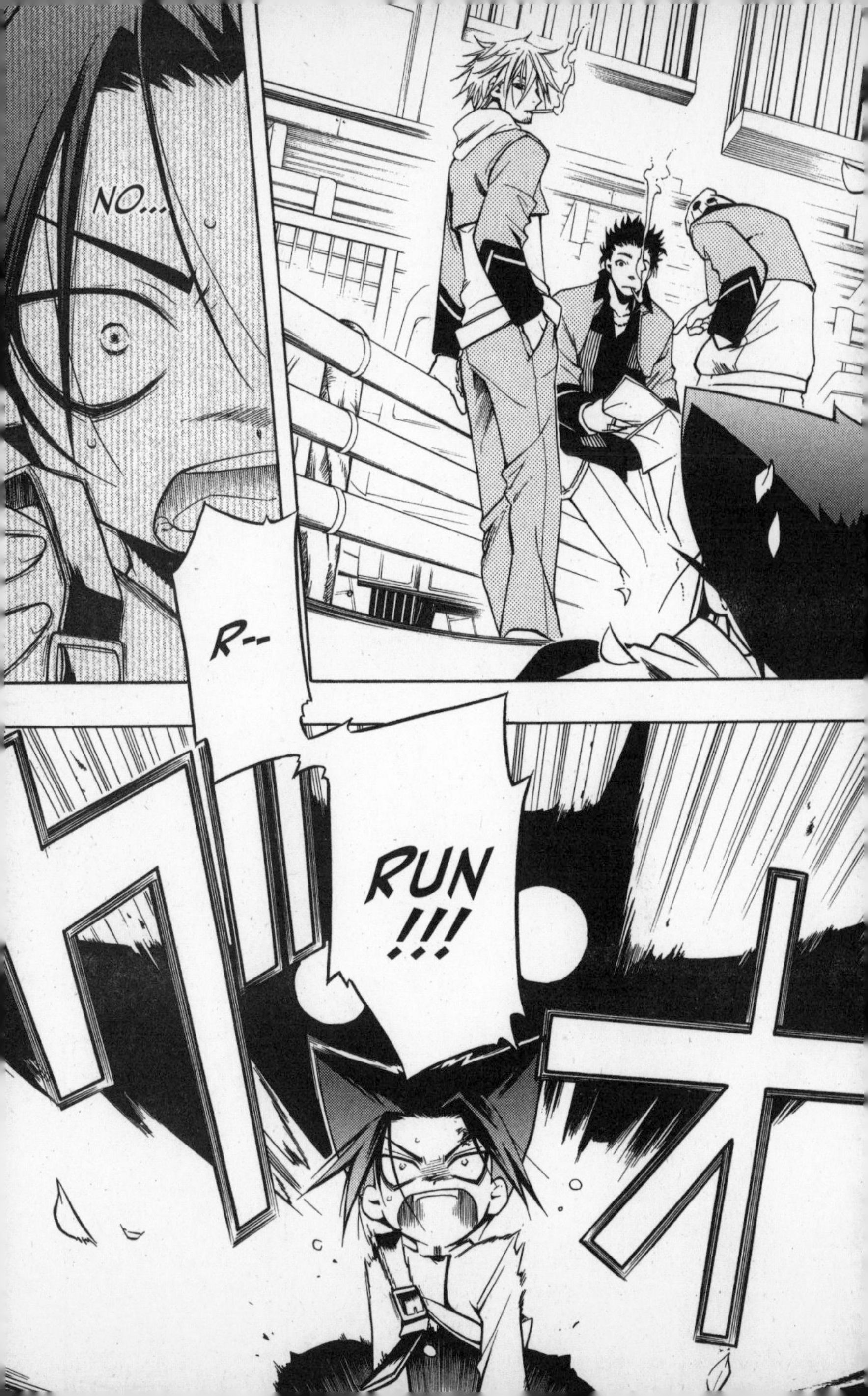
NO...
R--
RUN !!!

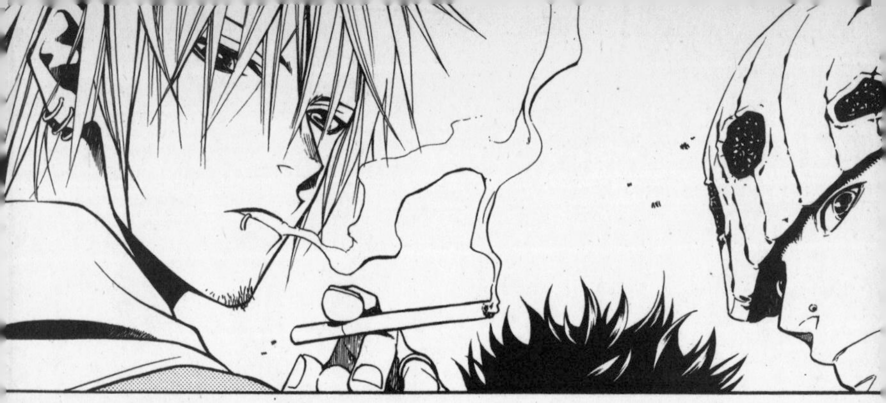
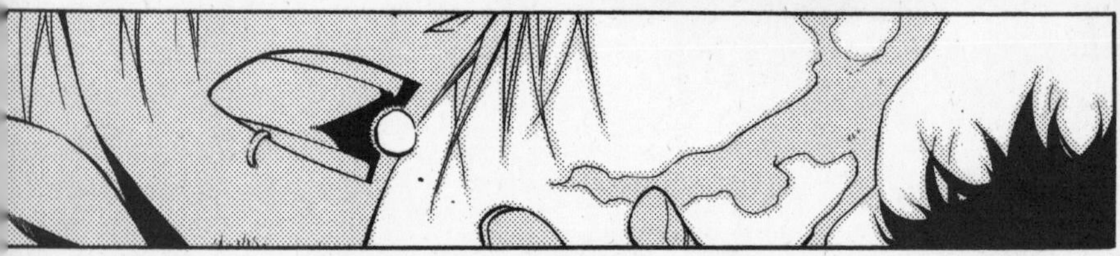
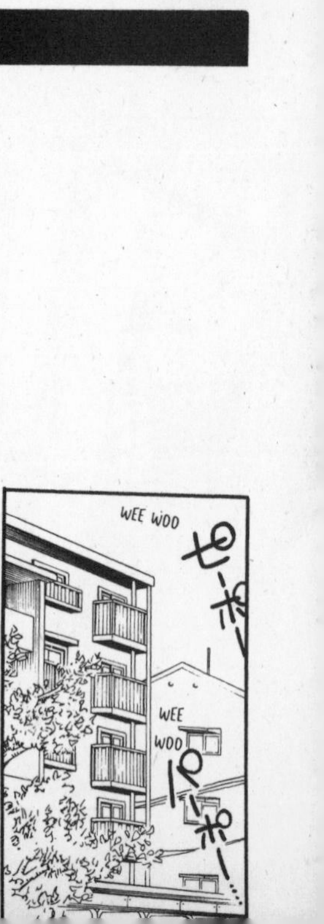
WEE WOO
ピーポー
WEE WOO
パーポー…
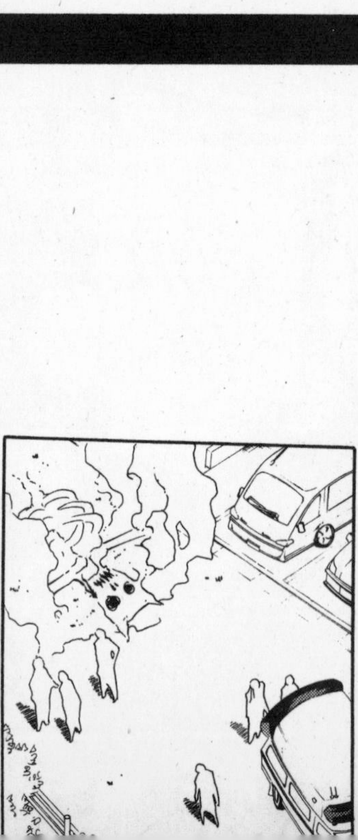
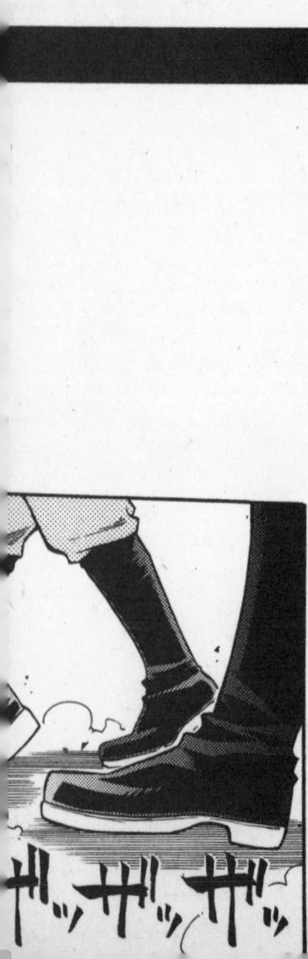
ザッザッザッ

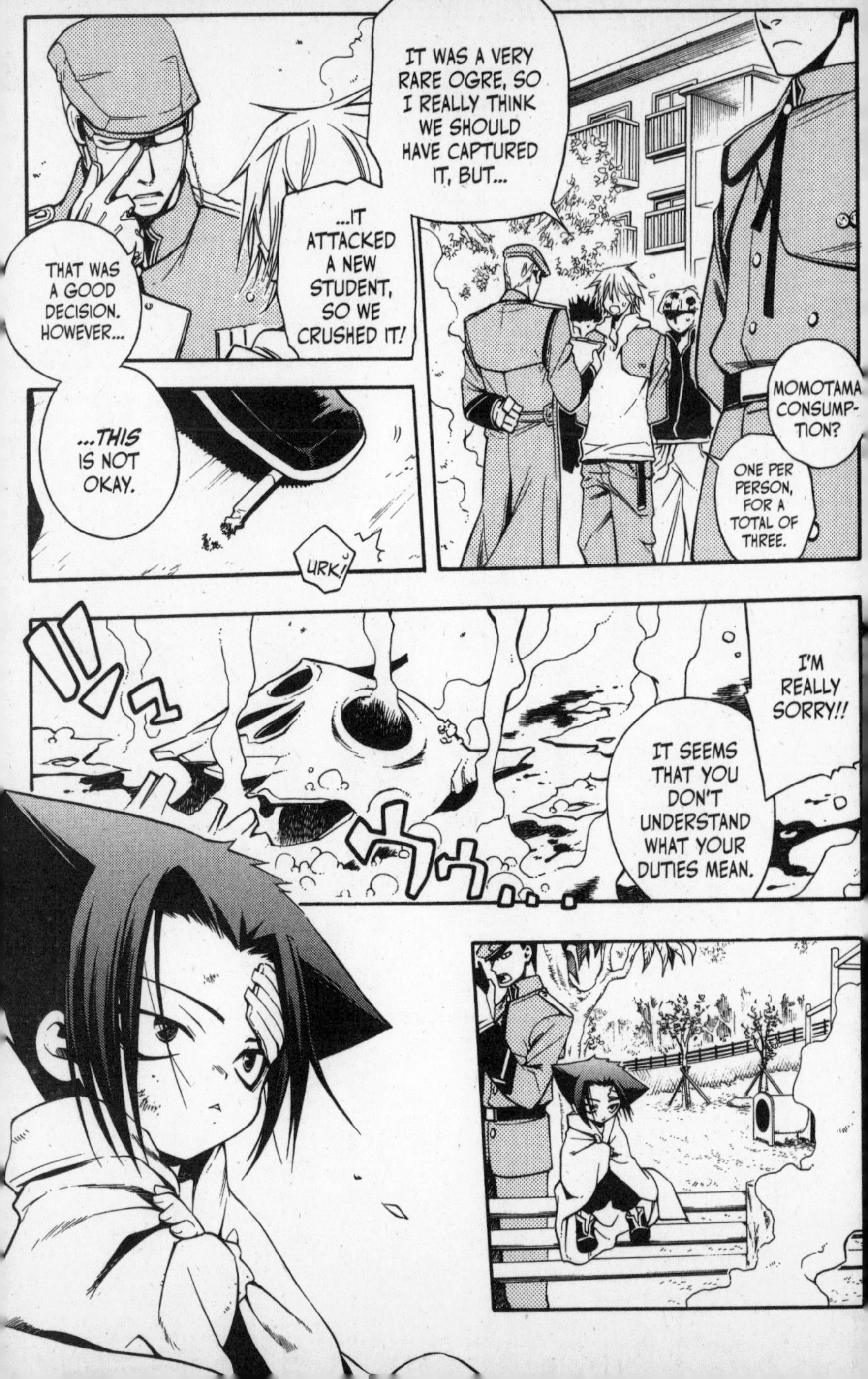
MOMOTAMA CONSUMPTION?
ONE PER PERSON, FOR A TOTAL OF THREE.
IT WAS A VERY RARE OGRE, SO I REALLY THINK WE SHOULD HAVE CAPTURED IT, BUT...
...IT ATTACKED A NEW STUDENT, SO WE CRUSHED IT!
THAT WAS A GOOD DECISION. HOWEVER...
...THIS IS NOT OKAY.
URK!
I'M REALLY SORRY!!
IT SEEMS THAT YOU DON'T UNDERSTAND WHAT YOUR DUTIES MEAN.

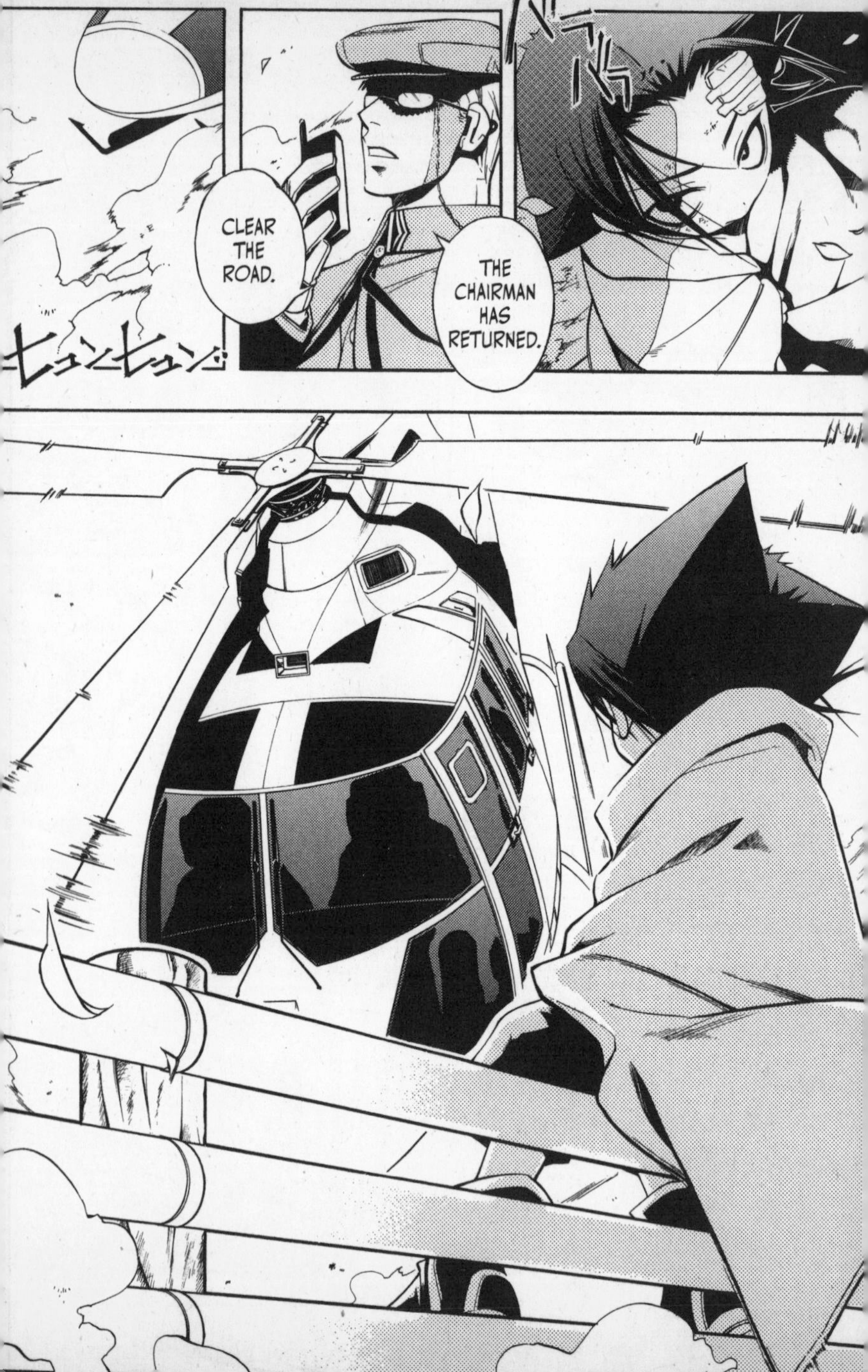
THE CHAIRMAN HAS RETURNED.
CLEAR THE ROAD.
ヒュンヒュン

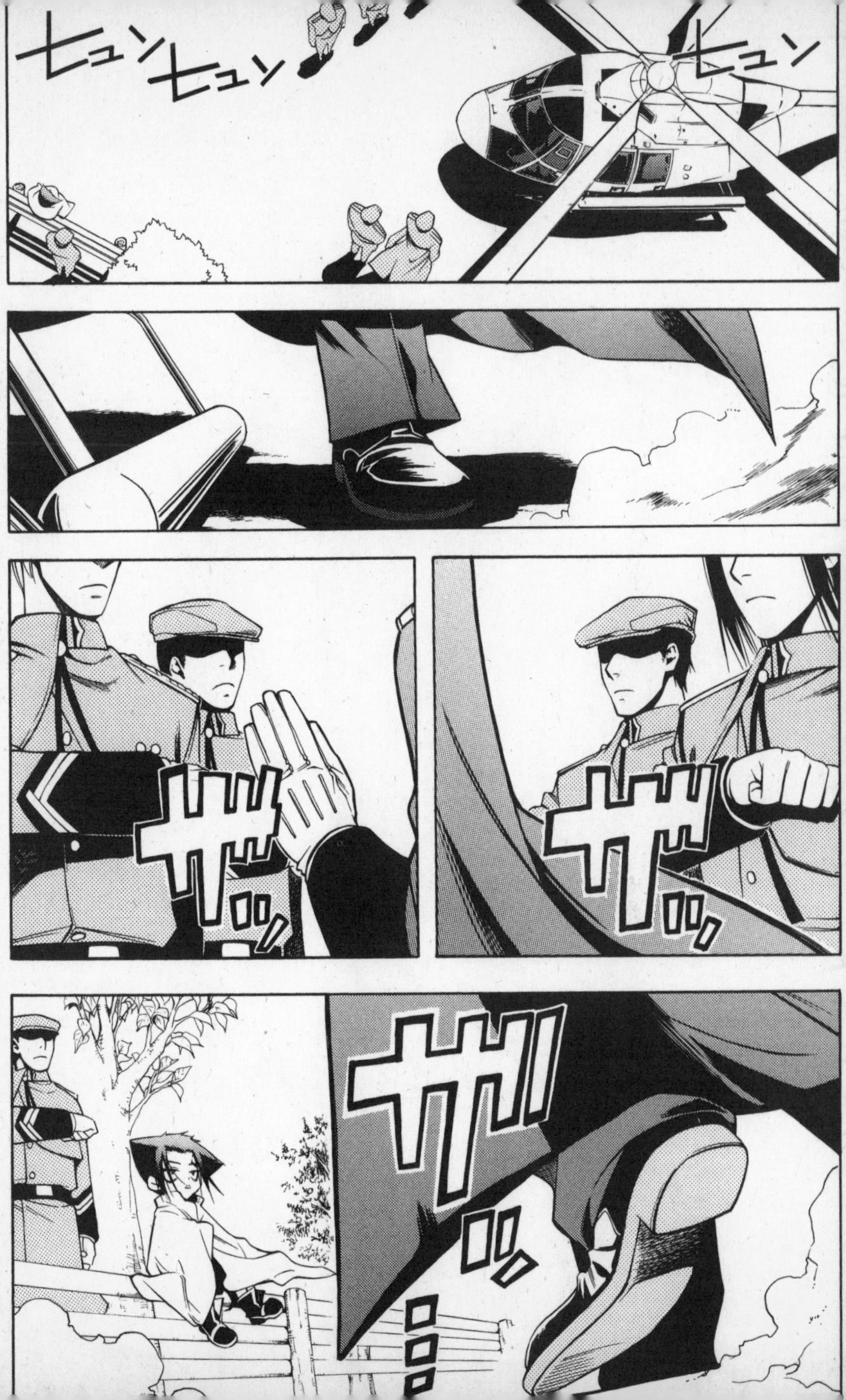
ヒュン
ヒュン
ヒュン
ザッ
ザッ
ザッ

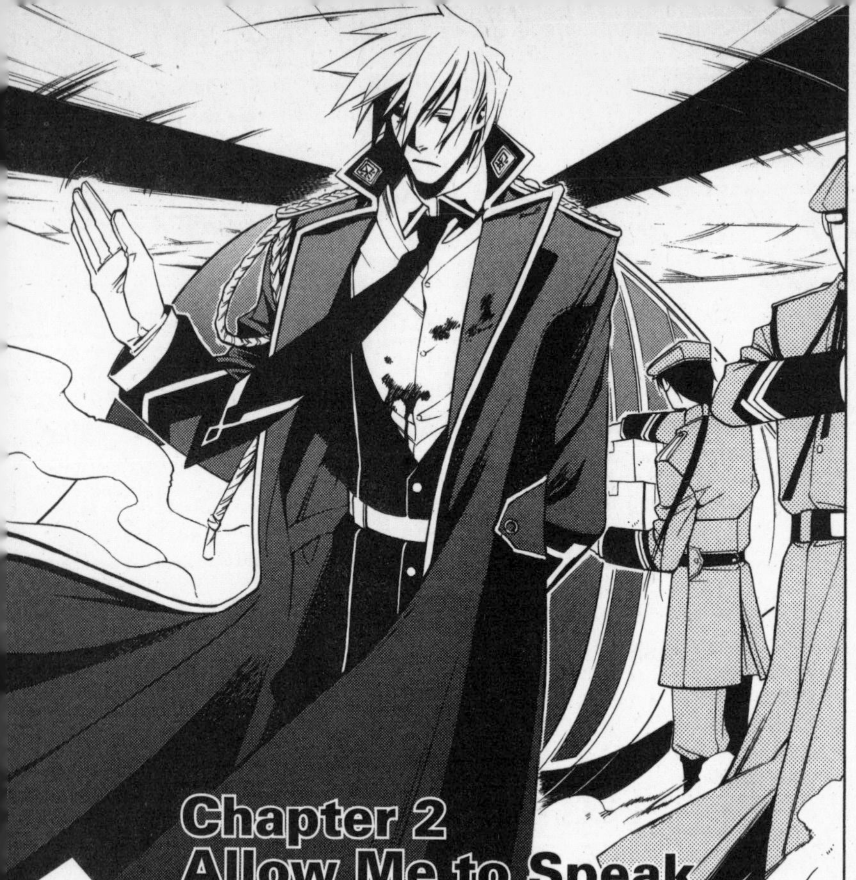
Chapter 2
Allow Me to Speak

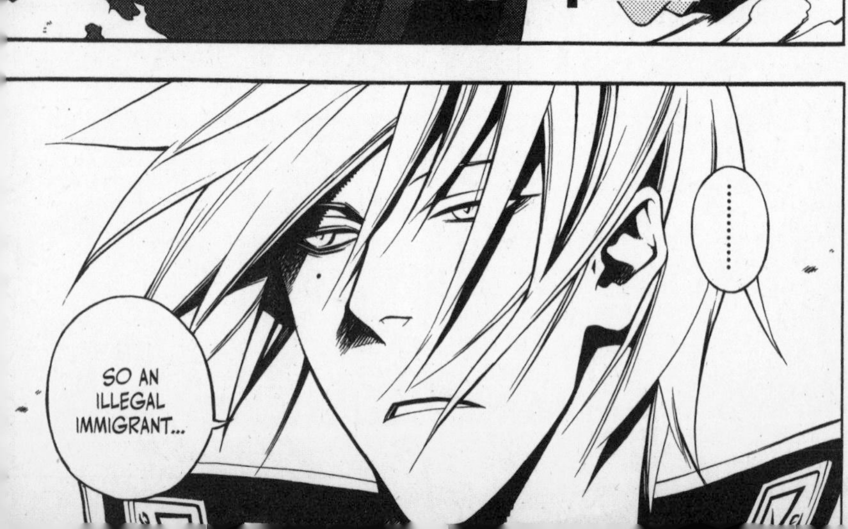
....
SO AN ILLEGAL IMMIGRANT...

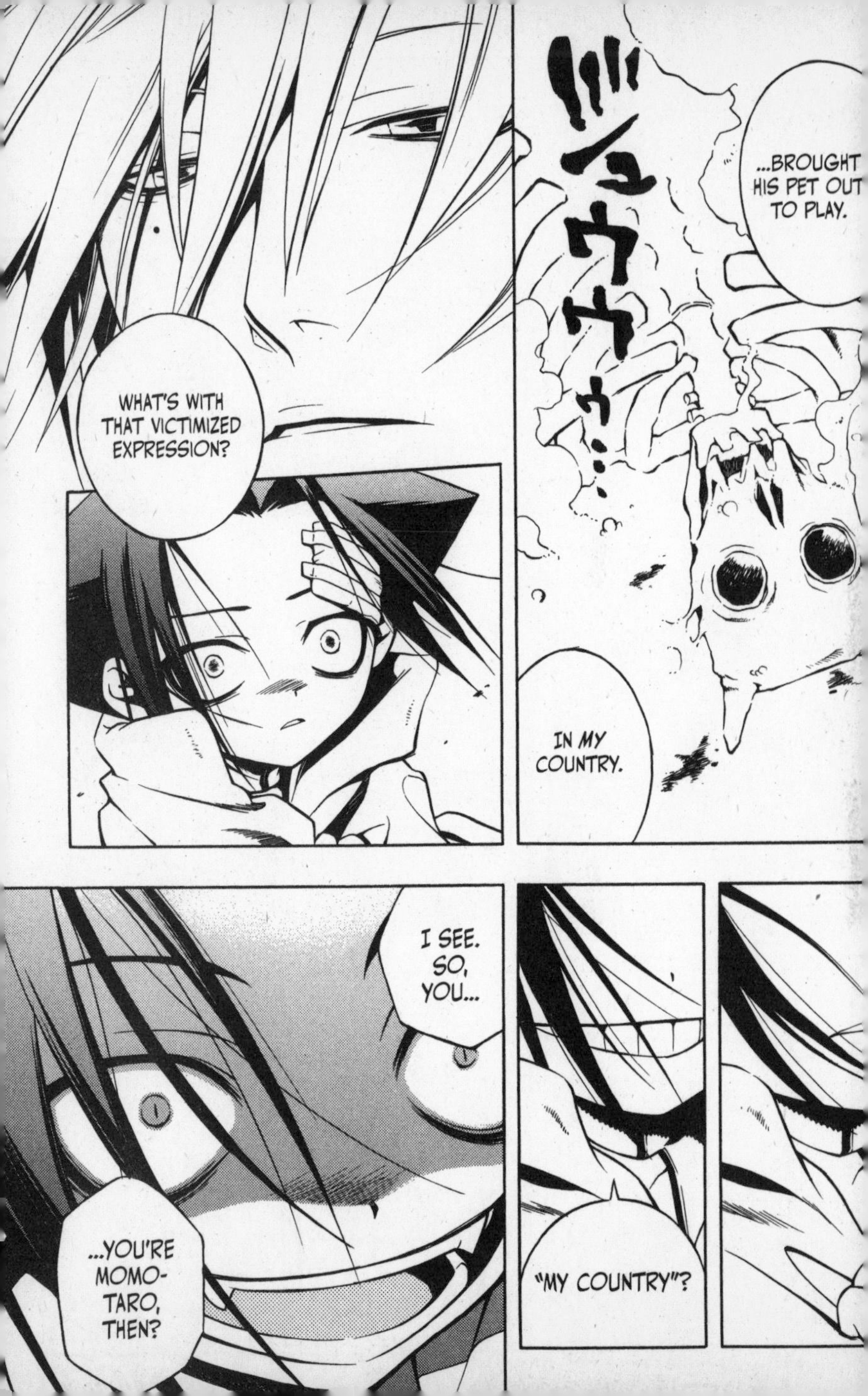
ジュウウゥ
...BROUGHT HIS PET OUT TO PLAY.
IN MY COUNTRY.
WHAT'S WITH THAT VICTIMIZED EXPRESSION?
"MY COUNTRY"?
I SEE. SO, YOU...
...YOU'RE MOMO-TARO, THEN?

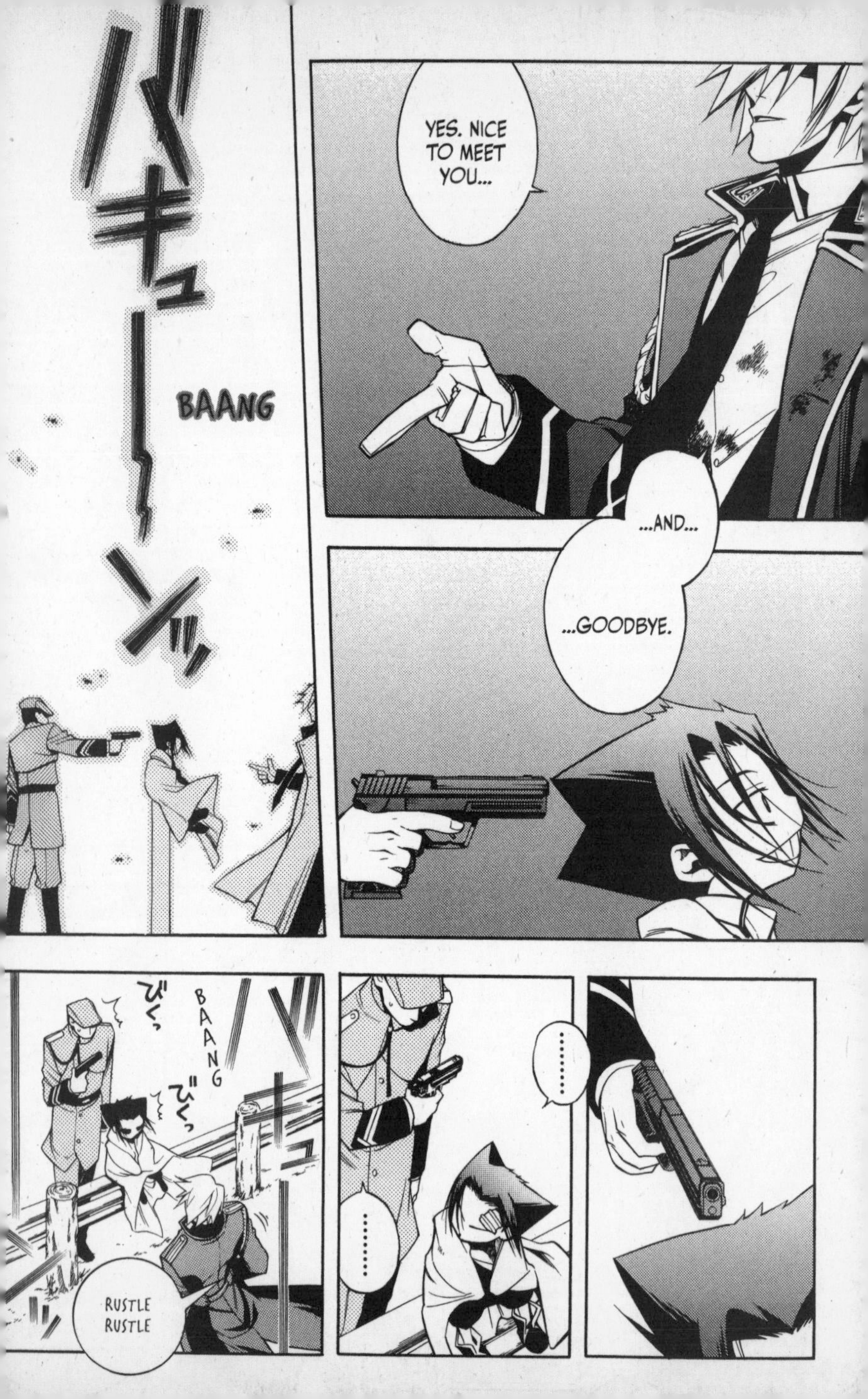
YES. NICE TO MEET YOU...
...AND...
...GOODBYE.
バキューンッ
BAANG
......
......
バキュ
BAANG
びくっ
びくっ
RUSTLE RUSTLE

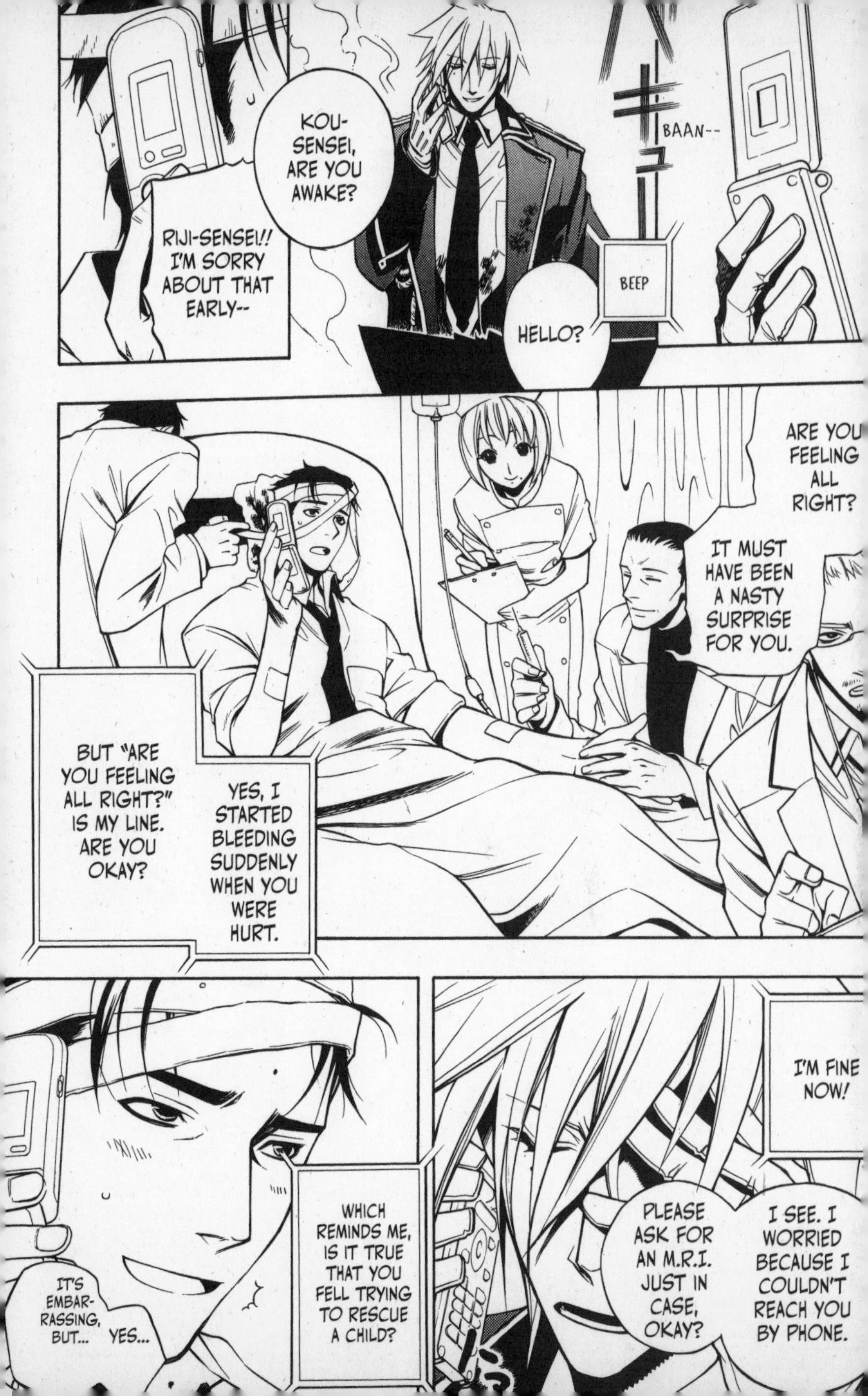
BAAN--
BEEP
HELLO?
KOU-SENSEI, ARE YOU AWAKE?
RIJI-SENSEI!! I'M SORRY ABOUT THAT EARLY--
ARE YOU FEELING ALL RIGHT?
IT MUST HAVE BEEN A NASTY SURPRISE FOR YOU.
YES, I STARTED BLEEDING SUDDENLY WHEN YOU WERE HURT.
BUT "ARE YOU FEELING ALL RIGHT?" IS MY LINE. ARE YOU OKAY?
I'M FINE NOW!
I SEE. I WORRIED BECAUSE I COULDN'T REACH YOU BY PHONE.
PLEASE ASK FOR AN M.R.I. JUST IN CASE, OKAY?
WHICH REMINDS ME, IS IT TRUE THAT YOU FELL TRYING TO RESCUE A CHILD?
IT'S EMBARRASSING, BUT...
YES...

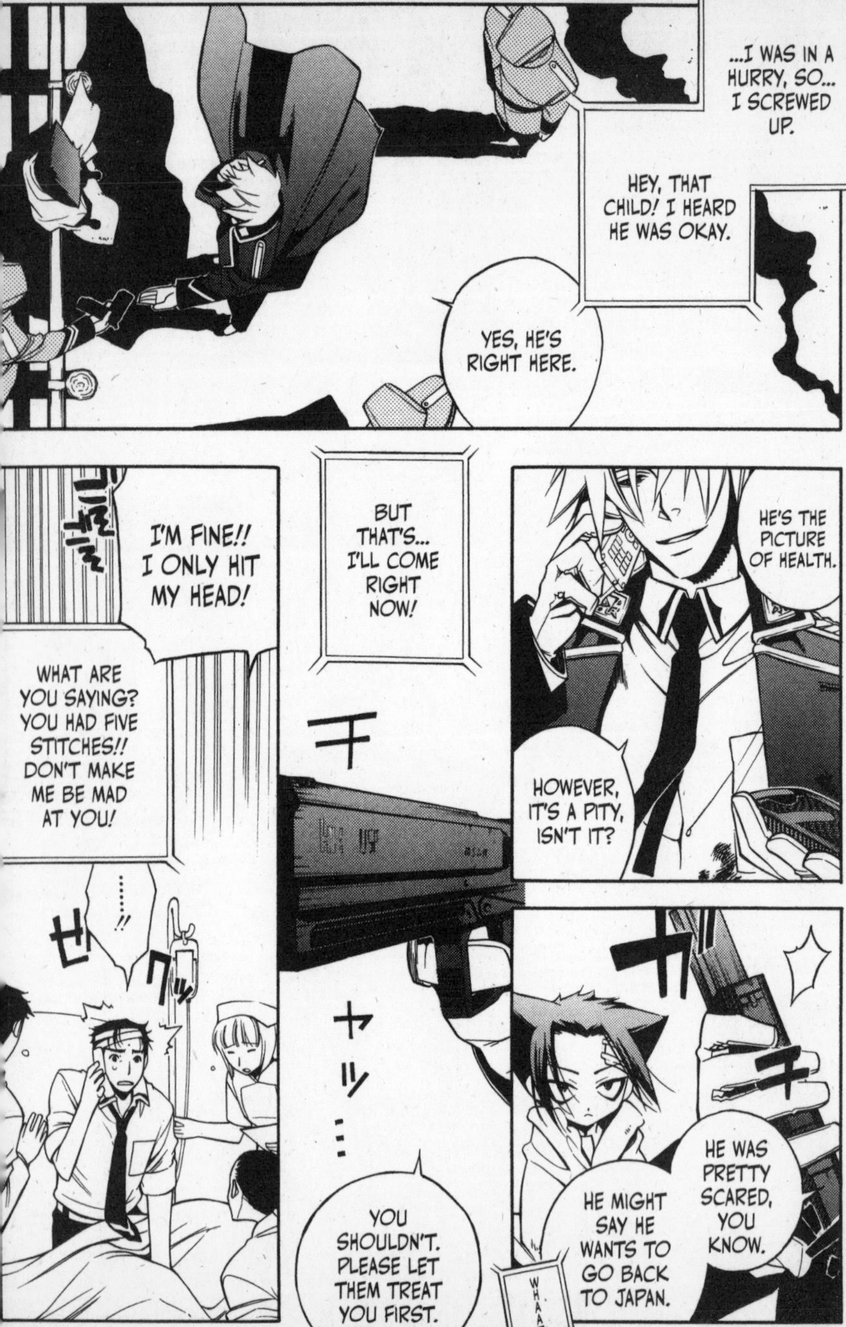
...I WAS IN A HURRY, SO... I SCREWED UP.
HEY, THAT CHILD! I HEARD HE WAS OKAY.
YES, HE'S RIGHT HERE.
HE'S THE PICTURE OF HEALTH.
HOWEVER, IT'S A PITY, ISN'T IT?
HE WAS PRETTY SCARED, YOU KNOW.
HE MIGHT SAY HE WANTS TO GO BACK TO JAPAN.
WHAAAT?!
BUT THAT'S... I'LL COME RIGHT NOW!
YOU SHOULDN'T. PLEASE LET THEM TREAT YOU FIRST.
I'M FINE!! I ONLY HIT MY HEAD!
WHAT ARE YOU SAYING? YOU HAD FIVE STITCHES!! DON'T MAKE ME BE MAD AT YOU!
......!!

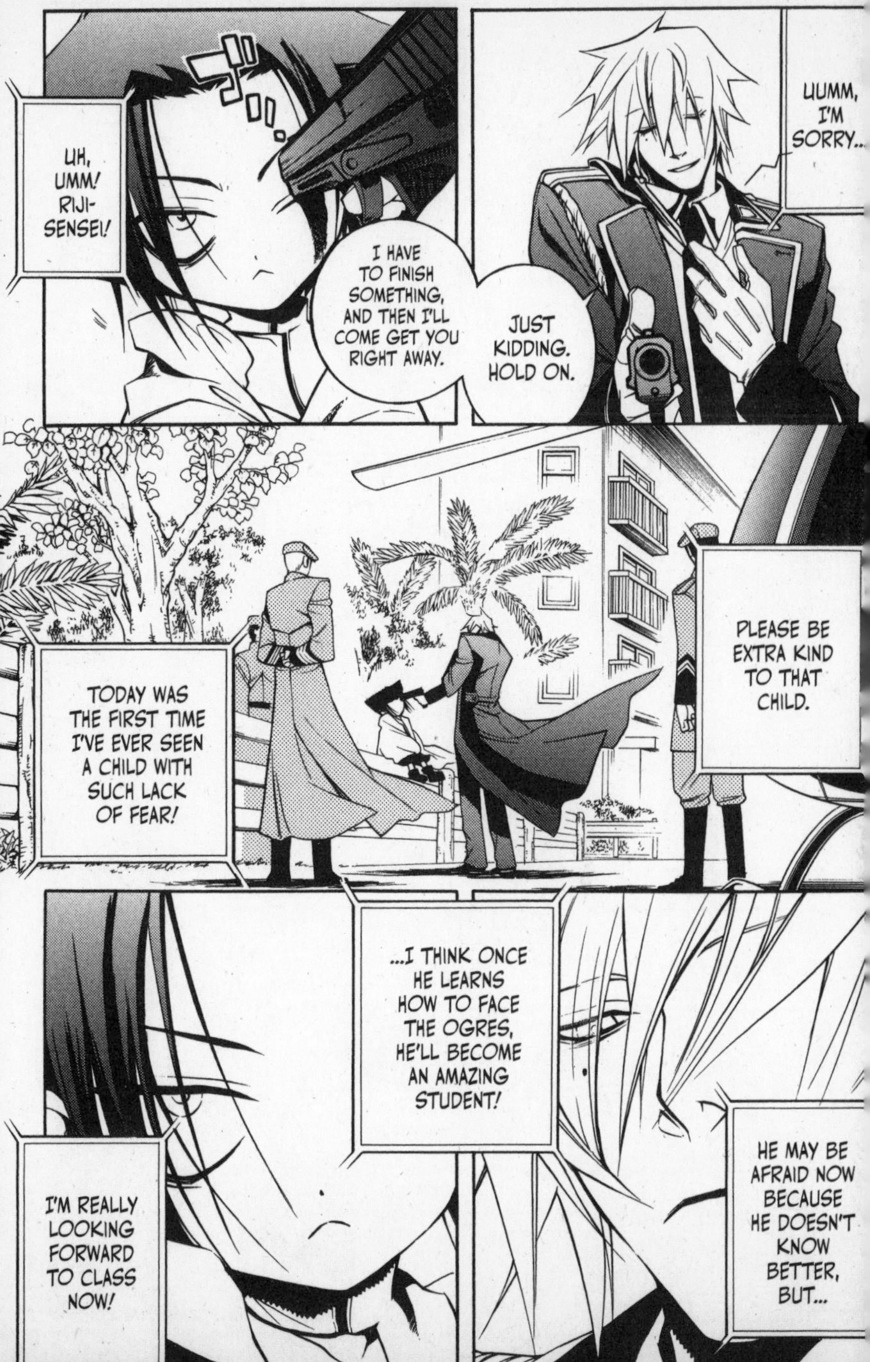
UUMM, I'M SORRY...
JUST KIDDING. HOLD ON.
I HAVE TO FINISH SOMETHING, AND THEN I'LL COME GET YOU RIGHT AWAY.
UH, UMM! RIJI-SENSEI!
PLEASE BE EXTRA KIND TO THAT CHILD.
TODAY WAS THE FIRST TIME I'VE EVER SEEN A CHILD WITH SUCH LACK OF FEAR!
HE MAY BE AFRAID NOW BECAUSE HE DOESN'T KNOW BETTER, BUT...
...I THINK ONCE HE LEARNS HOW TO FACE THE OGRES, HE'LL BECOME AN AMAZING STUDENT!
I'M REALLY LOOKING FORWARD TO CLASS NOW!

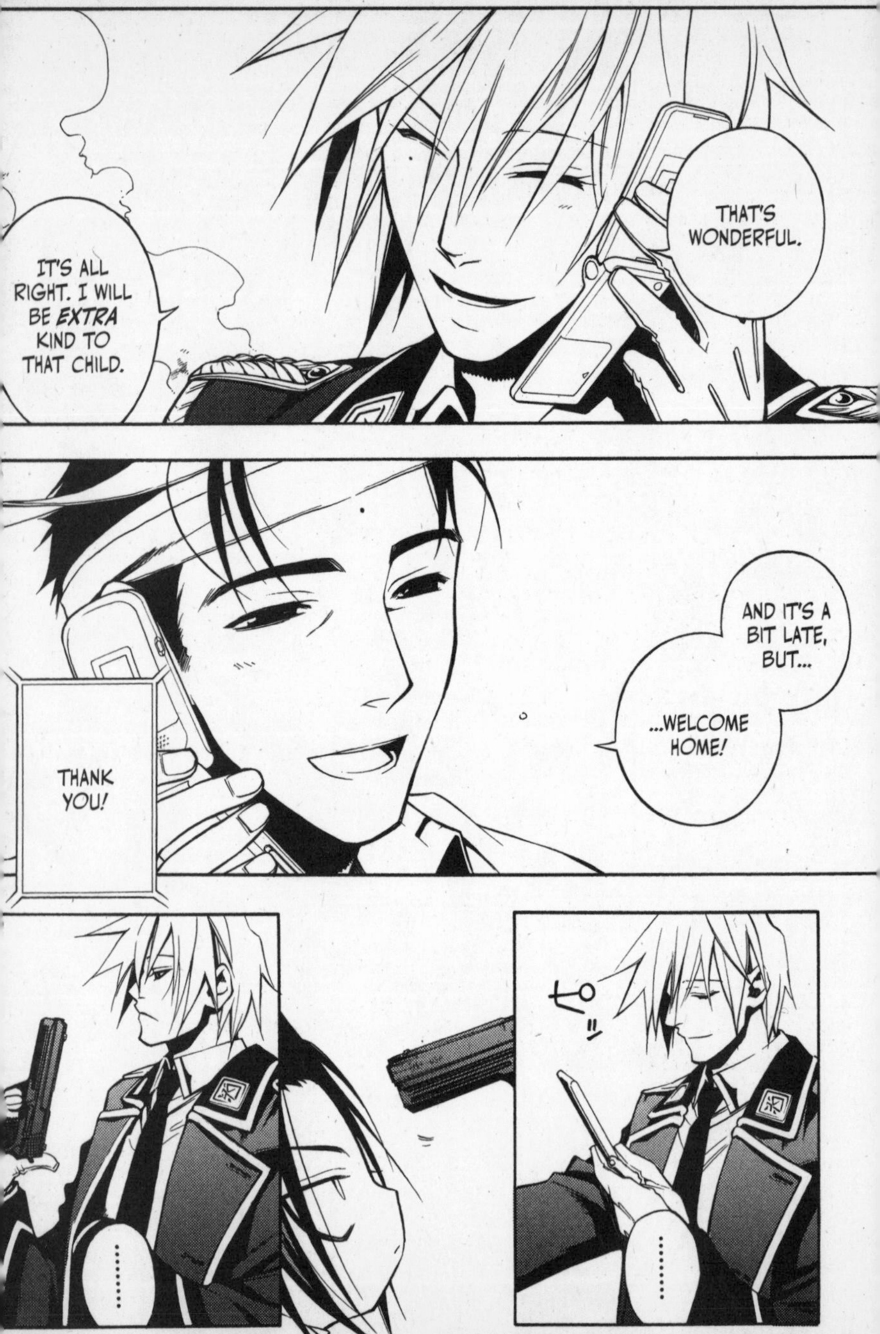

THAT'S WONDERFUL.
IT'S ALL RIGHT. I WILL BE *EXTRA* KIND TO THAT CHILD.
AND IT'S A BIT LATE, BUT...
...WELCOME HOME!
THANK YOU!
ピッ
......
......

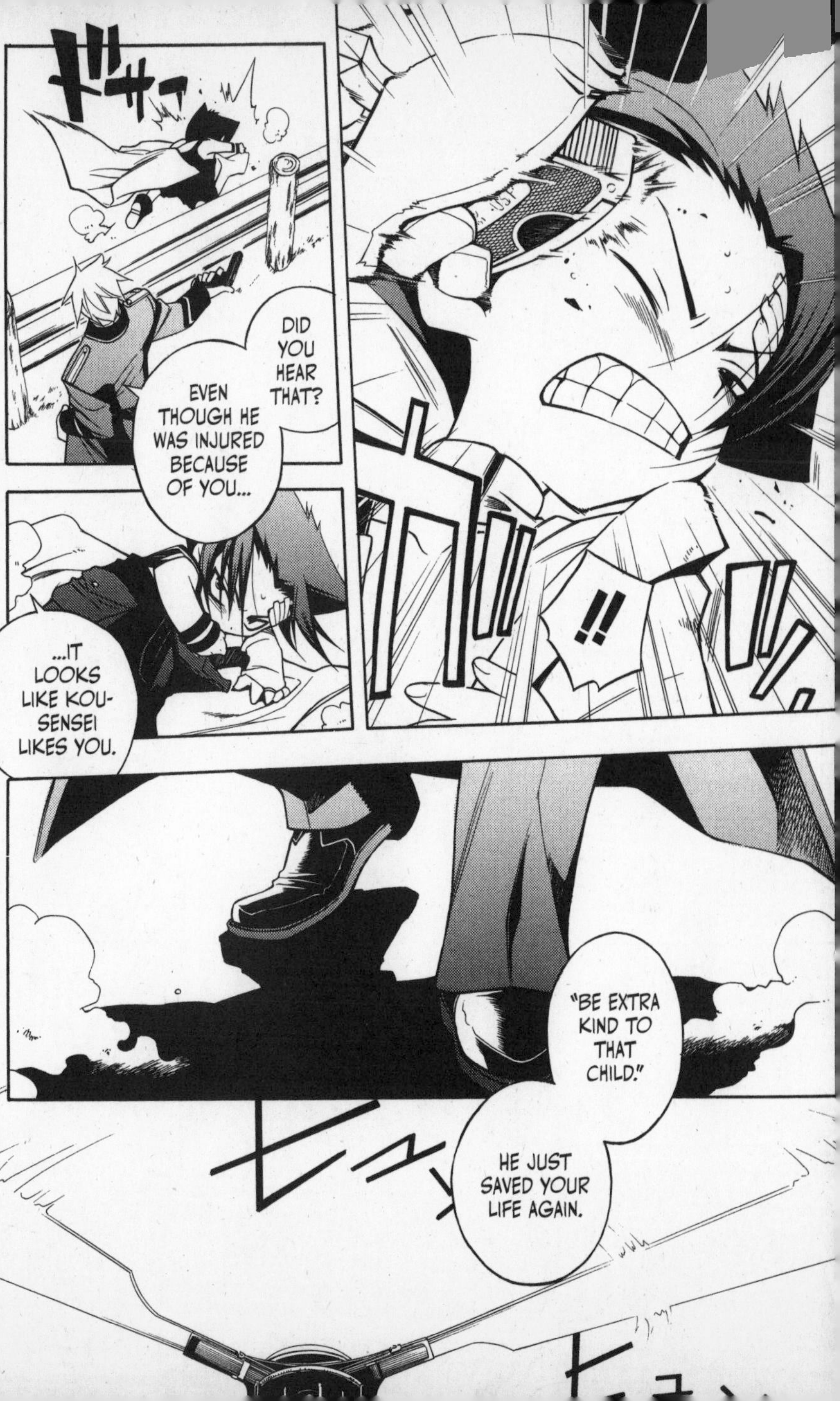
DID YOU HEAR THAT?
EVEN THOUGH HE WAS INJURED BECAUSE OF YOU...
...IT LOOKS LIKE KOU-SENSEI LIKES YOU.
"BE EXTRA KIND TO THAT CHILD."
HE JUST SAVED YOUR LIFE AGAIN.

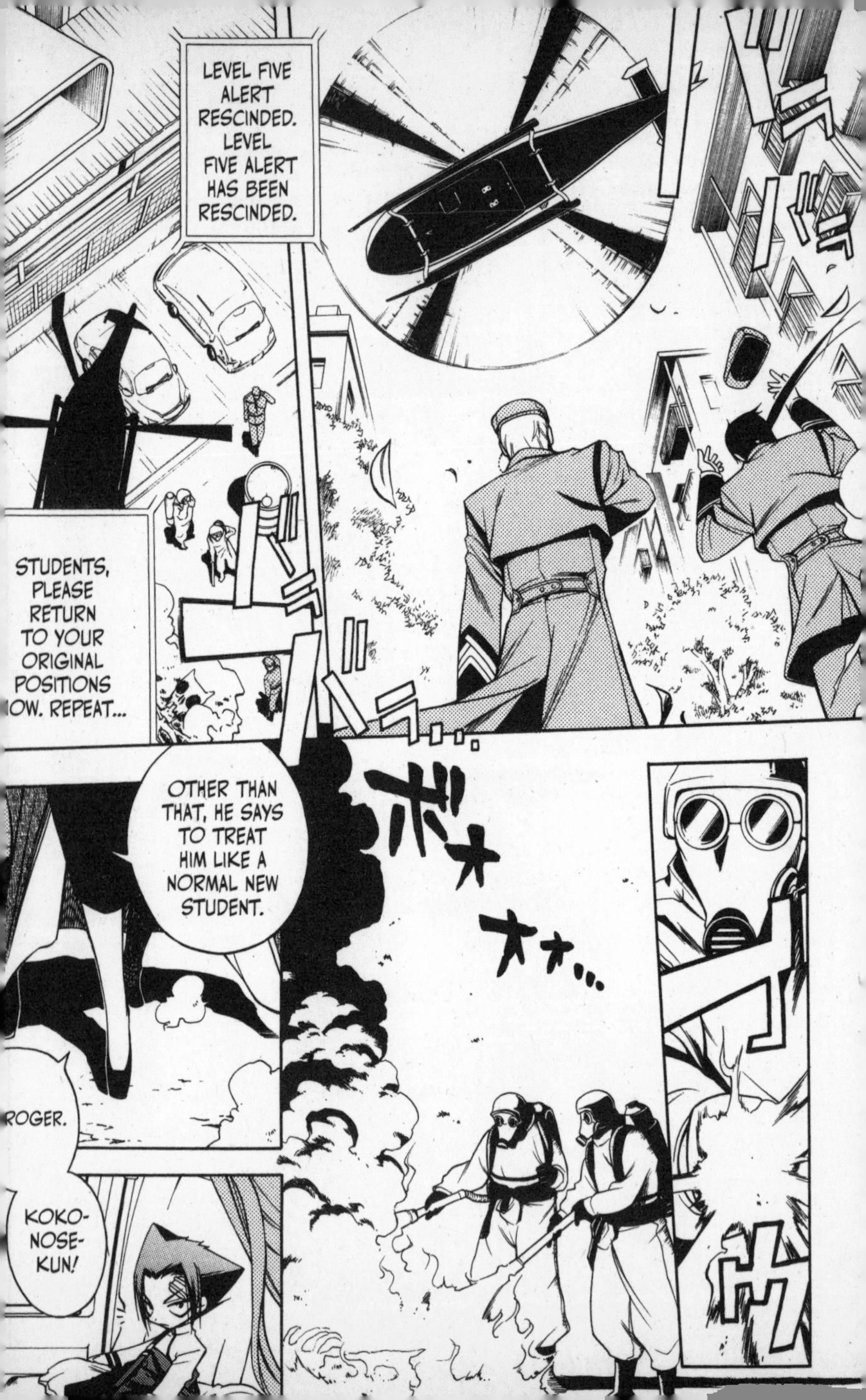
LEVEL FIVE ALERT RESCINDED. LEVEL FIVE ALERT HAS BEEN RESCINDED.
STUDENTS, PLEASE RETURN TO YOUR ORIGINAL POSITIONS NOW. REPEAT...
OTHER THAN THAT, HE SAYS TO TREAT HIM LIKE A NORMAL NEW STUDENT.
ROGER.
KOKO-NOSE-KUN!

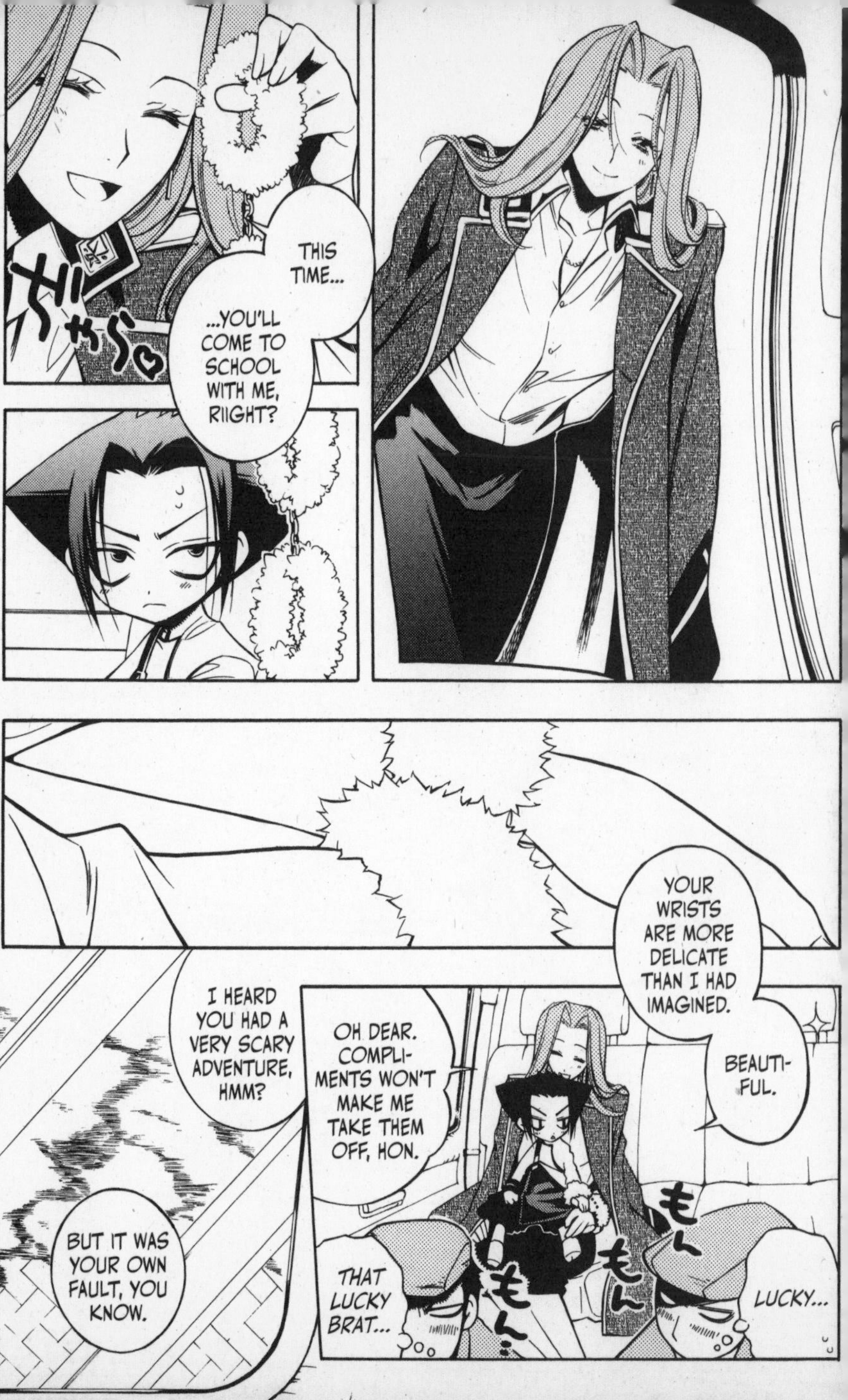
THIS TIME...
...YOU'LL COME TO SCHOOL WITH ME, RIIGHT?
YOUR WRISTS ARE MORE DELICATE THAN I HAD IMAGINED.
BEAUTIFUL.
OH DEAR. COMPLIMENTS WON'T MAKE ME TAKE THEM OFF, HON.
もん
もん
もん
LUCKY...
THAT LUCKY BRAT...
I HEARD YOU HAD A VERY SCARY ADVENTURE, HMM?
BUT IT WAS YOUR OWN FAULT, YOU KNOW.

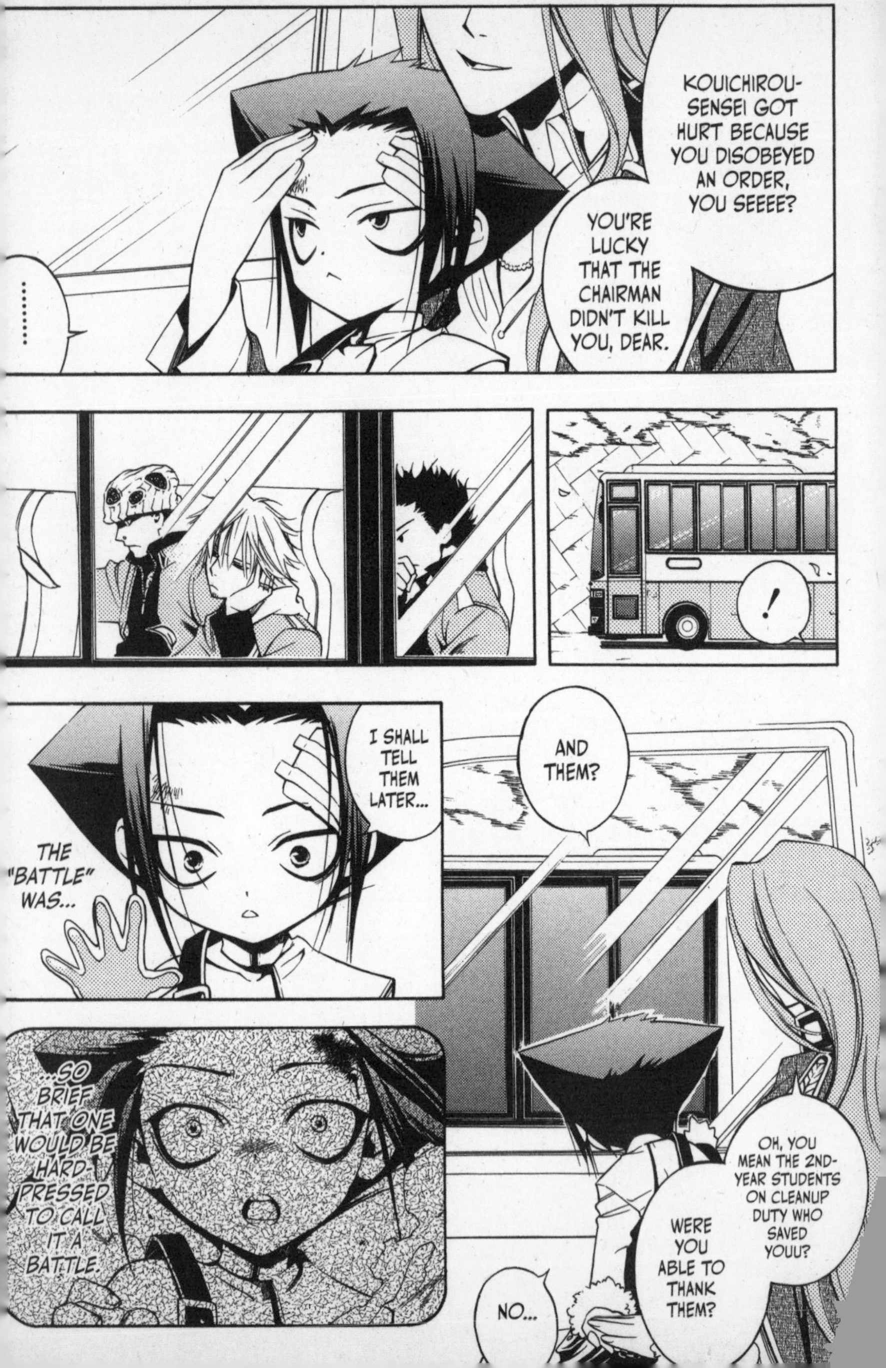
KOUICHIROU-SENSEI GOT HURT BECAUSE YOU DISOBEYED AN ORDER, YOU SEEEE?
YOU'RE LUCKY THAT THE CHAIRMAN DIDN'T KILL YOU, DEAR.
....
!
AND THEM?
I SHALL TELL THEM LATER...
THE "BATTLE" WAS...
OH, YOU MEAN THE 2ND-YEAR STUDENTS ON CLEANUP DUTY WHO SAVED YOUU?
WERE YOU ABLE TO THANK THEM?
NO...
...SO BRIEF THAT ONE WOULD BE HARD-PRESSED TO CALL IT A BATTLE.

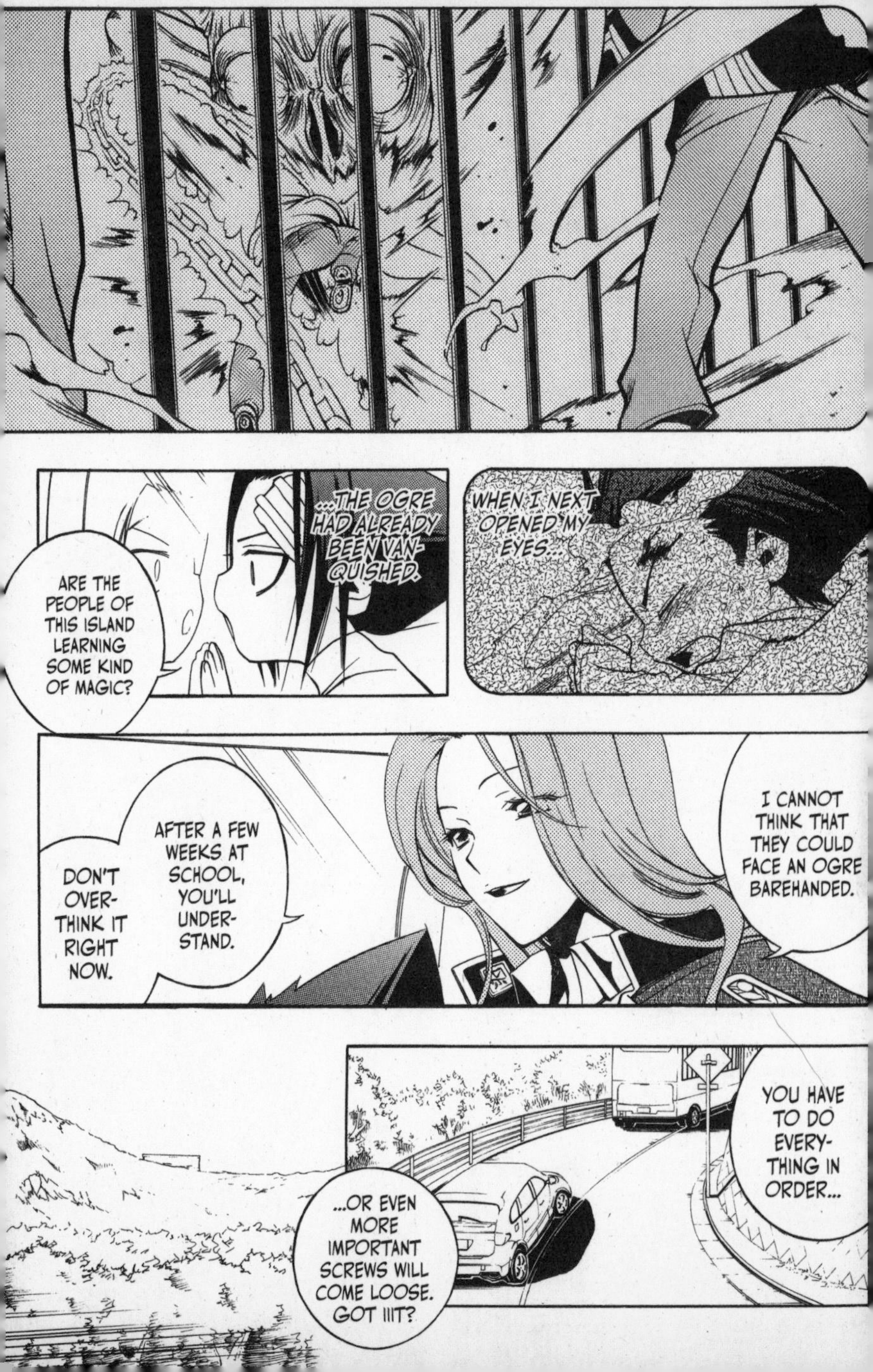
WHEN I NEXT OPENED MY EYES...
...THE OGRE HAD ALREADY BEEN VANQUISHED.
ARE THE PEOPLE OF THIS ISLAND LEARNING SOME KIND OF MAGIC?
I CANNOT THINK THAT THEY COULD FACE AN OGRE BAREHANDED.
AFTER A FEW WEEKS AT SCHOOL, YOU'LL UNDERSTAND.
DON'T OVERTHINK IT RIGHT NOW.
YOU HAVE TO DO EVERYTHING IN ORDER...
...OR EVEN MORE IMPORTANT SCREWS WILL COME LOOSE. GOT IIIT?

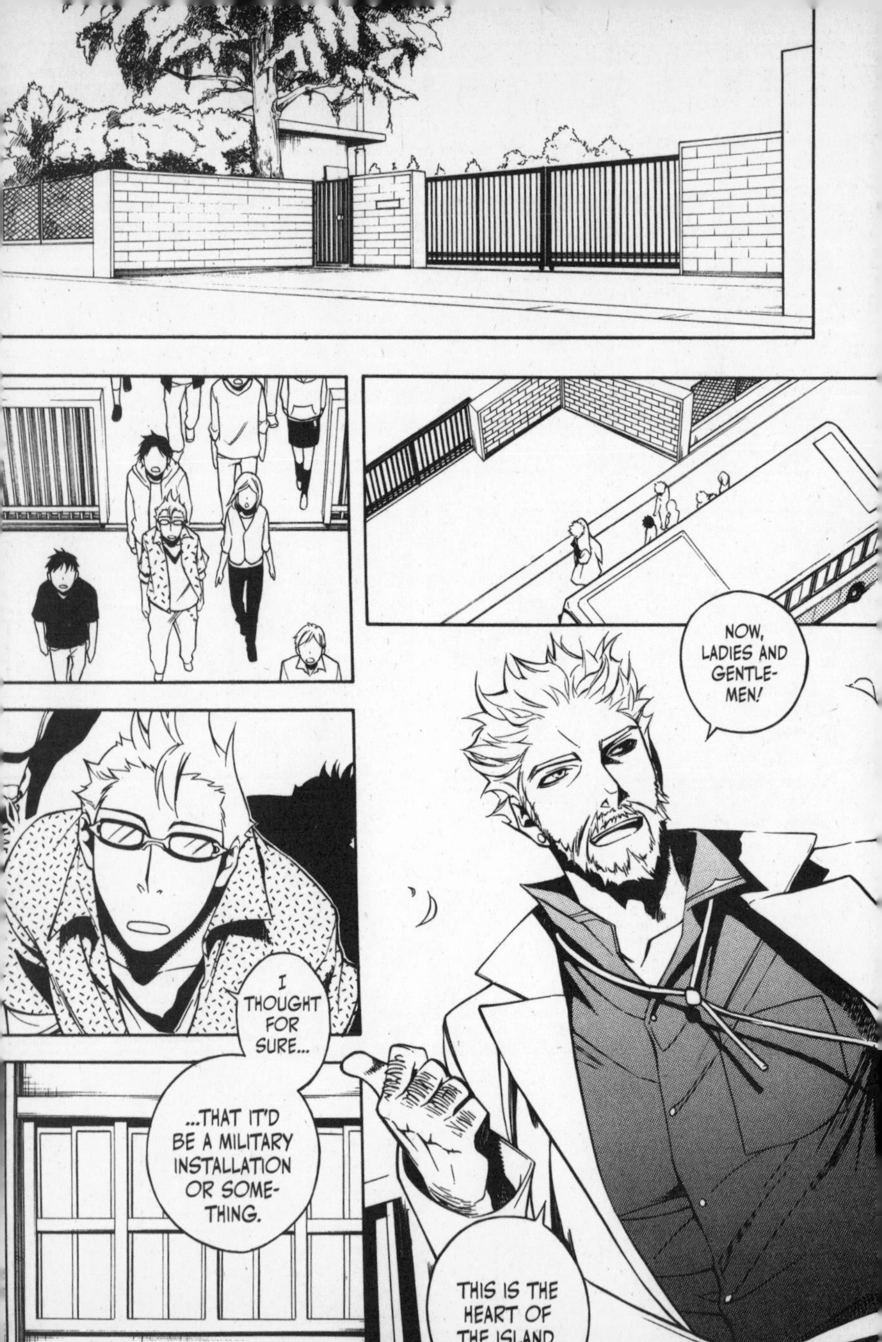
NOW, LADIES AND GENTLE-MEN!
THIS IS THE HEART OF THE ISLAND.
I THOUGHT FOR SURE...
...THAT IT'D BE A MILITARY INSTALLATION OR SOME-THING.

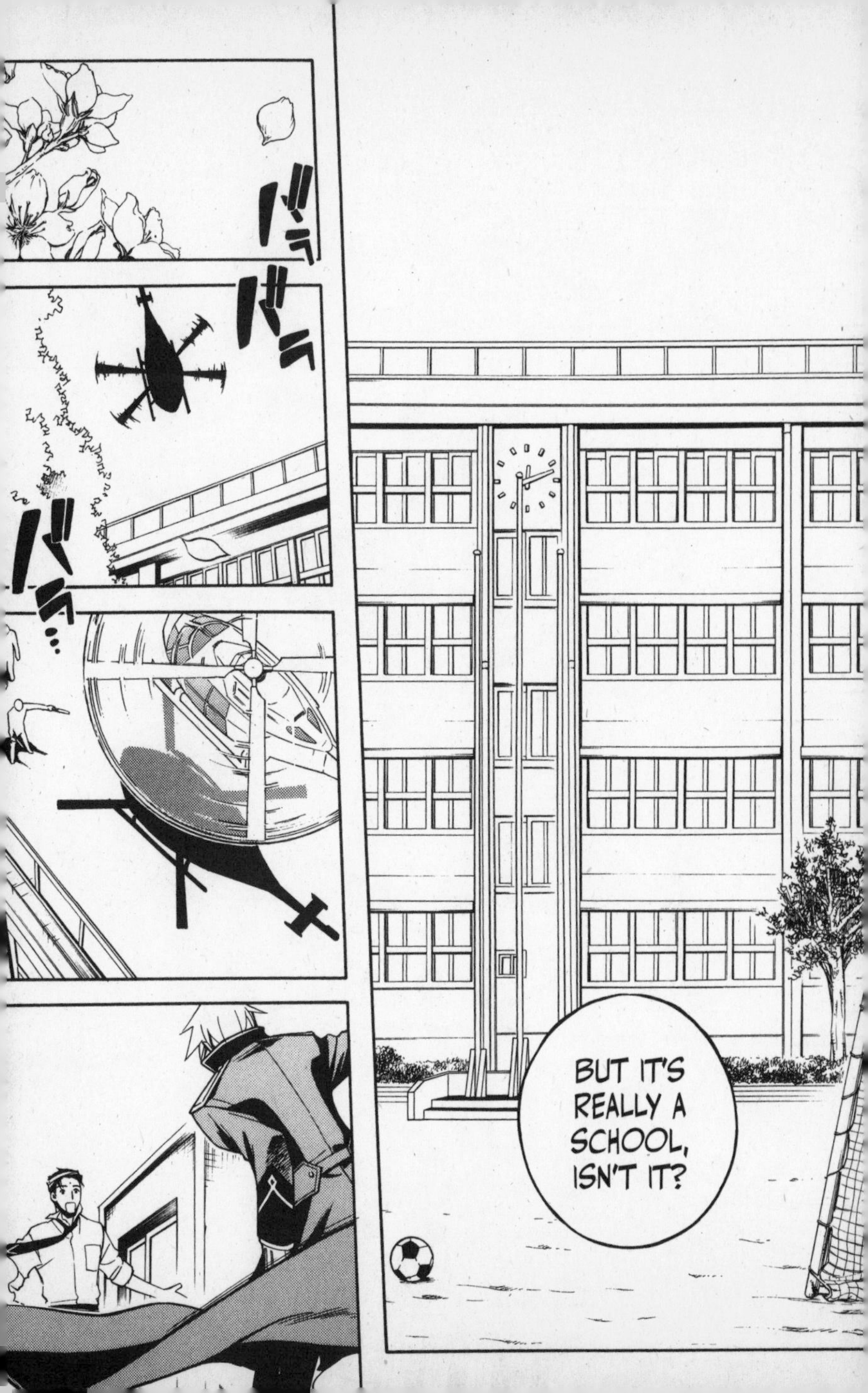
BUT IT'S REALLY A SCHOOL, ISN'T IT?
バラ
バラ
バラ...

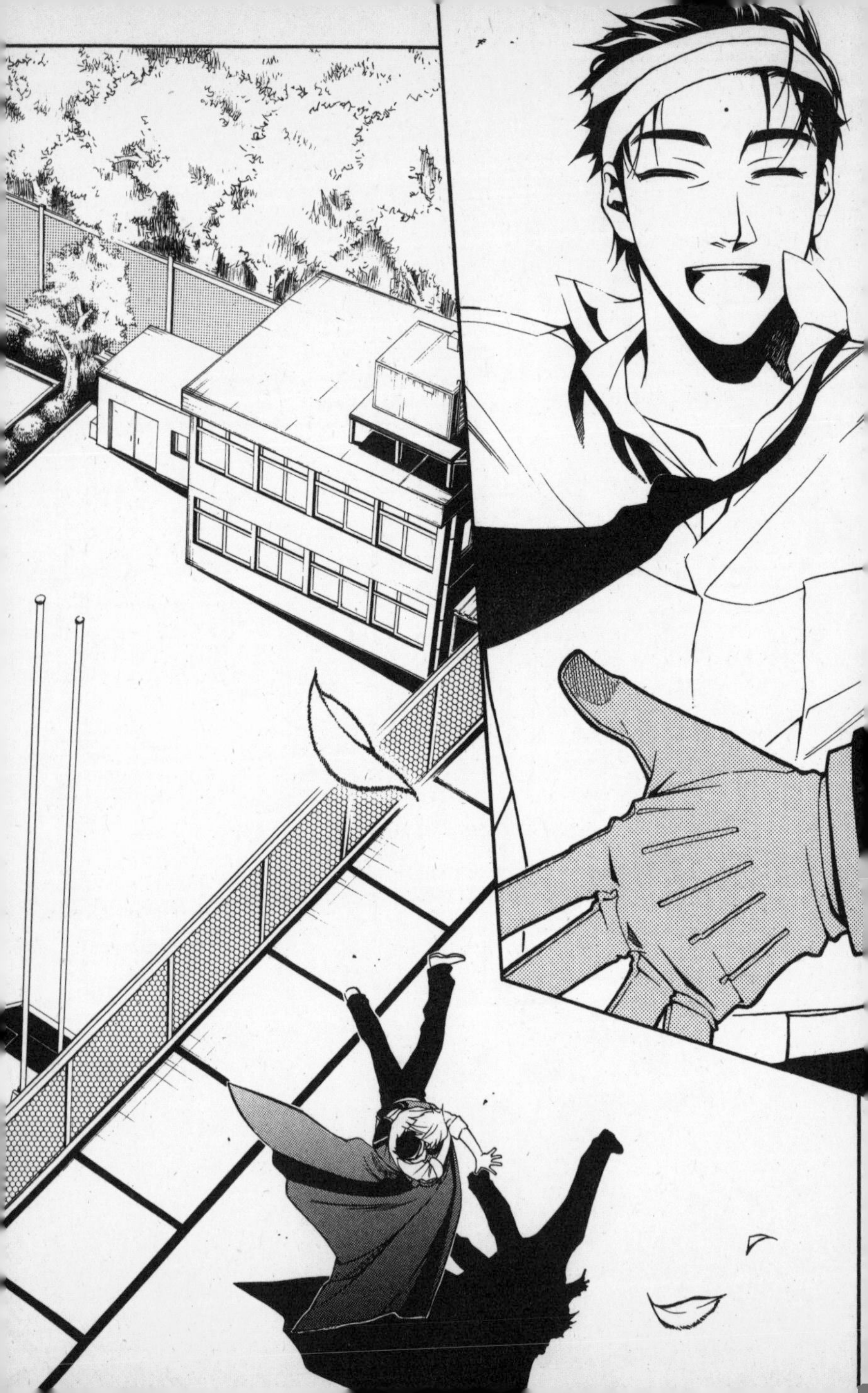

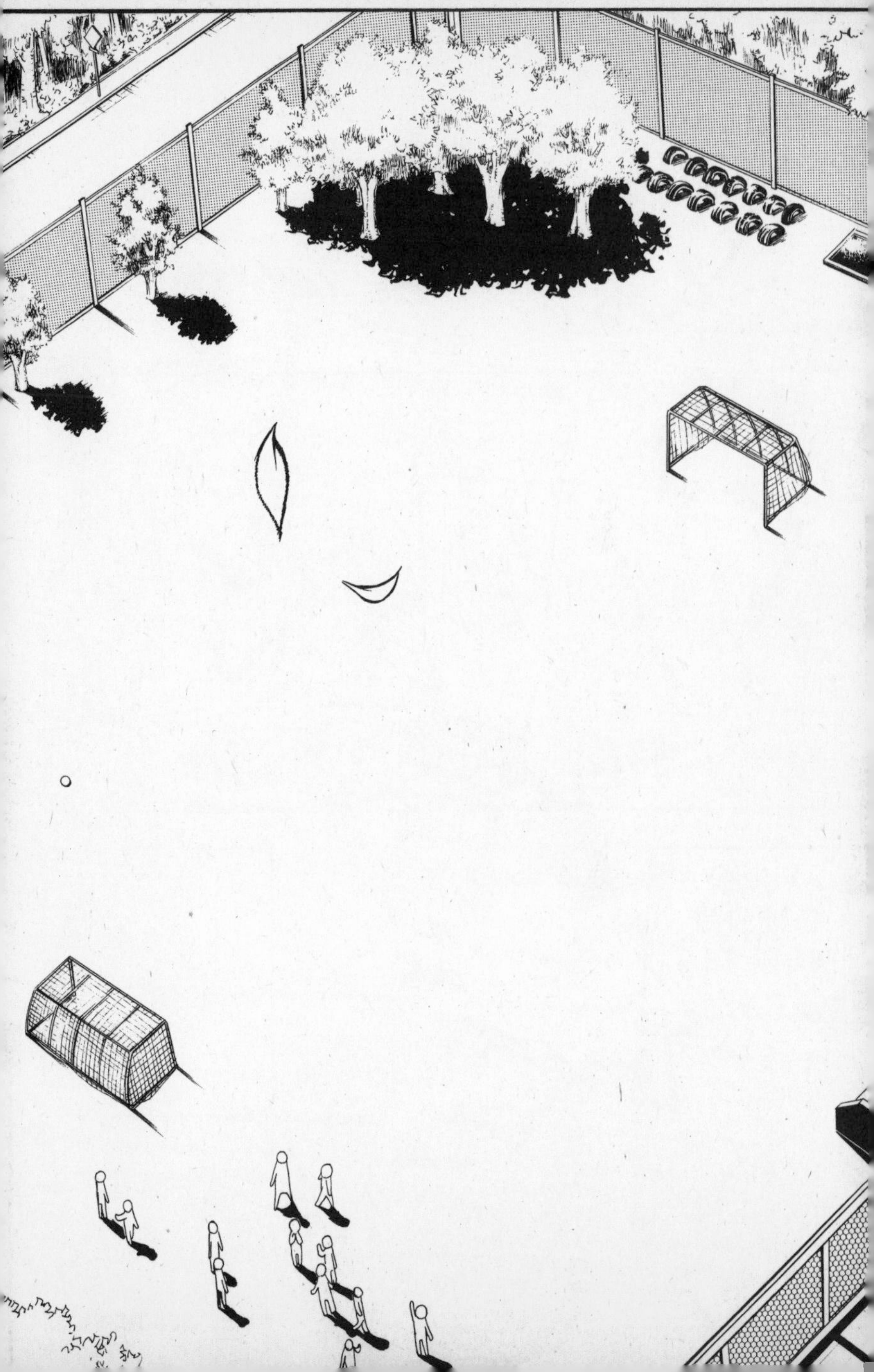

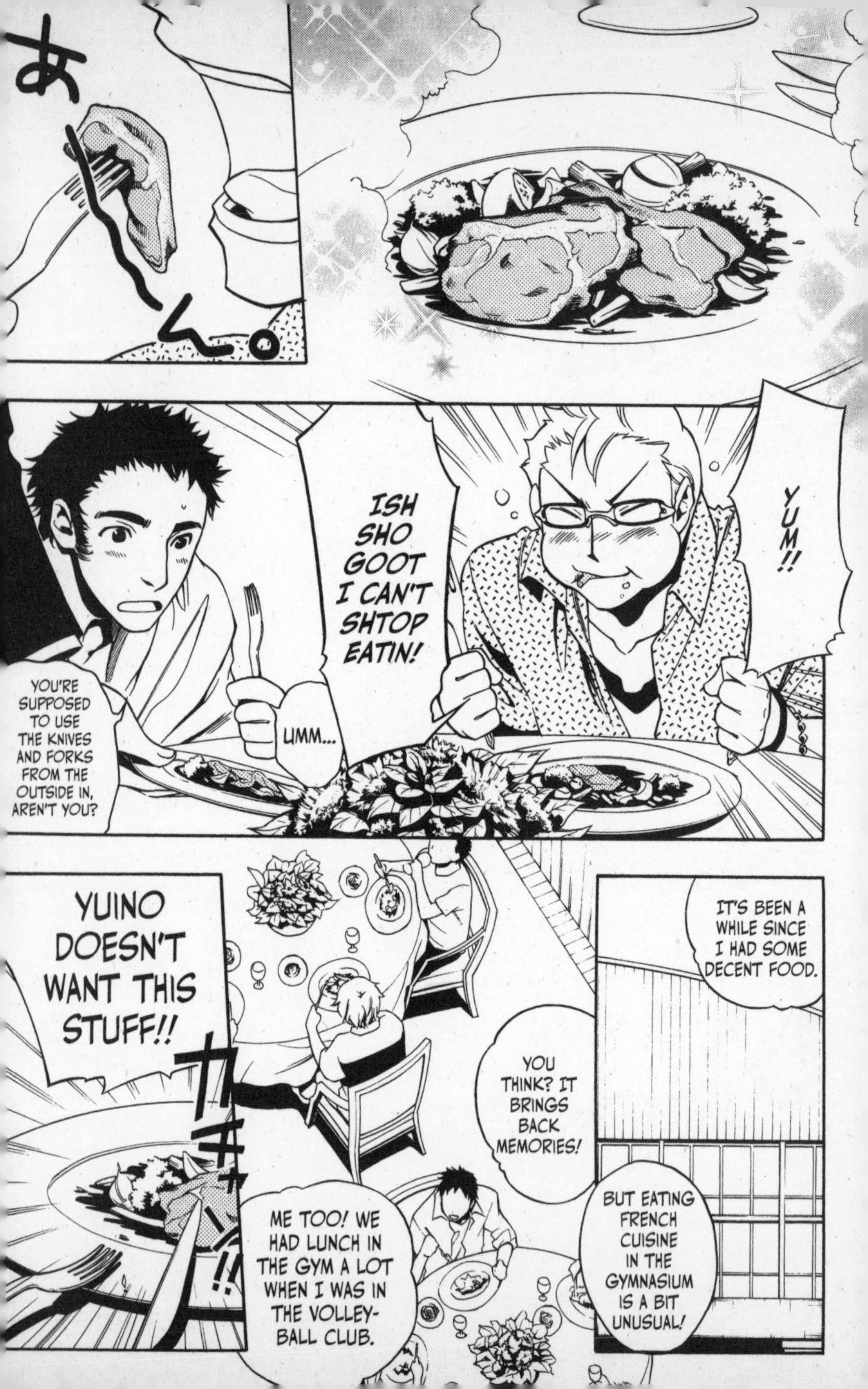
あ～ん。
YUM!!
ISH SHO GOOT I CAN'T SHTOP EATIN!
UMM...
YOU'RE SUPPOSED TO USE THE KNIVES AND FORKS FROM THE OUTSIDE IN, AREN'T YOU?
IT'S BEEN A WHILE SINCE I HAD SOME DECENT FOOD.
YOU THINK? IT BRINGS BACK MEMORIES!
BUT EATING FRENCH CUISINE IN THE GYMNASIUM IS A BIT UNUSUAL!
ME TOO! WE HAD LUNCH IN THE GYM A LOT WHEN I WAS IN THE VOLLEY-BALL CLUB.
YUINO DOESN'T WANT THIS STUFF!!
カチャ!!

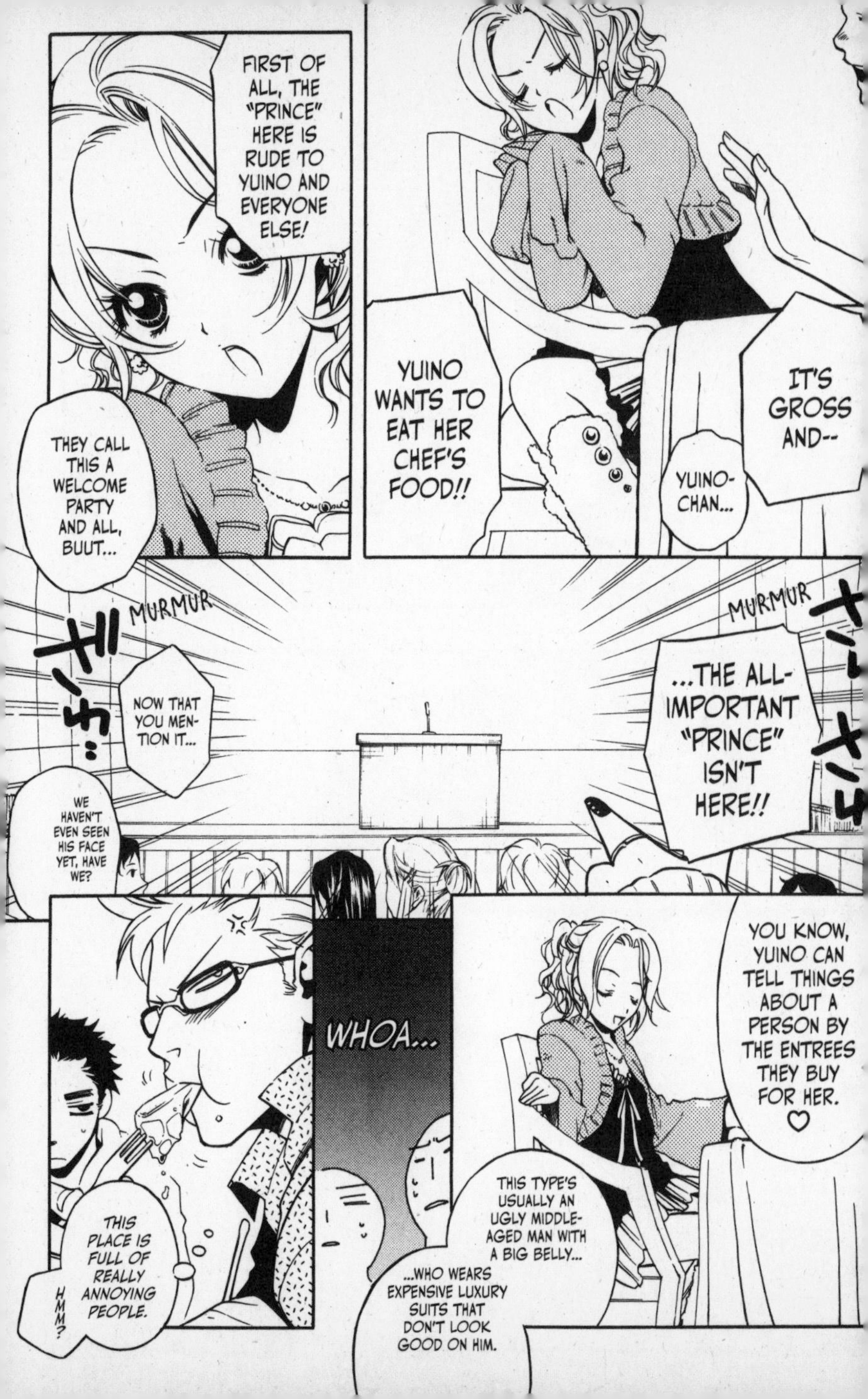
IT'S GROSS AND--
YUINO WANTS TO EAT HER CHEF'S FOOD!!
YUINO-CHAN...
FIRST OF ALL, THE "PRINCE" HERE IS RUDE TO YUINO AND EVERYONE ELSE!
THEY CALL THIS A WELCOME PARTY AND ALL, BUUT...
MURMUR
...THE ALL-IMPORTANT "PRINCE" ISN'T HERE!!
MURMUR
NOW THAT YOU MEN-TION IT...
WE HAVEN'T EVEN SEEN HIS FACE YET, HAVE WE?
YOU KNOW, YUINO CAN TELL THINGS ABOUT A PERSON BY THE ENTREES THEY BUY FOR HER. ♡
THIS TYPE'S USUALLY AN UGLY MIDDLE-AGED MAN WITH A BIG BELLY...
...WHO WEARS EXPENSIVE LUXURY SUITS THAT DON'T LOOK GOOD ON HIM.
WHOA...
THIS PLACE IS FULL OF REALLY ANNOYING PEOPLE.
HMM?

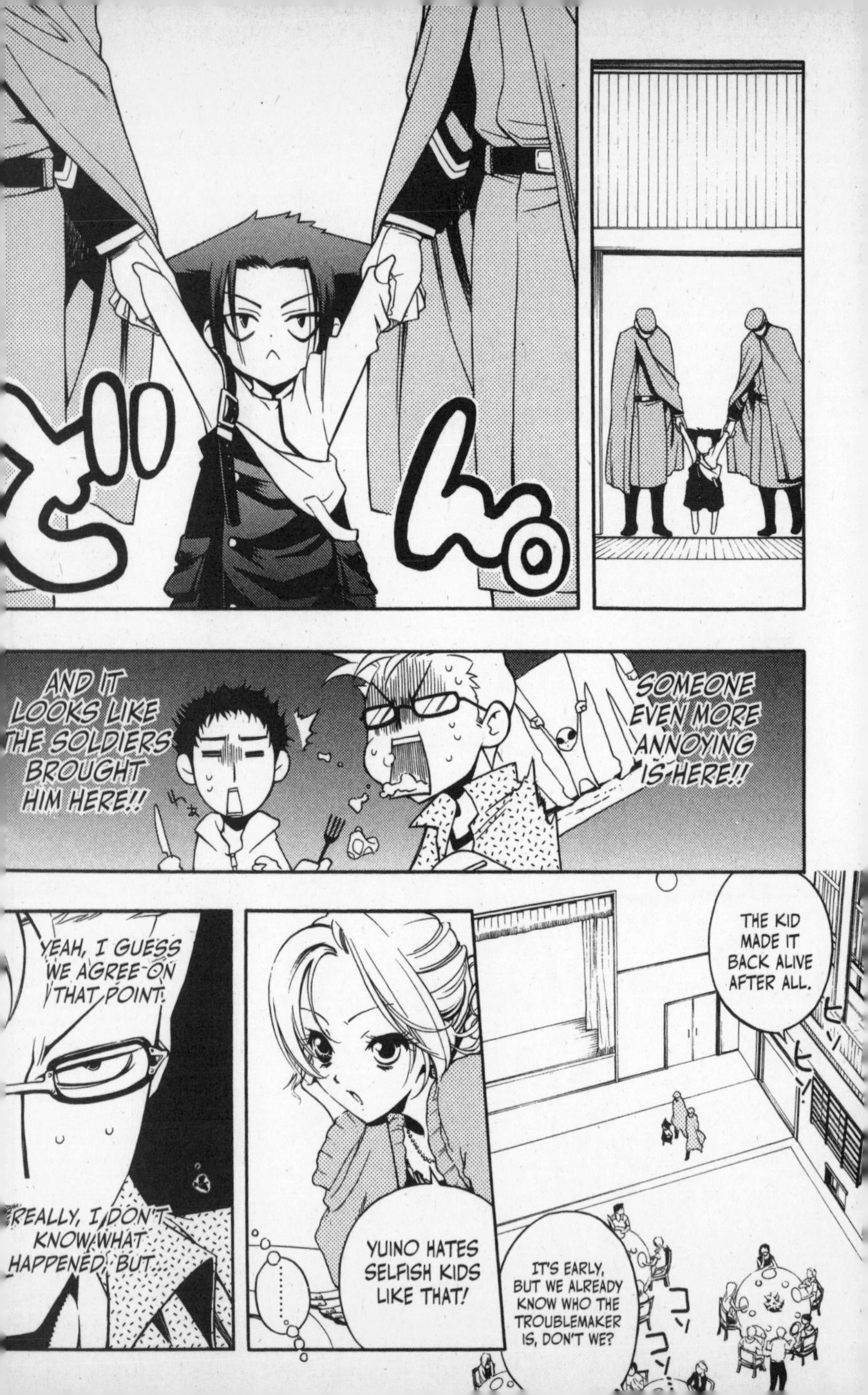
SOMEONE EVEN MORE ANNOYING IS HERE!!
AND IT LOOKS LIKE THE SOLDIERS BROUGHT HIM HERE!!
THE KID MADE IT BACK ALIVE AFTER ALL.
IT'S EARLY, BUT WE ALREADY KNOW WHO THE TROUBLEMAKER IS, DON'T WE?
YUINO HATES SELFISH KIDS LIKE THAT!
......
YEAH, I GUESS WE AGREE ON THAT POINT.
REALLY, I DON'T KNOW WHAT HAPPENED, BUT...

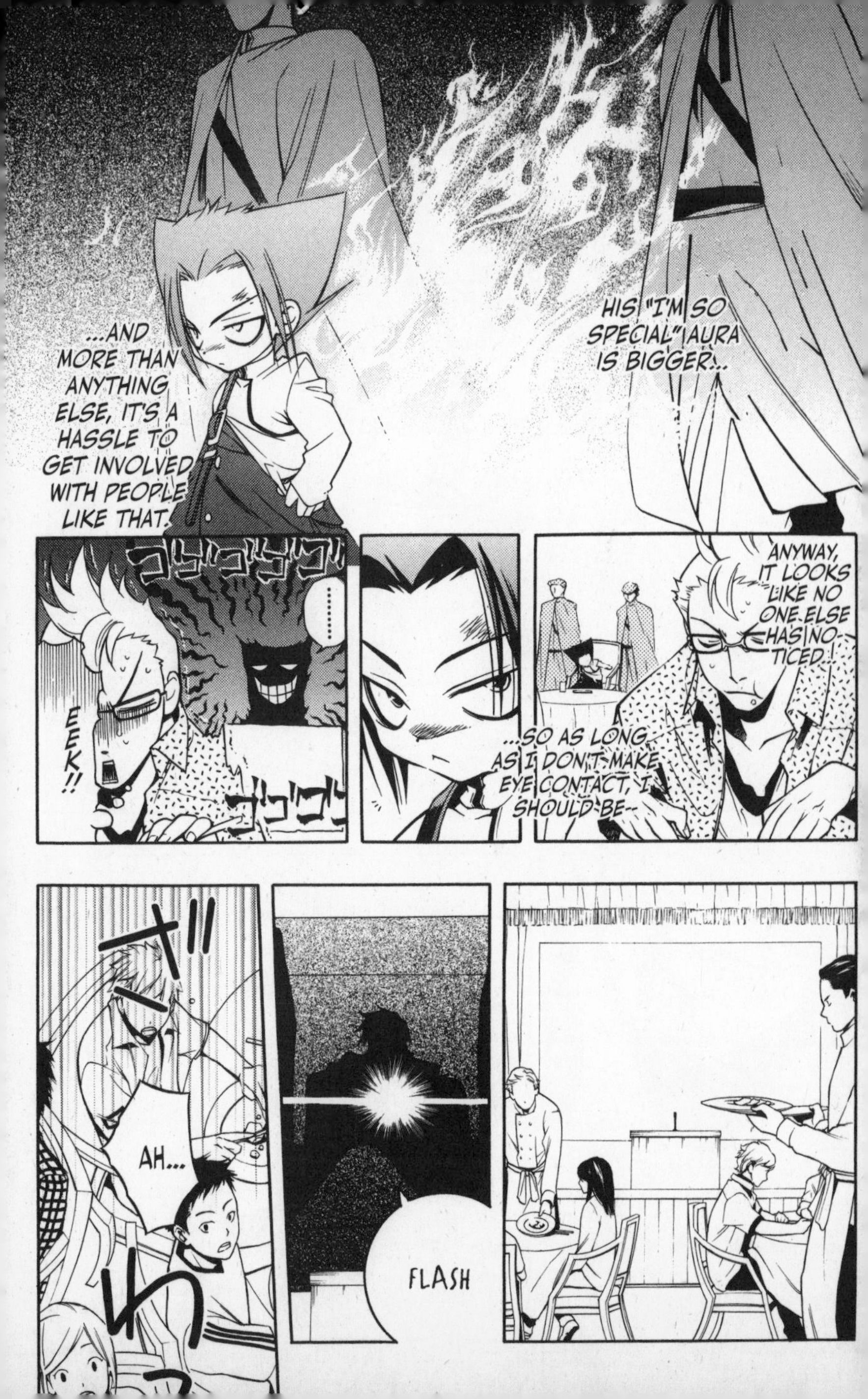
HIS "I'M SO SPECIAL" AURA IS BIGGER...
...AND MORE THAN ANYTHING ELSE, IT'S A HASSLE TO GET INVOLVED WITH PEOPLE LIKE THAT.
ANYWAY, IT LOOKS LIKE NO ONE ELSE HAS NOTICED...
...SO AS LONG AS I DON'T MAKE EYE CONTACT, I SHOULD BE--
......
EEK!!
FLASH
AH...

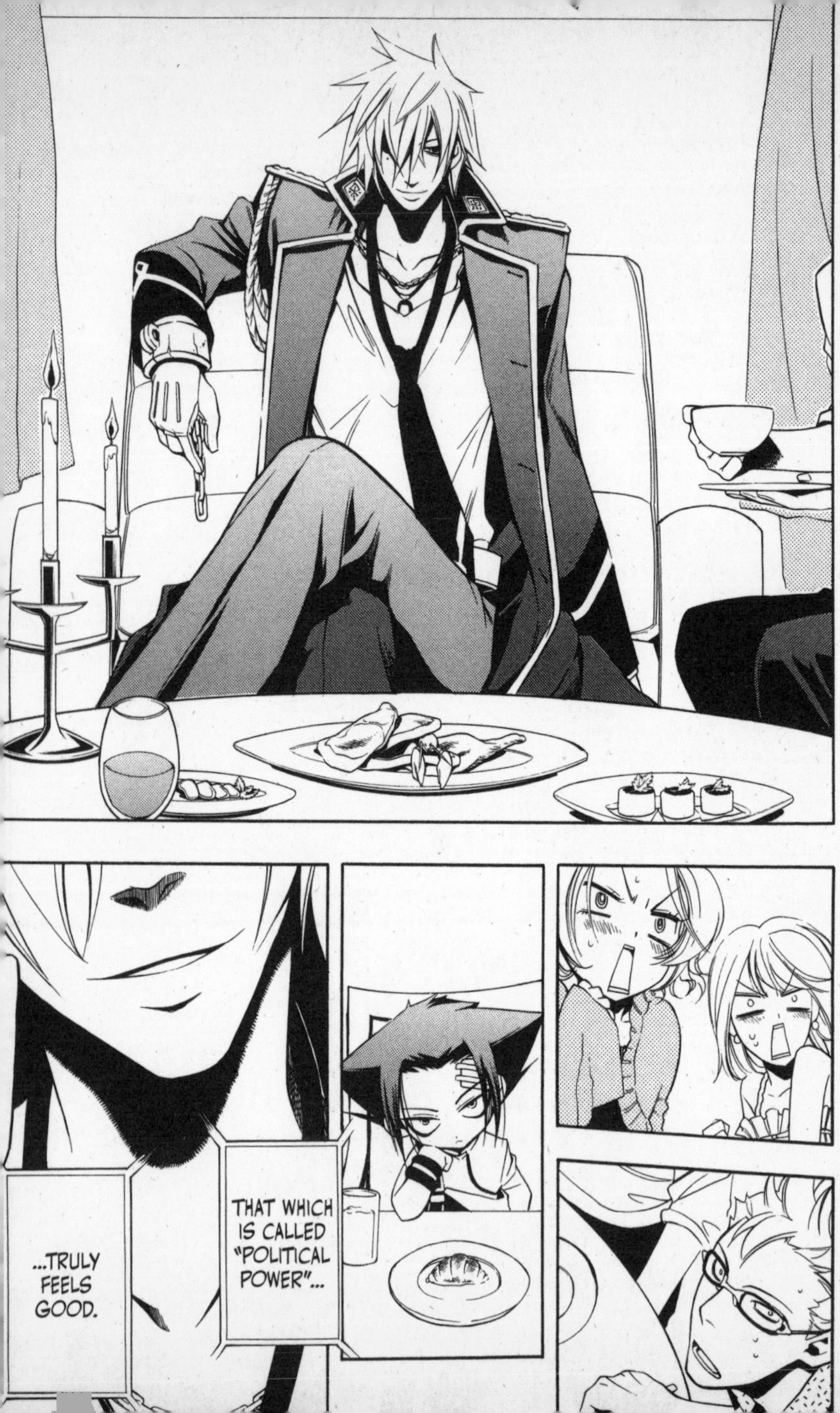
THAT WHICH IS CALLED "POLITICAL POWER"...
...TRULY FEELS GOOD.

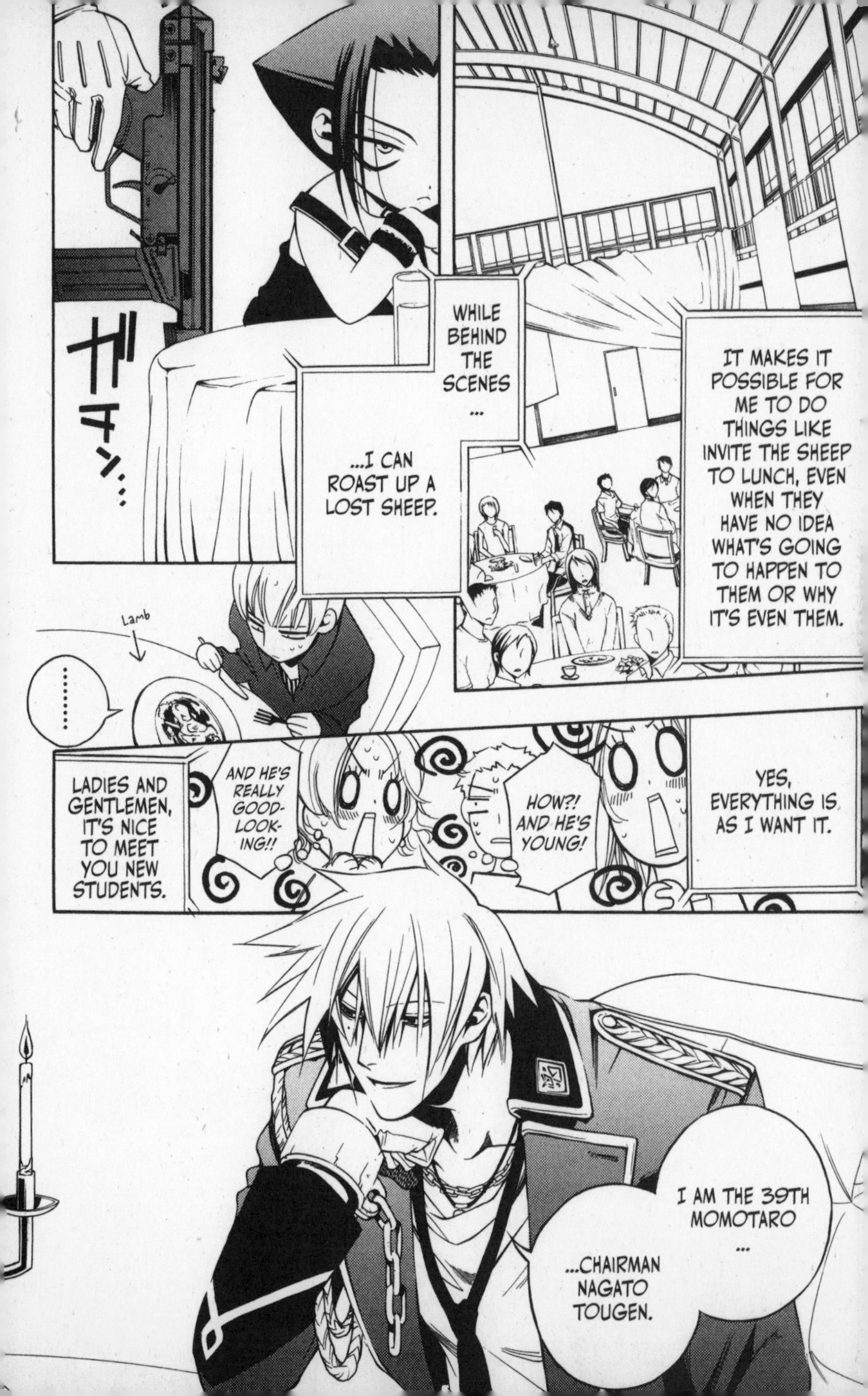
IT MAKES IT POSSIBLE FOR ME TO DO THINGS LIKE INVITE THE SHEEP TO LUNCH, EVEN WHEN THEY HAVE NO IDEA WHAT'S GOING TO HAPPEN TO THEM OR WHY IT'S EVEN THEM.
WHILE BEHIND THE SCENES ...
...I CAN ROAST UP A LOST SHEEP.
ガチャン…
Lamb
......
YES, EVERYTHING IS AS I WANT IT.
HOW?! AND HE'S YOUNG!
AND HE'S REALLY GOOD-LOOKING!!
LADIES AND GENTLEMEN, IT'S NICE TO MEET YOU NEW STUDENTS.
I AM THE 39TH MOMOTARO ...
...CHAIRMAN NAGATO TOUGEN.

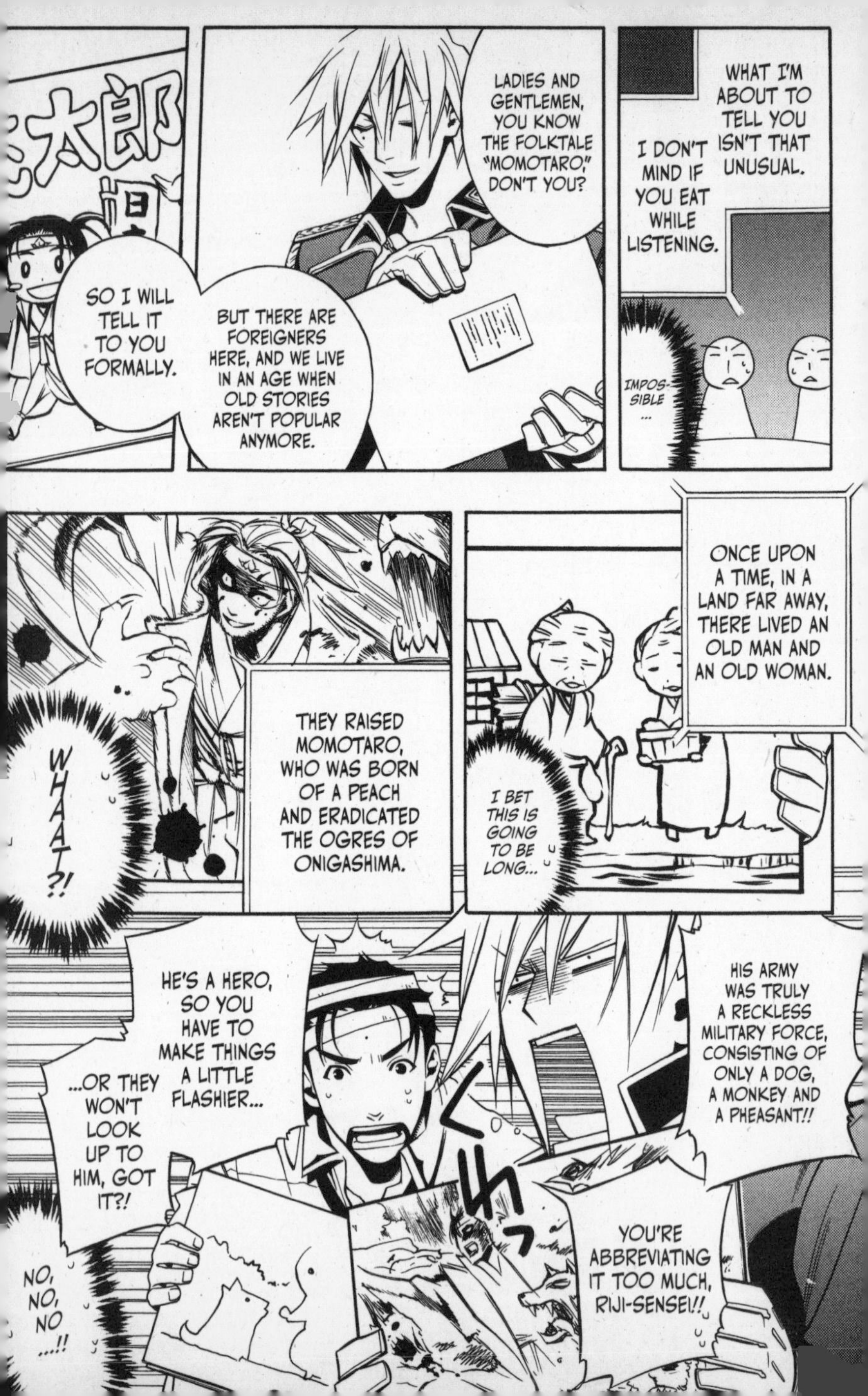
WHAT I'M ABOUT TO TELL YOU ISN'T THAT UNUSUAL.
I DON'T MIND IF YOU EAT WHILE LISTENING.
IMPOSSIBLE...
LADIES AND GENTLEMEN, YOU KNOW THE FOLKTALE "MOMOTARO," DON'T YOU?
BUT THERE ARE FOREIGNERS HERE, AND WE LIVE IN AN AGE WHEN OLD STORIES AREN'T POPULAR ANYMORE.
SO I WILL TELL IT TO YOU FORMALLY.
ONCE UPON A TIME, IN A LAND FAR AWAY, THERE LIVED AN OLD MAN AND AN OLD WOMAN.
I BET THIS IS GOING TO BE LONG...
THEY RAISED MOMOTARO, WHO WAS BORN OF A PEACH AND ERADICATED THE OGRES OF ONIGASHIMA.
WHAAAT?!
HIS ARMY WAS TRULY A RECKLESS MILITARY FORCE, CONSISTING OF ONLY A DOG, A MONKEY AND A PHEASANT!!
YOU'RE ABBREVIATING IT TOO MUCH, RIJI-SENSEI!!
HE'S A HERO, SO YOU HAVE TO MAKE THINGS A LITTLE FLASHIER...
...OR THEY WON'T LOOK UP TO HIM, GOT IT?!
NO, NO, NO...!!

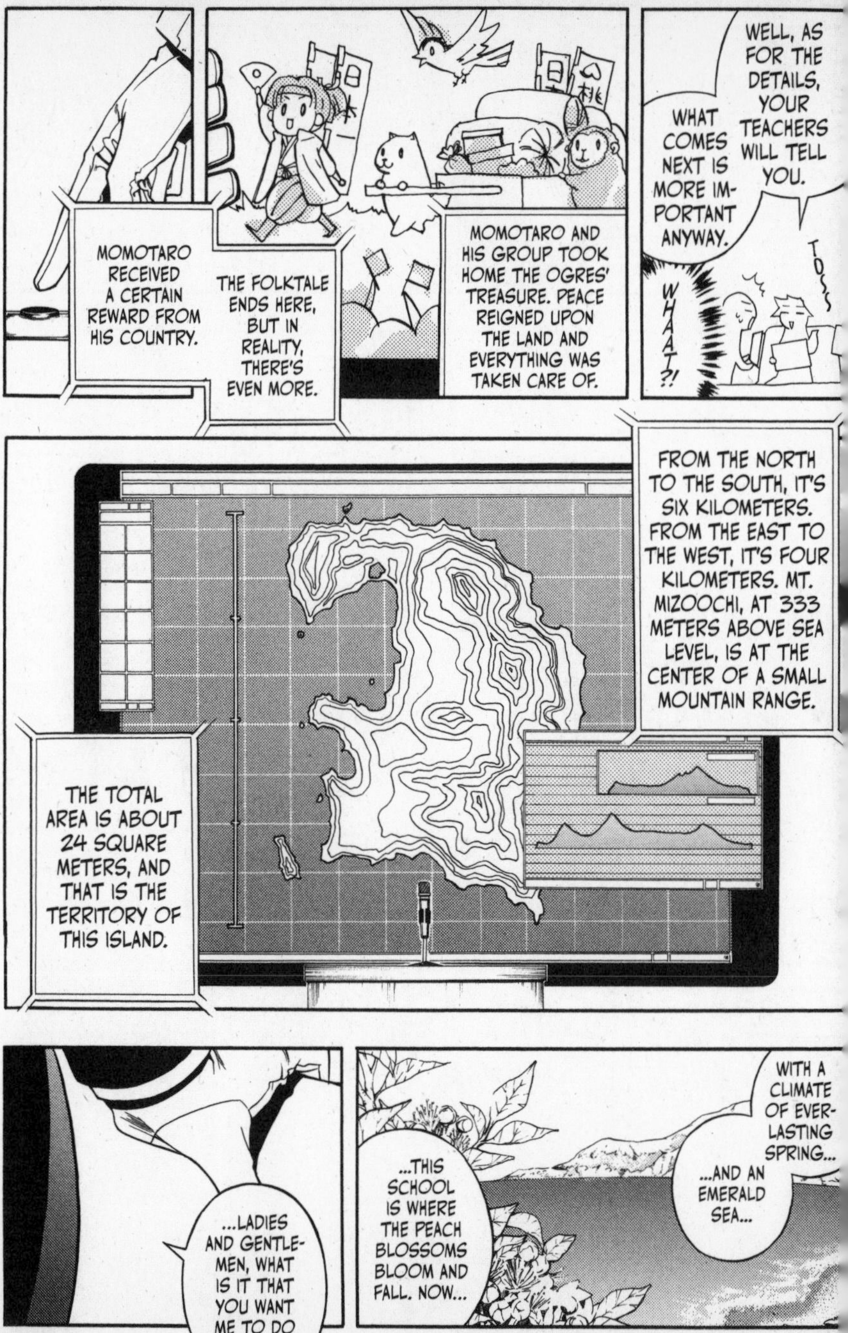
WELL, AS FOR THE DETAILS, YOUR TEACHERS WILL TELL YOU.
WHAT COMES NEXT IS MORE IMPORTANT ANYWAY.
WHAAT?!
TOSS
MOMOTARO AND HIS GROUP TOOK HOME THE OGRES' TREASURE. PEACE REIGNED UPON THE LAND AND EVERYTHING WAS TAKEN CARE OF.
THE FOLKTALE ENDS HERE, BUT IN REALITY, THERE'S EVEN MORE.
MOMOTARO RECEIVED A CERTAIN REWARD FROM HIS COUNTRY.
FROM THE NORTH TO THE SOUTH, IT'S SIX KILOMETERS. FROM THE EAST TO THE WEST, IT'S FOUR KILOMETERS. MT. MIZOOCHI, AT 333 METERS ABOVE SEA LEVEL, IS AT THE CENTER OF A SMALL MOUNTAIN RANGE.
THE TOTAL AREA IS ABOUT 24 SQUARE METERS, AND THAT IS THE TERRITORY OF THIS ISLAND.
WITH A CLIMATE OF EVER-LASTING SPRING...
...AND AN EMERALD SEA...
...THIS SCHOOL IS WHERE THE PEACH BLOSSOMS BLOOM AND FALL. NOW...
...LADIES AND GENTLE-MEN, WHAT IS IT THAT YOU WANT ME TO DO FOR YOU?

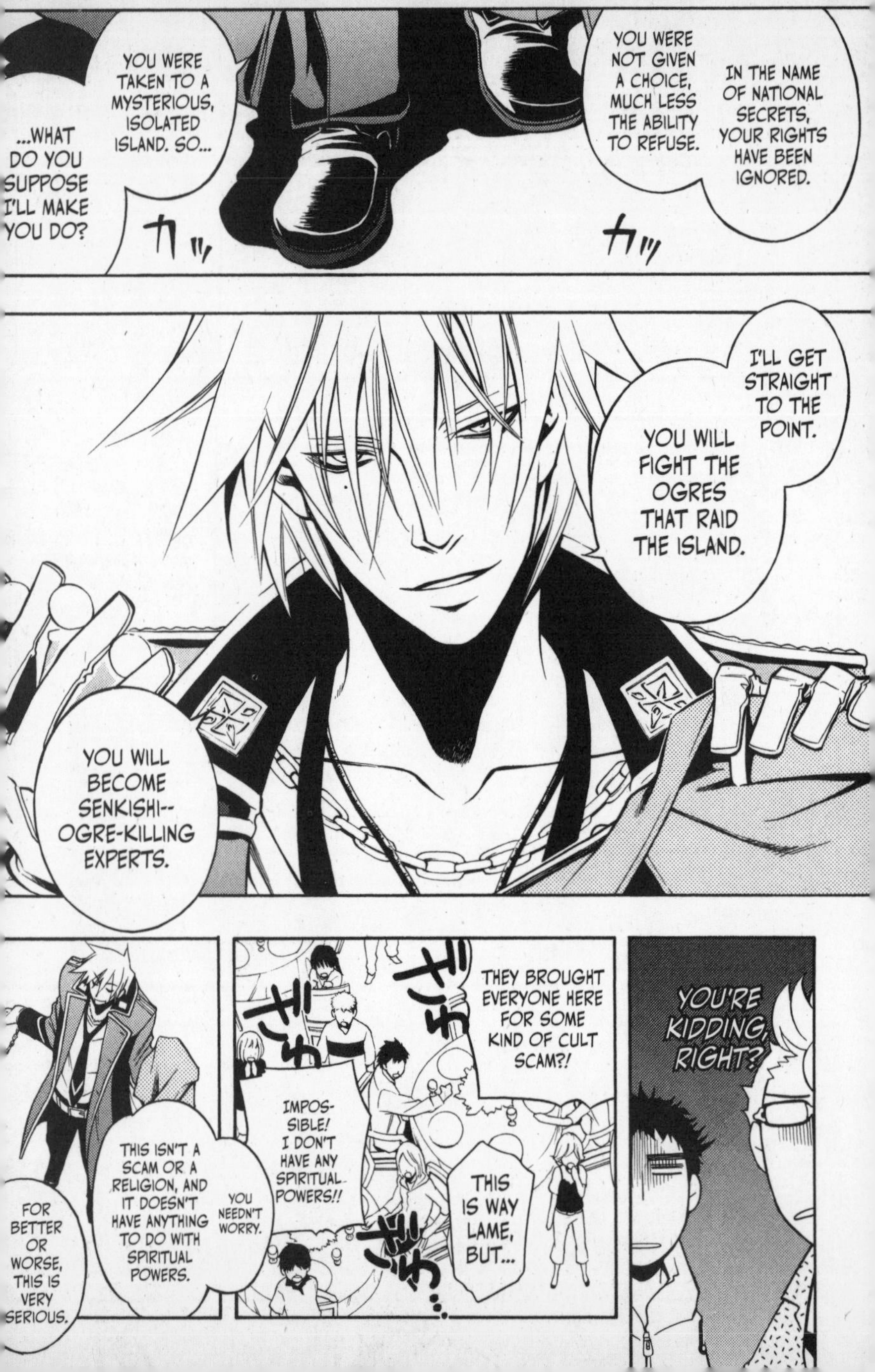
IN THE NAME OF NATIONAL SECRETS, YOUR RIGHTS HAVE BEEN IGNORED.
YOU WERE NOT GIVEN A CHOICE, MUCH LESS THE ABILITY TO REFUSE.
カッ
YOU WERE TAKEN TO A MYSTERIOUS, ISOLATED ISLAND. SO...
...WHAT DO YOU SUPPOSE I'LL MAKE YOU DO?
カッ
I'LL GET STRAIGHT TO THE POINT.
YOU WILL FIGHT THE OGRES THAT RAID THE ISLAND.
YOU WILL BECOME SENKISHI--OGRE-KILLING EXPERTS.
YOU'RE KIDDING, RIGHT?
THEY BROUGHT EVERYONE HERE FOR SOME KIND OF CULT SCAM?!
IMPOSSIBLE! I DON'T HAVE ANY SPIRITUAL POWERS!!
THIS IS WAY LAME, BUT...
YOU NEEDN'T WORRY.
THIS ISN'T A SCAM OR A RELIGION, AND IT DOESN'T HAVE ANYTHING TO DO WITH SPIRITUAL POWERS.
FOR BETTER OR WORSE, THIS IS VERY SERIOUS.

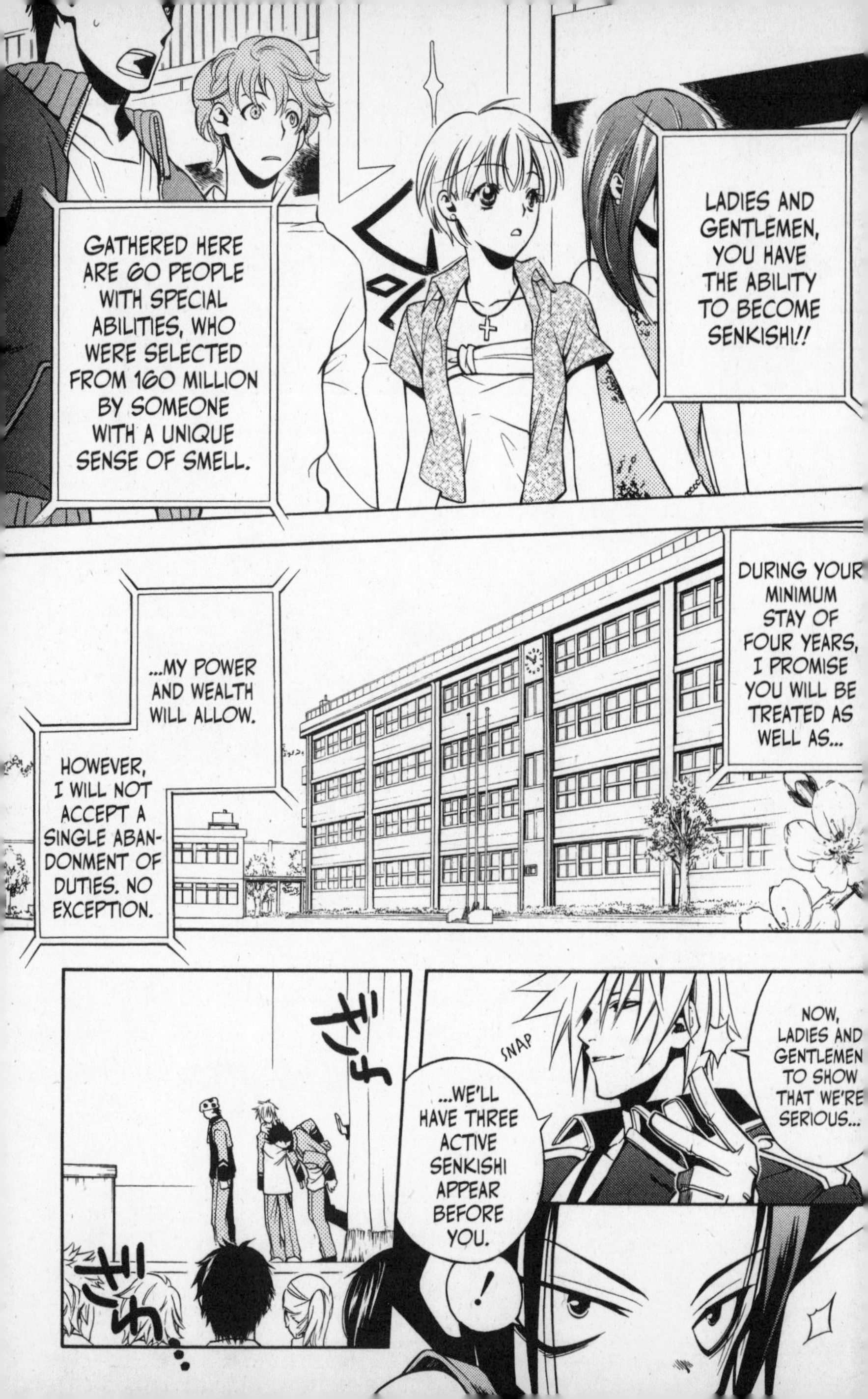
LADIES AND GENTLEMEN, YOU HAVE THE ABILITY TO BECOME SENKISHI!!
GATHERED HERE ARE 60 PEOPLE WITH SPECIAL ABILITIES, WHO WERE SELECTED FROM 160 MILLION BY SOMEONE WITH A UNIQUE SENSE OF SMELL.
DURING YOUR MINIMUM STAY OF FOUR YEARS, I PROMISE YOU WILL BE TREATED AS WELL AS...
...MY POWER AND WEALTH WILL ALLOW.
HOWEVER, I WILL NOT ACCEPT A SINGLE ABAN-DONMENT OF DUTIES. NO EXCEPTION.
NOW, LADIES AND GENTLEMEN TO SHOW THAT WE'RE SERIOUS...
SNAP
...WE'LL HAVE THREE ACTIVE SENKISHI APPEAR BEFORE YOU.
!

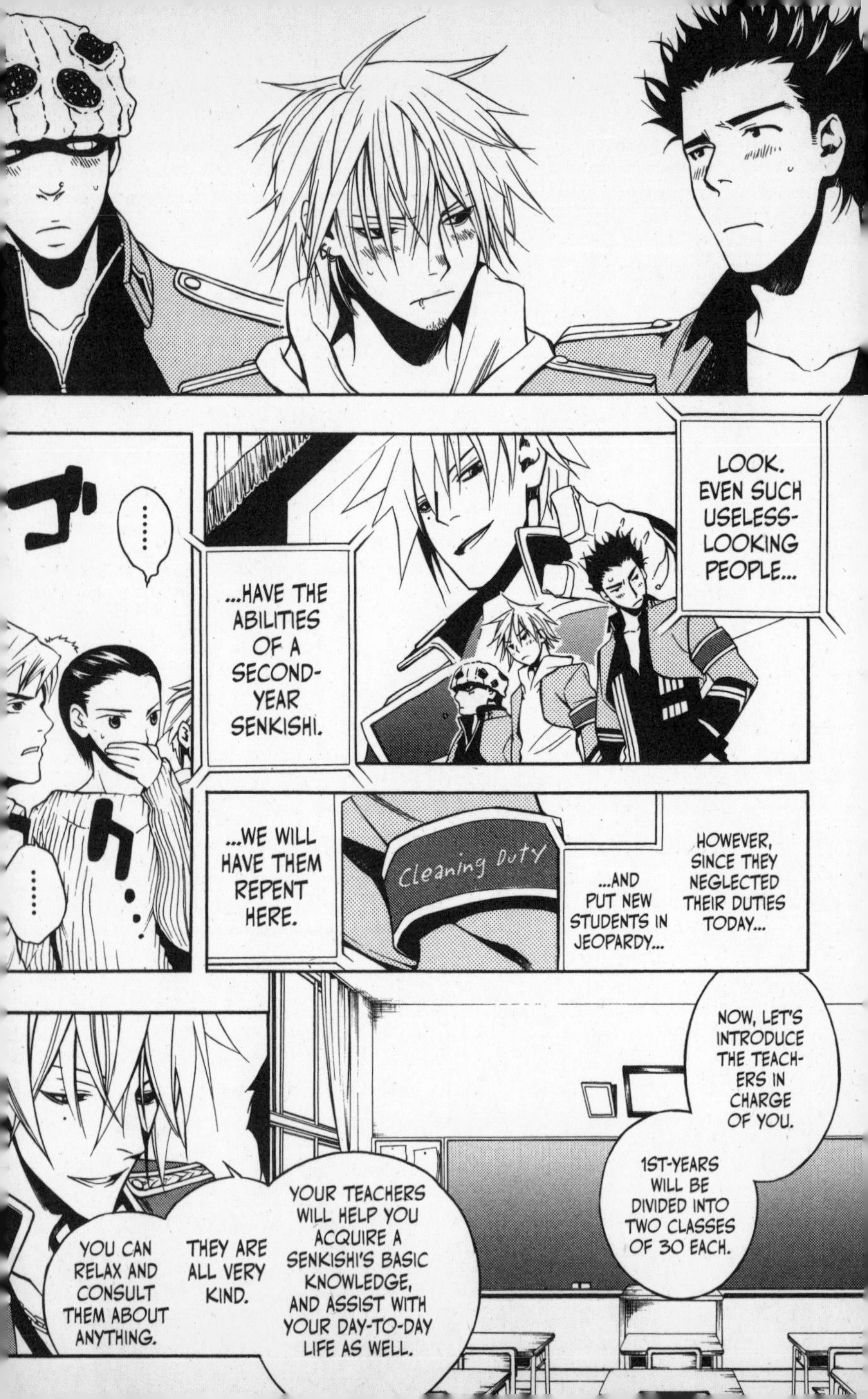
LOOK. EVEN SUCH USELESS-LOOKING PEOPLE...
...HAVE THE ABILITIES OF A SECOND-YEAR SENKISHI.
ゴ
......
ク
......
HOWEVER, SINCE THEY NEGLECTED THEIR DUTIES TODAY...
...AND PUT NEW STUDENTS IN JEOPARDY...
Cleaning Duty
...WE WILL HAVE THEM REPENT HERE.
NOW, LET'S INTRODUCE THE TEACHERS IN CHARGE OF YOU.
1ST-YEARS WILL BE DIVIDED INTO TWO CLASSES OF 30 EACH.
YOUR TEACHERS WILL HELP YOU ACQUIRE A SENKISHI'S BASIC KNOWLEDGE, AND ASSIST WITH YOUR DAY-TO-DAY LIFE AS WELL.
THEY ARE ALL VERY KIND.
YOU CAN RELAX AND CONSULT THEM ABOUT ANYTHING.

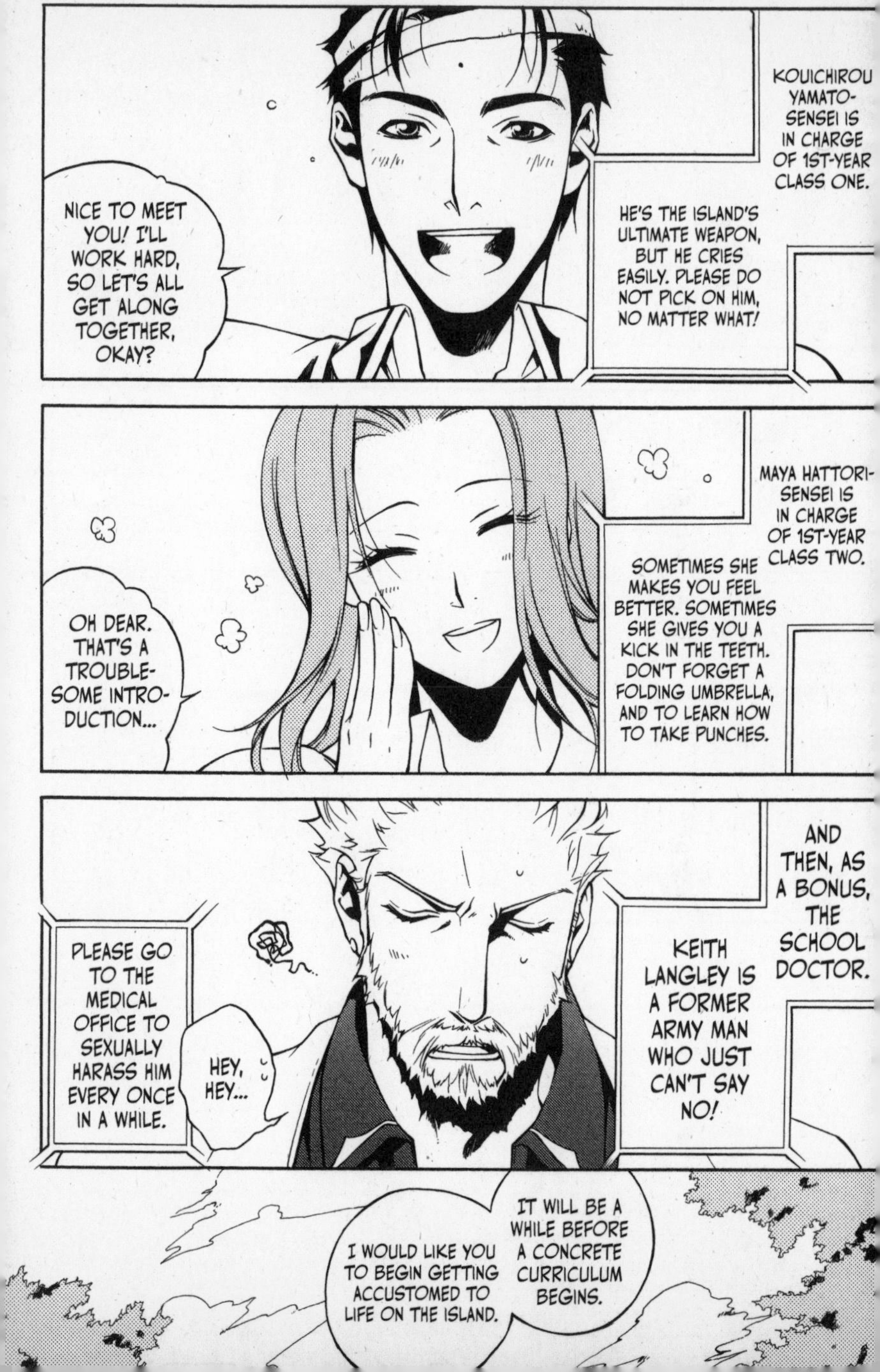
KOUICHIROU YAMATO-SENSEI IS IN CHARGE OF 1ST-YEAR CLASS ONE.
HE'S THE ISLAND'S ULTIMATE WEAPON, BUT HE CRIES EASILY. PLEASE DO NOT PICK ON HIM, NO MATTER WHAT!
NICE TO MEET YOU! I'LL WORK HARD, SO LET'S ALL GET ALONG TOGETHER, OKAY?
MAYA HATTORI-SENSEI IS IN CHARGE OF 1ST-YEAR CLASS TWO.
SOMETIMES SHE MAKES YOU FEEL BETTER. SOMETIMES SHE GIVES YOU A KICK IN THE TEETH. DON'T FORGET A FOLDING UMBRELLA, AND TO LEARN HOW TO TAKE PUNCHES.
OH DEAR. THAT'S A TROUBLE-SOME INTRO-DUCTION...
AND THEN, AS A BONUS, THE SCHOOL DOCTOR.
KEITH LANGLEY IS A FORMER ARMY MAN WHO JUST CAN'T SAY NO!
HEY, HEY...
PLEASE GO TO THE MEDICAL OFFICE TO SEXUALLY HARASS HIM EVERY ONCE IN A WHILE.
IT WILL BE A WHILE BEFORE A CONCRETE CURRICULUM BEGINS.
I WOULD LIKE YOU TO BEGIN GETTING ACCUSTOMED TO LIFE ON THE ISLAND.

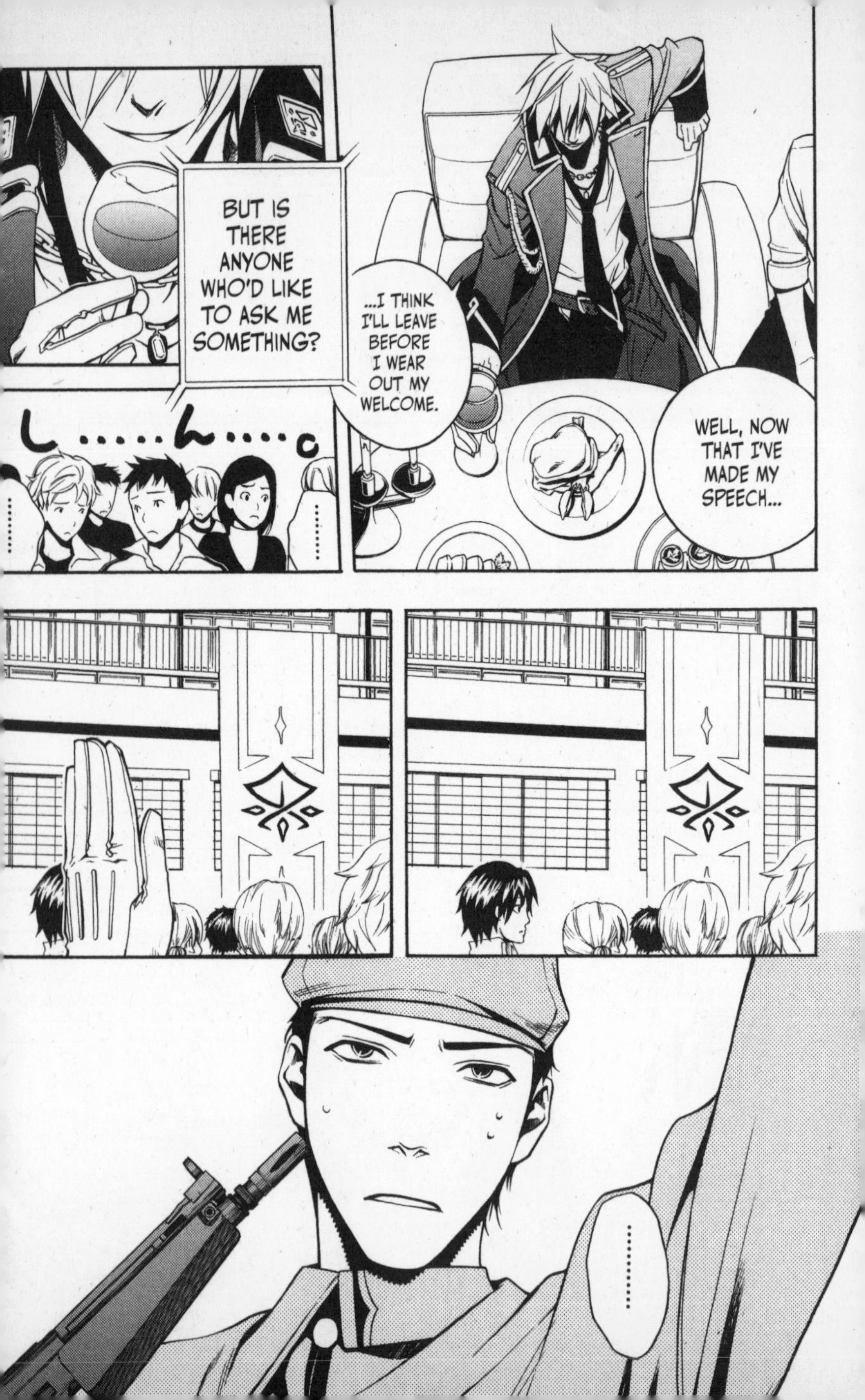
WELL, NOW THAT I'VE MADE MY SPEECH...
...I THINK I'LL LEAVE BEFORE I WEAR OUT MY WELCOME.
BUT IS THERE ANYONE WHO'D LIKE TO ASK ME SOMETHING?
......
......
......

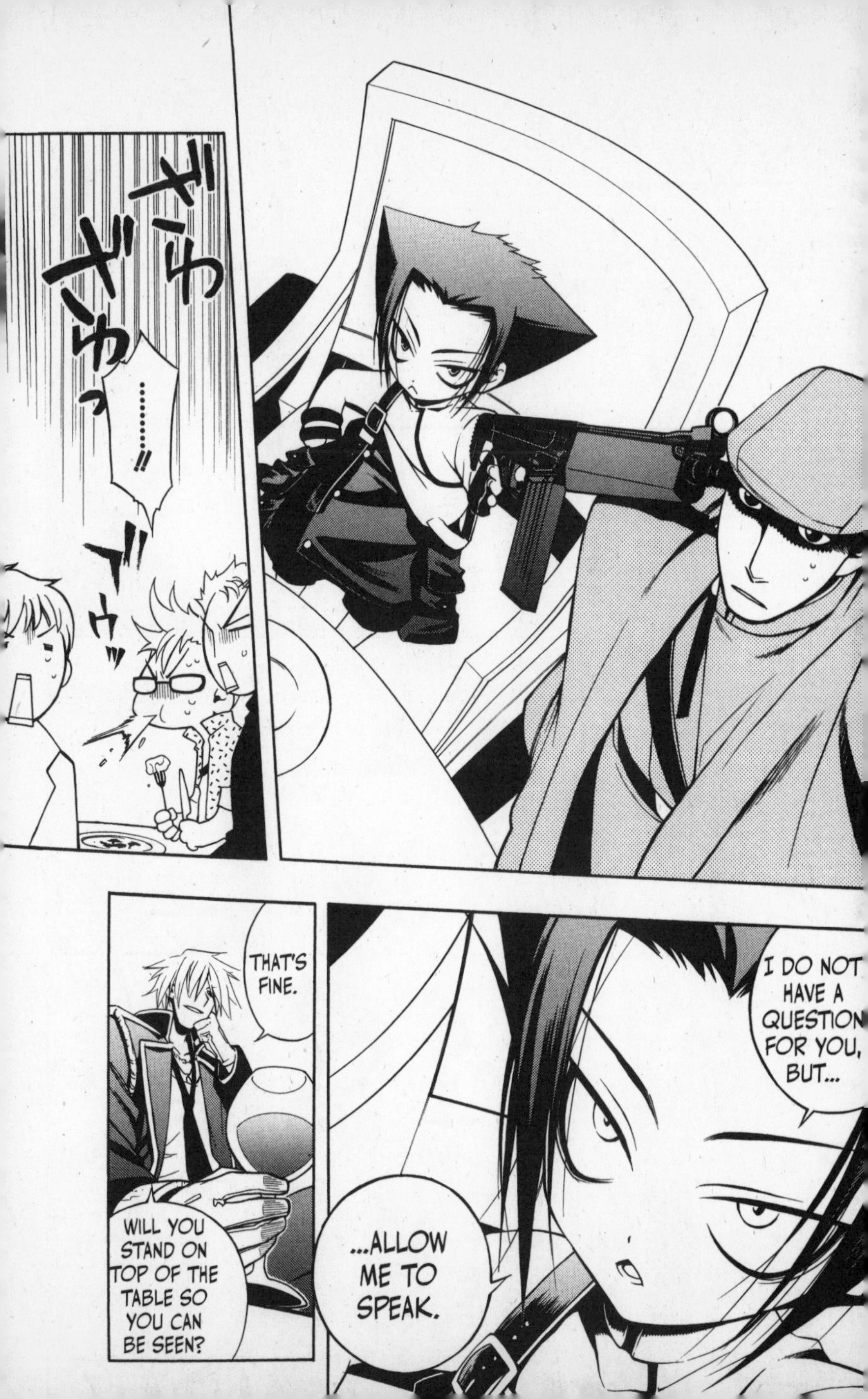
ざわざわっ
......!!
ブァウッ
I DO NOT HAVE A QUESTION FOR YOU, BUT...
...ALLOW ME TO SPEAK.
THAT'S FINE.
WILL YOU STAND ON TOP OF THE TABLE SO YOU CAN BE SEEN?

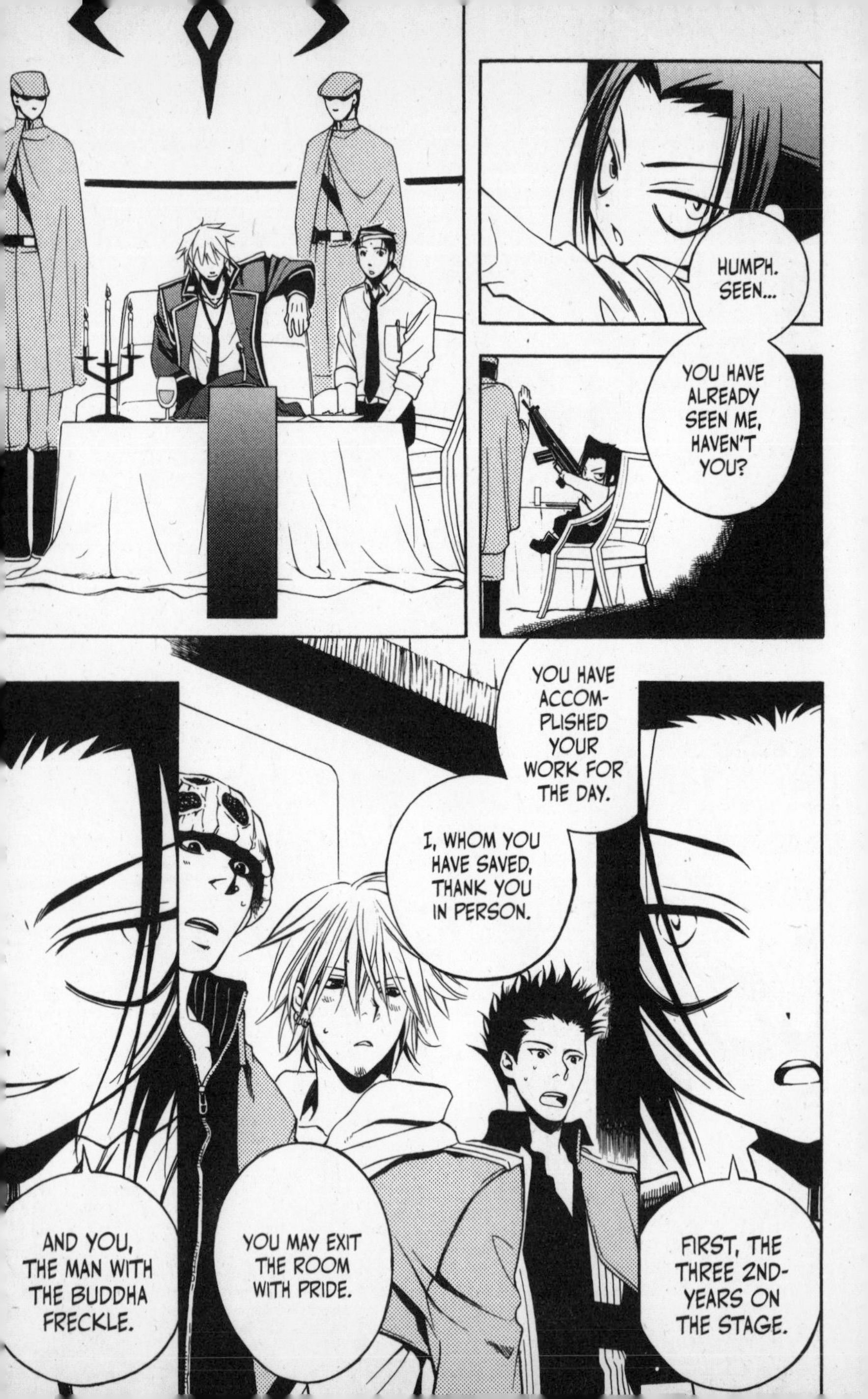
HUMPH. SEEN...
YOU HAVE ALREADY SEEN ME, HAVEN'T YOU?
YOU HAVE ACCOM-PLISHED YOUR WORK FOR THE DAY.
I, WHOM YOU HAVE SAVED, THANK YOU IN PERSON.
FIRST, THE THREE 2ND-YEARS ON THE STAGE.
YOU MAY EXIT THE ROOM WITH PRIDE.
AND YOU, THE MAN WITH THE BUDDHA FRECKLE.

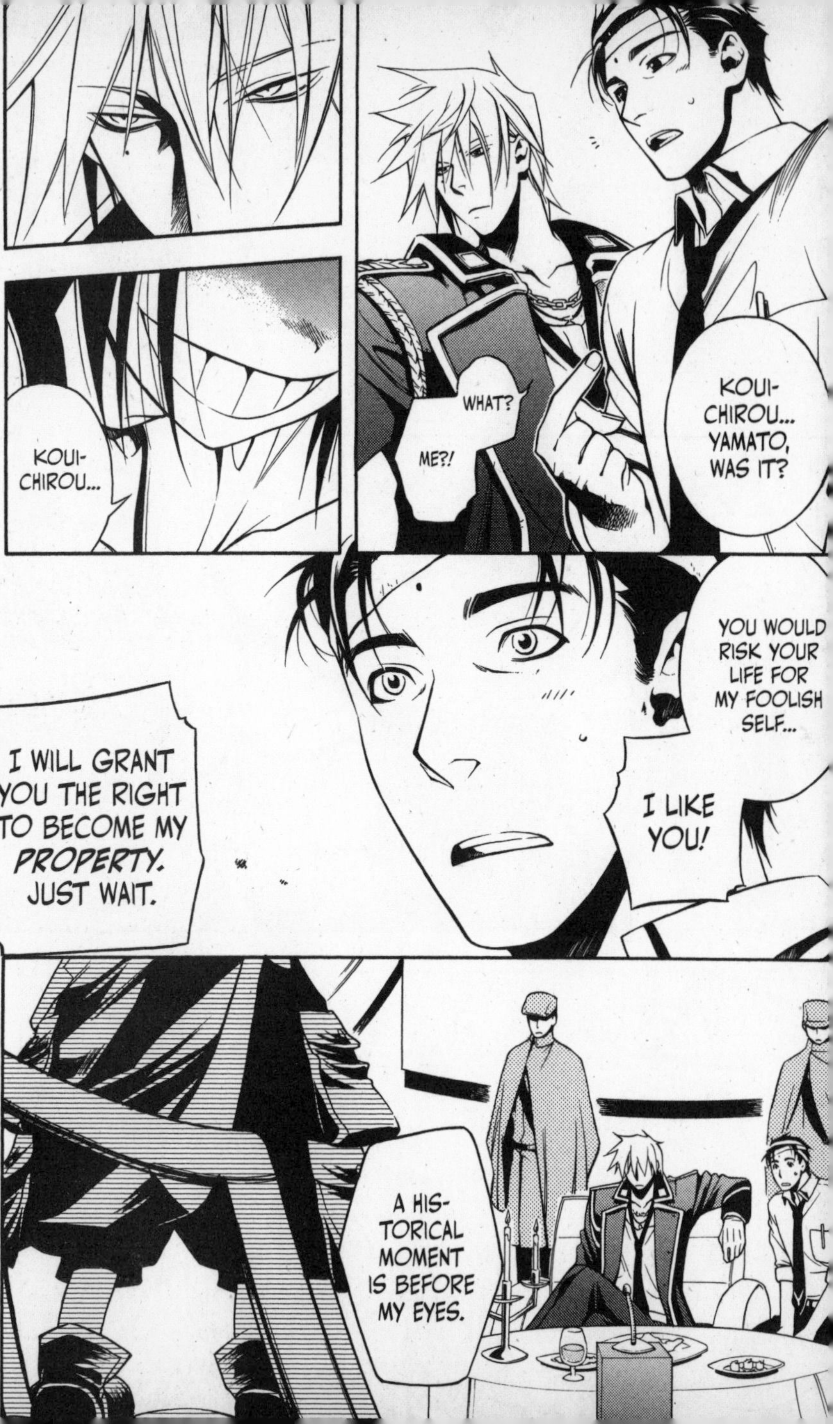
KOUI-CHIROU... YAMATO, WAS IT?
WHAT? ME?!
KOUI-CHIROU...
YOU WOULD RISK YOUR LIFE FOR MY FOOLISH SELF...
I LIKE YOU!
I WILL GRANT YOU THE RIGHT TO BECOME MY *PROPERTY*. JUST WAIT.
A HIS-TORICAL MOMENT IS BEFORE MY EYES.

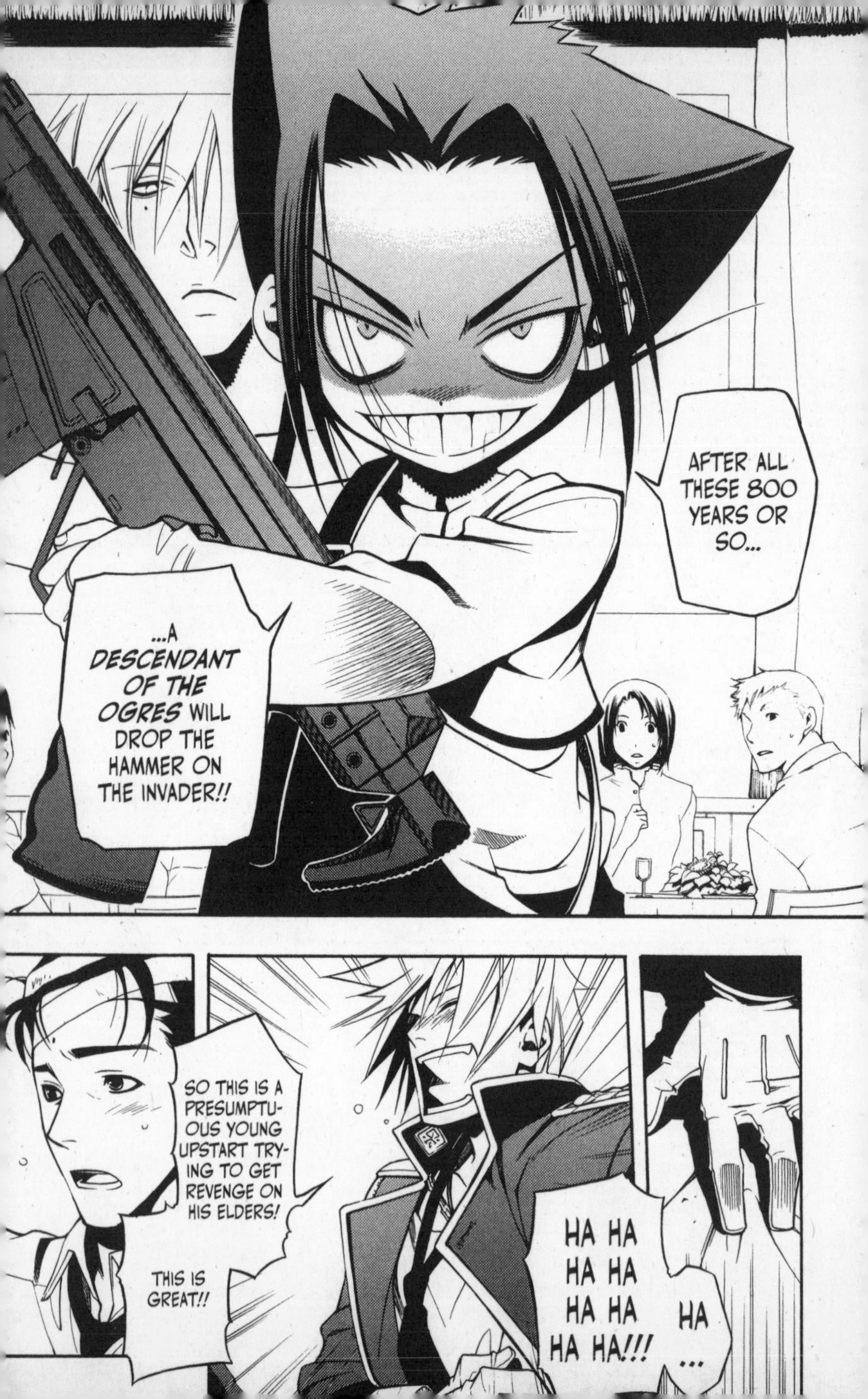
AFTER ALL THESE 800 YEARS OR SO...
...A *DESCENDANT OF THE OGRES* WILL DROP THE HAMMER ON THE INVADER!!
HA HA HA HA HA HA HA HA!!!
HA ...
SO THIS IS A PRESUMPTUOUS YOUNG UPSTART TRYING TO GET REVENGE ON HIS ELDERS!
THIS IS GREAT!!

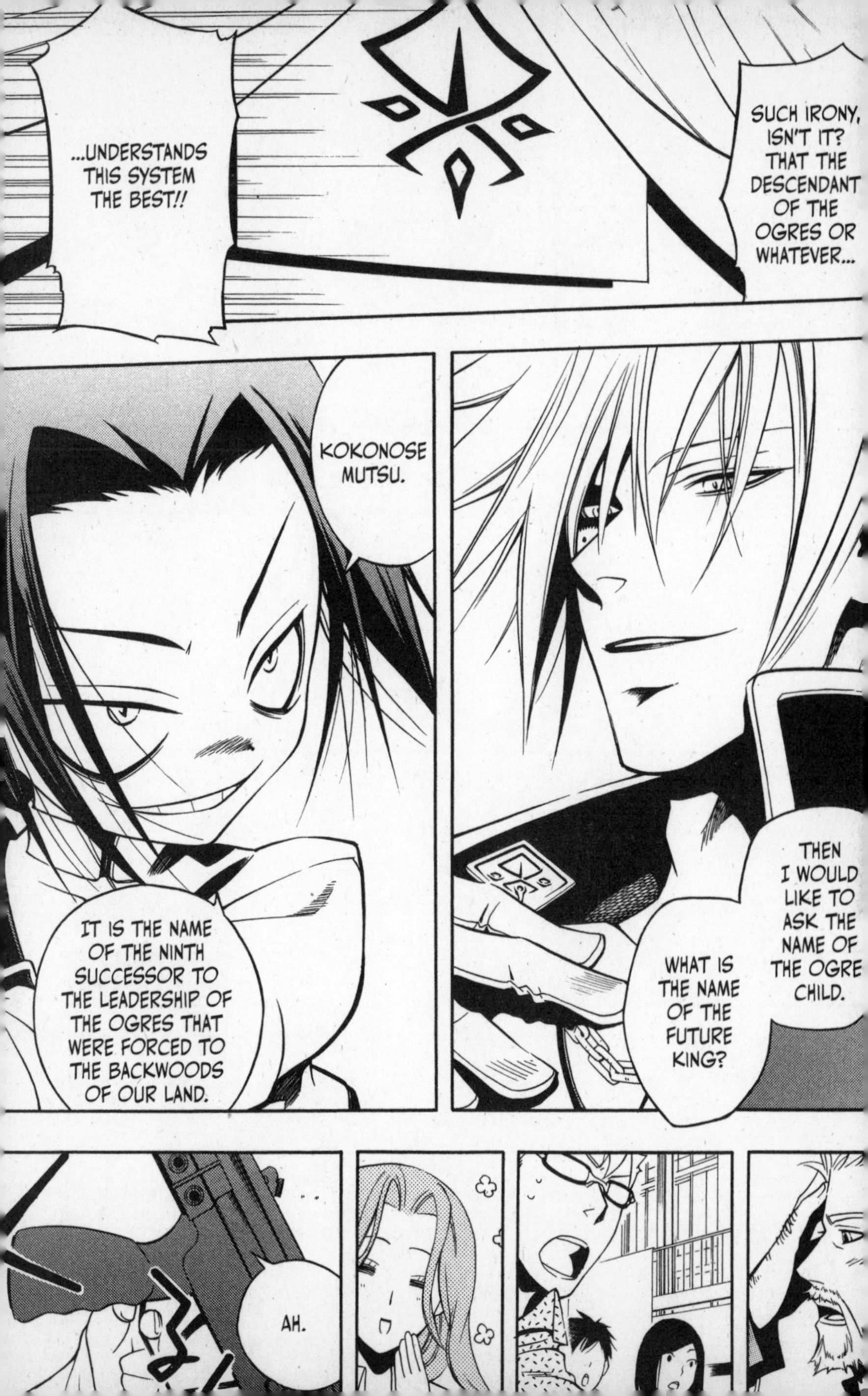
SUCH IRONY, ISN'T IT? THAT THE DESCENDANT OF THE OGRES OR WHATEVER...
...UNDERSTANDS THIS SYSTEM THE BEST!!
THEN I WOULD LIKE TO ASK THE NAME OF THE OGRE CHILD.
WHAT IS THE NAME OF THE FUTURE KING?
KOKONOSE MUTSU.
IT IS THE NAME OF THE NINTH SUCCESSOR TO THE LEADERSHIP OF THE OGRES THAT WERE FORCED TO THE BACKWOODS OF OUR LAND.
AH.

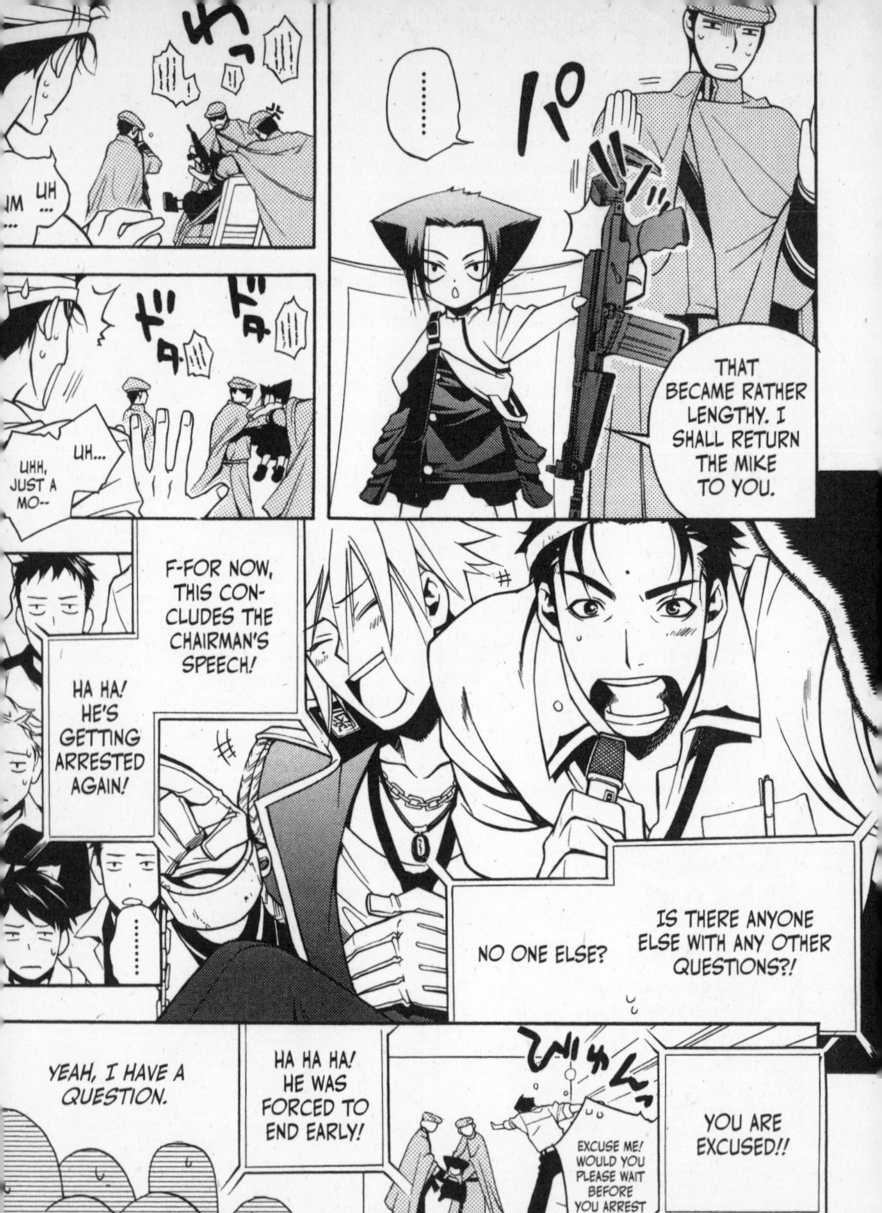
......
THAT BECAME RATHER LENGTHY. I SHALL RETURN THE MIKE TO YOU.
UH ...
UH...
UHH, JUST A MO--
IS THERE ANYONE ELSE WITH ANY OTHER QUESTIONS?!
NO ONE ELSE?
F-FOR NOW, THIS CONCLUDES THE CHAIRMAN'S SPEECH!
HA HA! HE'S GETTING ARRESTED AGAIN!
......
YOU ARE EXCUSED!!
EXCUSE ME! WOULD YOU PLEASE WAIT BEFORE YOU ARREST THAT CHILD?!
HA HA HA! HE WAS FORCED TO END EARLY!
YEAH, I HAVE A QUESTION.

CAN I GO BACK HOME?

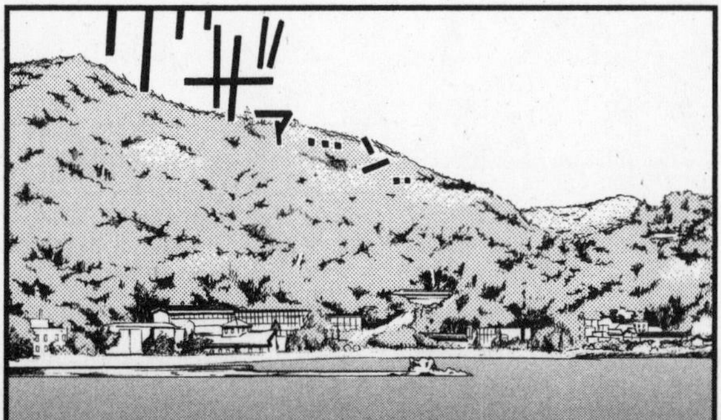
ザザァ…ン…

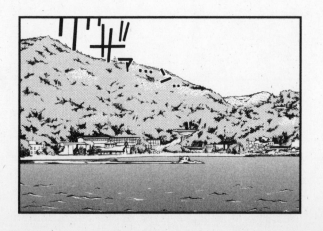

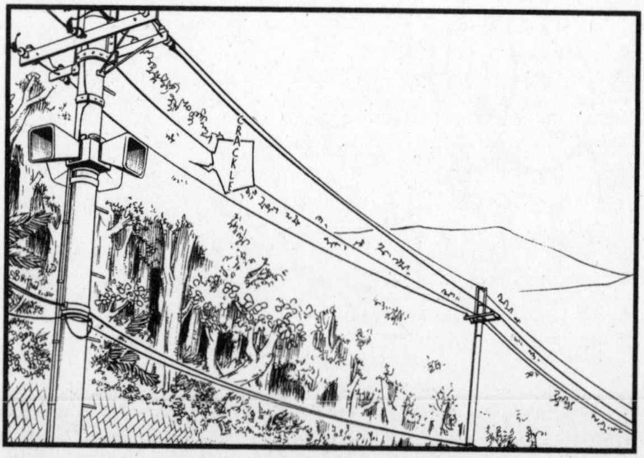
CRACKLE

MOMOTARO

ONCE UPON A TIME, IN A LAND FAR AWAY, THERE LIVED AN OLD MAN AND
OLD WOMAN. THE OLD MAN WENT TO THE MOUNTAIN TO CUT GRASS.
THE OLD WOMAN WENT TO THE RIVER TO DO THE LAUNDRY.

THE OLD WOMAN WAS DOING THE LAUNDRY WHEN A VERY BIG PEACH CAME
ROLLING AND TUMBLING, ROLLING AND TUMBLING DOWN THE RIVER. THE
OLD WOMAN WAS VERY HAPPY WHEN SHE WAS ABLE TO PICK UP THE PEACH.
SHE TOOK THE PEACH HOME AND DECIDED TO EAT IT WITH THE OLD MAN.

WHEN THE OLD MAN SPLIT OPEN THE PEACH, A HEALTHY BABY BOY APPEARED.
THE OLD MAN AND OLD WOMAN DIDN'T HAVE ANY CHILDREN, SO THEY
NAMED THE BABY MOMOTARO AND RAISED HIM WITH LOVE AND CARE.

IN TIME, MOMOTARO BECAME A WONDERFUL YOUNG MAN. HE DECIDED TO GET RID OF THE OGRES THAT REGULARLY ATTACKED HIS VILLAGE. MOMOTARO TOOK THE SWEET DUMPLINGS THAT THE OLD WOMAN MADE FOR HIM AND SET OUT FOR ONIGASHIMA, THE ISLAND OF THE OGRES.

HE WALKED FOR A WHILE AND MET A DOG, WHO SAID,
"MOMOTARO-SAN, PLEASE GIVE ME ONE OF THOSE SWEET DUMPLINGS."

"I'LL GIVE YOU ONE IF YOU'LL FOLLOW ME," MOMOTARO REPLIED.
THAT'S HOW THE DOG STARTED FOLLOWING MOMOTARO.

THEY WALKED FOR A WHILE AND MET A MONKEY.
"MOMOTARO-SAN, PLEASE GIVE ME ONE OF THOSE SWEET DUMPLINGS," SAID THE MONKEY.

"I'LL GIVE YOU ONE IF YOU'LL FOLLOW ME," MOMOTARO REPLIED.
THAT'S HOW THE MONKEY STARTED FOLLOWING MOMOTARO.

THEY WALKED FOR A WHILE AND MET A PHEASANT.
"MOMOTARO-SAN, PLEASE GIVE ME ONE OF THOSE SWEET DUMPLINGS," SAID THE PHEASANT.

"I'LL GIVE YOU ONE IF YOU'LL FOLLOW ME," MOMOTARO REPLIED.
THAT'S HOW THE PHEASANT STARTED FOLLOWING MOMOTARO.

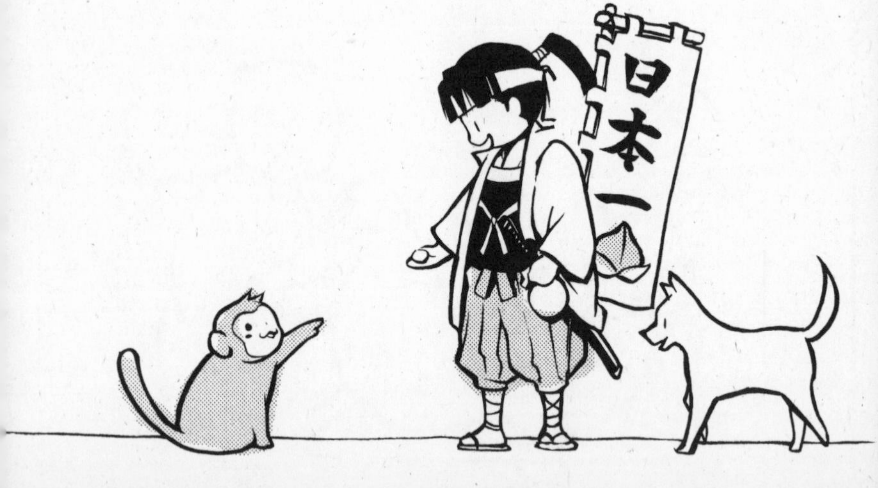
日本一

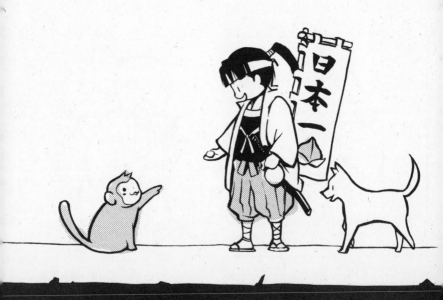

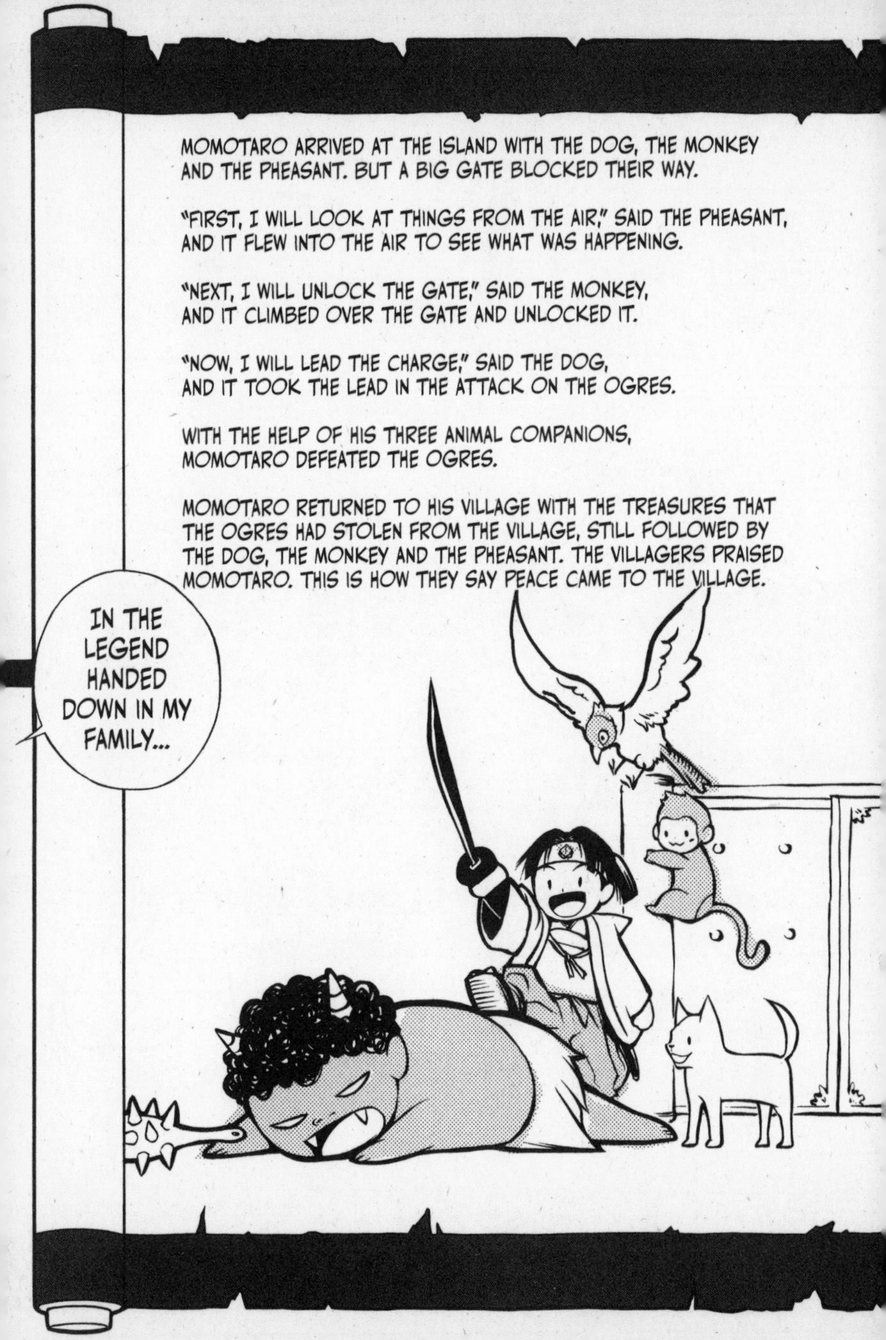
MOMOTARO ARRIVED AT THE ISLAND WITH THE DOG, THE MONKEY AND THE PHEASANT. BUT A BIG GATE BLOCKED THEIR WAY.
"FIRST, I WILL LOOK AT THINGS FROM THE AIR," SAID THE PHEASANT, AND IT FLEW INTO THE AIR TO SEE WHAT WAS HAPPENING.
"NEXT, I WILL UNLOCK THE GATE," SAID THE MONKEY, AND IT CLIMBED OVER THE GATE AND UNLOCKED IT.
"NOW, I WILL LEAD THE CHARGE," SAID THE DOG, AND IT TOOK THE LEAD IN THE ATTACK ON THE OGRES.
WITH THE HELP OF HIS THREE ANIMAL COMPANIONS, MOMOTARO DEFEATED THE OGRES.
MOMOTARO RETURNED TO HIS VILLAGE WITH THE TREASURES THAT THE OGRES HAD STOLEN FROM THE VILLAGE, STILL FOLLOWED BY THE DOG, THE MONKEY AND THE PHEASANT. THE VILLAGERS PRAISED MOMOTARO. THIS IS HOW THEY SAY PEACE CAME TO THE VILLAGE.
IN THE LEGEND HANDED DOWN IN MY FAMILY...

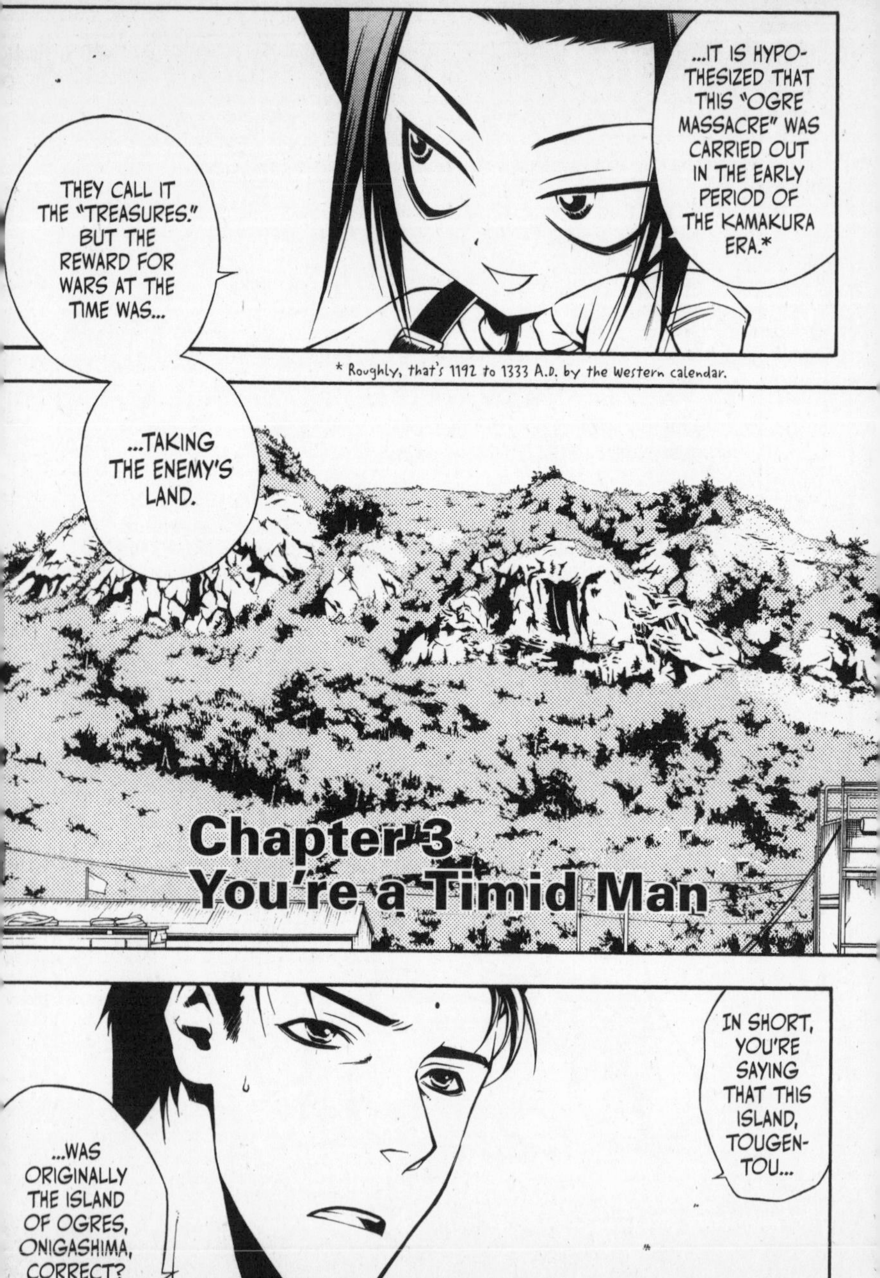
...IT IS HYPOTHESIZED THAT THIS "OGRE MASSACRE" WAS CARRIED OUT IN THE EARLY PERIOD OF THE KAMAKURA ERA.*
THEY CALL IT THE "TREASURES." BUT THE REWARD FOR WARS AT THE TIME WAS...
...TAKING THE ENEMY'S LAND.
Chapter 3
You're a Timid Man
IN SHORT, YOU'RE SAYING THAT THIS ISLAND, TOUGEN-TOU...
...WAS ORIGINALLY THE ISLAND OF OGRES, ONIGASHIMA, CORRECT?

* Roughly, that's 1192 to 1333 A.D. by the Western calendar.

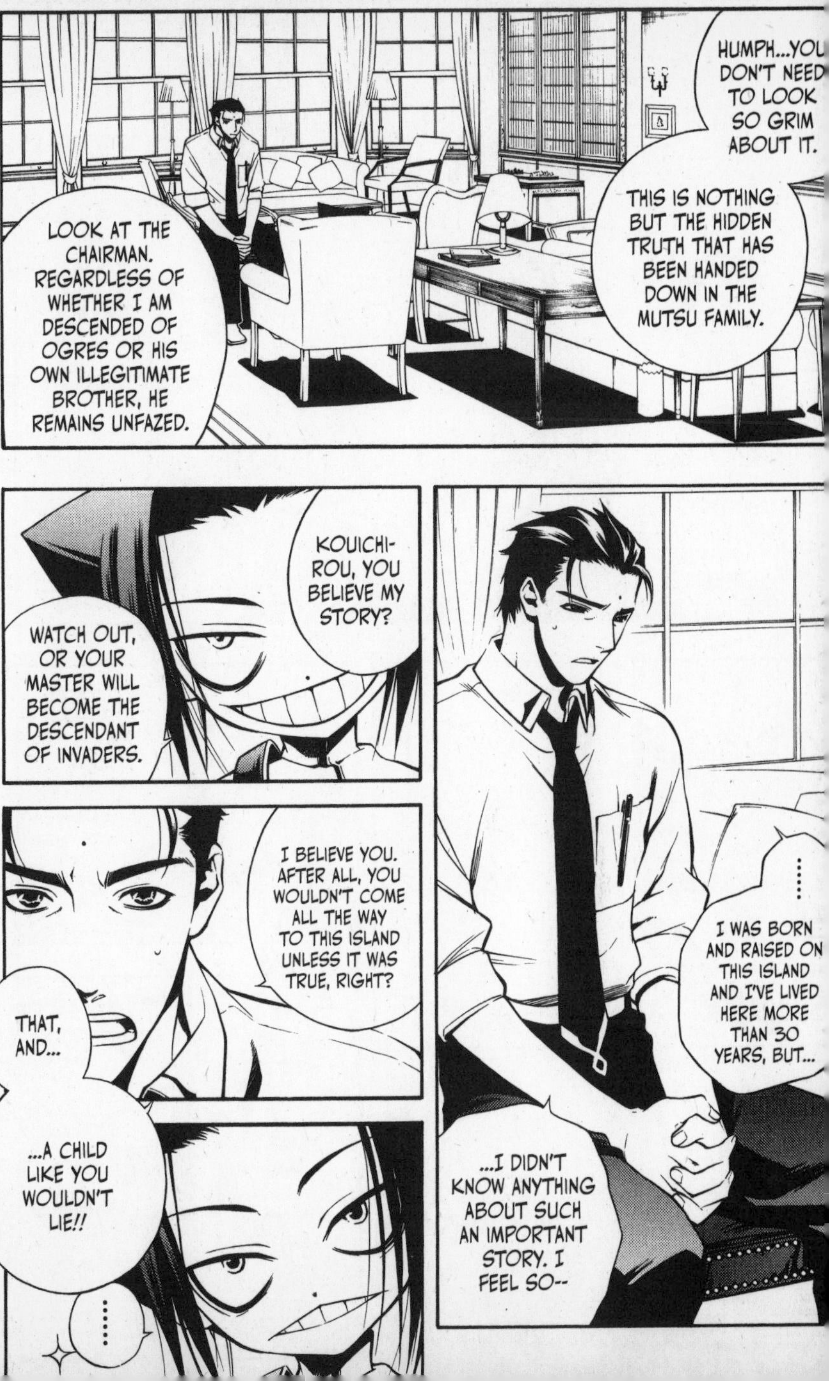
HUMPH...YOU DON'T NEED TO LOOK SO GRIM ABOUT IT.
THIS IS NOTHING BUT THE HIDDEN TRUTH THAT HAS BEEN HANDED DOWN IN THE MUTSU FAMILY.
LOOK AT THE CHAIRMAN. REGARDLESS OF WHETHER I AM DESCENDED OF OGRES OR HIS OWN ILLEGITIMATE BROTHER, HE REMAINS UNFAZED.
......
I WAS BORN AND RAISED ON THIS ISLAND AND I'VE LIVED HERE MORE THAN 30 YEARS, BUT...
...I DIDN'T KNOW ANYTHING ABOUT SUCH AN IMPORTANT STORY. I FEEL SO--
KOUICHIROU, YOU BELIEVE MY STORY?
WATCH OUT, OR YOUR MASTER WILL BECOME THE DESCENDANT OF INVADERS.
I BELIEVE YOU. AFTER ALL, YOU WOULDN'T COME ALL THE WAY TO THIS ISLAND UNLESS IT WAS TRUE, RIGHT?
THAT, AND...
...A CHILD LIKE YOU WOULDN'T LIE!!
......

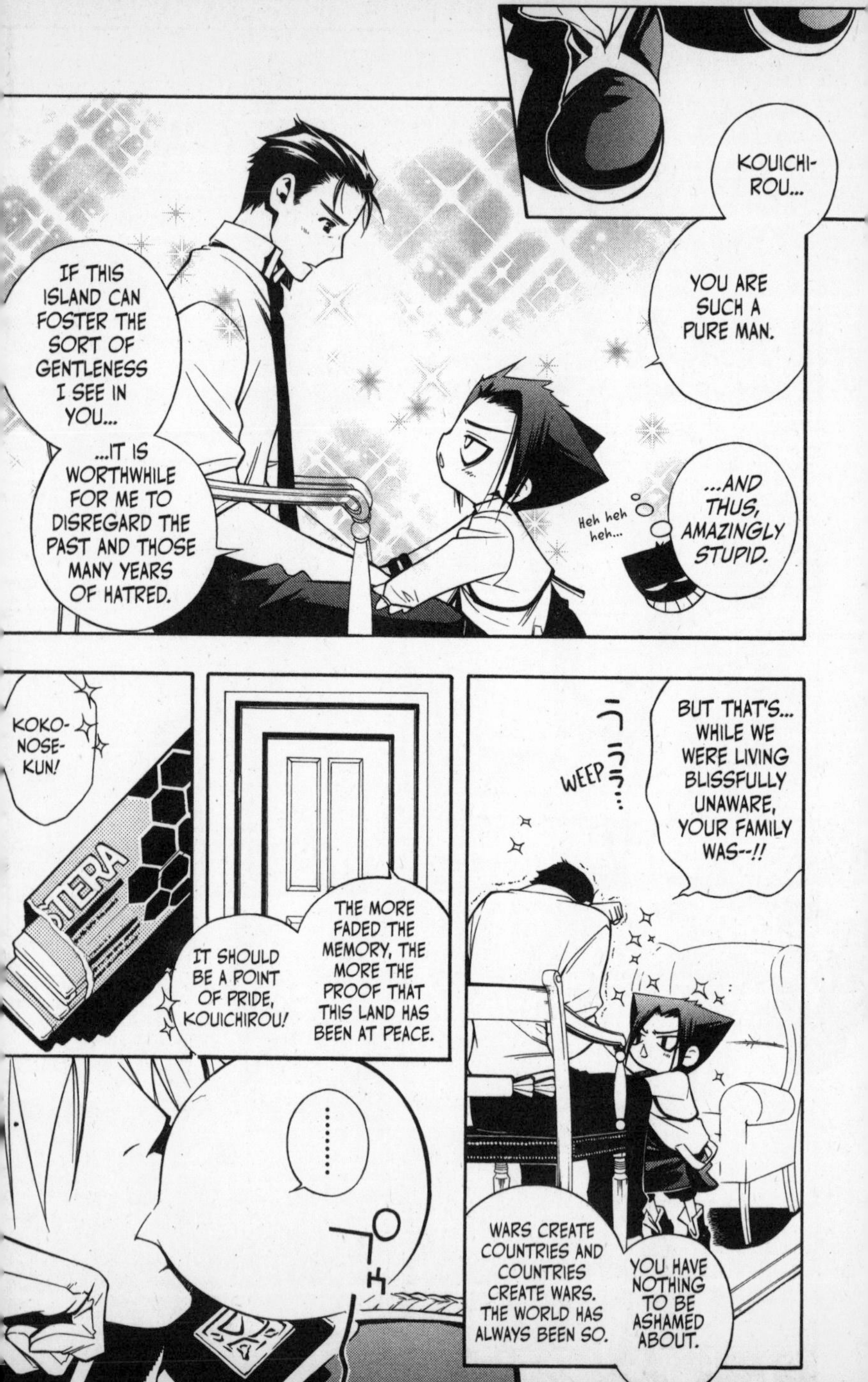
KOUICHI-ROU...
YOU ARE SUCH A PURE MAN.
...AND THUS, AMAZINGLY STUPID.
Heh heh heh...
IF THIS ISLAND CAN FOSTER THE SORT OF GENTLENESS I SEE IN YOU...
...IT IS WORTHWHILE FOR ME TO DISREGARD THE PAST AND THOSE MANY YEARS OF HATRED.
BUT THAT'S... WHILE WE WERE LIVING BLISSFULLY UNAWARE, YOUR FAMILY WAS--!!
WEEP
THE MORE FADED THE MEMORY, THE MORE THE PROOF THAT THIS LAND HAS BEEN AT PEACE.
IT SHOULD BE A POINT OF PRIDE, KOUICHIROU!
KOKO-NOSE-KUN!
STERA
YOU HAVE NOTHING TO BE ASHAMED ABOUT.
WARS CREATE COUNTRIES AND COUNTRIES CREATE WARS. THE WORLD HAS ALWAYS BEEN SO.
......

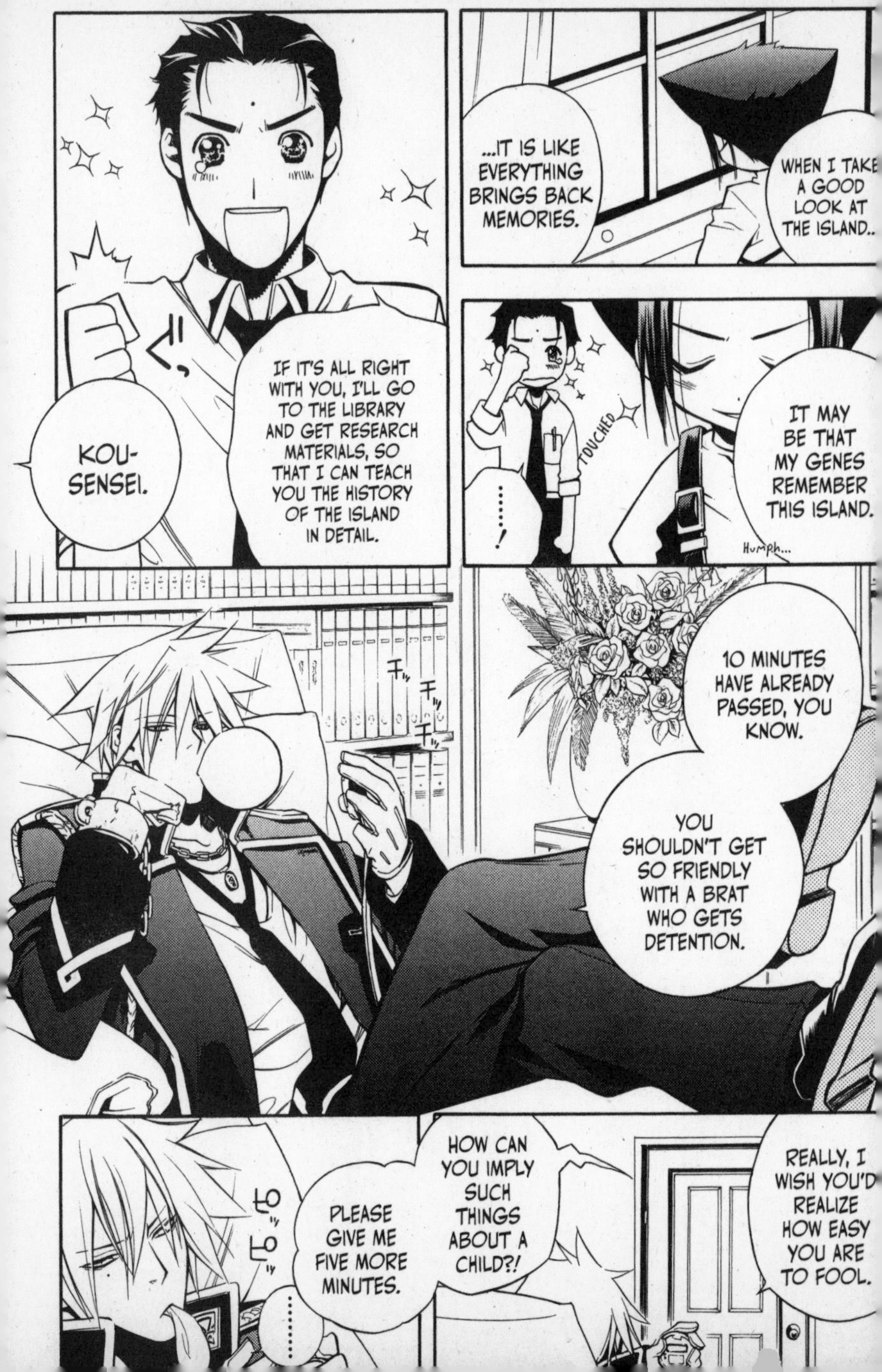
WHEN I TAKE A GOOD LOOK AT THE ISLAND...
...IT IS LIKE EVERYTHING BRINGS BACK MEMORIES.
IT MAY BE THAT MY GENES REMEMBER THIS ISLAND.
Humph...
TOUCHED
......!
IF IT'S ALL RIGHT WITH YOU, I'LL GO TO THE LIBRARY AND GET RESEARCH MATERIALS, SO THAT I CAN TEACH YOU THE HISTORY OF THE ISLAND IN DETAIL.
KOU-SENSEI.
10 MINUTES HAVE ALREADY PASSED, YOU KNOW.
YOU SHOULDN'T GET SO FRIENDLY WITH A BRAT WHO GETS DETENTION.
チッ
チッ
チッ
REALLY, I WISH YOU'D REALIZE HOW EASY YOU ARE TO FOOL.
HOW CAN YOU IMPLY SUCH THINGS ABOUT A CHILD?!
PLEASE GIVE ME FIVE MORE MINUTES.
......

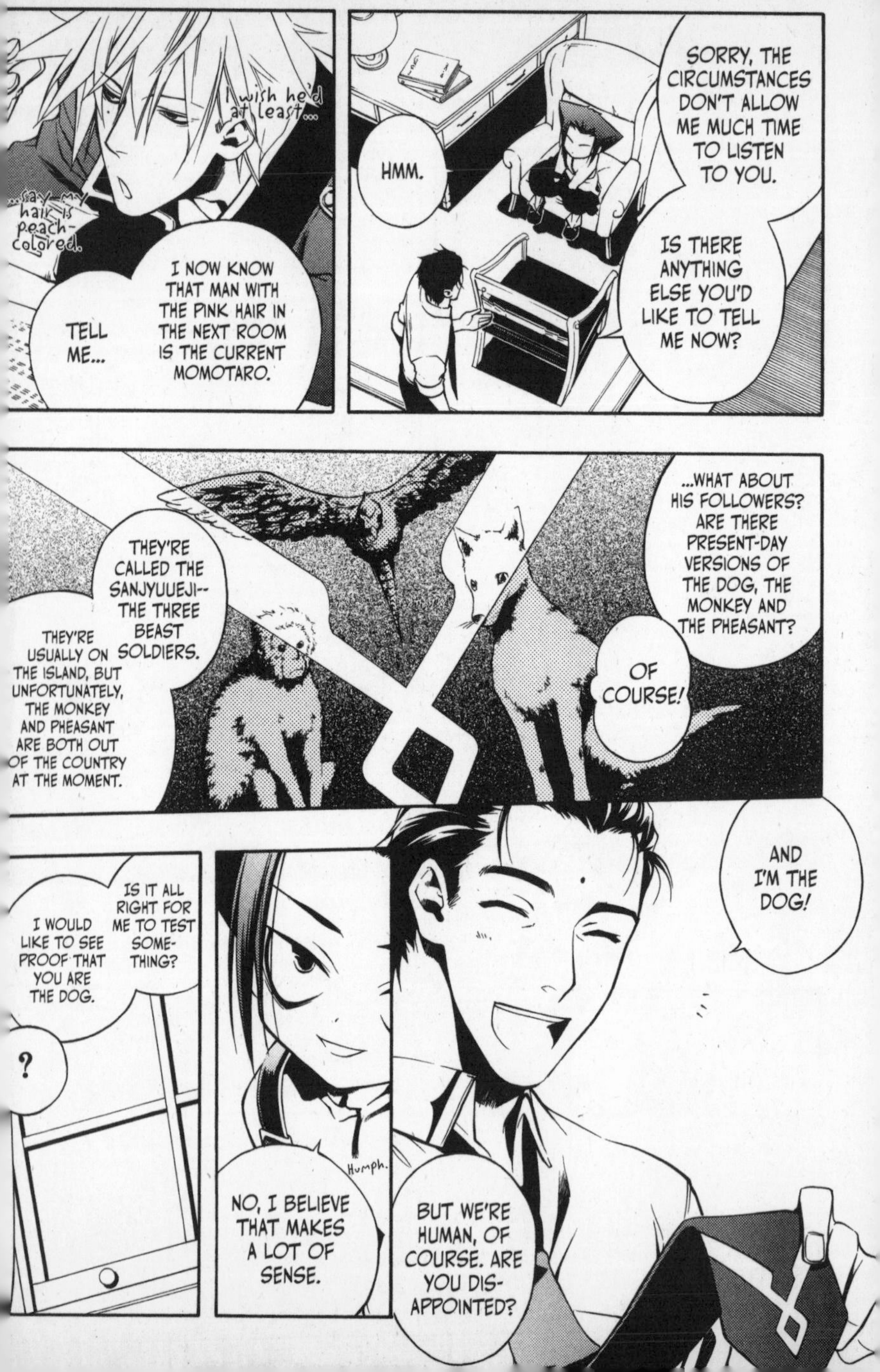
SORRY, THE CIRCUMSTANCES DON'T ALLOW ME MUCH TIME TO LISTEN TO YOU.
IS THERE ANYTHING ELSE YOU'D LIKE TO TELL ME NOW?
HMM.
I wish he'd at least...
...say my hair is peach-colored.
I NOW KNOW THAT MAN WITH THE PINK HAIR IN THE NEXT ROOM IS THE CURRENT MOMOTARO.
TELL ME...
...WHAT ABOUT HIS FOLLOWERS? ARE THERE PRESENT-DAY VERSIONS OF THE DOG, THE MONKEY AND THE PHEASANT?
OF COURSE!
THEY'RE CALLED THE SANJYUUEJI-- THE THREE BEAST SOLDIERS.
THEY'RE USUALLY ON THE ISLAND, BUT UNFORTUNATELY, THE MONKEY AND PHEASANT ARE BOTH OUT OF THE COUNTRY AT THE MOMENT.
AND I'M THE DOG!
BUT WE'RE HUMAN, OF COURSE. ARE YOU DIS-APPOINTED?
Humph.
NO, I BELIEVE THAT MAKES A LOT OF SENSE.
IS IT ALL RIGHT FOR ME TO TEST SOME-THING?
I WOULD LIKE TO SEE PROOF THAT YOU ARE THE DOG.
?

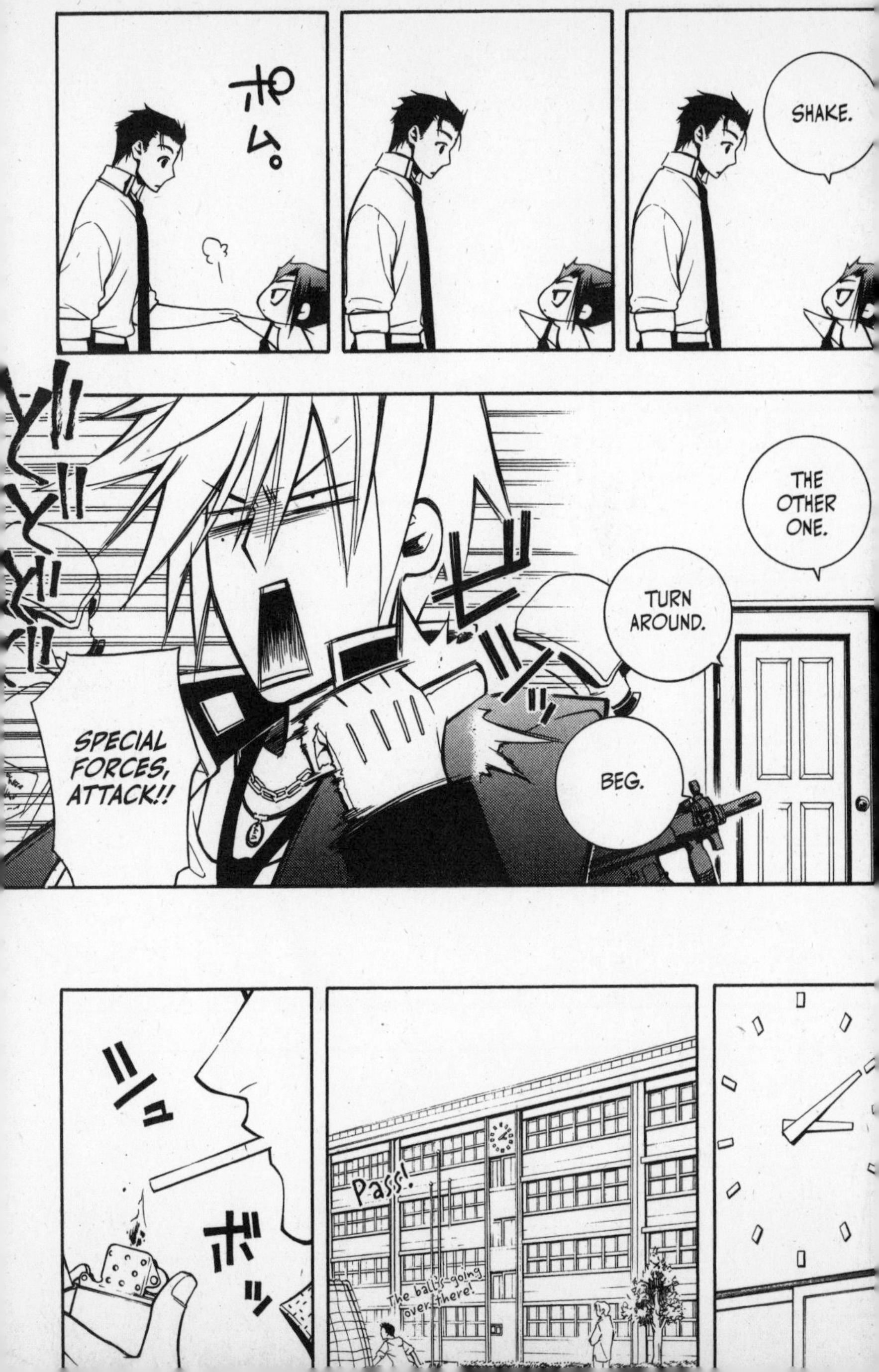
SHAKE.
ポム。
THE OTHER ONE.
TURN AROUND.
BEG.
SPECIAL FORCES, ATTACK!!
Pass!
The ball's going over there!
ボッ
ニュ

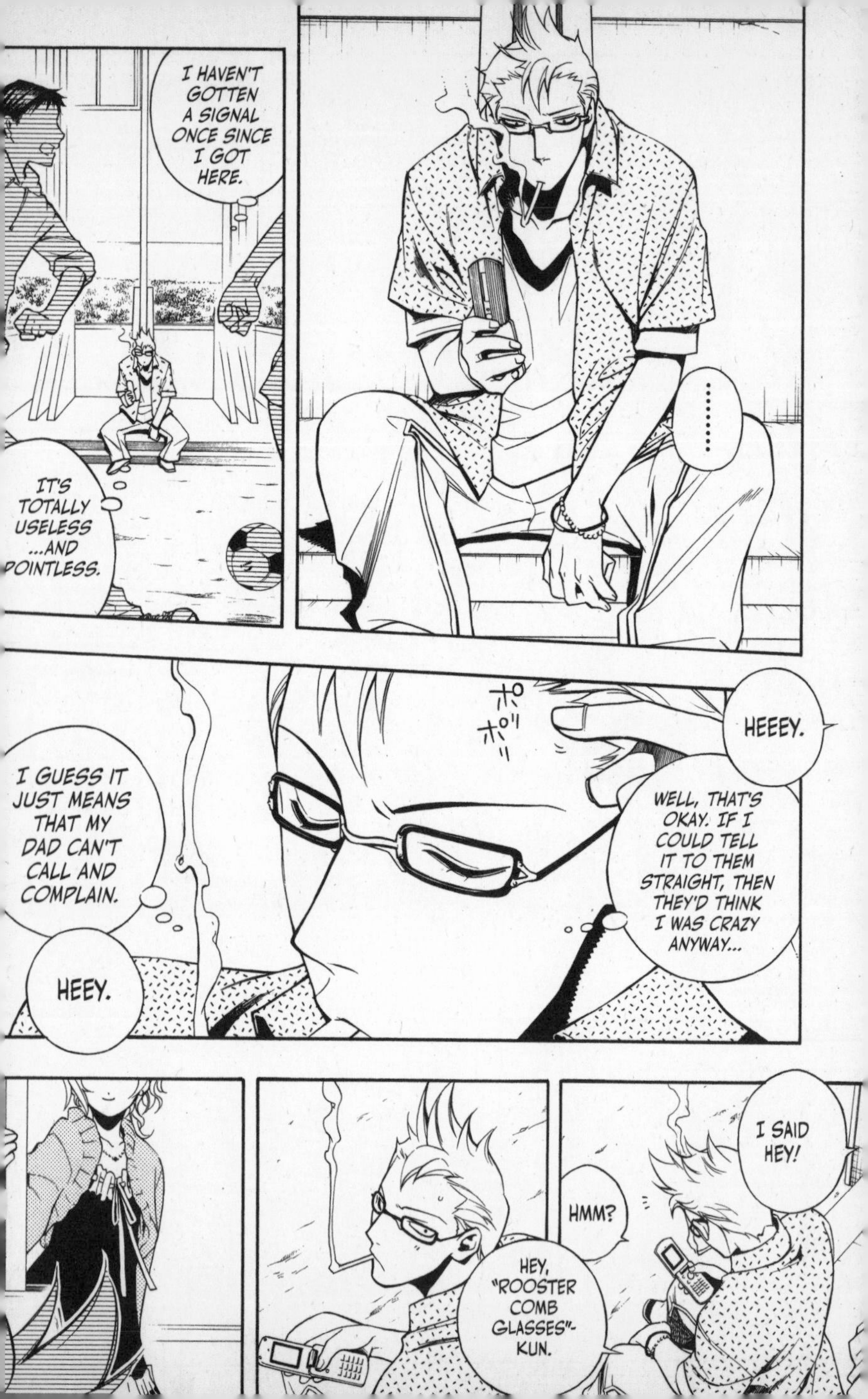
......
I HAVEN'T GOTTEN A SIGNAL ONCE SINCE I GOT HERE.
IT'S TOTALLY USELESS ...AND POINTLESS.
HEEEY.
WELL, THAT'S OKAY. IF I COULD TELL IT TO THEM STRAIGHT, THEN THEY'D THINK I WAS CRAZY ANYWAY...
ポリポリ
I GUESS IT JUST MEANS THAT MY DAD CAN'T CALL AND COMPLAIN.
HEEY.
I SAID HEY!
HMM?
HEY, "ROOSTER COMB GLASSES"-KUN.

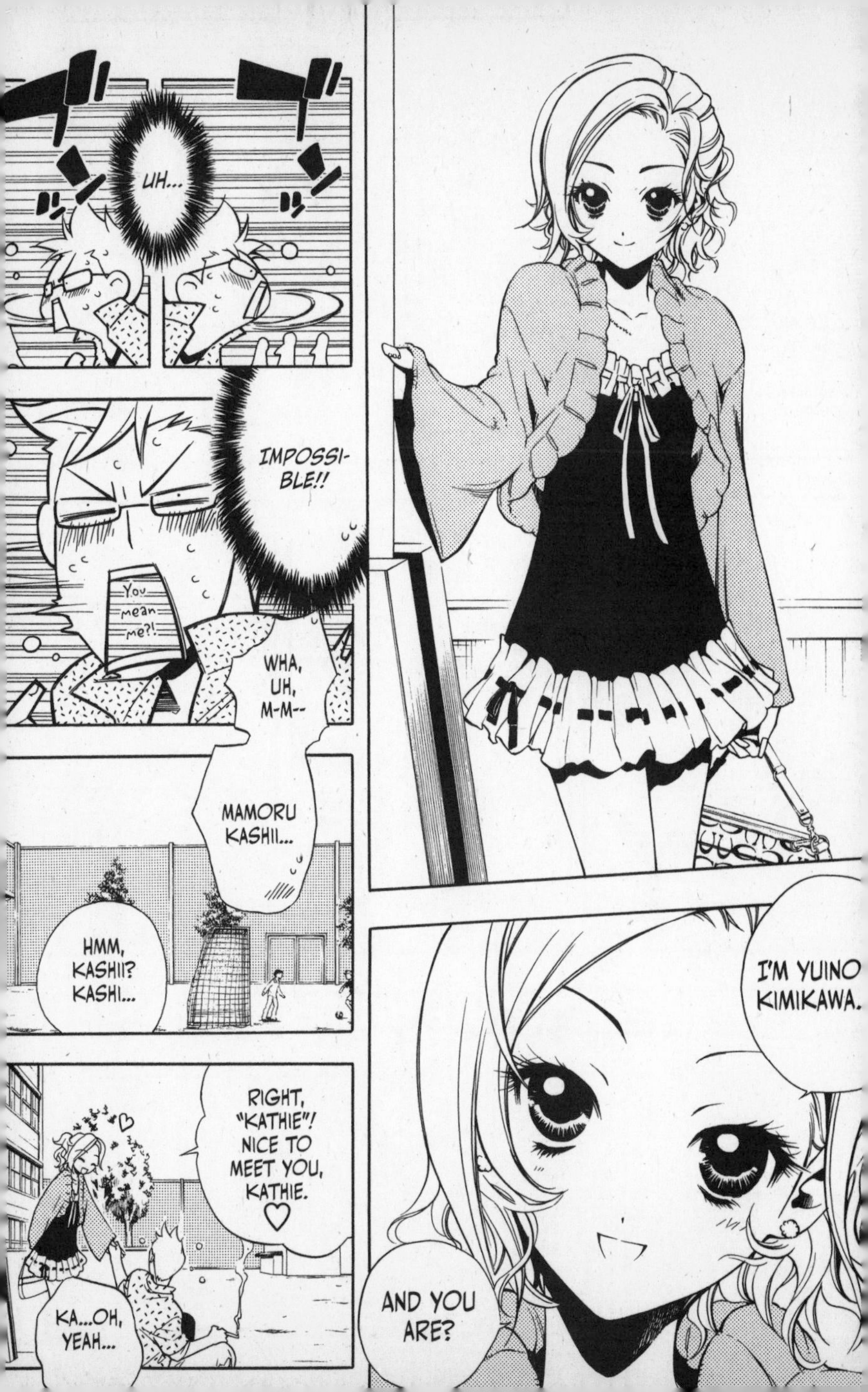
I'M YUINO KIMIKAWA.
AND YOU ARE?
UH...
IMPOSSIBLE!!
You mean me?!
WHA, UH, M-M--
MAMORU KASHII...
HMM, KASHII? KASHI...
RIGHT, "KATHIE"! NICE TO MEET YOU, KATHIE. ♡
KA...OH, YEAH...

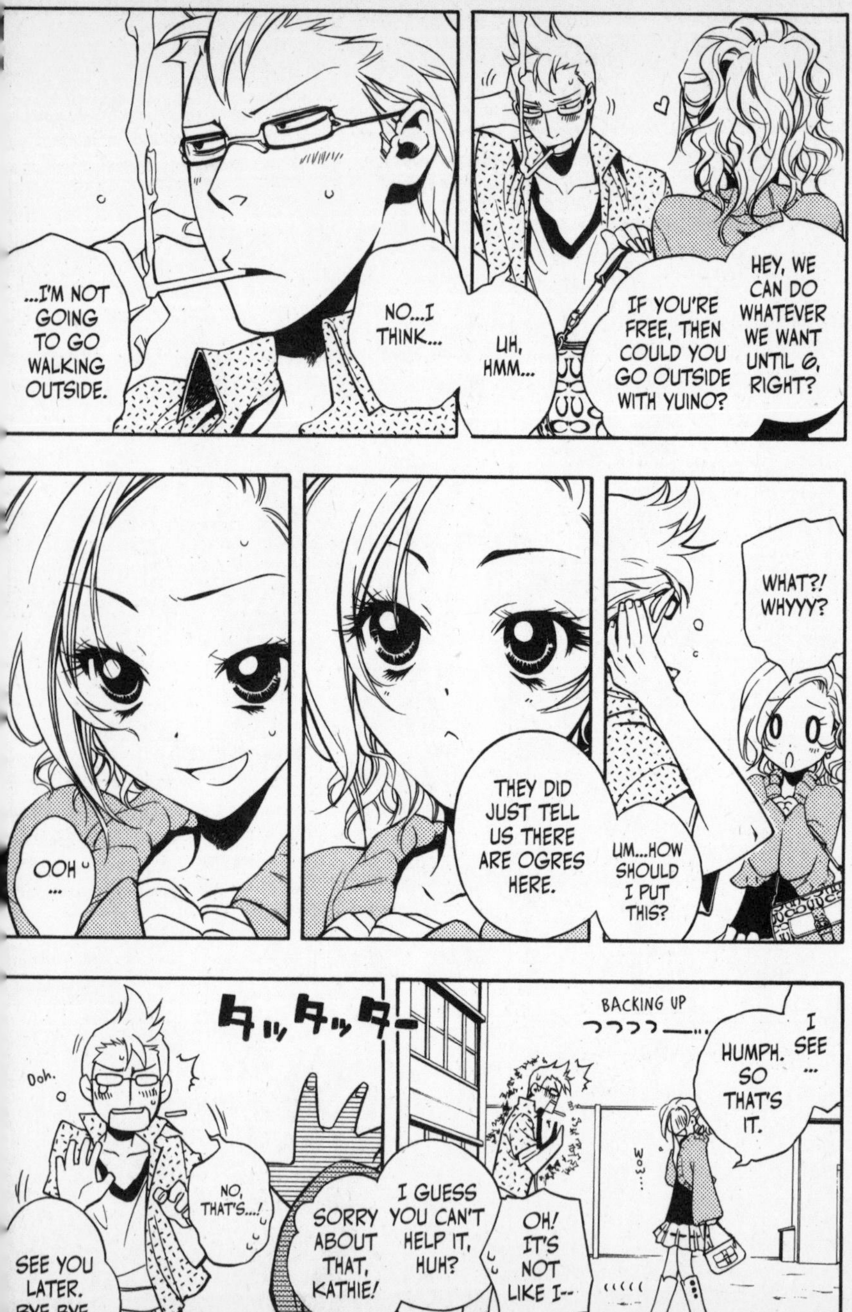
HEY, WE CAN DO WHATEVER WE WANT UNTIL 6, RIGHT?
IF YOU'RE FREE, THEN COULD YOU GO OUTSIDE WITH YUINO?
UH, HMM...
NO...I THINK...
...I'M NOT GOING TO GO WALKING OUTSIDE.
WHAT?! WHYYY?
UM...HOW SHOULD I PUT THIS?
THEY DID JUST TELL US THERE ARE OGRES HERE.
OOH ...
BACKING UP
つつつつ――...
I SEE ...
HUMPH. SO THAT'S IT.
WOW...
OH! IT'S NOT LIKE I--
タッタッター
I GUESS YOU CAN'T HELP IT, HUH?
SORRY ABOUT THAT, KATHIE!
NO, THAT'S...!
Ooh.
SEE YOU LATER. BYE BYE.

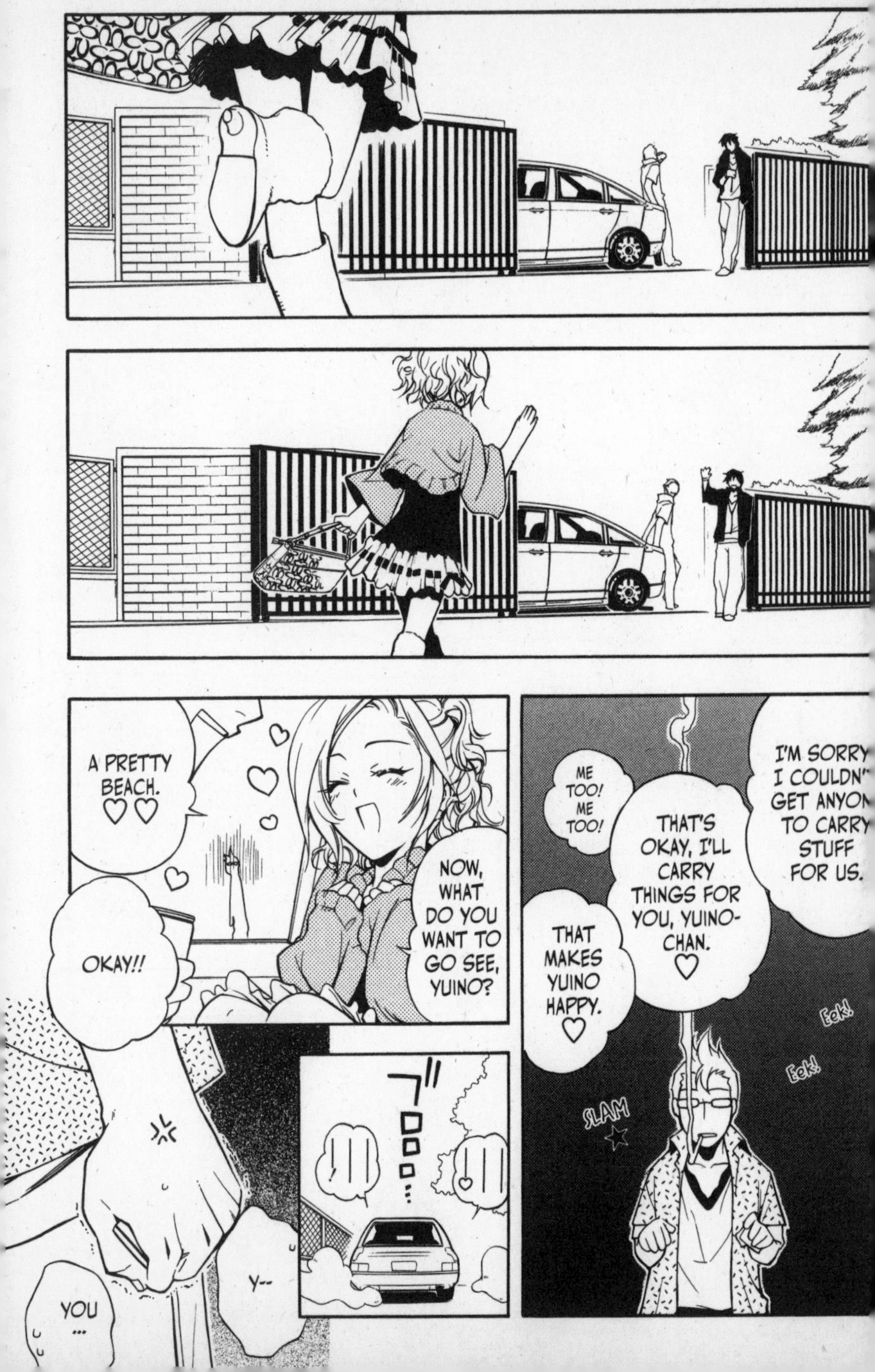
I'M SORRY I COULDN' GET ANYON TO CARRY STUFF FOR US.
THAT'S OKAY, I'LL CARRY THINGS FOR YOU, YUINO-CHAN. ♡
ME TOO! ME TOO!
THAT MAKES YUINO HAPPY. ♡
Eek!
Eek!
SLAM
NOW, WHAT DO YOU WANT TO GO SEE, YUINO?
A PRETTY BEACH. ♡♡
OKAY!!
ブロロロ...
Y--
YOU ...

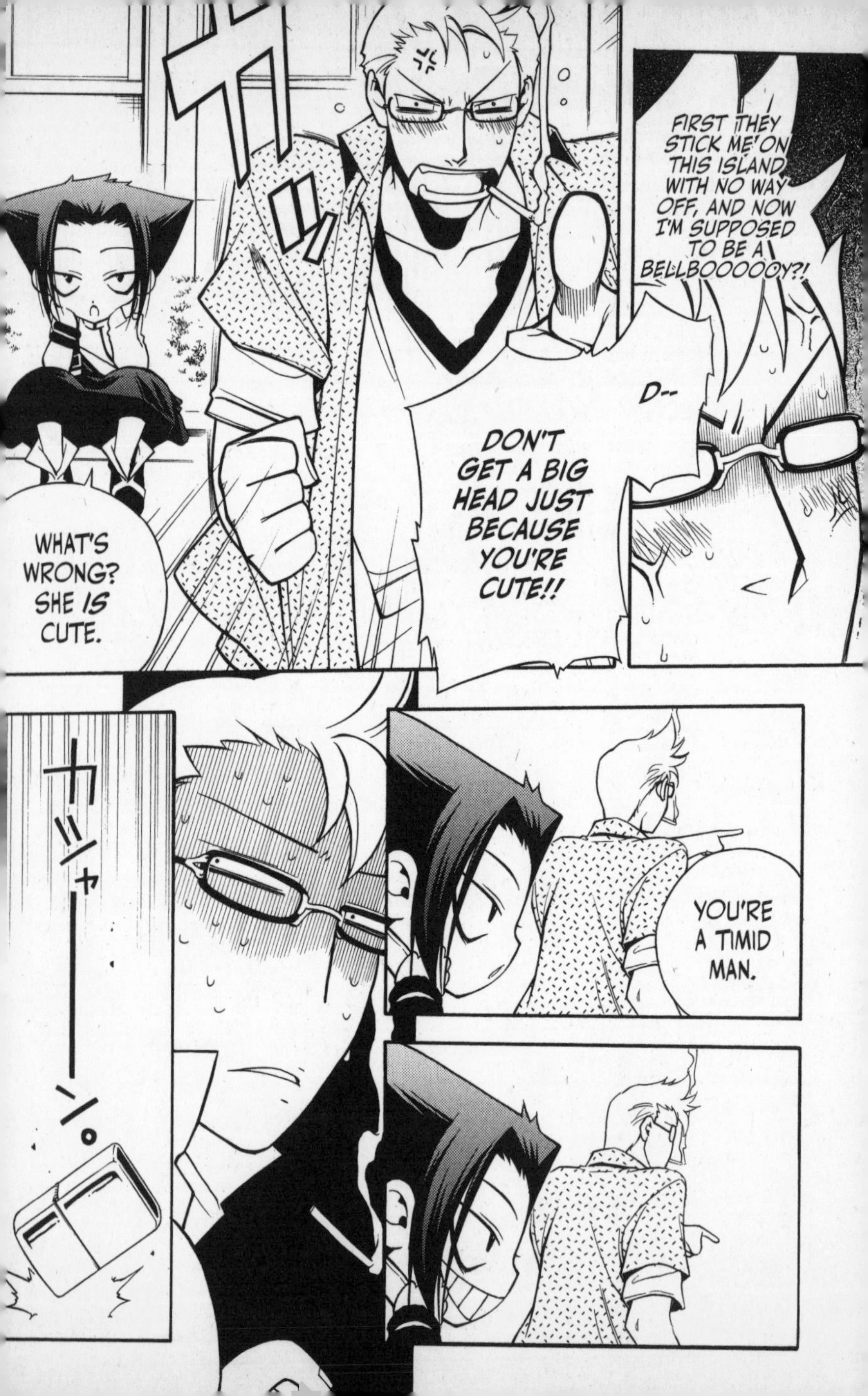
FIRST THEY STICK ME ON THIS ISLAND WITH NO WAY OFF, AND NOW I'M SUPPOSED TO BE A BELLBOOOOOOY?!
D--
DON'T GET A BIG HEAD JUST BECAUSE YOU'RE CUTE!!
WHAT'S WRONG? SHE *IS* CUTE.
YOU'RE A TIMID MAN.

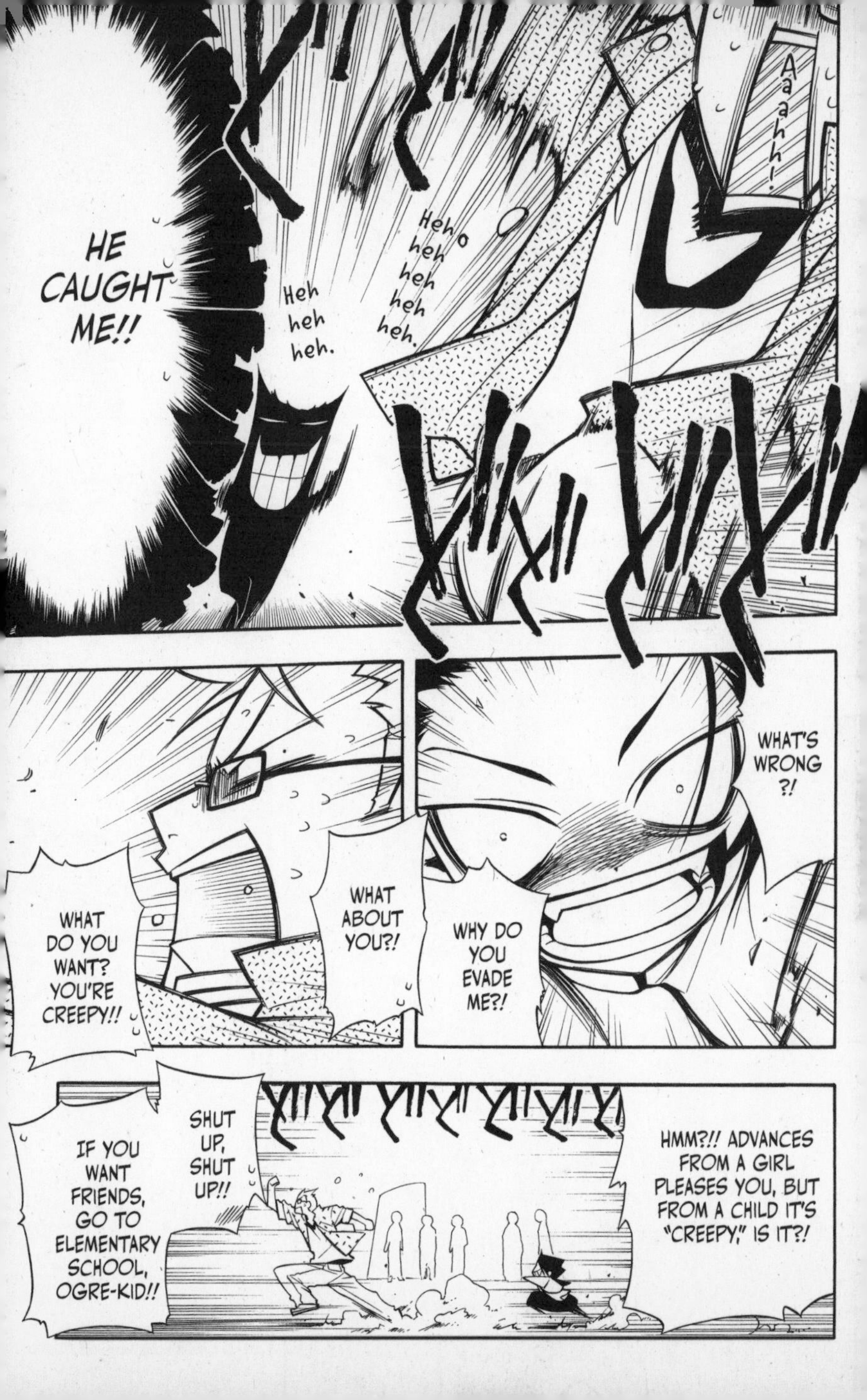
Aaahh!
Heh heh heh heh heh.
Heh heh heh.
HE CAUGHT ME!!
WHAT'S WRONG?!
WHY DO YOU EVADE ME?!
WHAT ABOUT YOU?!
WHAT DO YOU WANT? YOU'RE CREEPY!!
HMM?!! ADVANCES FROM A GIRL PLEASES YOU, BUT FROM A CHILD IT'S "CREEPY," IS IT?!
SHUT UP, SHUT UP!!
IF YOU WANT FRIENDS, GO TO ELEMENTARY SCHOOL, OGRE-KID!!

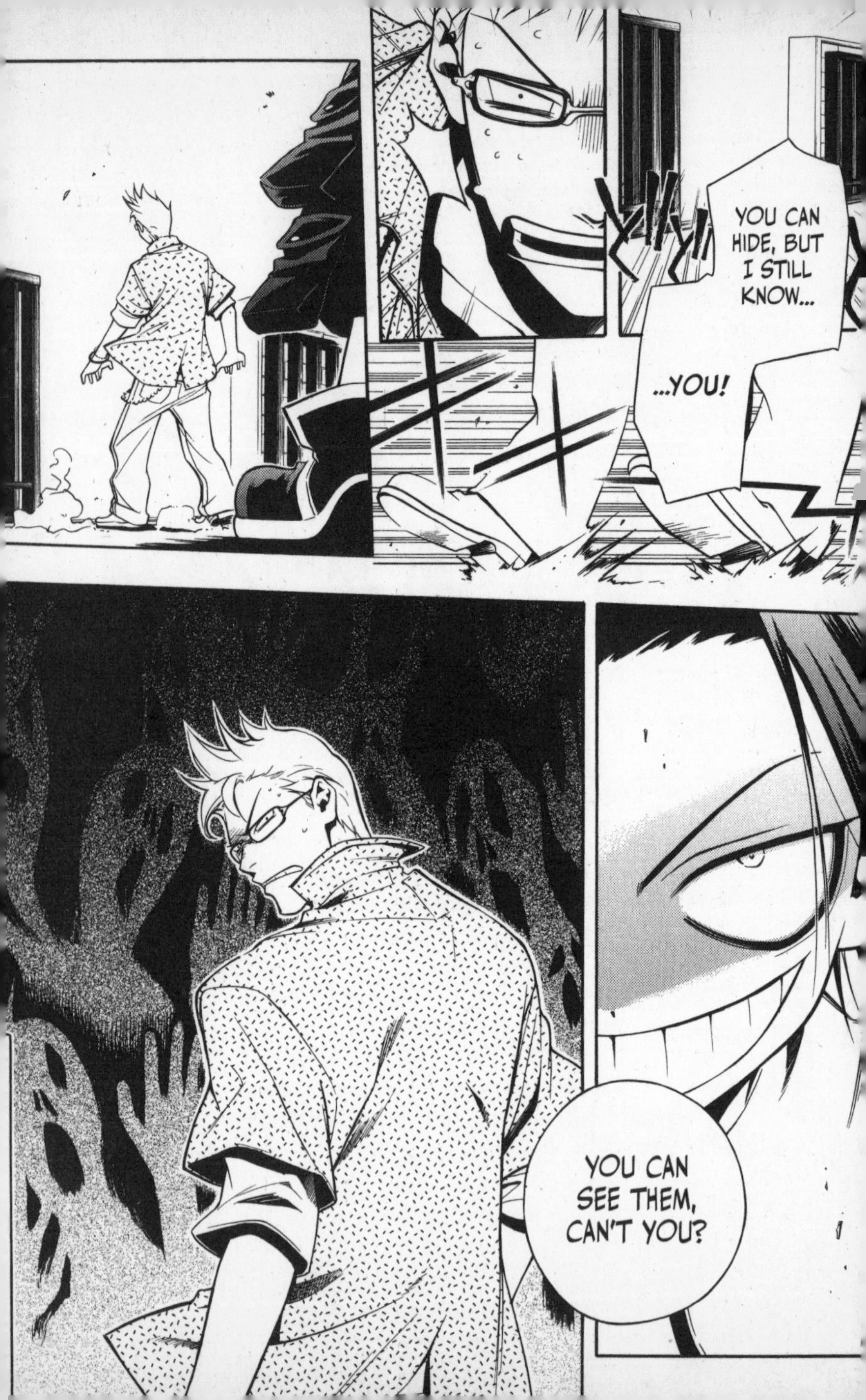
YOU CAN HIDE, BUT I STILL KNOW...
...YOU!
YOU CAN SEE THEM, CAN'T YOU?

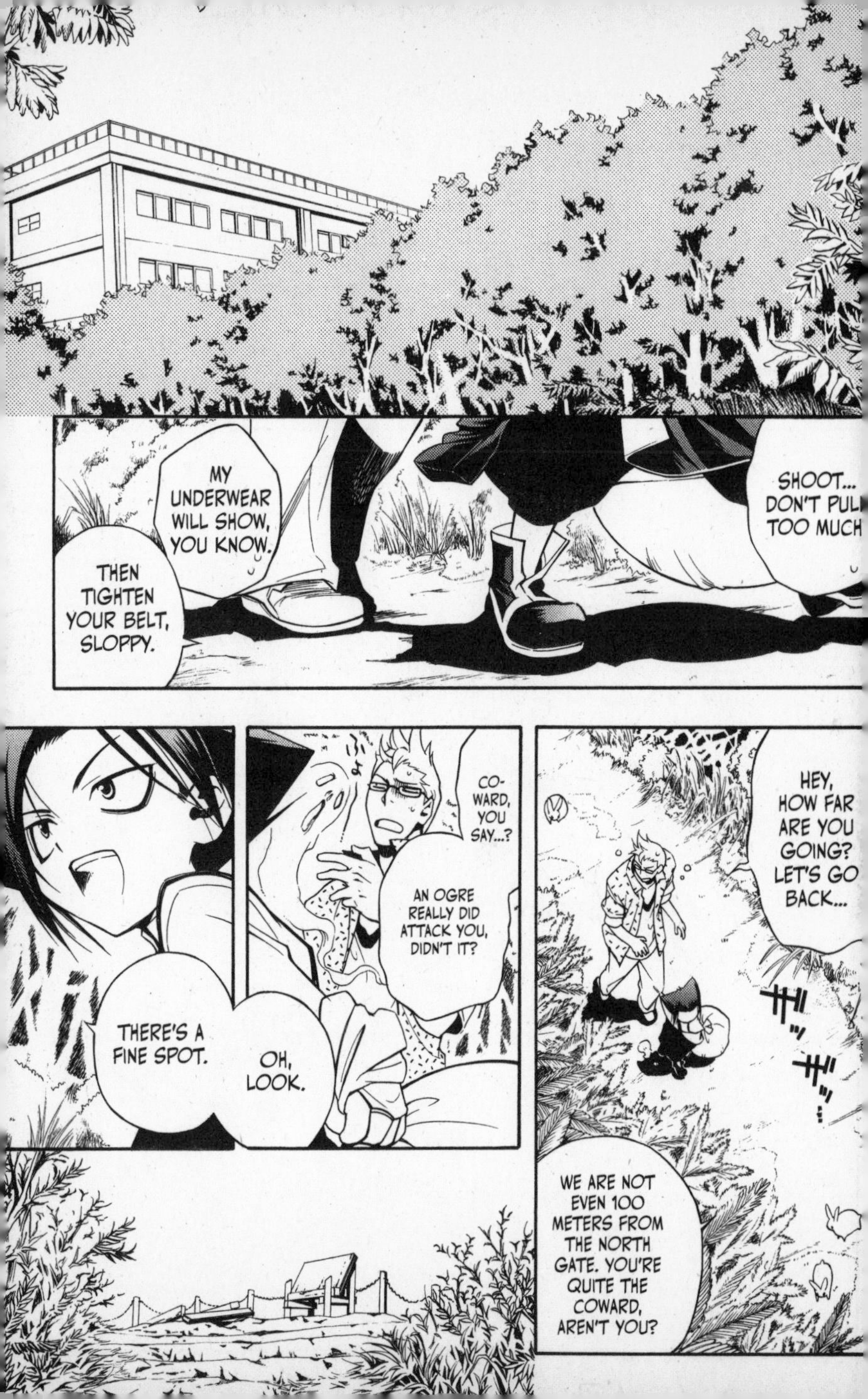
SHOOT... DON'T PUL TOO MUCH
MY UNDERWEAR WILL SHOW, YOU KNOW.
THEN TIGHTEN YOUR BELT, SLOPPY.
HEY, HOW FAR ARE YOU GOING? LET'S GO BACK...
ギッ
ギッ
WE ARE NOT EVEN 100 METERS FROM THE NORTH GATE. YOU'RE QUITE THE COWARD, AREN'T YOU?
CO-WARD, YOU SAY...?
AN OGRE REALLY DID ATTACK YOU, DIDN'T IT?
OH, LOOK.
THERE'S A FINE SPOT.

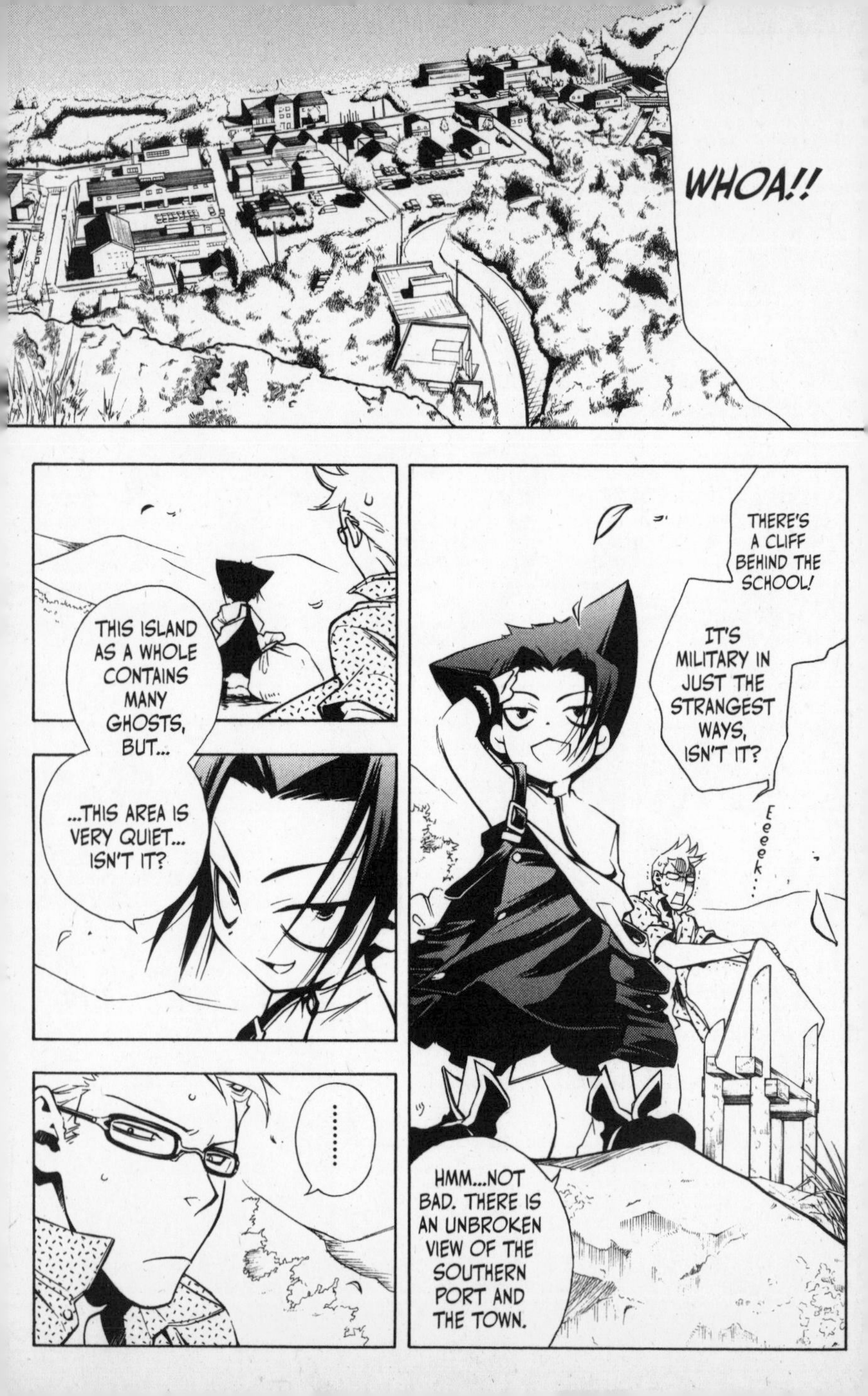
WHOA!!
THERE'S A CLIFF BEHIND THE SCHOOL!
IT'S MILITARY IN JUST THE STRANGEST WAYS, ISN'T IT?
Eeeek...
HMM...NOT BAD. THERE IS AN UNBROKEN VIEW OF THE SOUTHERN PORT AND THE TOWN.
THIS ISLAND AS A WHOLE CONTAINS MANY GHOSTS, BUT...
...THIS AREA IS VERY QUIET... ISN'T IT?
......

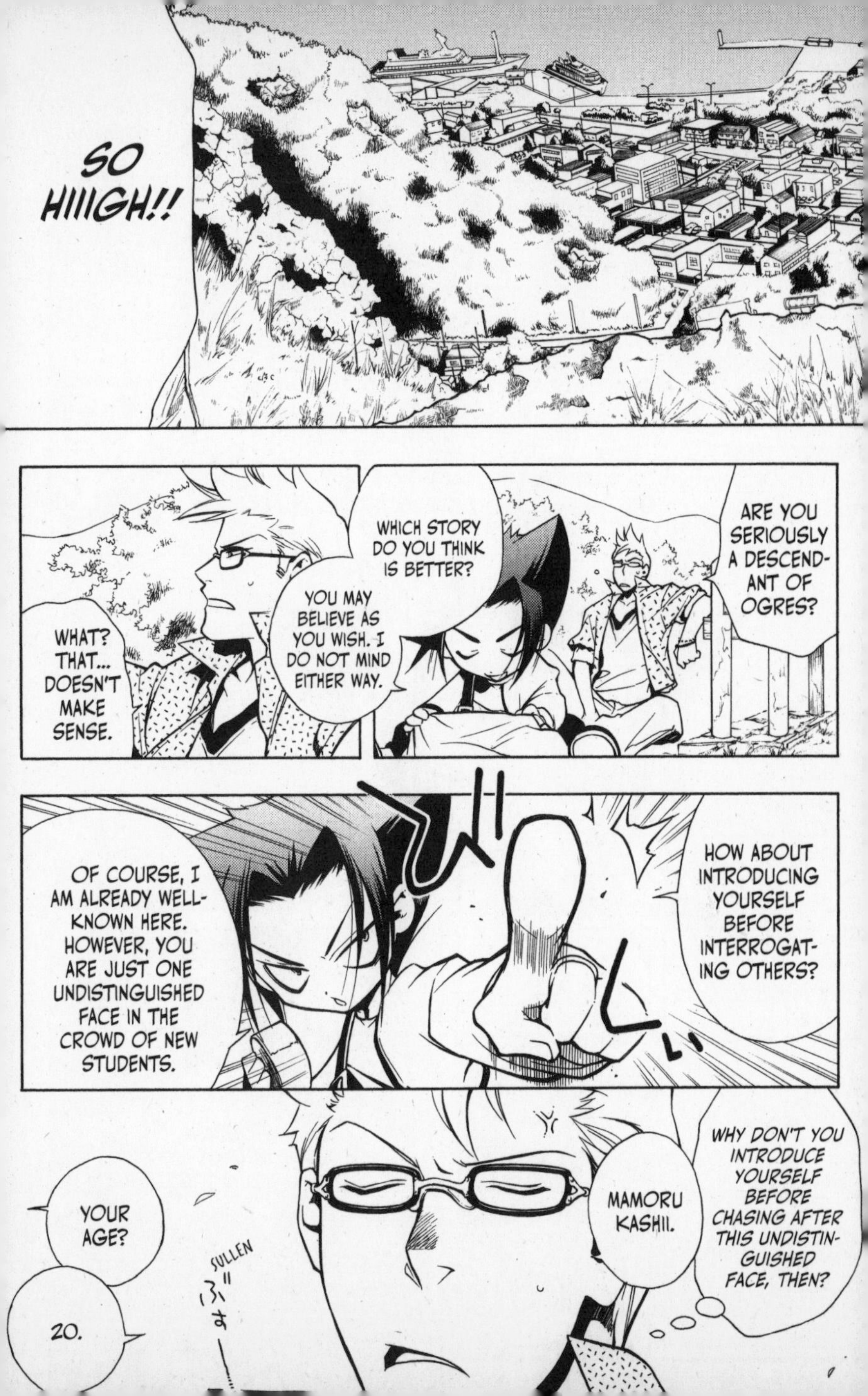
SO HIIIGH!!
ARE YOU SERIOUSLY A DESCENDANT OF OGRES?
WHICH STORY DO YOU THINK IS BETTER?
YOU MAY BELIEVE AS YOU WISH. I DO NOT MIND EITHER WAY.
WHAT? THAT... DOESN'T MAKE SENSE.
HOW ABOUT INTRODUCING YOURSELF BEFORE INTERROGATING OTHERS?
OF COURSE, I AM ALREADY WELL-KNOWN HERE. HOWEVER, YOU ARE JUST ONE UNDISTINGUISHED FACE IN THE CROWD OF NEW STUDENTS.
WHY DON'T YOU INTRODUCE YOURSELF BEFORE CHASING AFTER THIS UNDISTINGUISHED FACE, THEN?
MAMORU KASHII.
SULLEN
ふす
YOUR AGE?
20.

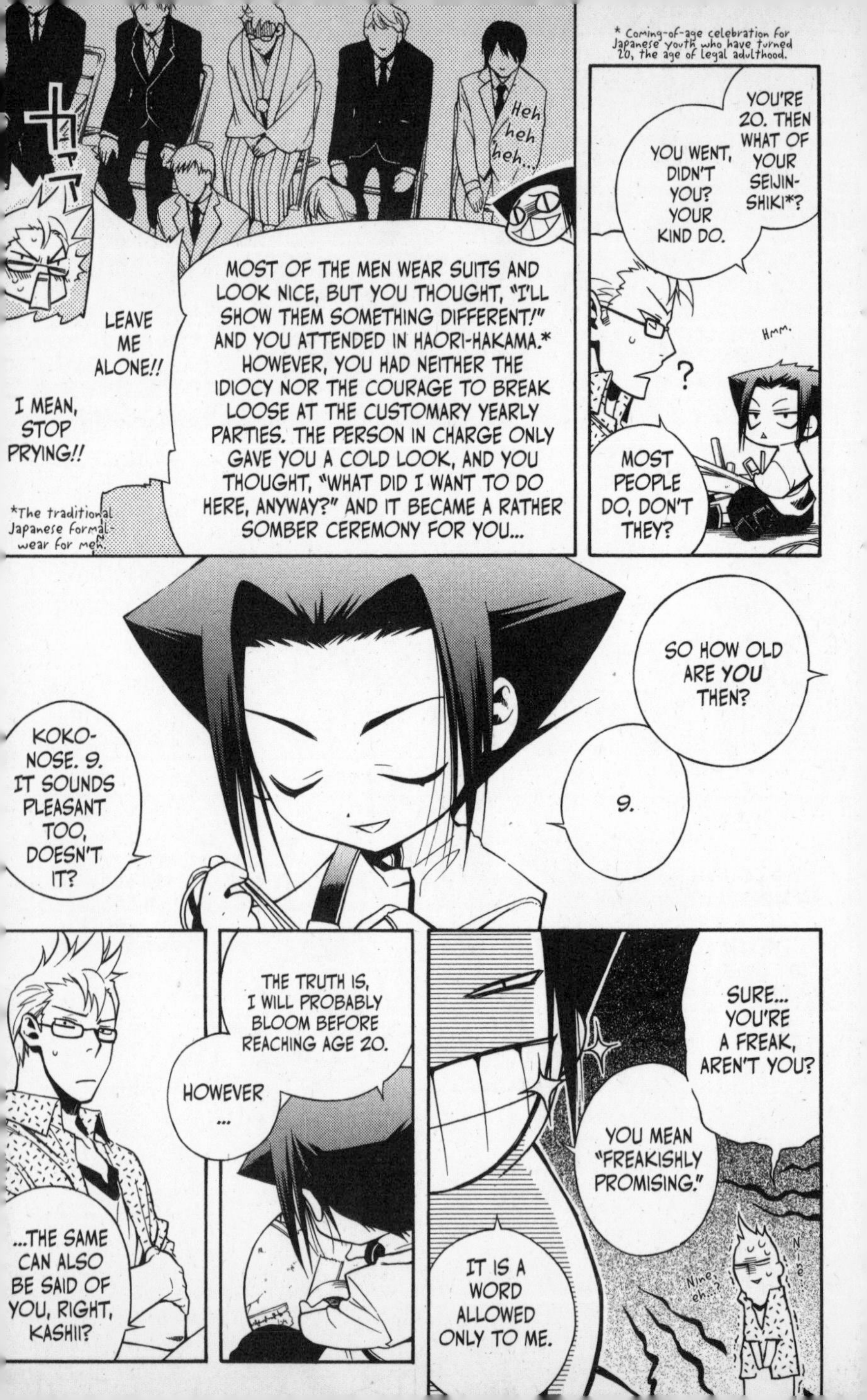
* Coming-of-age celebration for Japanese youth who have turned 20, the age of legal adulthood.
YOU'RE 20. THEN WHAT OF YOUR SEIJIN-SHIKI*?
YOU WENT, DIDN'T YOU? YOUR KIND DO.
Hmm.
?
MOST PEOPLE DO, DON'T THEY?
Heh heh heh...
MOST OF THE MEN WEAR SUITS AND LOOK NICE, BUT YOU THOUGHT, "I'LL SHOW THEM SOMETHING DIFFERENT!" AND YOU ATTENDED IN HAORI-HAKAMA.* HOWEVER, YOU HAD NEITHER THE IDIOCY NOR THE COURAGE TO BREAK LOOSE AT THE CUSTOMARY YEARLY PARTIES. THE PERSON IN CHARGE ONLY GAVE YOU A COLD LOOK, AND YOU THOUGHT, "WHAT DID I WANT TO DO HERE, ANYWAY?" AND IT BECAME A RATHER SOMBER CEREMONY FOR YOU...
LEAVE ME ALONE!!
I MEAN, STOP PRYING!!
*The traditional Japanese formal-wear for men.
SO HOW OLD ARE YOU THEN?
9.
KOKO-NOSE. 9. IT SOUNDS PLEASANT TOO, DOESN'T IT?
SURE... YOU'RE A FREAK, AREN'T YOU?
YOU MEAN "FREAKISHLY PROMISING."
Nine...
Nine, eh...?
IT IS A WORD ALLOWED ONLY TO ME.
THE TRUTH IS, I WILL PROBABLY BLOOM BEFORE REACHING AGE 20.
HOWEVER ...
...THE SAME CAN ALSO BE SAID OF YOU, RIGHT, KASHII?

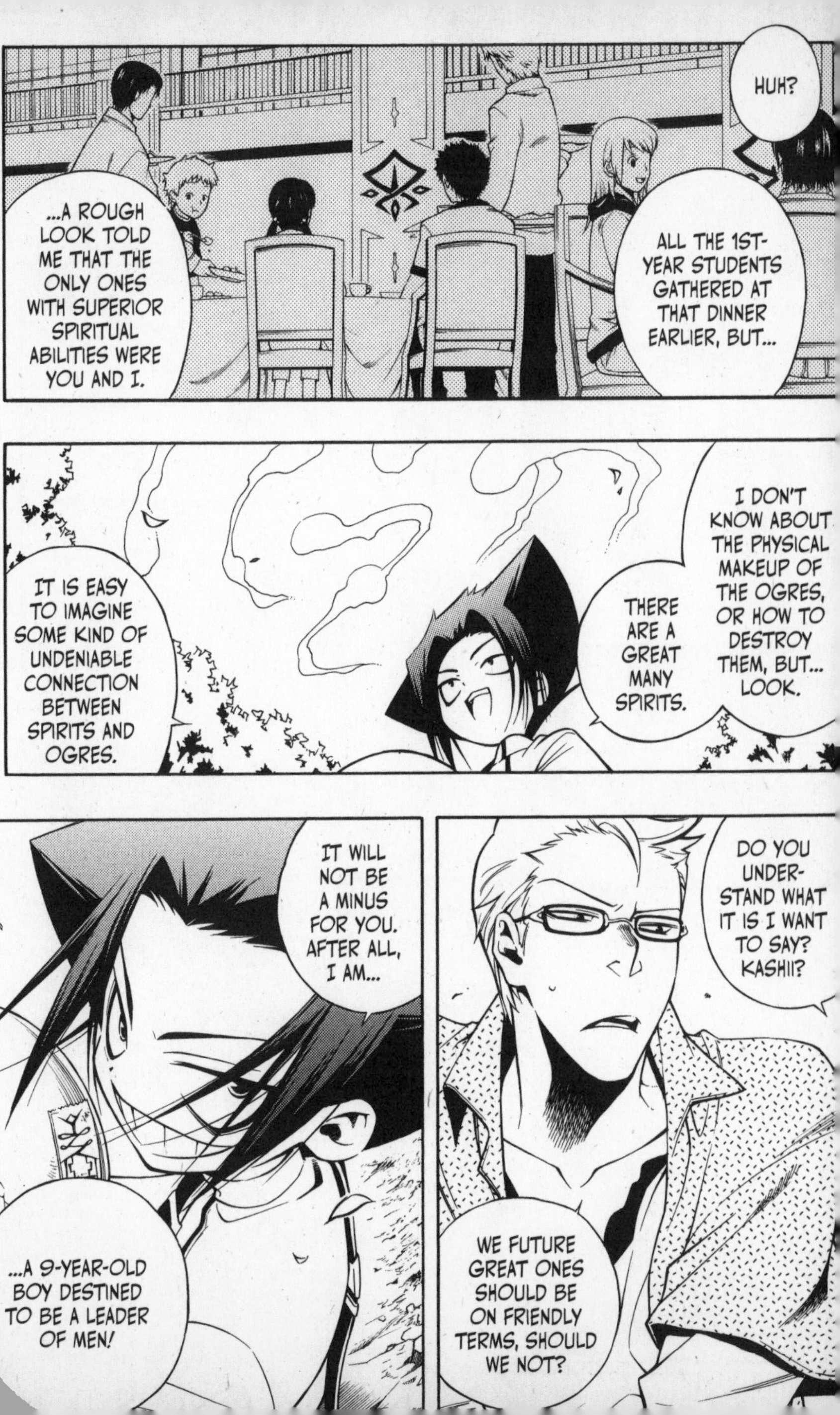
HUH?
ALL THE 1ST-YEAR STUDENTS GATHERED AT THAT DINNER EARLIER, BUT...
...A ROUGH LOOK TOLD ME THAT THE ONLY ONES WITH SUPERIOR SPIRITUAL ABILITIES WERE YOU AND I.
I DON'T KNOW ABOUT THE PHYSICAL MAKEUP OF THE OGRES, OR HOW TO DESTROY THEM, BUT... LOOK.
THERE ARE A GREAT MANY SPIRITS.
IT IS EASY TO IMAGINE SOME KIND OF UNDENIABLE CONNECTION BETWEEN SPIRITS AND OGRES.
DO YOU UNDER-STAND WHAT IT IS I WANT TO SAY? KASHII?
WE FUTURE GREAT ONES SHOULD BE ON FRIENDLY TERMS, SHOULD WE NOT?
IT WILL NOT BE A MINUS FOR YOU. AFTER ALL, I AM...
...A 9-YEAR-OLD BOY DESTINED TO BE A LEADER OF MEN!

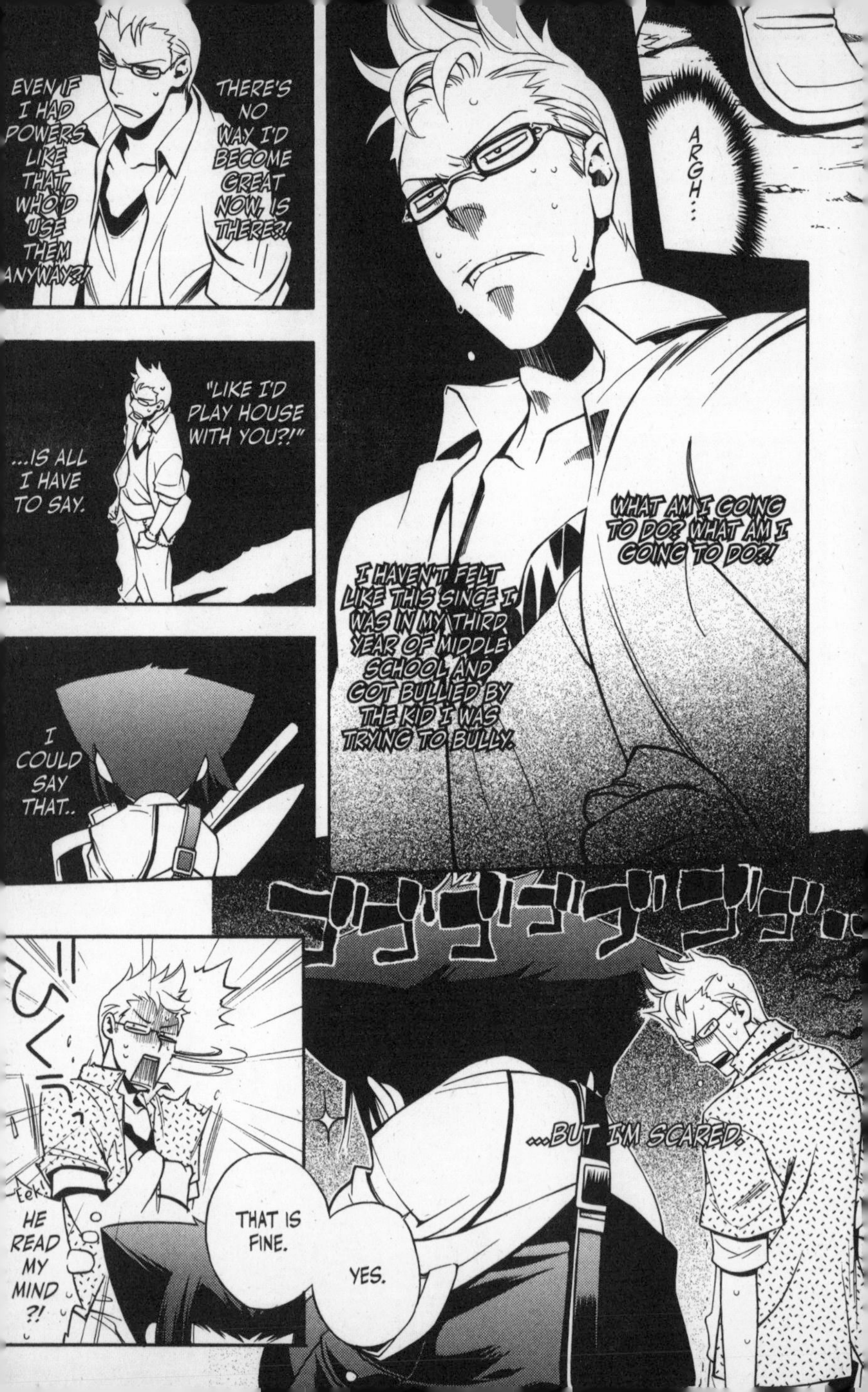
ARGH...
WHAT AM I GOING TO DO? WHAT AM I GOING TO DO?!
I HAVEN'T FELT LIKE THIS SINCE I WAS IN MY THIRD YEAR OF MIDDLE SCHOOL AND GOT BULLIED BY THE KID I WAS TRYING TO BULLY.
THERE'S NO WAY I'D BECOME GREAT NOW, IS THERE?!
EVEN IF I HAD POWERS LIKE THAT, WHO'D USE THEM ANYWAY?!
"LIKE I'D PLAY HOUSE WITH YOU?!"
...IS ALL I HAVE TO SAY.
I COULD SAY THAT..
...BUT I'M SCARED.
THAT IS FINE.
YES.
Eek!
HE READ MY MIND?!

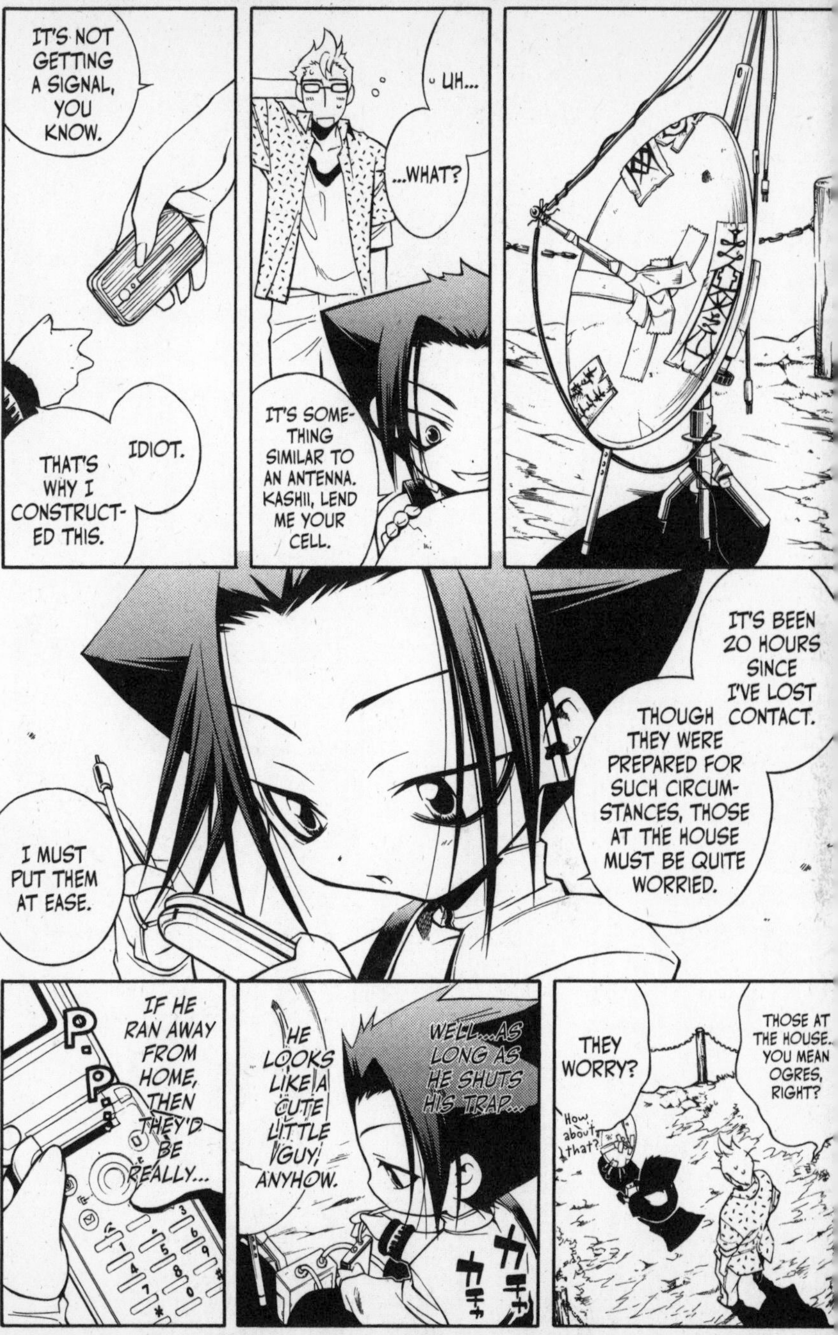
UH...
...WHAT?
IT'S SOMETHING SIMILAR TO AN ANTENNA. KASHII, LEND ME YOUR CELL.
IT'S NOT GETTING A SIGNAL, YOU KNOW.
IDIOT.
THAT'S WHY I CONSTRUCTED THIS.
IT'S BEEN 20 HOURS SINCE I'VE LOST CONTACT.
THOUGH THEY WERE PREPARED FOR SUCH CIRCUMSTANCES, THOSE AT THE HOUSE MUST BE QUITE WORRIED.
I MUST PUT THEM AT EASE.
THOSE AT THE HOUSE.. YOU MEAN OGRES, RIGHT?
THEY WORRY?
How about that?
WELL...AS LONG AS HE SHUTS HIS TRAP...
HE LOOKS LIKE A CUTE LITTLE GUY, ANYHOW.
カチカチ
カチカチ
P
P
IF HE RAN AWAY FROM HOME, THEN THEY'D BE REALLY...

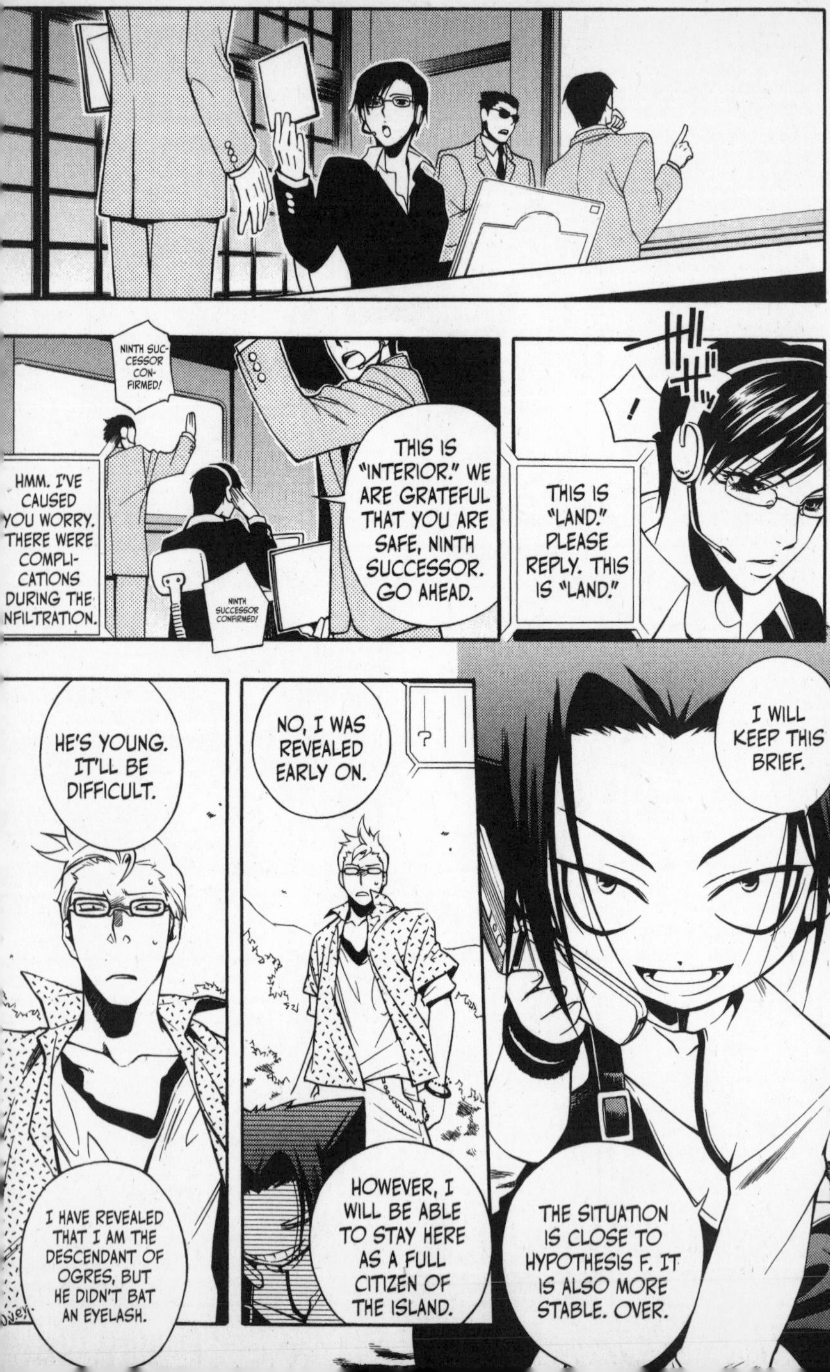
!
THIS IS "LAND." PLEASE REPLY. THIS IS "LAND."
NINTH SUCCESSOR CONFIRMED!
THIS IS "INTERIOR." WE ARE GRATEFUL THAT YOU ARE SAFE, NINTH SUCCESSOR. GO AHEAD.
HMM. I'VE CAUSED YOU WORRY. THERE WERE COMPLICATIONS DURING THE INFILTRATION.
NINTH SUCCESSOR CONFIRMED!
I WILL KEEP THIS BRIEF.
THE SITUATION IS CLOSE TO HYPOTHESIS F. IT IS ALSO MORE STABLE. OVER.
NO, I WAS REVEALED EARLY ON.
HOWEVER, I WILL BE ABLE TO STAY HERE AS A FULL CITIZEN OF THE ISLAND.
HE'S YOUNG. IT'LL BE DIFFICULT.
I HAVE REVEALED THAT I AM THE DESCENDANT OF OGRES, BUT HE DIDN'T BAT AN EYELASH.

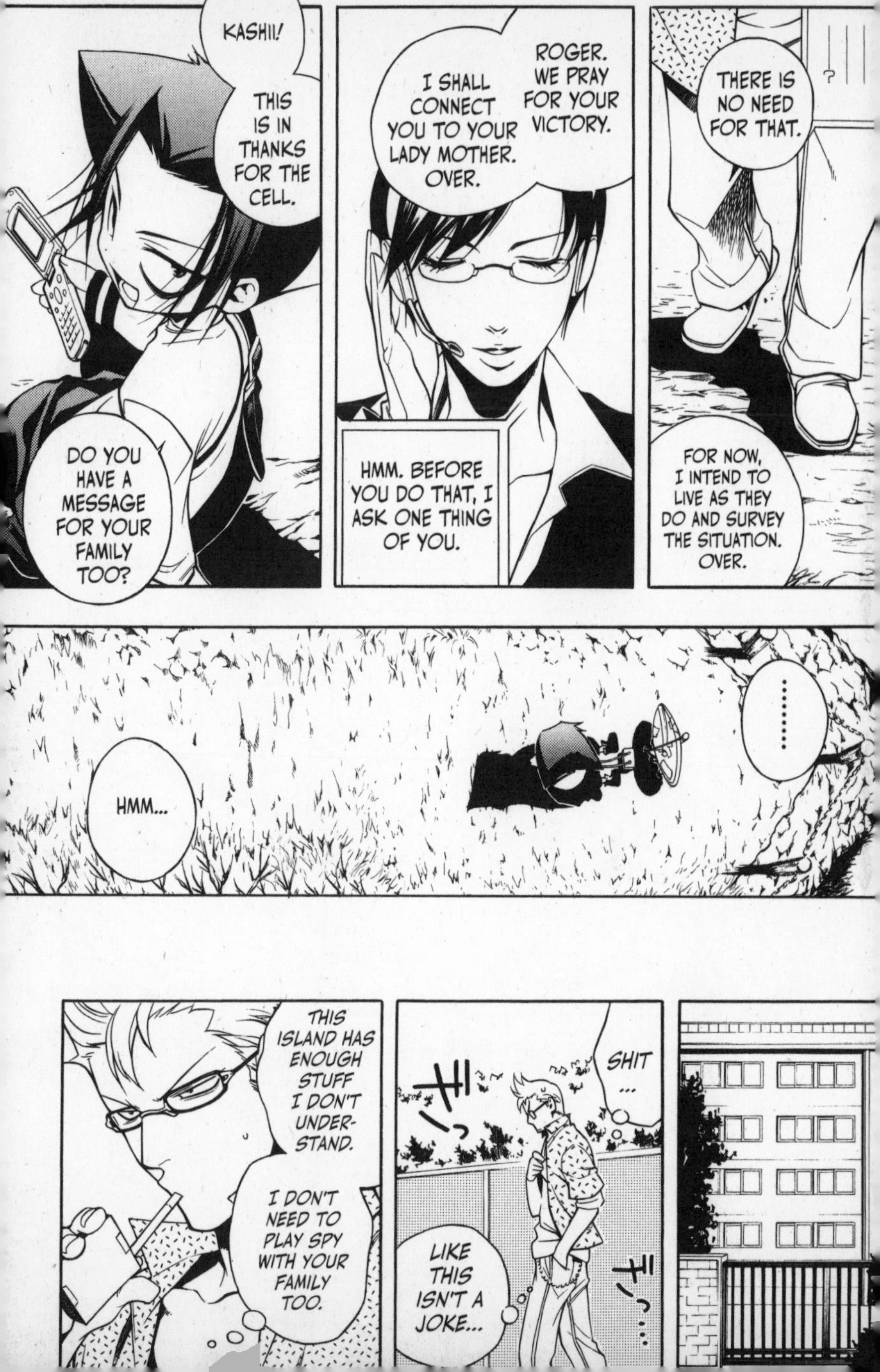
THERE IS NO NEED FOR THAT.
FOR NOW, I INTEND TO LIVE AS THEY DO AND SURVEY THE SITUATION. OVER.
ROGER. WE PRAY FOR YOUR VICTORY.
I SHALL CONNECT YOU TO YOUR LADY MOTHER. OVER.
HMM. BEFORE YOU DO THAT, I ASK ONE THING OF YOU.
KASHII!
THIS IS IN THANKS FOR THE CELL.
DO YOU HAVE A MESSAGE FOR YOUR FAMILY TOO?
......
HMM...
SHIT ...
LIKE THIS ISN'T A JOKE...
THIS ISLAND HAS ENOUGH STUFF I DON'T UNDER-STAND.
I DON'T NEED TO PLAY SPY WITH YOUR FAMILY TOO.

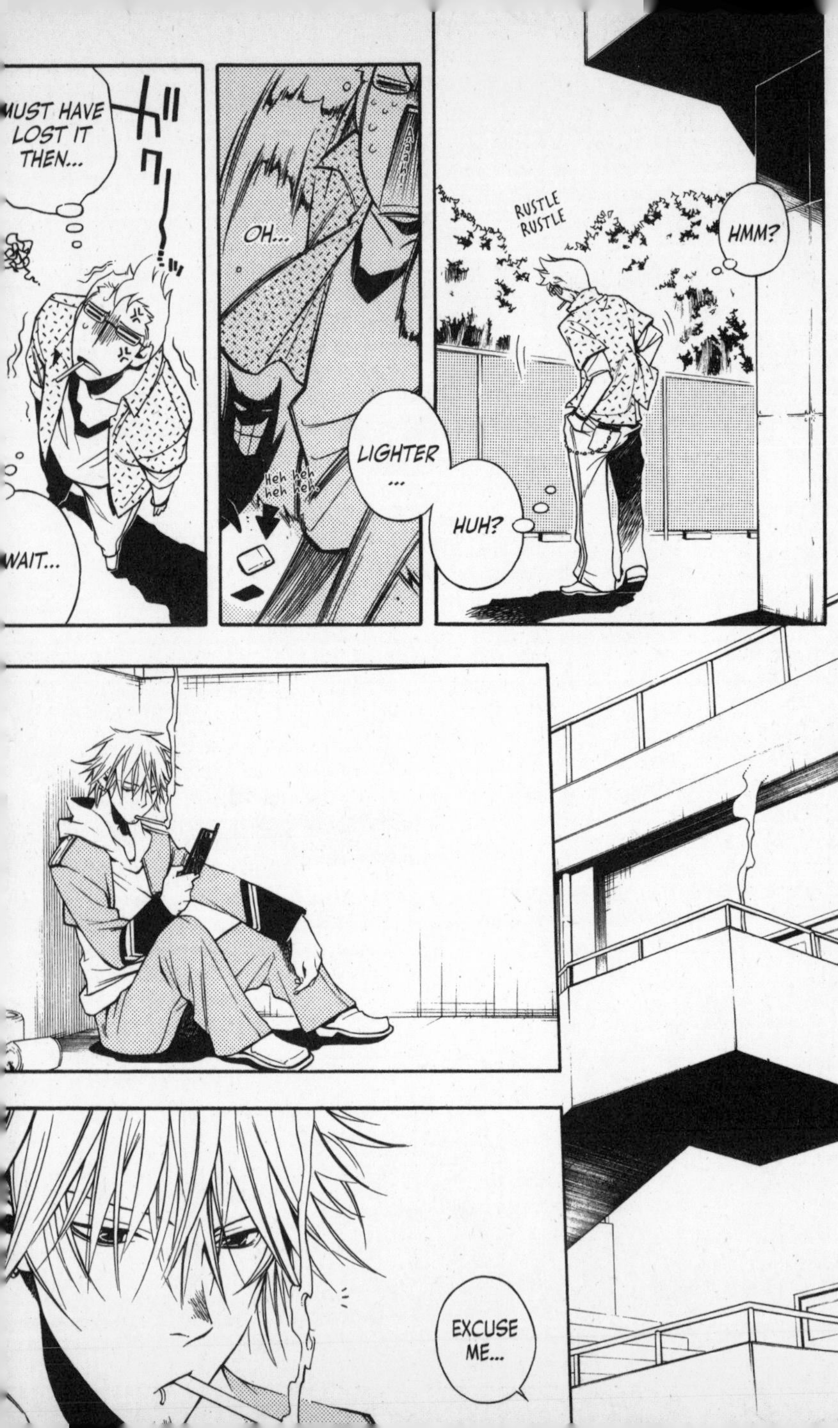

HMM?
RUSTLE RUSTLE
HUH?
Aaah
OH...
LIGHTER ...
Heh heh heh heh
MUST HAVE LOST IT THEN...
WAIT...
EXCUSE ME...

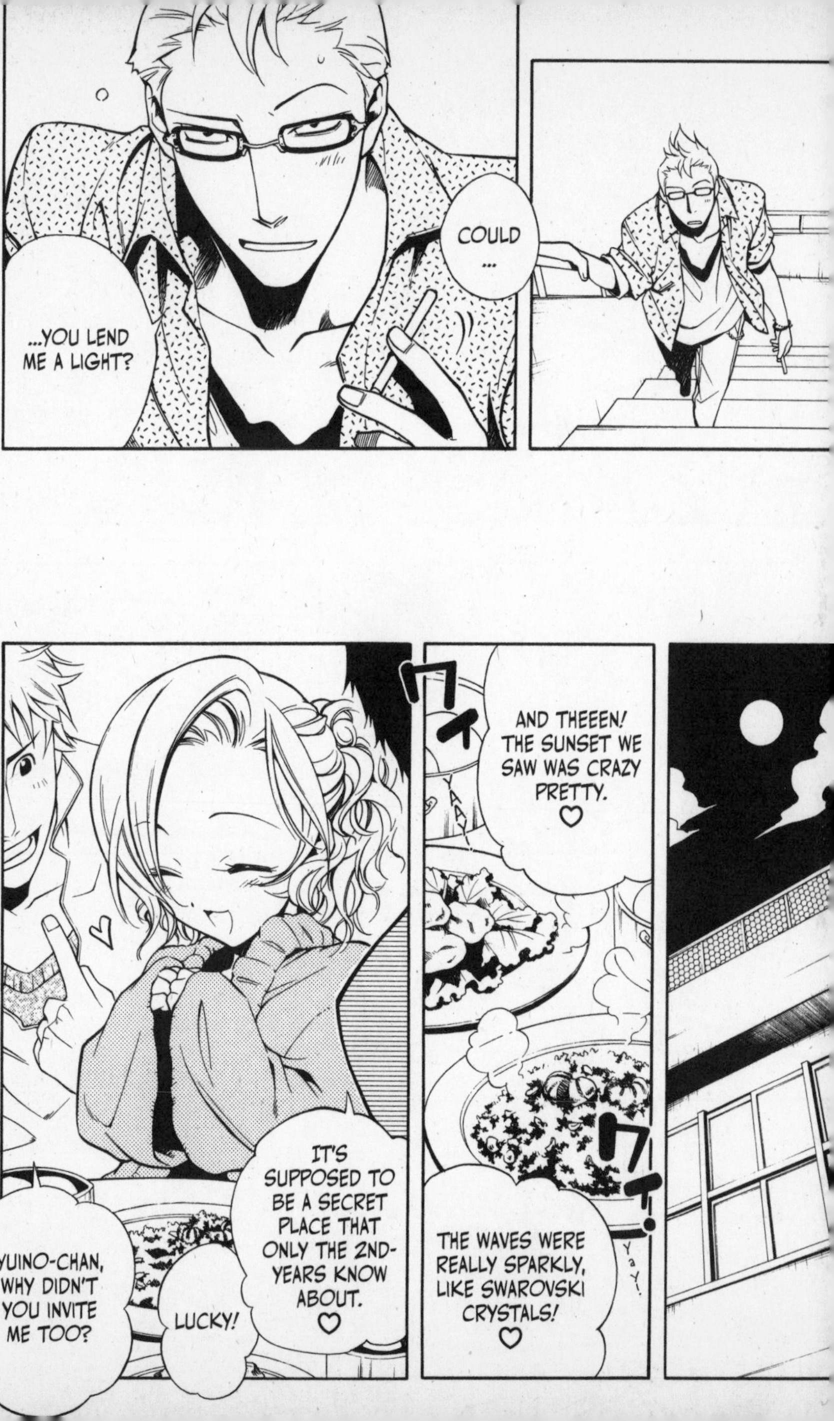
COULD ...
...YOU LEND ME A LIGHT?
AND THEEEN! THE SUNSET WE SAW WAS CRAZY PRETTY. ♡
YAAY
THE WAVES WERE REALLY SPARKLY, LIKE SWAROVSKI CRYSTALS! ♡
YaY!
IT'S SUPPOSED TO BE A SECRET PLACE THAT ONLY THE 2ND-YEARS KNOW ABOUT. ♡
LUCKY!
YUINO-CHAN, WHY DIDN'T YOU INVITE ME TOO?

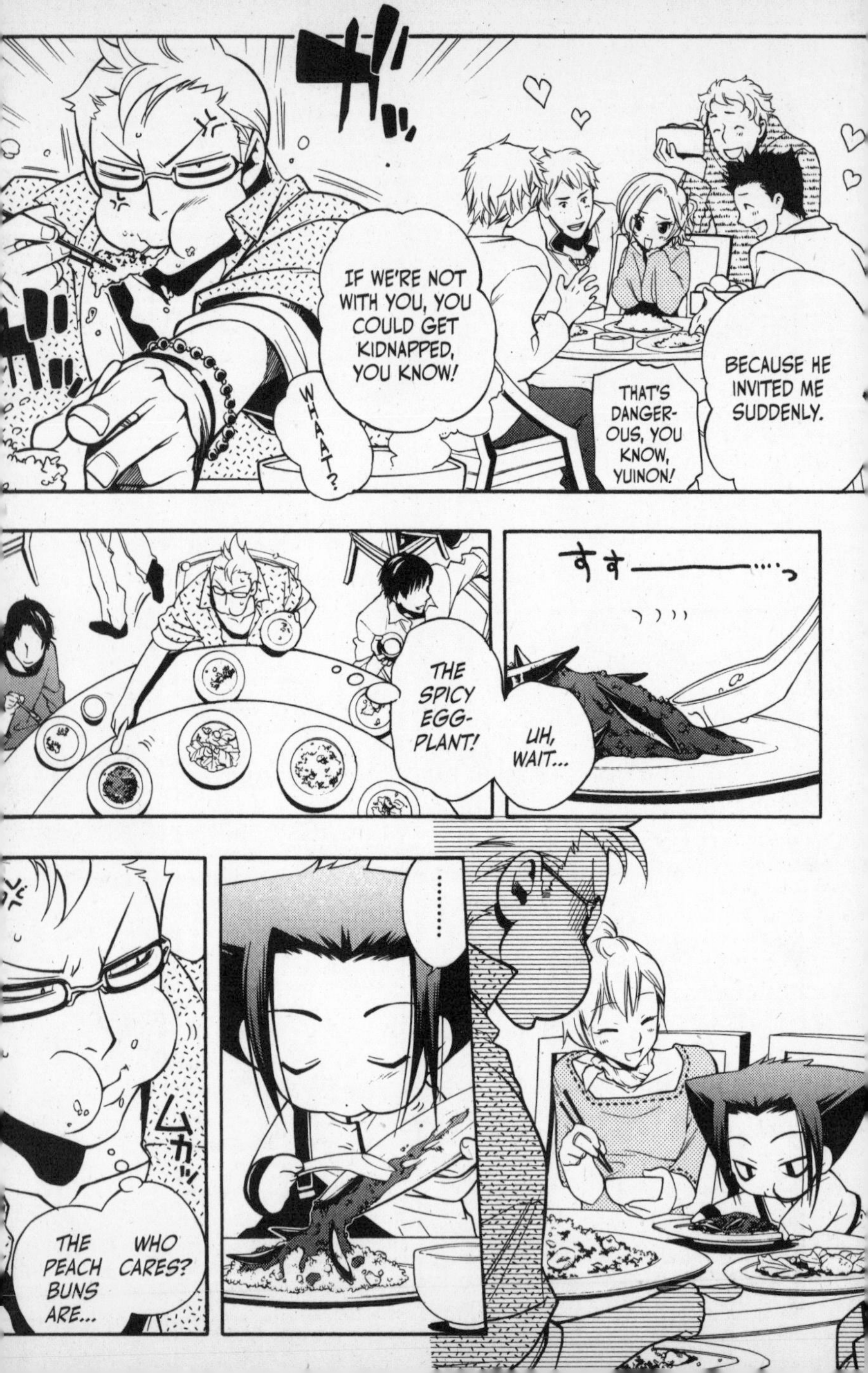
BECAUSE HE INVITED ME SUDDENLY.
THAT'S DANGER-OUS, YOU KNOW, YUINON!
IF WE'RE NOT WITH YOU, YOU COULD GET KIDNAPPED, YOU KNOW!
WHAAT?
すす――――…っ
UH, WAIT...
THE SPICY EGG-PLANT!
……
ムカッ
WHO CARES?
THE PEACH BUNS ARE...

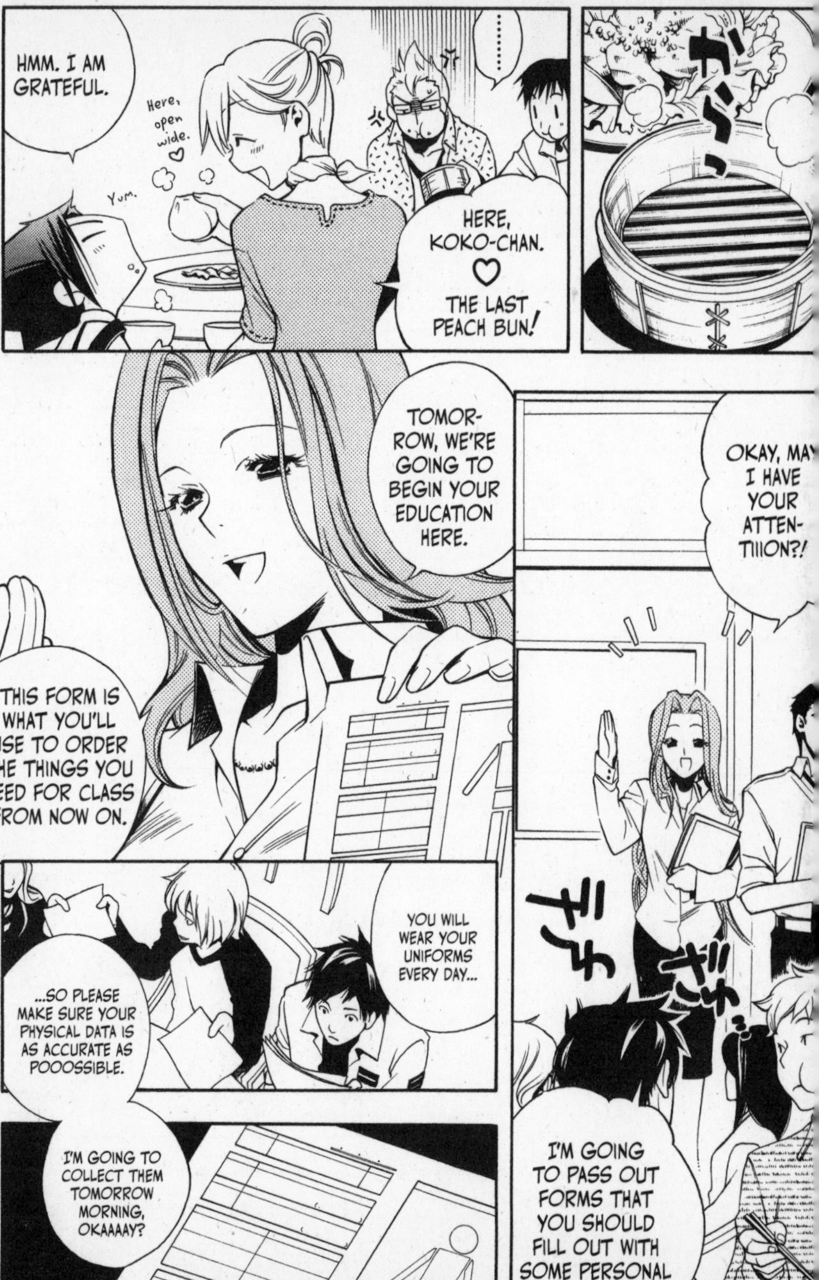
......
HERE, KOKO-CHAN. ♥ THE LAST PEACH BUN!
Here, open wide. ♥
Yum.
HMM. I AM GRATEFUL.
OKAY, MAY I HAVE YOUR ATTEN-TIIION?!
I'M GOING TO PASS OUT FORMS THAT YOU SHOULD FILL OUT WITH SOME PERSONAL INFORMAAATION.
TOMOR-ROW, WE'RE GOING TO BEGIN YOUR EDUCATION HERE.
THIS FORM IS WHAT YOU'LL USE TO ORDER THE THINGS YOU NEED FOR CLASS FROM NOW ON.
YOU WILL WEAR YOUR UNIFORMS EVERY DAY...
...SO PLEASE MAKE SURE YOUR PHYSICAL DATA IS AS ACCURATE AS POOOSSIBLE.
I'M GOING TO COLLECT THEM TOMORROW MORNING, OKAAAAY?

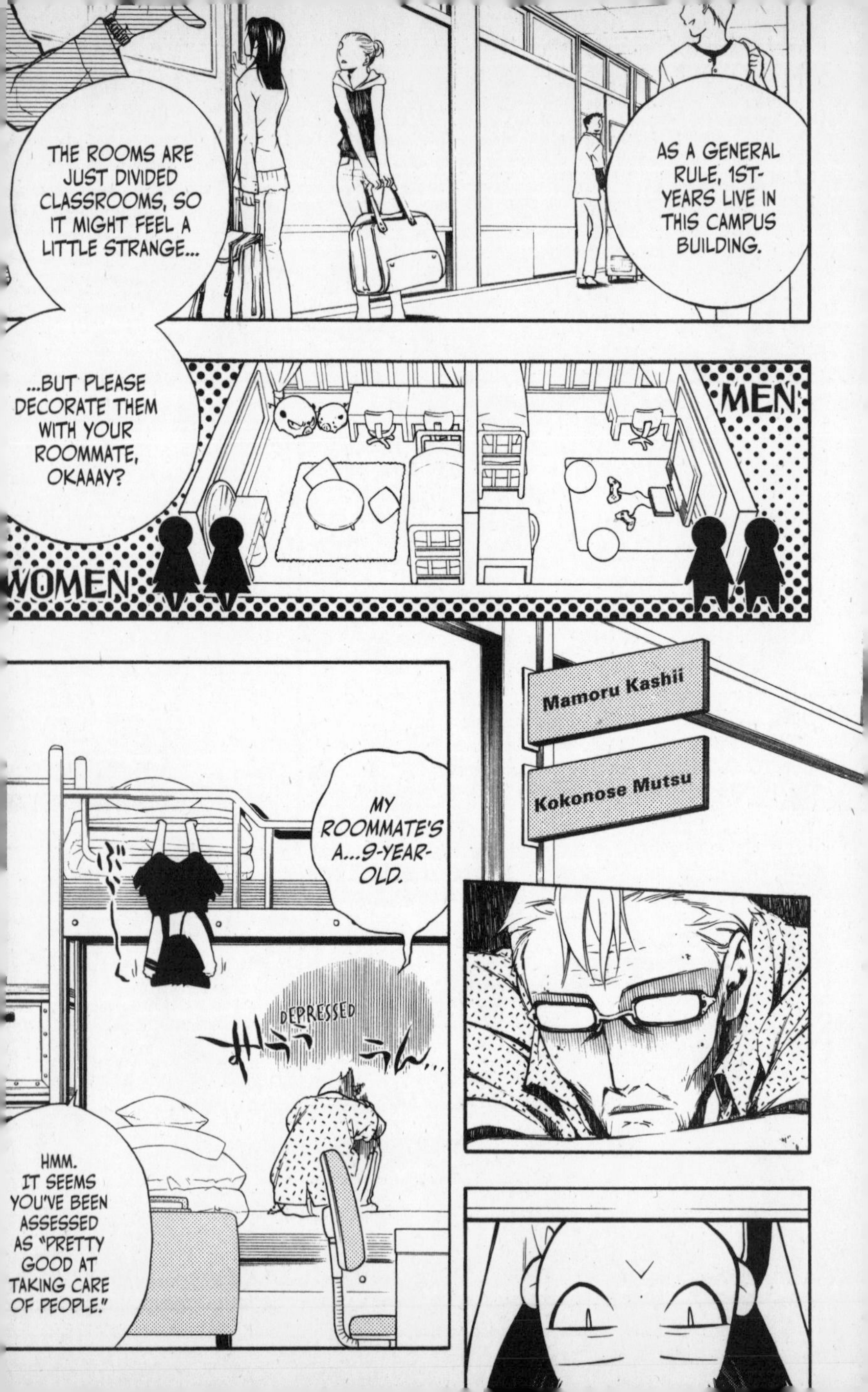
AS A GENERAL RULE, 1ST-YEARS LIVE IN THIS CAMPUS BUILDING.
THE ROOMS ARE JUST DIVIDED CLASSROOMS, SO IT MIGHT FEEL A LITTLE STRANGE...
MEN
...BUT PLEASE DECORATE THEM WITH YOUR ROOMMATE, OKAAAY?
WOMEN
Mamoru Kashii
Kokonose Mutsu
MY ROOMMATE'S A...9-YEAR-OLD.
DEPRESSED
HMM. IT SEEMS YOU'VE BEEN ASSESSED AS "PRETTY GOOD AT TAKING CARE OF PEOPLE."

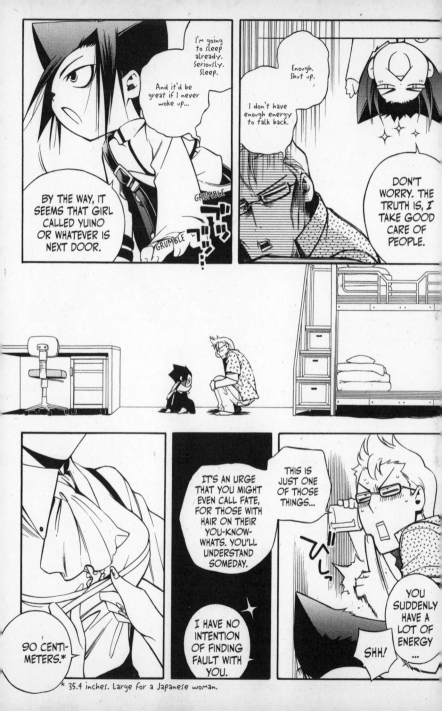

DON'T WORRY. THE TRUTH IS, I TAKE GOOD CARE OF PEOPLE.
Enough. Shut up.
I don't have enough energy to talk back.
I'm going to sleep already. Seriously. Sleep.
And it'd be great if I never woke up...
BY THE WAY, IT SEEMS THAT GIRL CALLED YUINO OR WHATEVER IS NEXT DOOR.
GRUMBLE
GRUMBLE
THIS IS JUST ONE OF THOSE THINGS...
YOU SUDDENLY HAVE A LOT OF ENERGY ...
SHH!
IT'S AN URGE THAT YOU MIGHT EVEN CALL FATE, FOR THOSE WITH HAIR ON THEIR YOU-KNOW-WHATS. YOU'LL UNDERSTAND SOMEDAY.
I HAVE NO INTENTION OF FINDING FAULT WITH YOU.
90 CENTI-METERS.*

* 35.4 inches. Large for a Japanese woman.

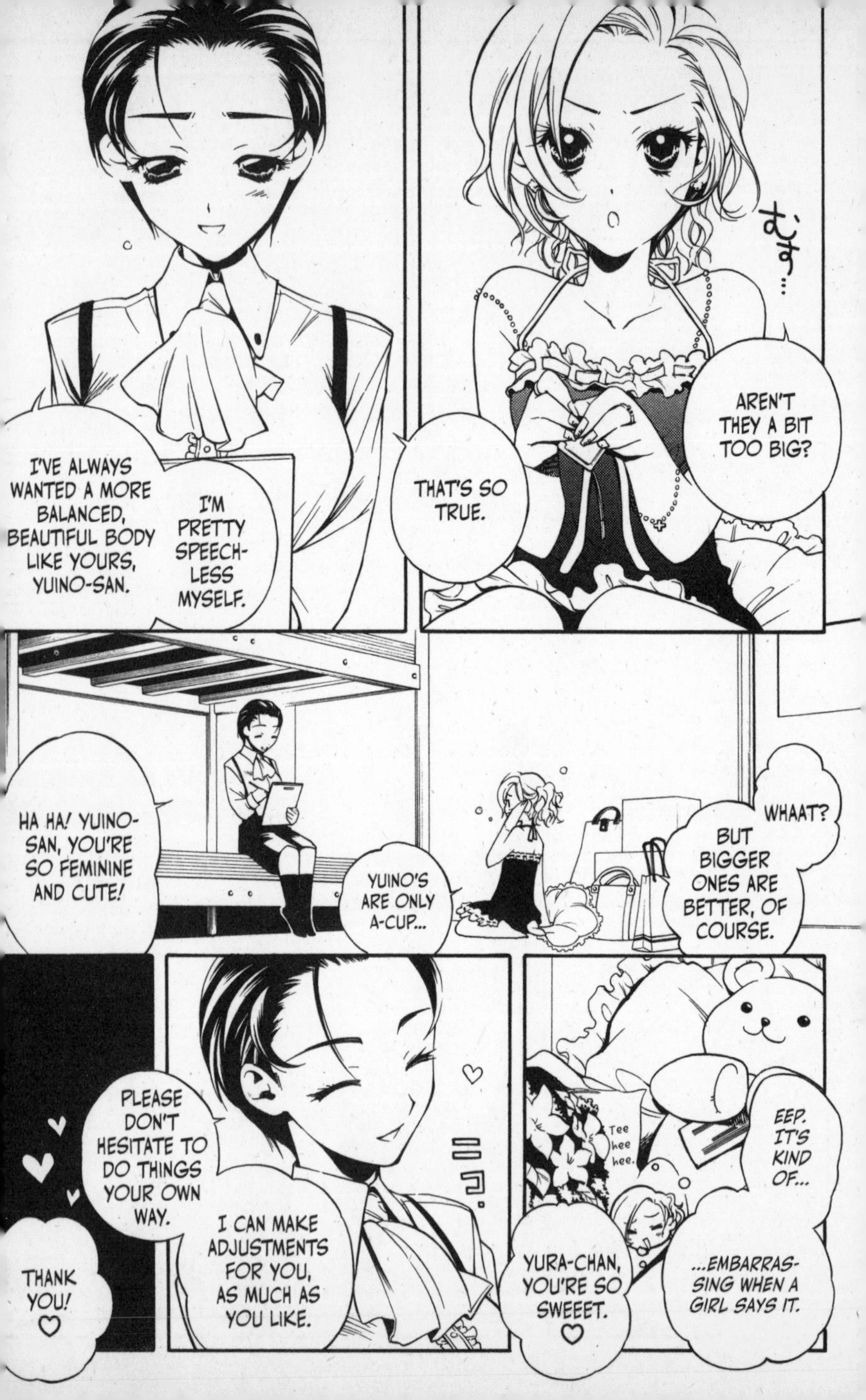
むす…
AREN'T THEY A BIT TOO BIG?
THAT'S SO TRUE.
I'M PRETTY SPEECH-LESS MYSELF.
I'VE ALWAYS WANTED A MORE BALANCED, BEAUTIFUL BODY LIKE YOURS, YUINO-SAN.
WHAAT?
BUT BIGGER ONES ARE BETTER, OF COURSE.
YUINO'S ARE ONLY A-CUP...
HA HA! YUINO-SAN, YOU'RE SO FEMININE AND CUTE!
EEP. IT'S KIND OF...
Tee hee hee.
...EMBARRAS-SING WHEN A GIRL SAYS IT.
YURA-CHAN, YOU'RE SO SWEEET. ♡
ニコ。
PLEASE DON'T HESITATE TO DO THINGS YOUR OWN WAY.
I CAN MAKE ADJUSTMENTS FOR YOU, AS MUCH AS YOU LIKE.
THANK YOU! ♡

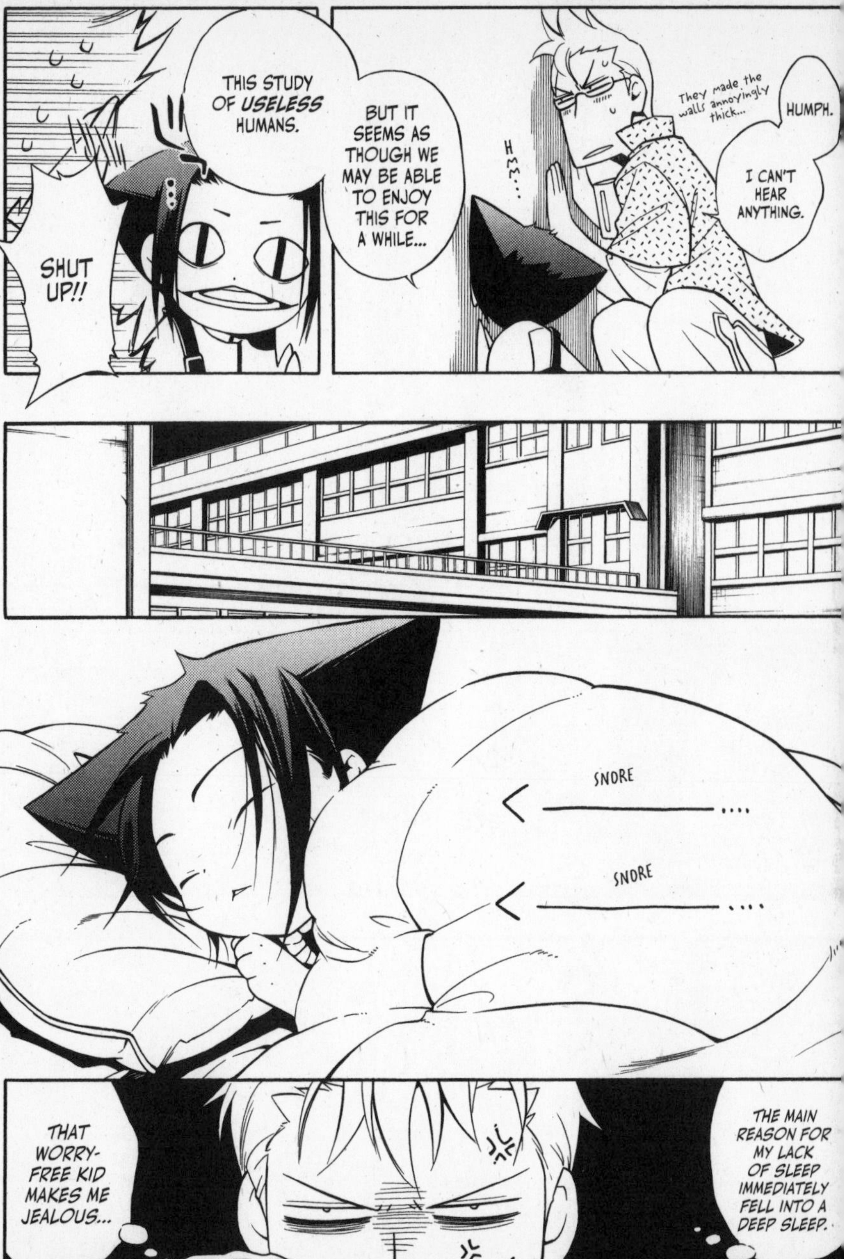

They made the walls annoyingly thick...
HUMPH.
I CAN'T HEAR ANYTHING.
HMM...
BUT IT SEEMS AS THOUGH WE MAY BE ABLE TO ENJOY THIS FOR A WHILE...
THIS STUDY OF *USELESS* HUMANS.
SHUT UP!!
SNORE
<————....
SNORE
<————....
THE MAIN REASON FOR MY LACK OF SLEEP IMMEDIATELY FELL INTO A DEEP SLEEP.
THAT WORRY-FREE KID MAKES ME JEALOUS...
<————....
SNORE

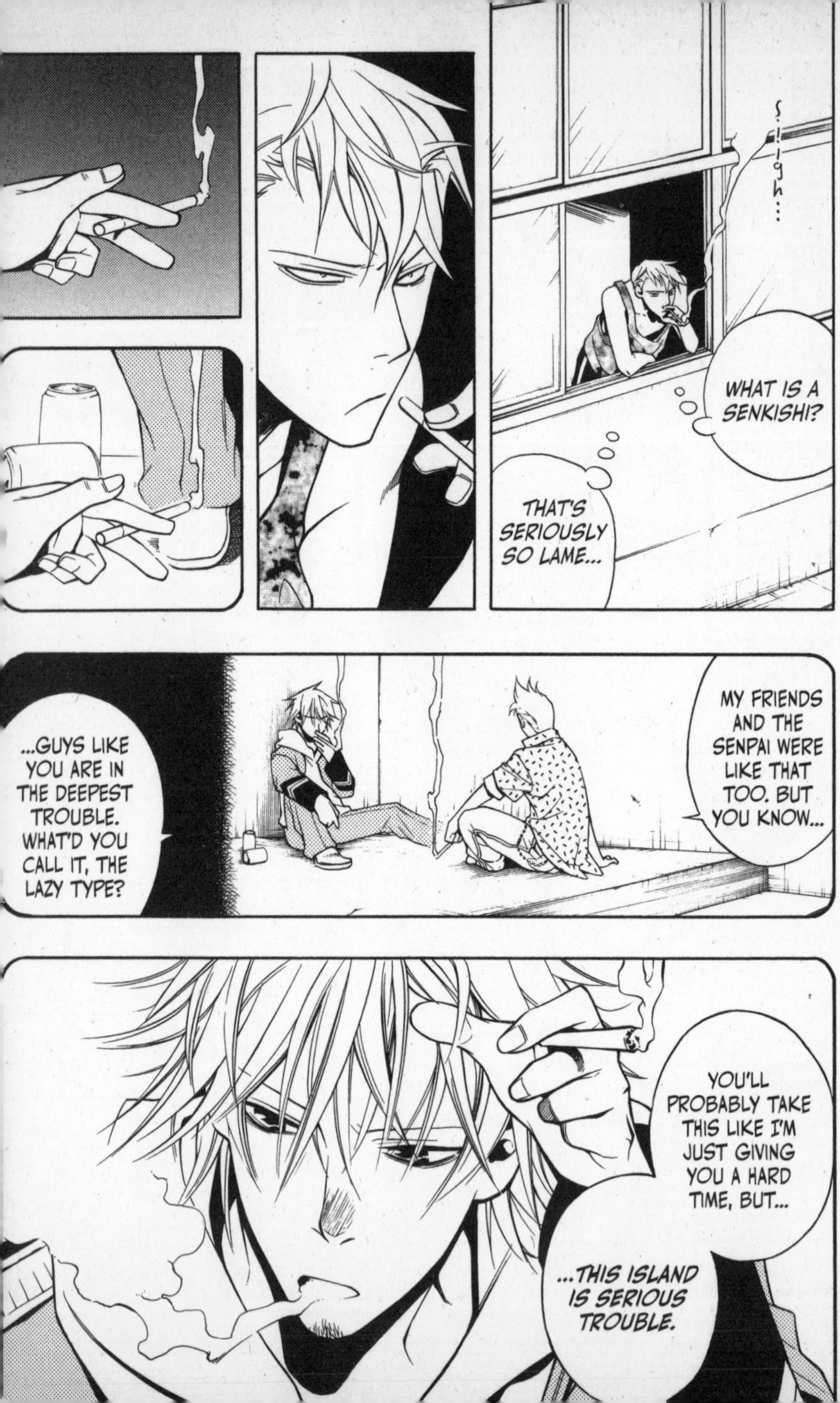
S-i-i-g-h...
WHAT IS A SENKISHI?
THAT'S SERIOUSLY SO LAME...
MY FRIENDS AND THE SENPAI WERE LIKE THAT TOO. BUT YOU KNOW...
...GUYS LIKE YOU ARE IN THE DEEPEST TROUBLE. WHAT'D YOU CALL IT, THE LAZY TYPE?
YOU'LL PROBABLY TAKE THIS LIKE I'M JUST GIVING YOU A HARD TIME, BUT...
...THIS ISLAND IS SERIOUS TROUBLE.

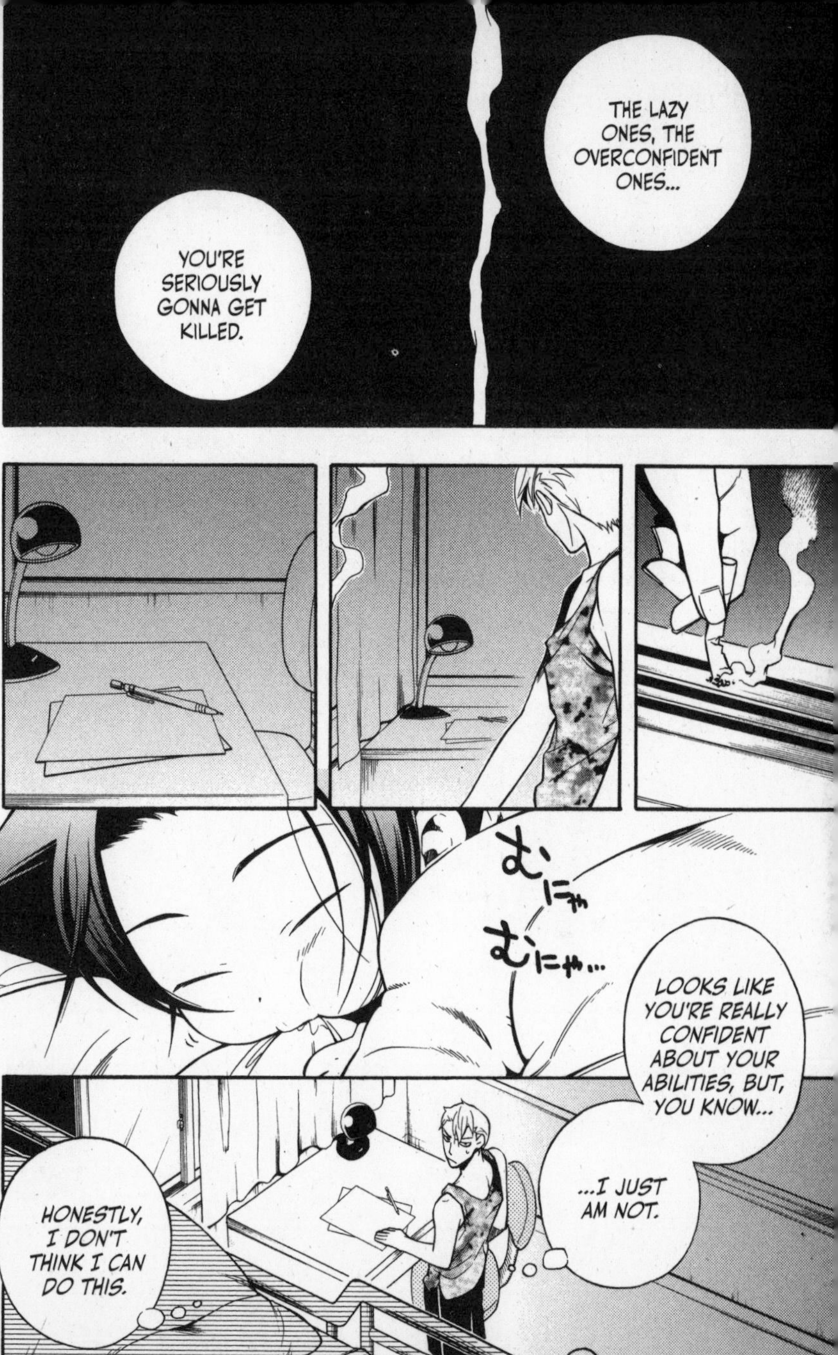
THE LAZY ONES, THE OVERCONFIDENT ONES...
YOU'RE SERIOUSLY GONNA GET KILLED.
むにゃむにゃ...
LOOKS LIKE YOU'RE REALLY CONFIDENT ABOUT YOUR ABILITIES, BUT, YOU KNOW...
...I JUST AM NOT.
HONESTLY, I DON'T THINK I CAN DO THIS.

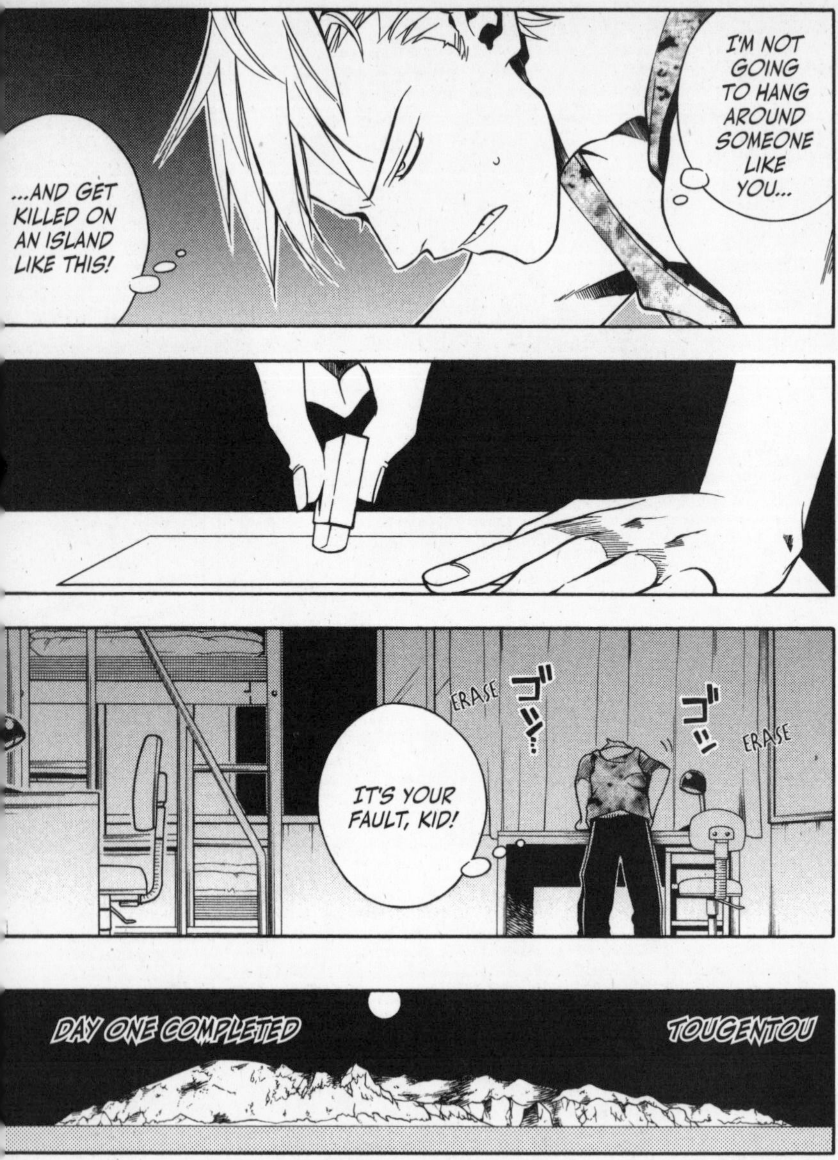
I'M NOT GOING TO HANG AROUND SOMEONE LIKE YOU...
...AND GET KILLED ON AN ISLAND LIKE THIS!
ERASE
ゴシ
ERASE
ゴシ...
IT'S YOUR FAULT, KID!
TOUGENTOU
DAY ONE COMPLETED

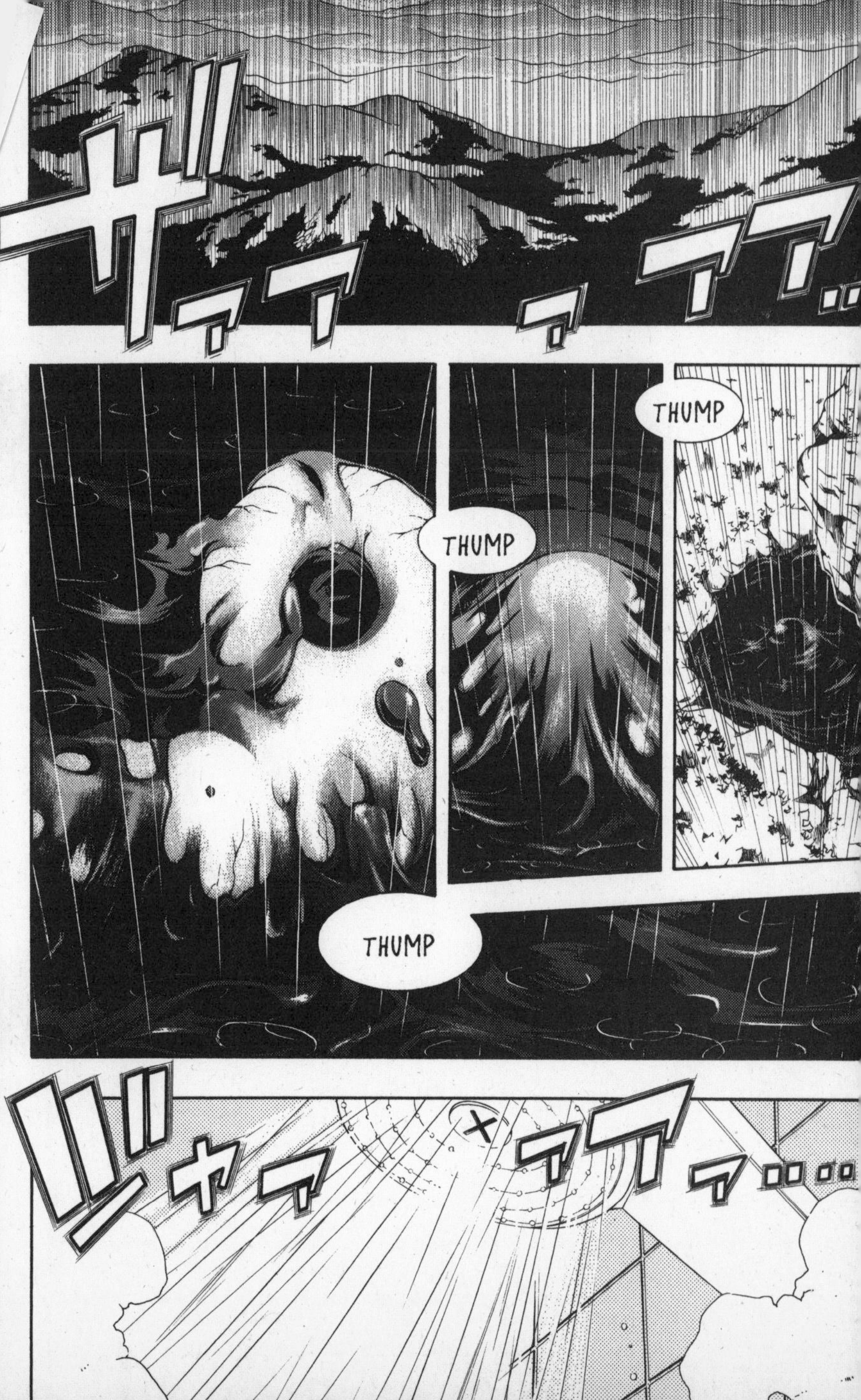
ザァアァアア‥
THUMP
THUMP
THUMP
ジャアアアァ‥‥

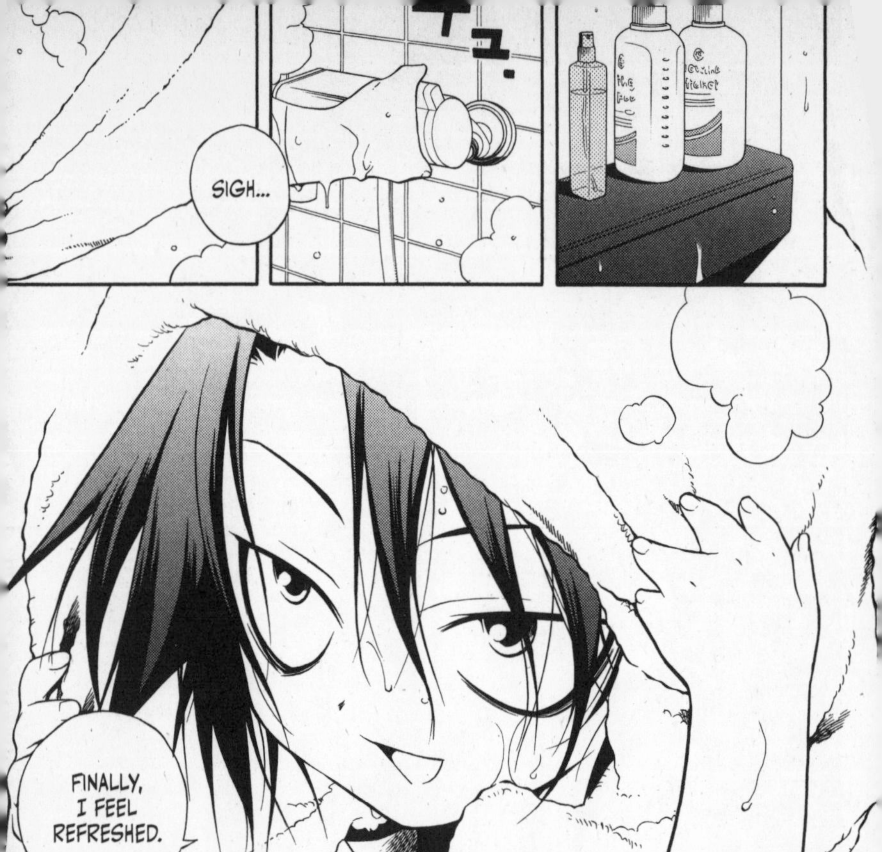
キュ.
SIGH...
FINALLY, I FEEL REFRESHED.

Chapter 4
The Land of Our Forefathers Is...

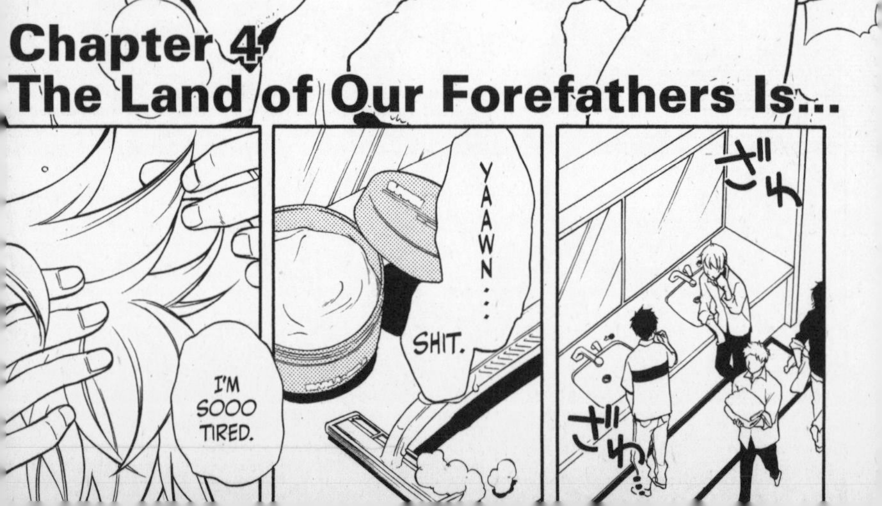
ざわ
ざわ...
YAAWN...
SHIT.
I'M SOOO TIRED.

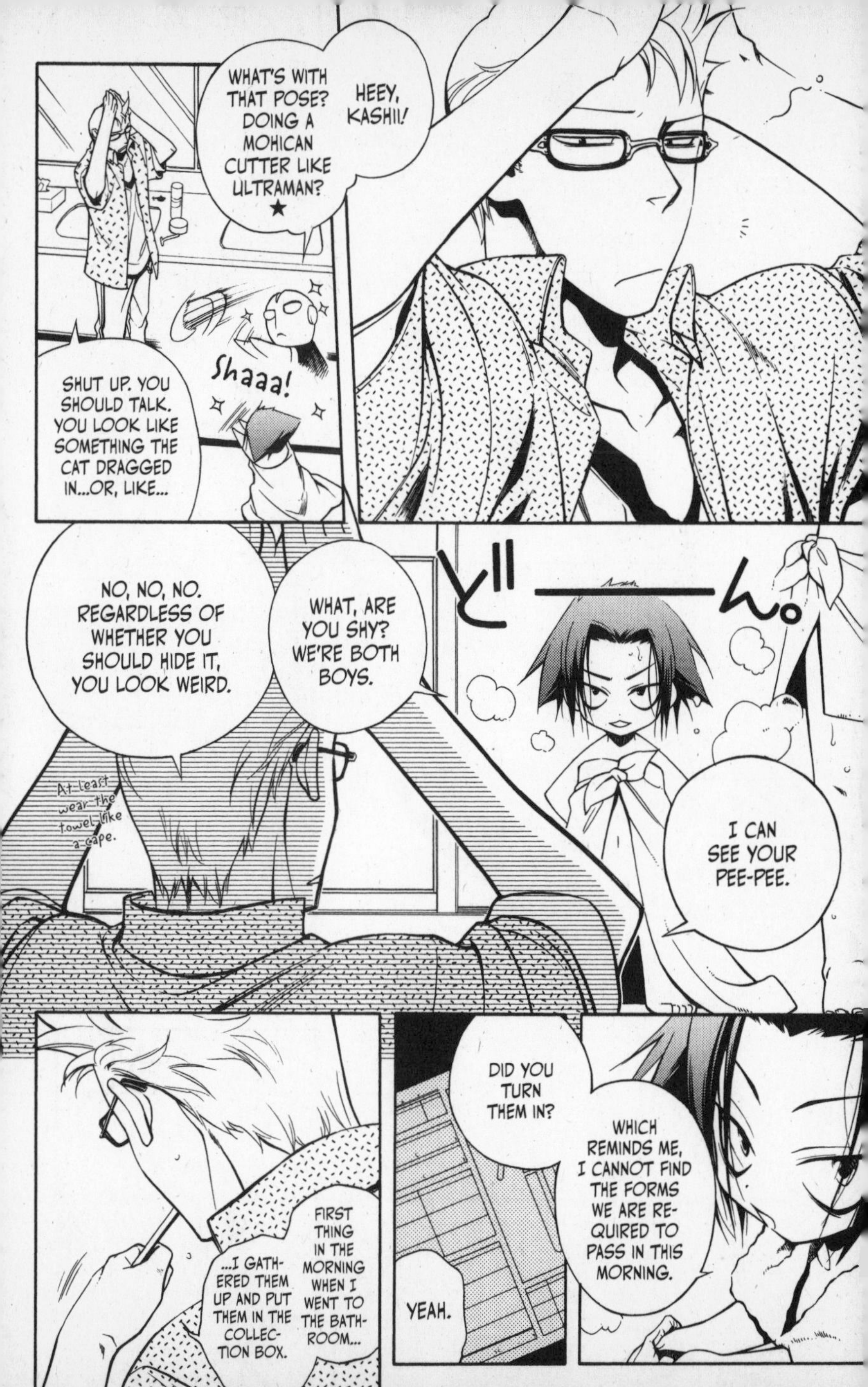
HEEY, KASHII!
WHAT'S WITH THAT POSE? DOING A MOHICAN CUTTER LIKE ULTRAMAN? ★
Shaaa!
SHUT UP. YOU SHOULD TALK. YOU LOOK LIKE SOMETHING THE CAT DRAGGED IN...OR, LIKE...
どーーーん。
I CAN SEE YOUR PEE-PEE.
WHAT, ARE YOU SHY? WE'RE BOTH BOYS.
NO, NO, NO. REGARDLESS OF WHETHER YOU SHOULD HIDE IT, YOU LOOK WEIRD.
At least wear the towel like a cape.
WHICH REMINDS ME, I CANNOT FIND THE FORMS WE ARE REQUIRED TO PASS IN THIS MORNING.
DID YOU TURN THEM IN?
YEAH.
FIRST THING IN THE MORNING WHEN I WENT TO THE BATHROOM...
...I GATHERED THEM UP AND PUT THEM IN THE COLLECTION BOX.

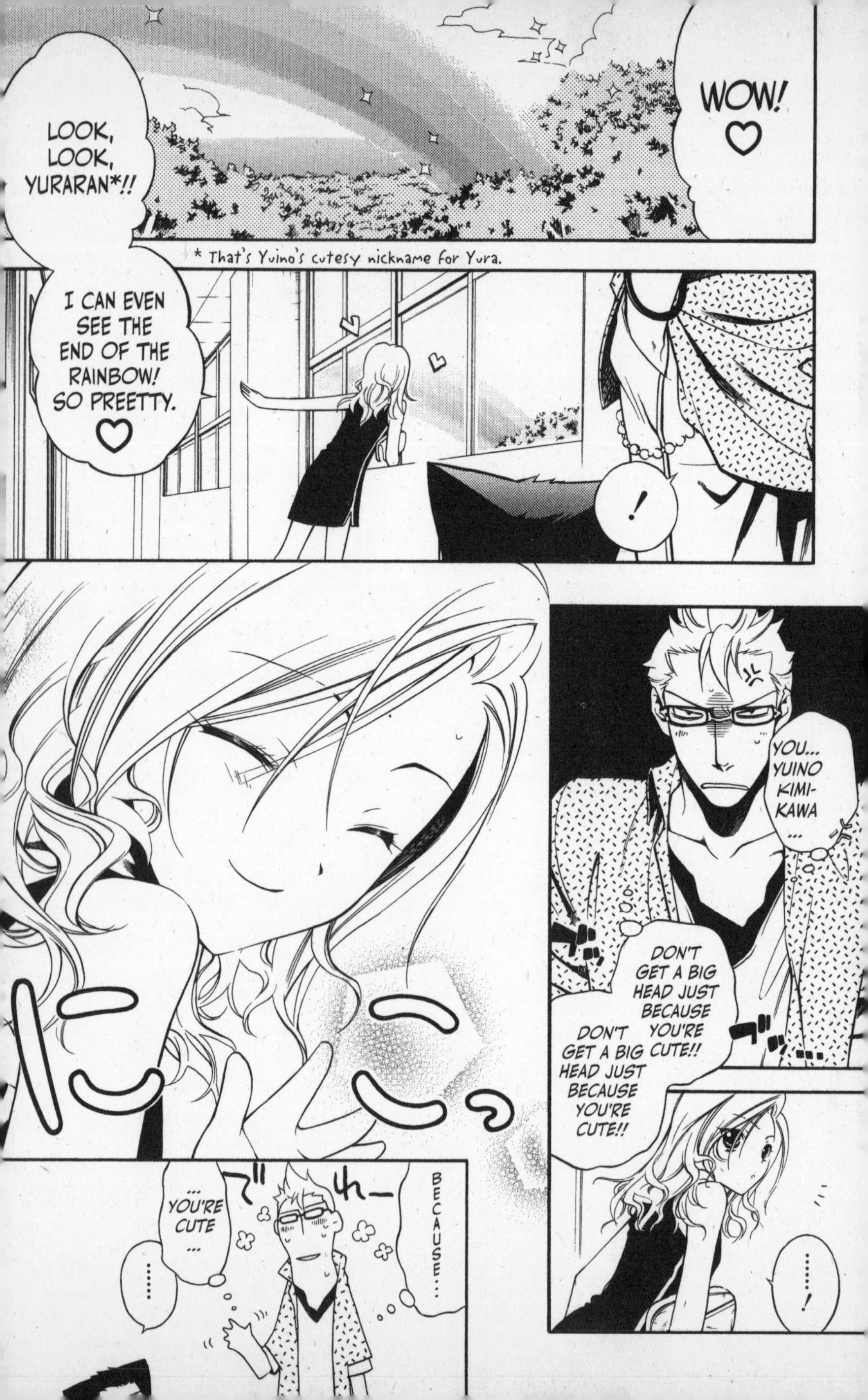
WOW! ♥
LOOK, LOOK, YURARAN*!!
* That's Yuino's cutesy nickname for Yura.
!
I CAN EVEN SEE THE END OF THE RAINBOW! SO PREETTY. ♥
YOU... YUINO KIMIKAWA ...
DON'T GET A BIG HEAD JUST BECAUSE YOU'RE CUTE!!
DON'T GET A BIG HEAD JUST BECAUSE YOU'RE CUTE!!
......!
BECAUSE...
... YOU'RE CUTE ...
......

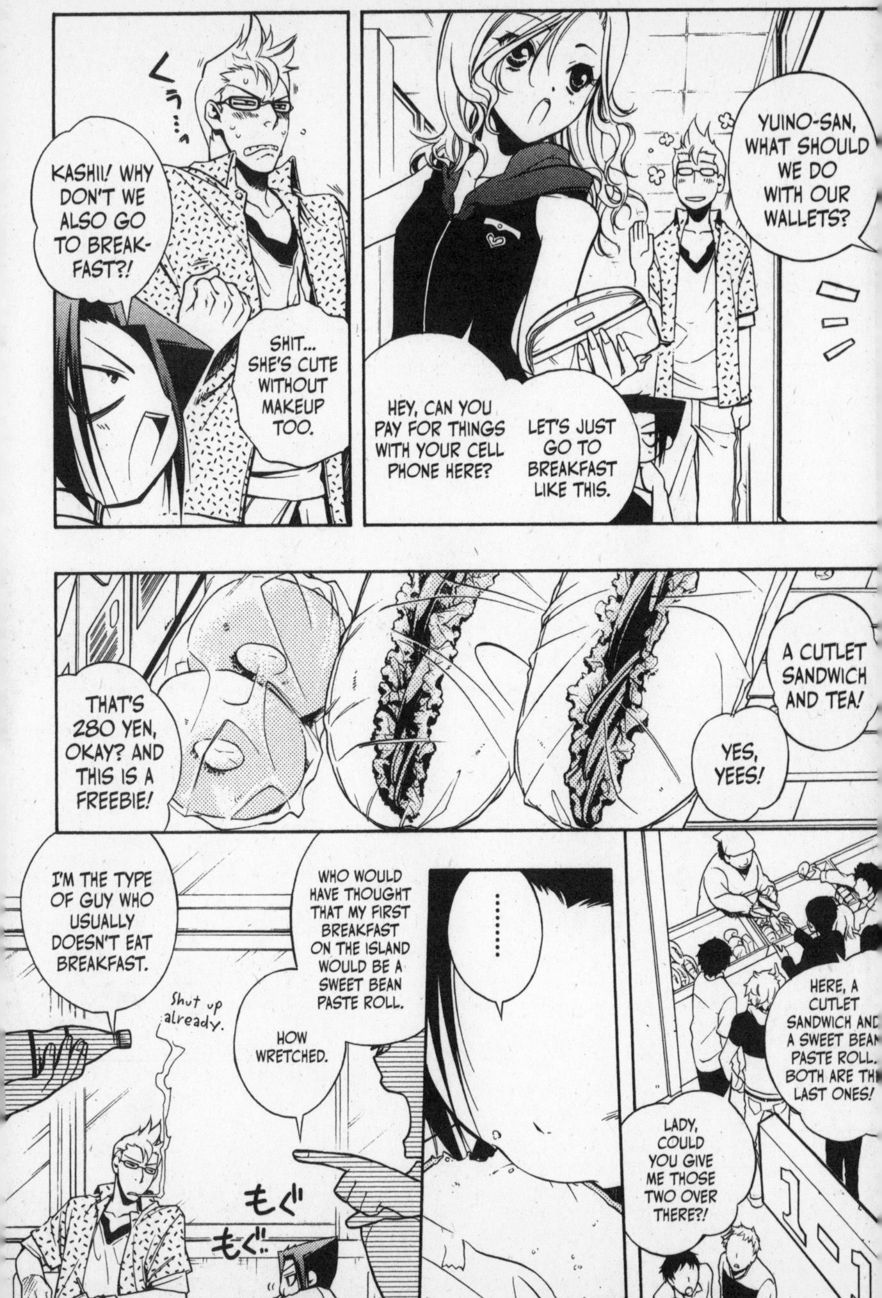
YUINO-SAN, WHAT SHOULD WE DO WITH OUR WALLETS?
LET'S JUST GO TO BREAKFAST LIKE THIS.
HEY, CAN YOU PAY FOR THINGS WITH YOUR CELL PHONE HERE?
くら…
KASHII! WHY DON'T WE ALSO GO TO BREAK-FAST?!
SHIT... SHE'S CUTE WITHOUT MAKEUP TOO.
A CUTLET SANDWICH AND TEA!
YES, YEES!
THAT'S 280 YEN, OKAY? AND THIS IS A FREEBIE!
HERE, A CUTLET SANDWICH AN A SWEET BEA PASTE ROLL. BOTH ARE TH LAST ONES!
LADY, COULD YOU GIVE ME THOSE TWO OVER THERE?!
……
WHO WOULD HAVE THOUGHT THAT MY FIRST BREAKFAST ON THE ISLAND WOULD BE A SWEET BEAN PASTE ROLL.
HOW WRETCHED.
I'M THE TYPE OF GUY WHO USUALLY DOESN'T EAT BREAKFAST.
Shut up already.
もぐ
もぐ

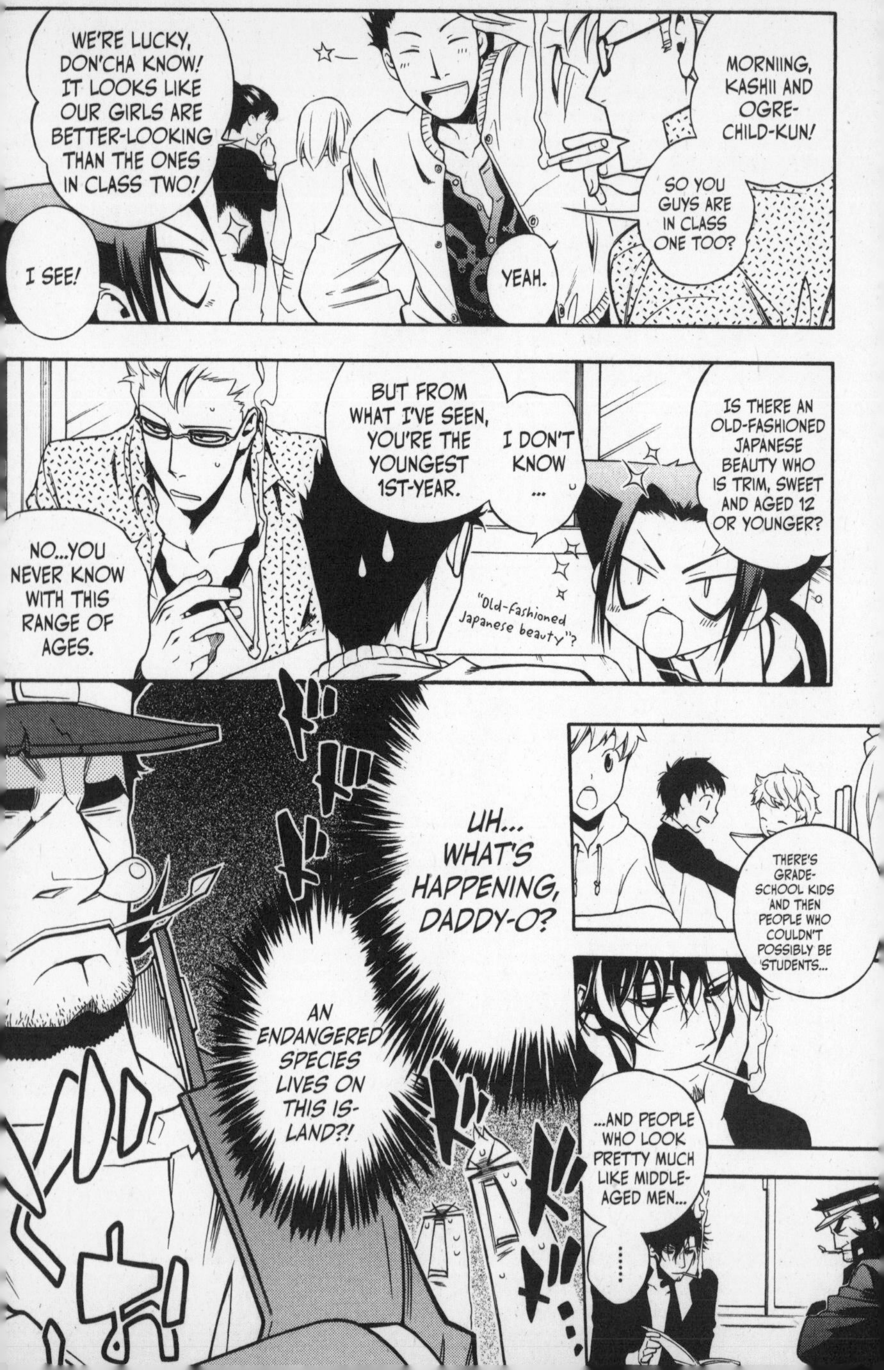
MORNIIING, KASHII AND OGRE-CHILD-KUN!
SO YOU GUYS ARE IN CLASS ONE TOO?
YEAH.
WE'RE LUCKY, DON'CHA KNOW! IT LOOKS LIKE OUR GIRLS ARE BETTER-LOOKING THAN THE ONES IN CLASS TWO!
I SEE!
IS THERE AN OLD-FASHIONED JAPANESE BEAUTY WHO IS TRIM, SWEET AND AGED 12 OR YOUNGER?
"Old-fashioned Japanese beauty"?
I DON'T KNOW ...
BUT FROM WHAT I'VE SEEN, YOU'RE THE YOUNGEST 1ST-YEAR.
NO...YOU NEVER KNOW WITH THIS RANGE OF AGES.
THERE'S GRADE-SCHOOL KIDS AND THEN PEOPLE WHO COULDN'T POSSIBLY BE STUDENTS...
...AND PEOPLE WHO LOOK PRETTY MUCH LIKE MIDDLE-AGED MEN...
......
UH... WHAT'S HAPPENING, DADDY-O?
AN ENDANGERED SPECIES LIVES ON THIS IS-LAND?!

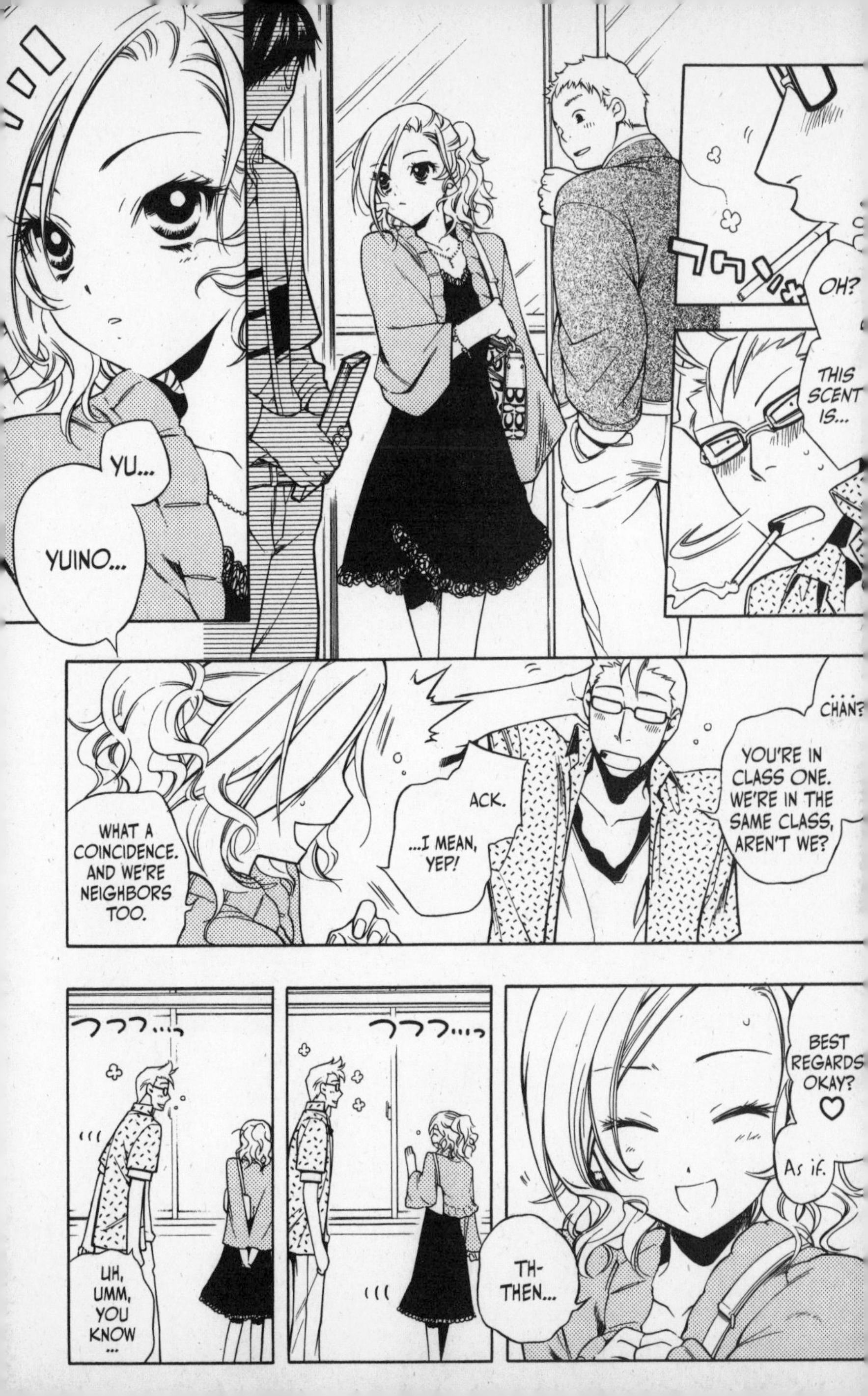
OH?
THIS SCENT IS...
YU...
YUINO...
CHAN?
YOU'RE IN CLASS ONE. WE'RE IN THE SAME CLASS, AREN'T WE?
ACK.
...I MEAN, YEP!
WHAT A COINCIDENCE. AND WE'RE NEIGHBORS TOO.
BEST REGARDS OKAY? ♡
As if.
TH-THEN...
UH, UMM, YOU KNOW ...

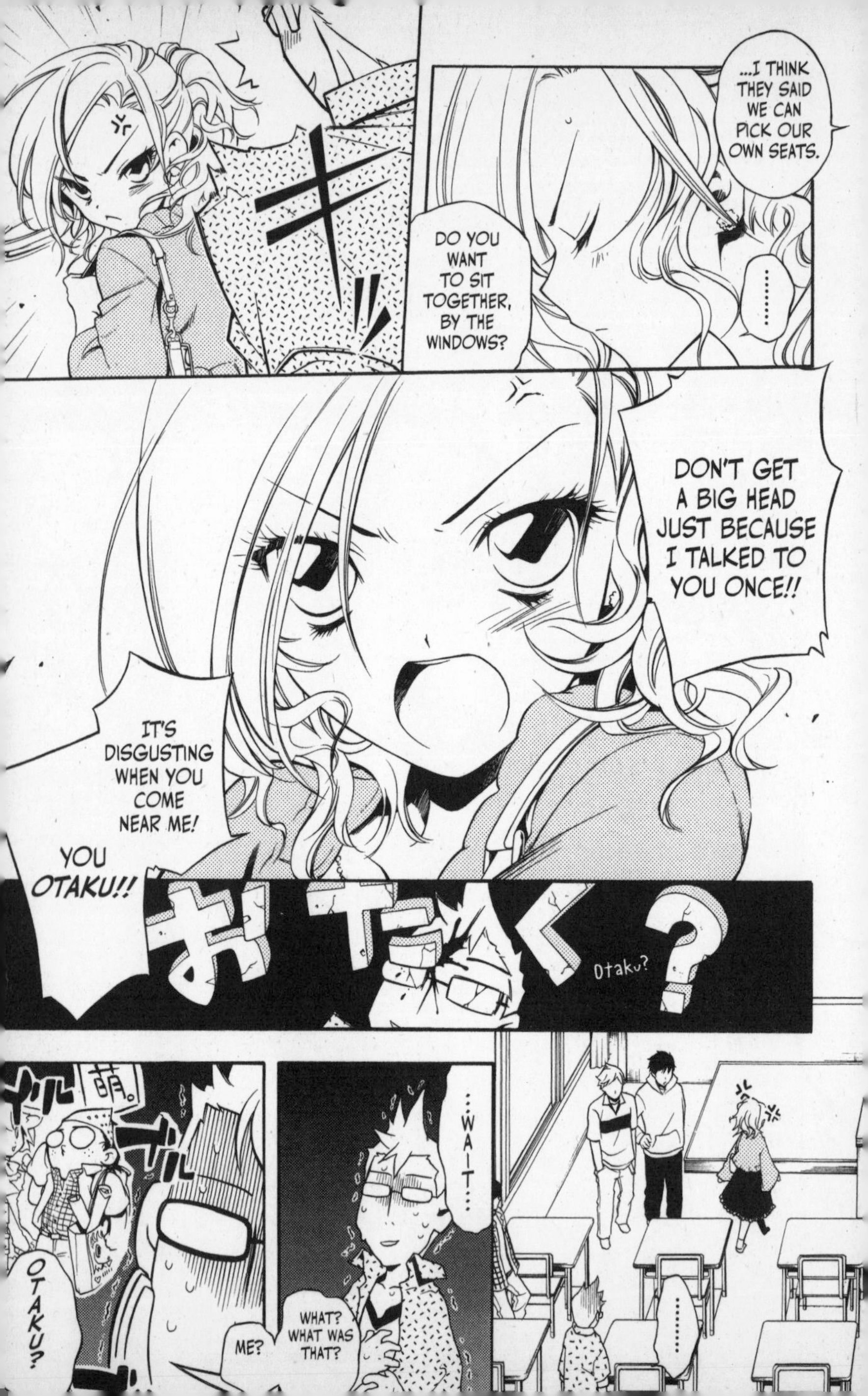
...I THINK THEY SAID WE CAN PICK OUR OWN SEATS.
DO YOU WANT TO SIT TOGETHER, BY THE WINDOWS?
......
DON'T GET A BIG HEAD JUST BECAUSE I TALKED TO YOU ONCE!!
IT'S DISGUSTING WHEN YOU COME NEAR ME!
YOU OTAKU!!
おたく?
Otaku?
......
...WAIT...
WHAT? WHAT WAS THAT?
ME?
萌。
OTAKU?

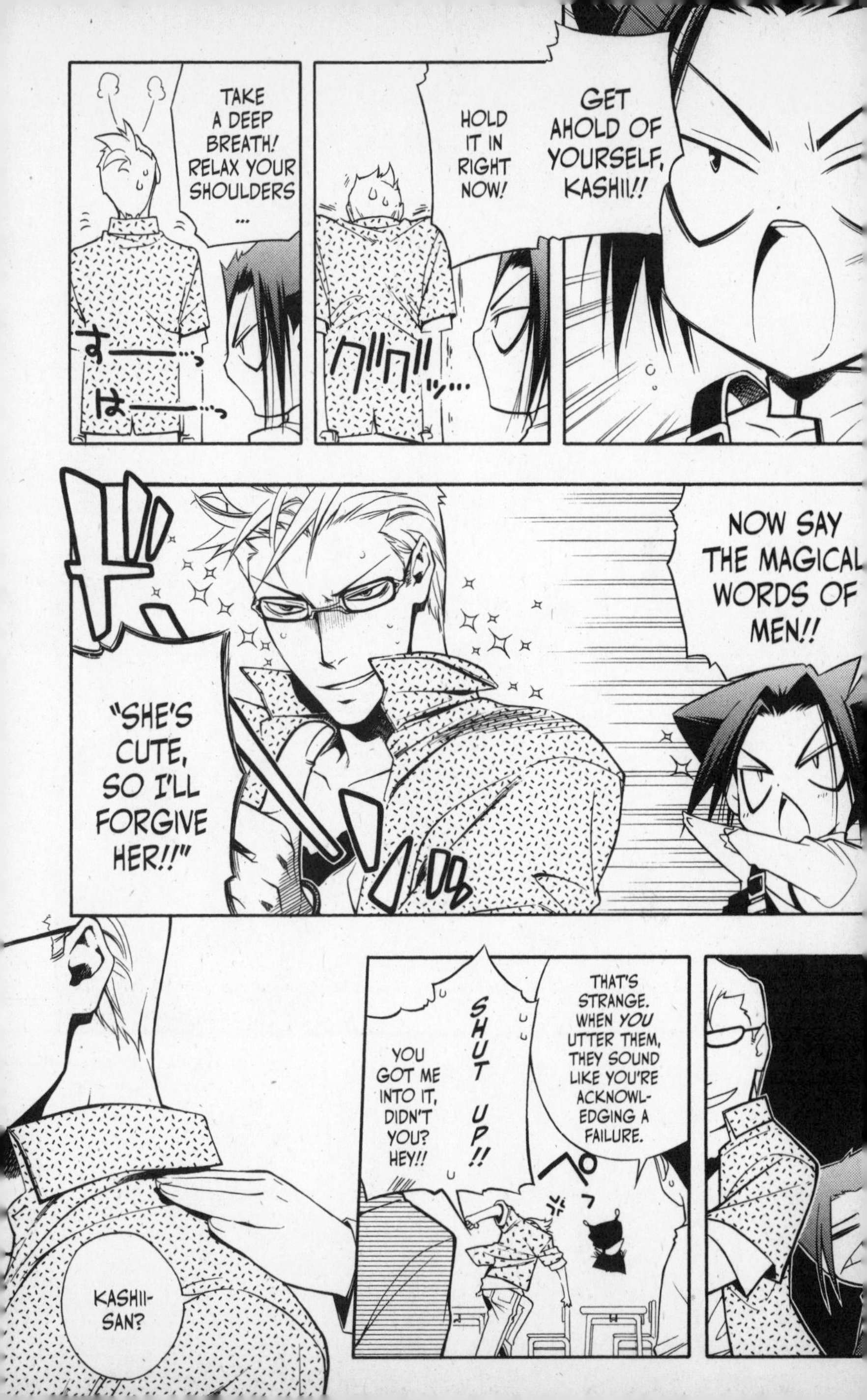
GET AHOLD OF YOURSELF, KASHII!!
HOLD IT IN RIGHT NOW!
グッグッ…
TAKE A DEEP BREATH! RELAX YOUR SHOULDERS ...
すーー…っ
はーー…っ
NOW SAY THE MAGICAL WORDS OF MEN!!
"SHE'S CUTE, SO I'LL FORGIVE HER!!"
THAT'S STRANGE. WHEN *YOU* UTTER THEM, THEY SOUND LIKE YOU'RE ACKNOWL-EDGING A FAILURE.
SHUT UP!!
YOU GOT ME INTO IT, DIDN'T YOU? HEY!!
KASHII-SAN?

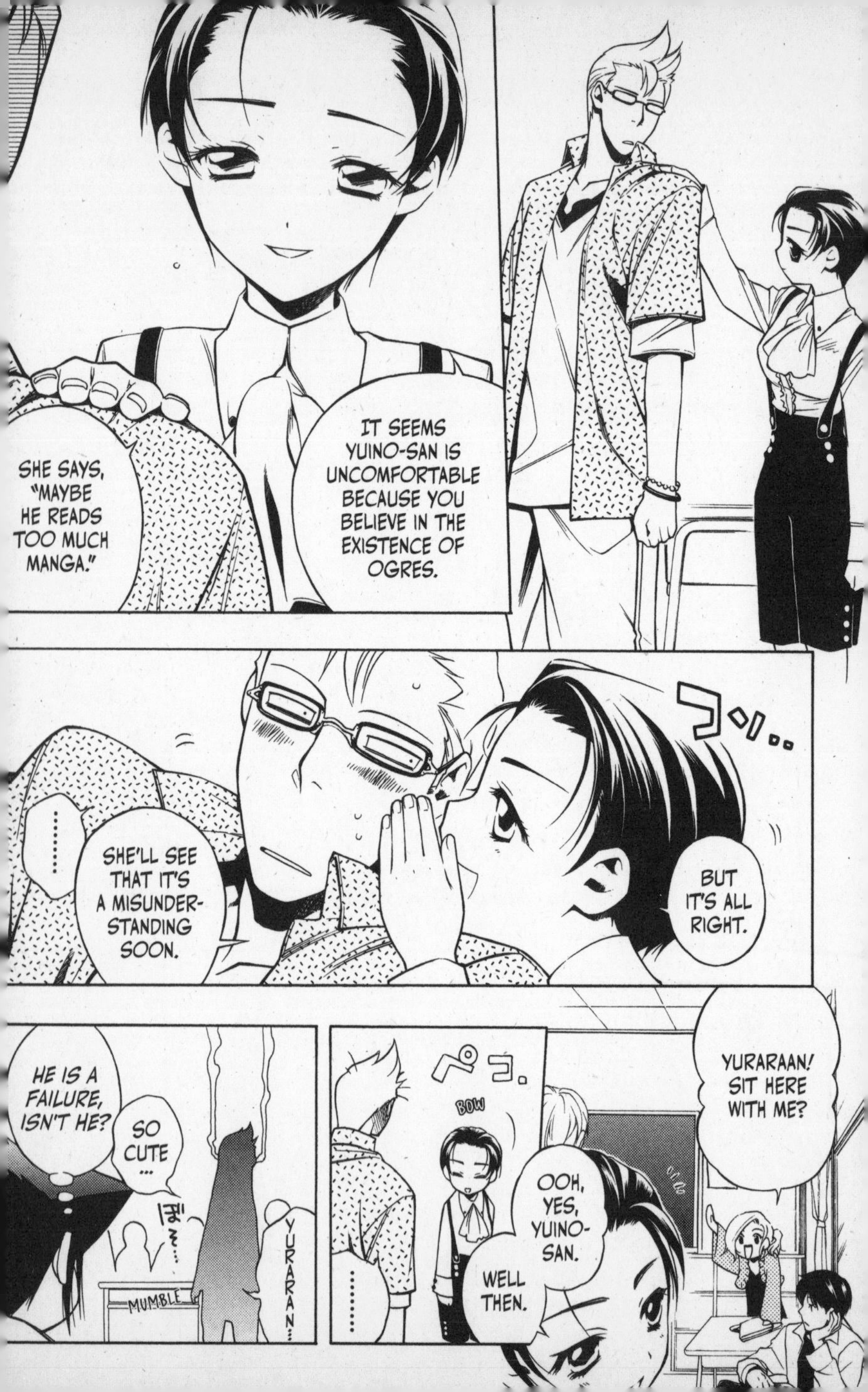
IT SEEMS YUINO-SAN IS UNCOMFORTABLE BECAUSE YOU BELIEVE IN THE EXISTENCE OF OGRES.
SHE SAYS, "MAYBE HE READS TOO MUCH MANGA."
BUT IT'S ALL RIGHT.
SHE'LL SEE THAT IT'S A MISUNDERSTANDING SOON.
......
YURARAAN! SIT HERE WITH ME?
ペコ。
BOW
OOH, YES, YUINO-SAN.
WELL THEN.
......
YURARAN...
MUMBLE
SO CUTE...
HE IS A FAILURE, ISN'T HE?

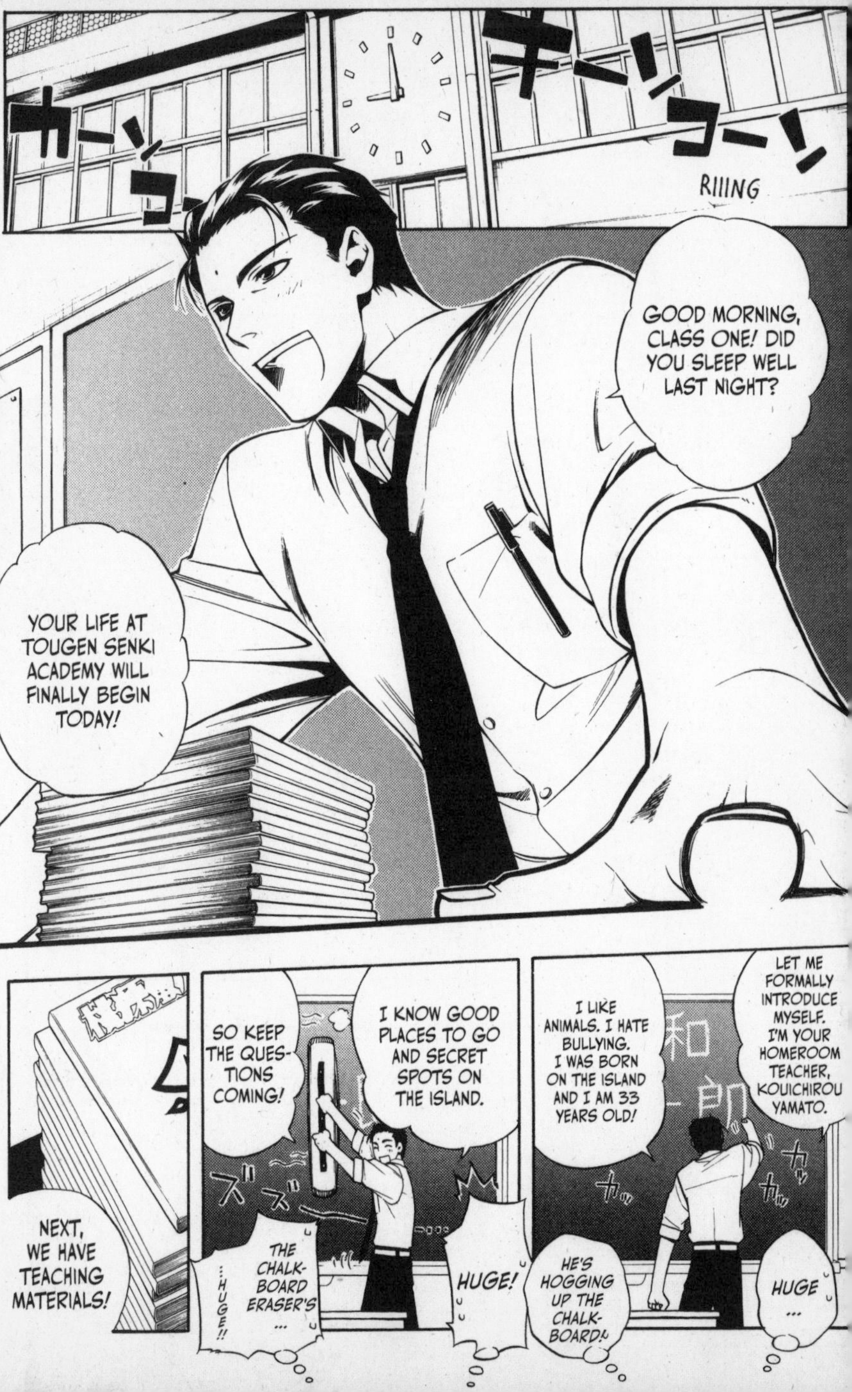

キーンコーン!
RIIING
カーンコー
GOOD MORNING, CLASS ONE! DID YOU SLEEP WELL LAST NIGHT?
YOUR LIFE AT TOUGEN SENKI ACADEMY WILL FINALLY BEGIN TODAY!
LET ME FORMALLY INTRODUCE MYSELF. I'M YOUR HOMEROOM TEACHER, KOUICHIROU YAMATO.
I LIKE ANIMALS. I HATE BULLYING. I WAS BORN ON THE ISLAND AND I AM 33 YEARS OLD!
HUGE ...
HE'S HOGGING UP THE CHALK-BOARD!
I KNOW GOOD PLACES TO GO AND SECRET SPOTS ON THE ISLAND.
SO KEEP THE QUES-TIONS COMING!
HUGE!
THE CHALK-BOARD ERASER'S ...
...HUGE!!
NEXT, WE HAVE TEACHING MATERIALS!

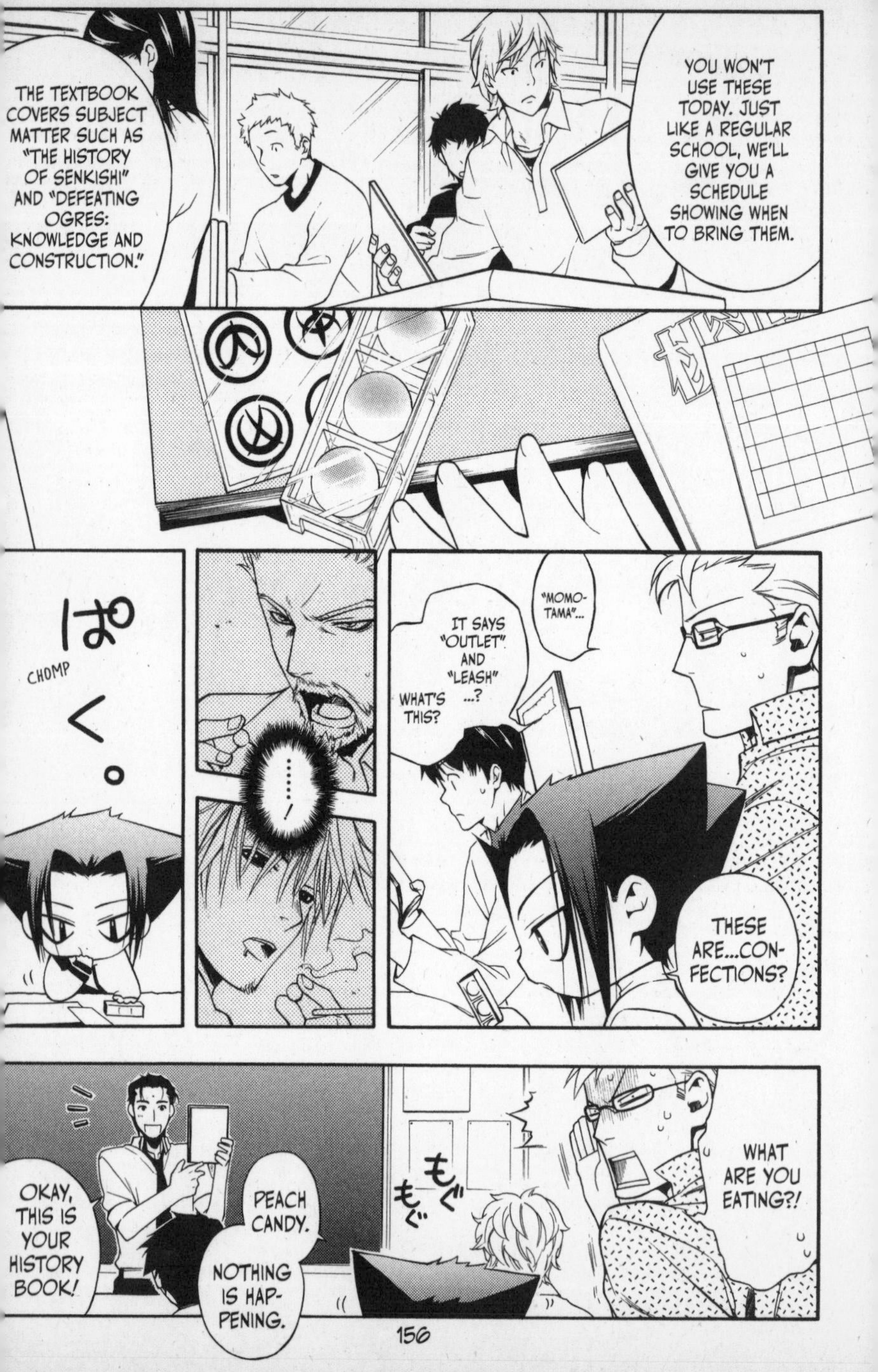
YOU WON'T USE THESE TODAY. JUST LIKE A REGULAR SCHOOL, WE'LL GIVE YOU A SCHEDULE SHOWING WHEN TO BRING THEM.
THE TEXTBOOK COVERS SUBJECT MATTER SUCH AS "THE HISTORY OF SENKISHI" AND "DEFEATING OGRES: KNOWLEDGE AND CONSTRUCTION."
"MOMO-TAMA"...
IT SAYS "OUTLET" AND "LEASH" ...?
WHAT'S THIS?
THESE ARE...CONFECTIONS?
......!
ぱく。
CHOMP
WHAT ARE YOU EATING?!
もぐもぐ
PEACH CANDY.
NOTHING IS HAP-PENING.
OKAY, THIS IS YOUR HISTORY BOOK!

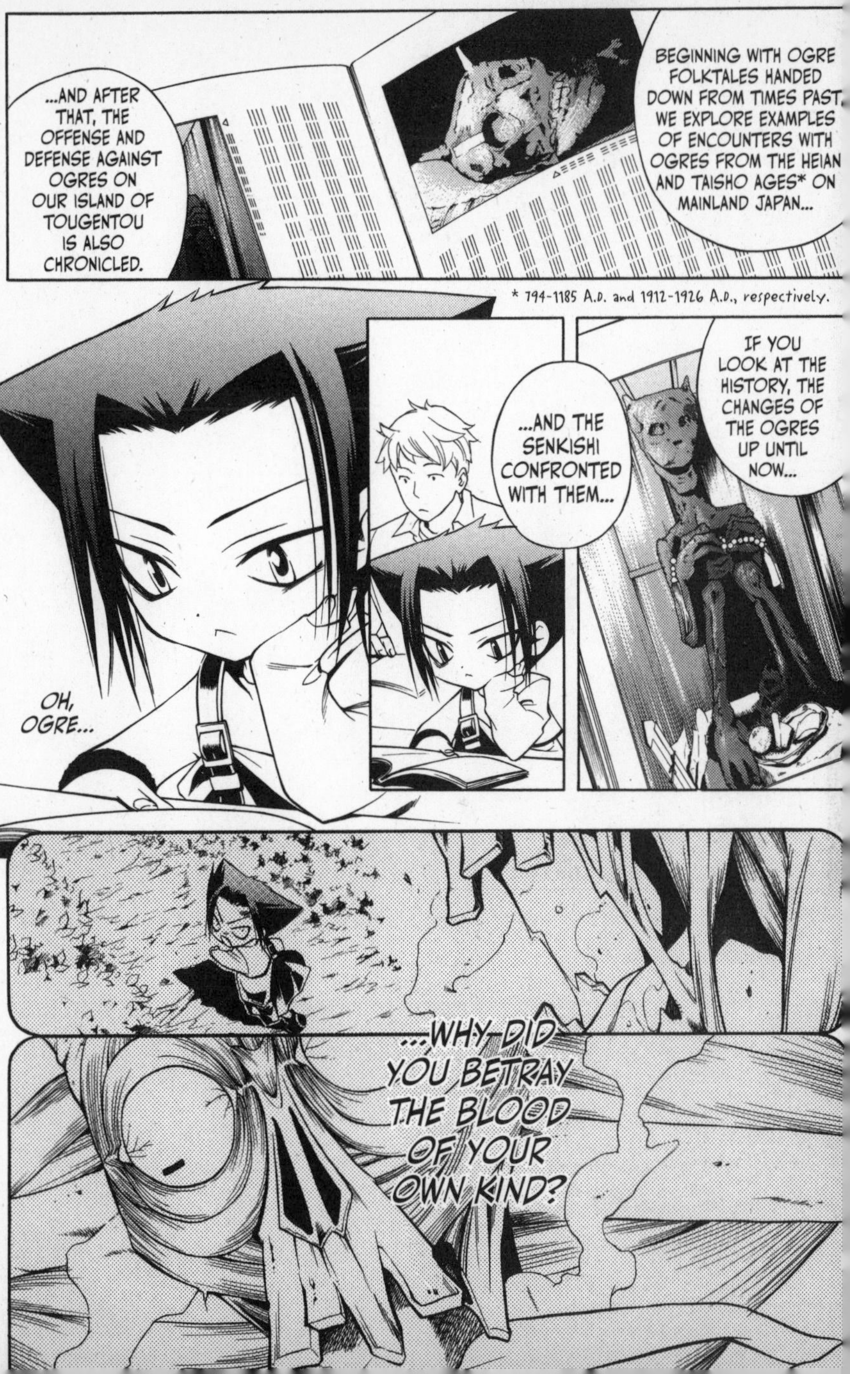
BEGINNING WITH OGRE FOLKTALES HANDED DOWN FROM TIMES PAST, WE EXPLORE EXAMPLES OF ENCOUNTERS WITH OGRES FROM THE HEIAN AND TAISHO AGES* ON MAINLAND JAPAN...
...AND AFTER THAT, THE OFFENSE AND DEFENSE AGAINST OGRES ON OUR ISLAND OF TOUGENTOU IS ALSO CHRONICLED.
* 794-1185 A.D. and 1912-1926 A.D., respectively.
IF YOU LOOK AT THE HISTORY, THE CHANGES OF THE OGRES UP UNTIL NOW...
...AND THE SENKISHI CONFRONTED WITH THEM...
OH, OGRE...
...WHY DID YOU BETRAY THE BLOOD OF YOUR OWN KIND?

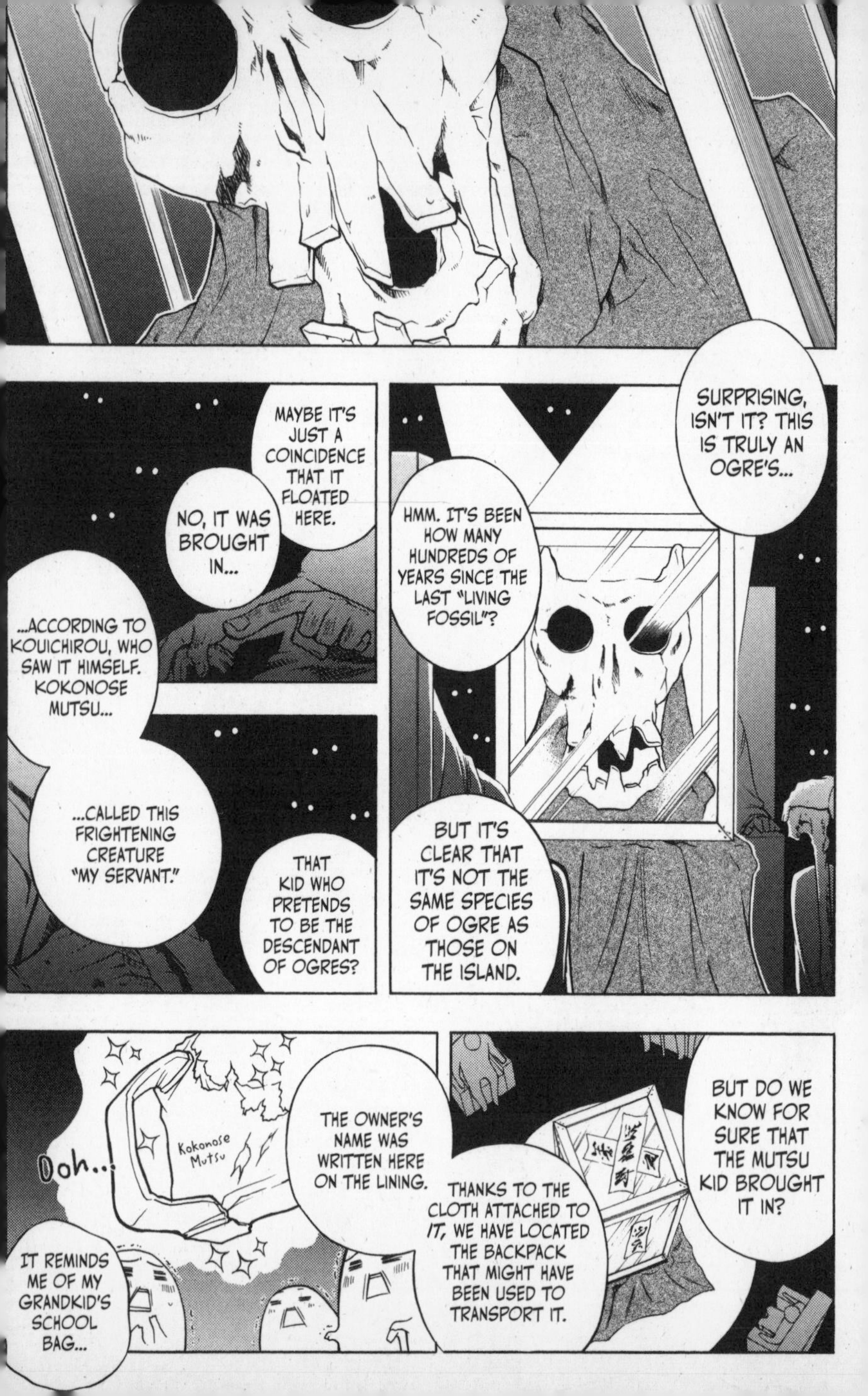

SURPRISING, ISN'T IT? THIS IS TRULY AN OGRE'S...
HMM. IT'S BEEN HOW MANY HUNDREDS OF YEARS SINCE THE LAST "LIVING FOSSIL"?
BUT IT'S CLEAR THAT IT'S NOT THE SAME SPECIES OF OGRE AS THOSE ON THE ISLAND.
MAYBE IT'S JUST A COINCIDENCE THAT IT FLOATED HERE.
NO, IT WAS BROUGHT IN...
...ACCORDING TO KOUICHIROU, WHO SAW IT HIMSELF. KOKONOSE MUTSU...
...CALLED THIS FRIGHTENING CREATURE "MY SERVANT."
THAT KID WHO PRETENDS TO BE THE DESCENDANT OF OGRES?
BUT DO WE KNOW FOR SURE THAT THE MUTSU KID BROUGHT IT IN?
THANKS TO THE CLOTH ATTACHED TO *IT*, WE HAVE LOCATED THE BACKPACK THAT MIGHT HAVE BEEN USED TO TRANSPORT IT.
THE OWNER'S NAME WAS WRITTEN HERE ON THE LINING.
Kokonose Mutsu
Ooh...
IT REMINDS ME OF MY GRANDKID'S SCHOOL BAG...

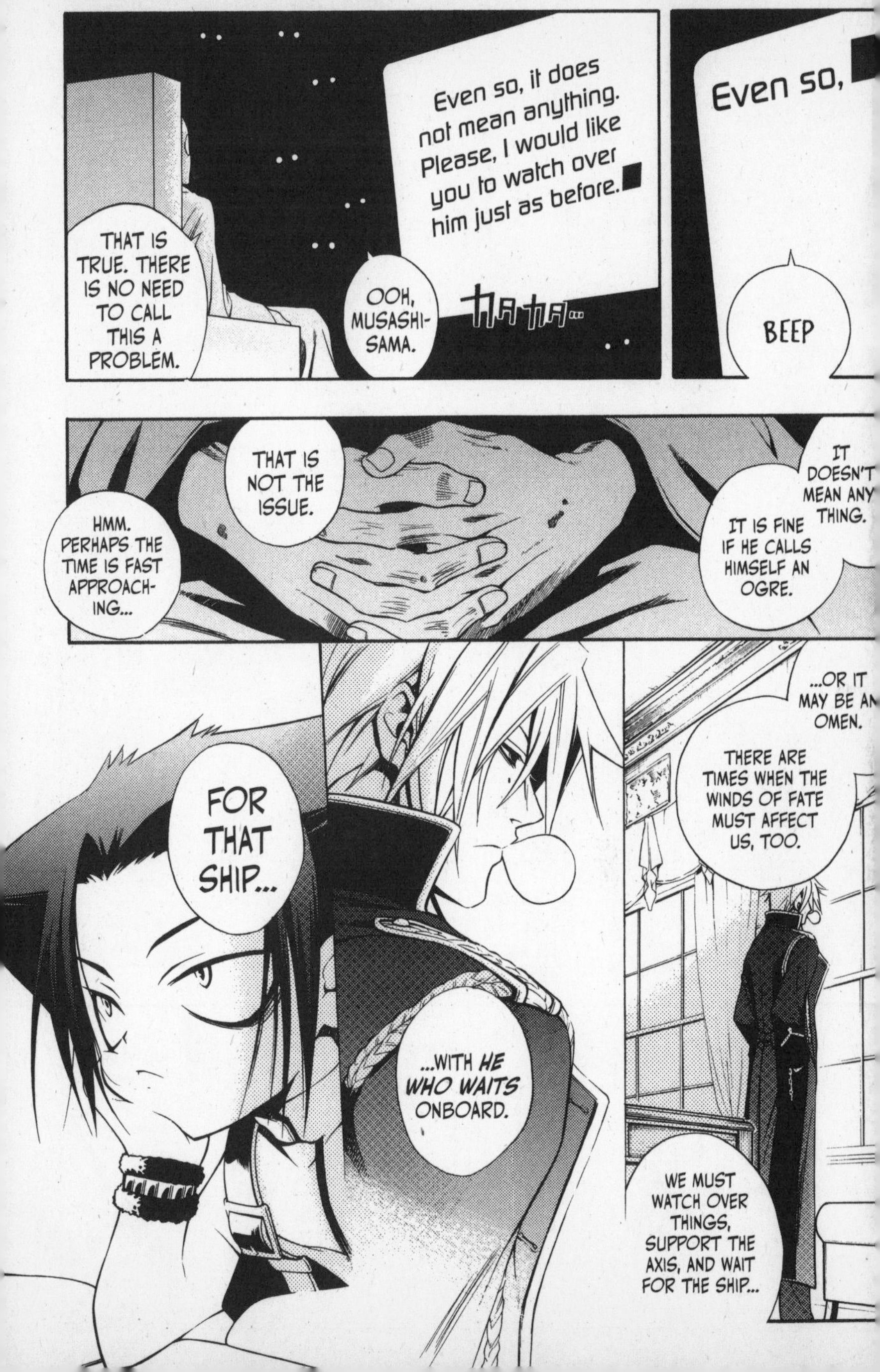
Even so,
BEEP
Even so, it does not mean anything. Please, I would like you to watch over him just as before.
カタカタ...
OOH, MUSASHI-SAMA.
THAT IS TRUE. THERE IS NO NEED TO CALL THIS A PROBLEM.
IT DOESN'T MEAN ANY THING.
IT IS FINE IF HE CALLS HIMSELF AN OGRE.
THAT IS NOT THE ISSUE.
HMM. PERHAPS THE TIME IS FAST APPROACHING...
...OR IT MAY BE AN OMEN.
THERE ARE TIMES WHEN THE WINDS OF FATE MUST AFFECT US, TOO.
WE MUST WATCH OVER THINGS, SUPPORT THE AXIS, AND WAIT FOR THE SHIP...
FOR THAT SHIP...
...WITH *HE WHO WAITS* ONBOARD.

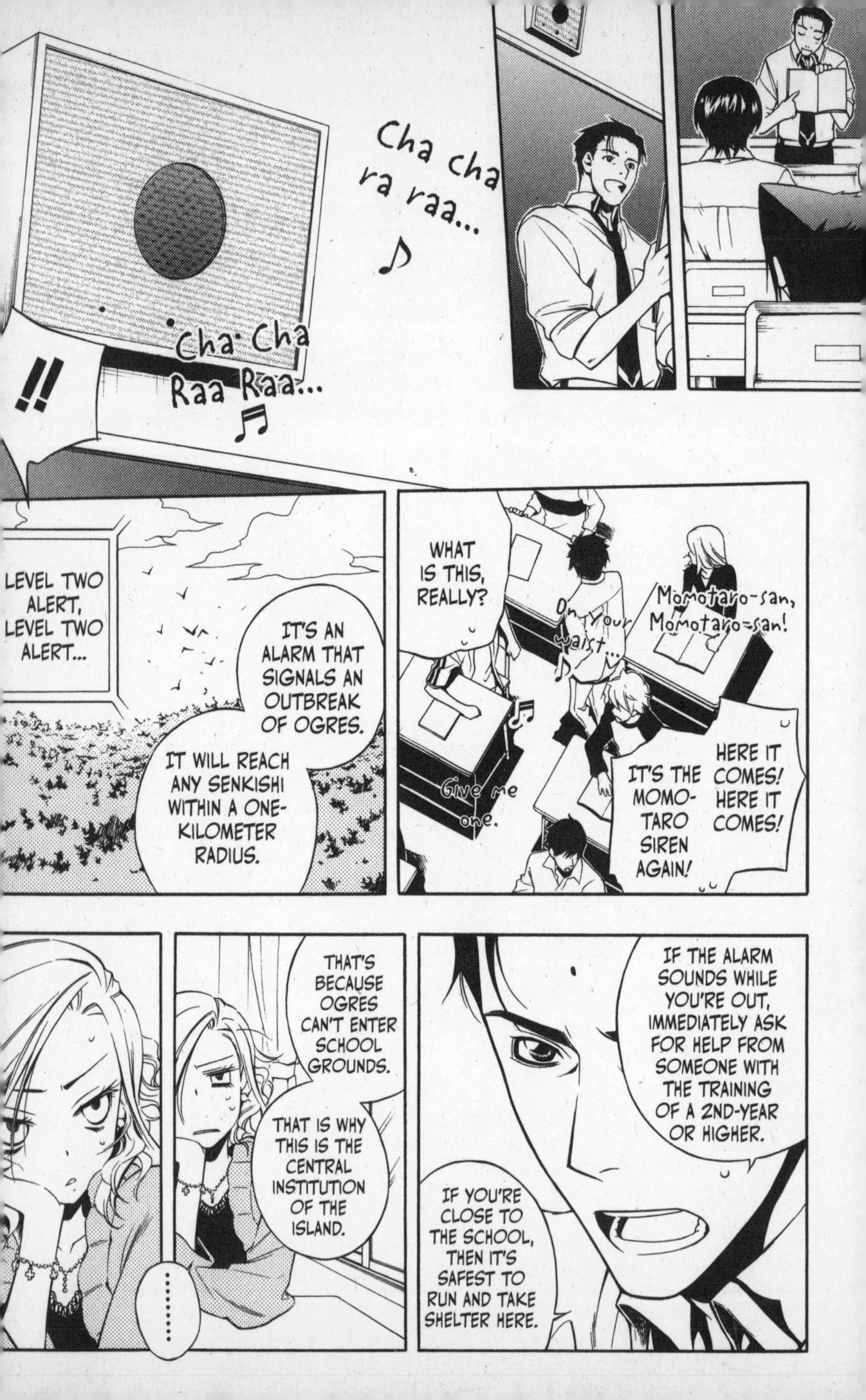
Cha cha ra raa... ♪
Cha Cha Raa Raa... ♫
!!
WHAT IS THIS, REALLY?
Momotaro-san, Momotaro-san!
On your waist... ♪
Give me one.
HERE IT COMES! HERE IT COMES!
IT'S THE MOMO-TARO SIREN AGAIN!
LEVEL TWO ALERT, LEVEL TWO ALERT...
IT'S AN ALARM THAT SIGNALS AN OUTBREAK OF OGRES.
IT WILL REACH ANY SENKISHI WITHIN A ONE-KILOMETER RADIUS.
IF THE ALARM SOUNDS WHILE YOU'RE OUT, IMMEDIATELY ASK FOR HELP FROM SOMEONE WITH THE TRAINING OF A 2ND-YEAR OR HIGHER.
IF YOU'RE CLOSE TO THE SCHOOL, THEN IT'S SAFEST TO RUN AND TAKE SHELTER HERE.
THAT'S BECAUSE OGRES CAN'T ENTER SCHOOL GROUNDS.
THAT IS WHY THIS IS THE CENTRAL INSTITUTION OF THE ISLAND.
......

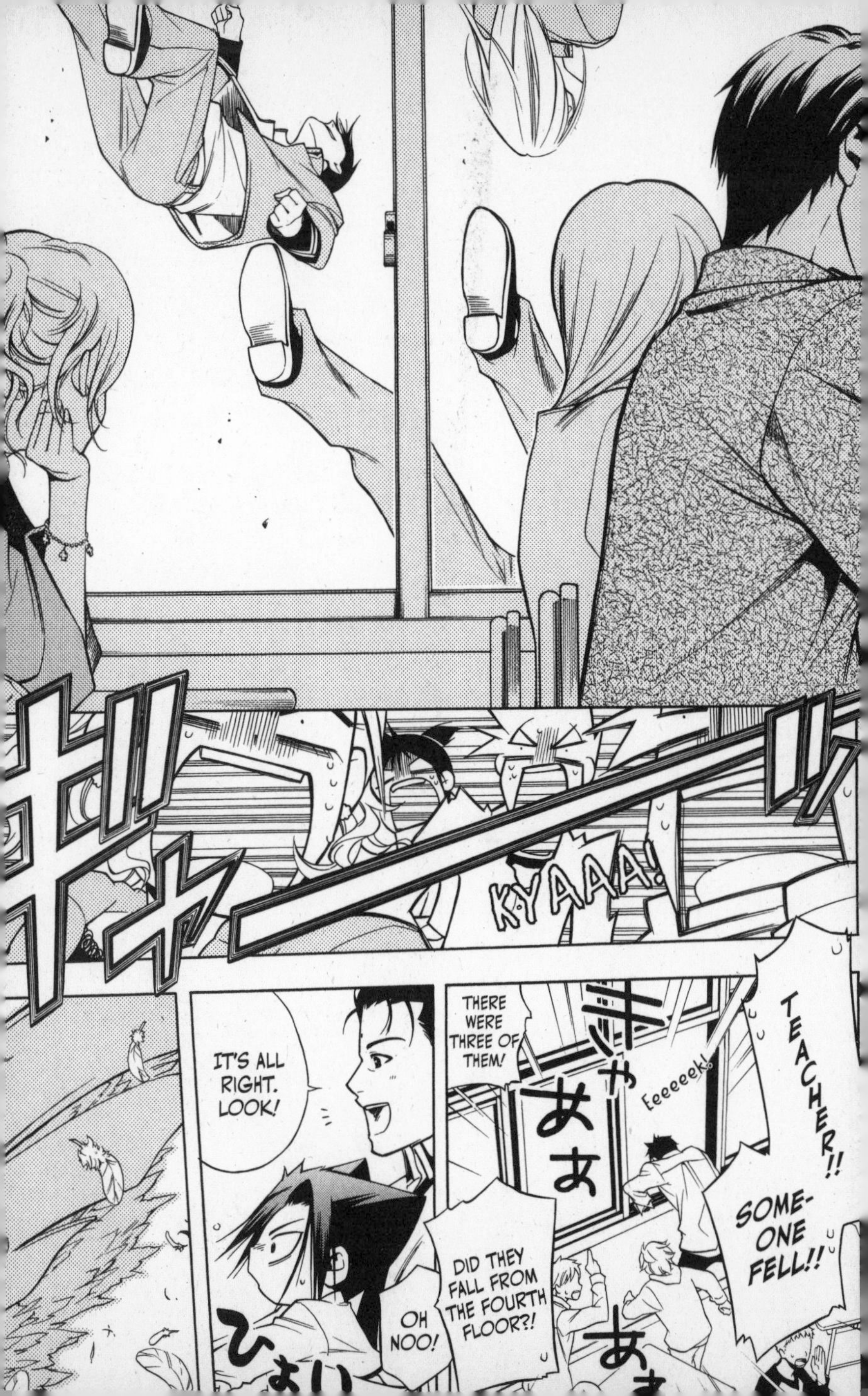
KYAAA!
TEACHER!!
SOME-ONE FELL!!
Eeeeeek!
THERE WERE THREE OF THEM!
DID THEY FALL FROM THE FOURTH FLOOR?!
OH NOO!
IT'S ALL RIGHT. LOOK!
ひょい

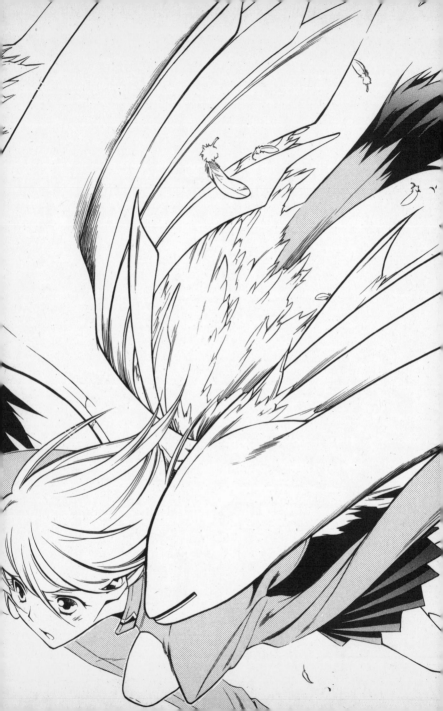

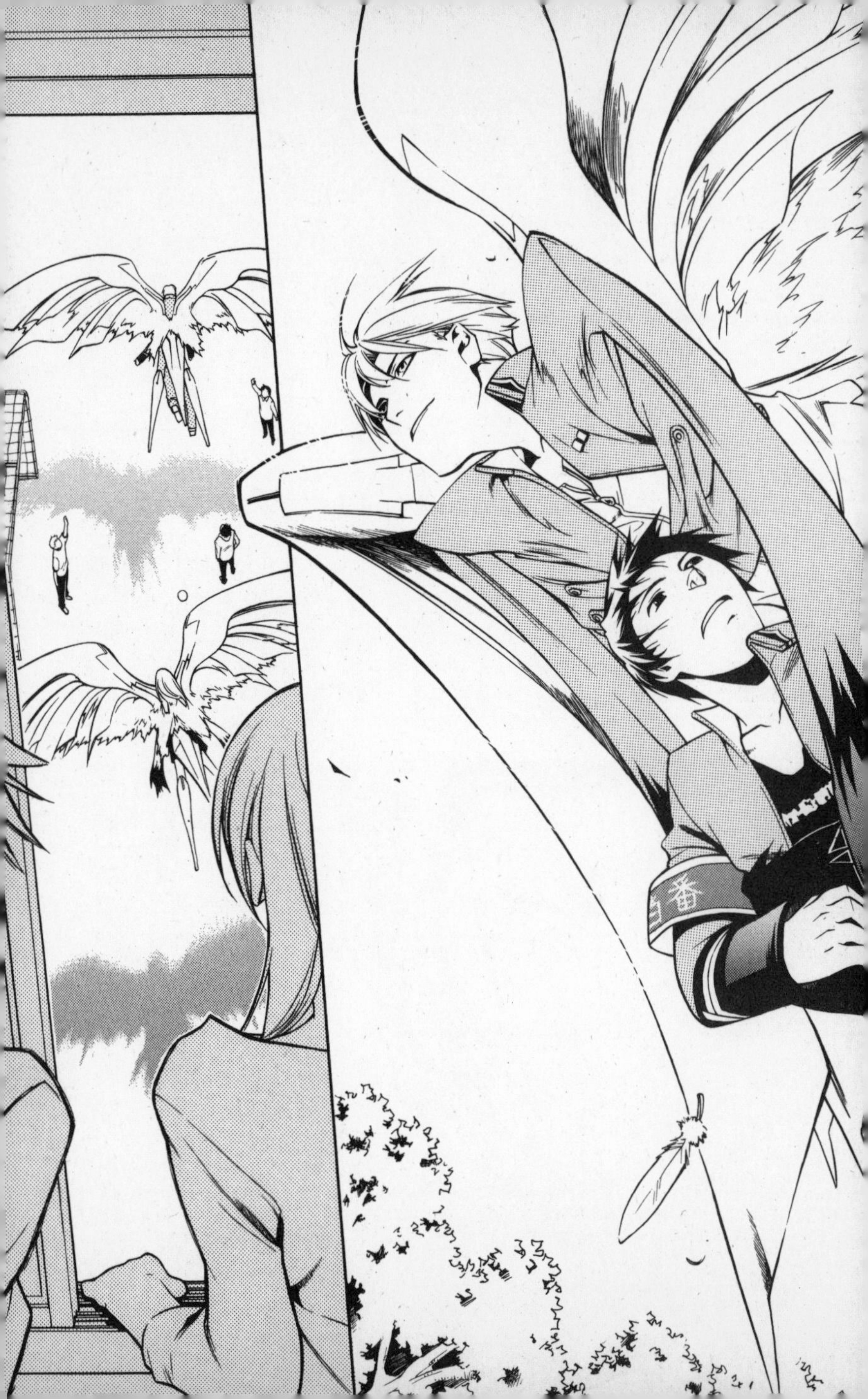

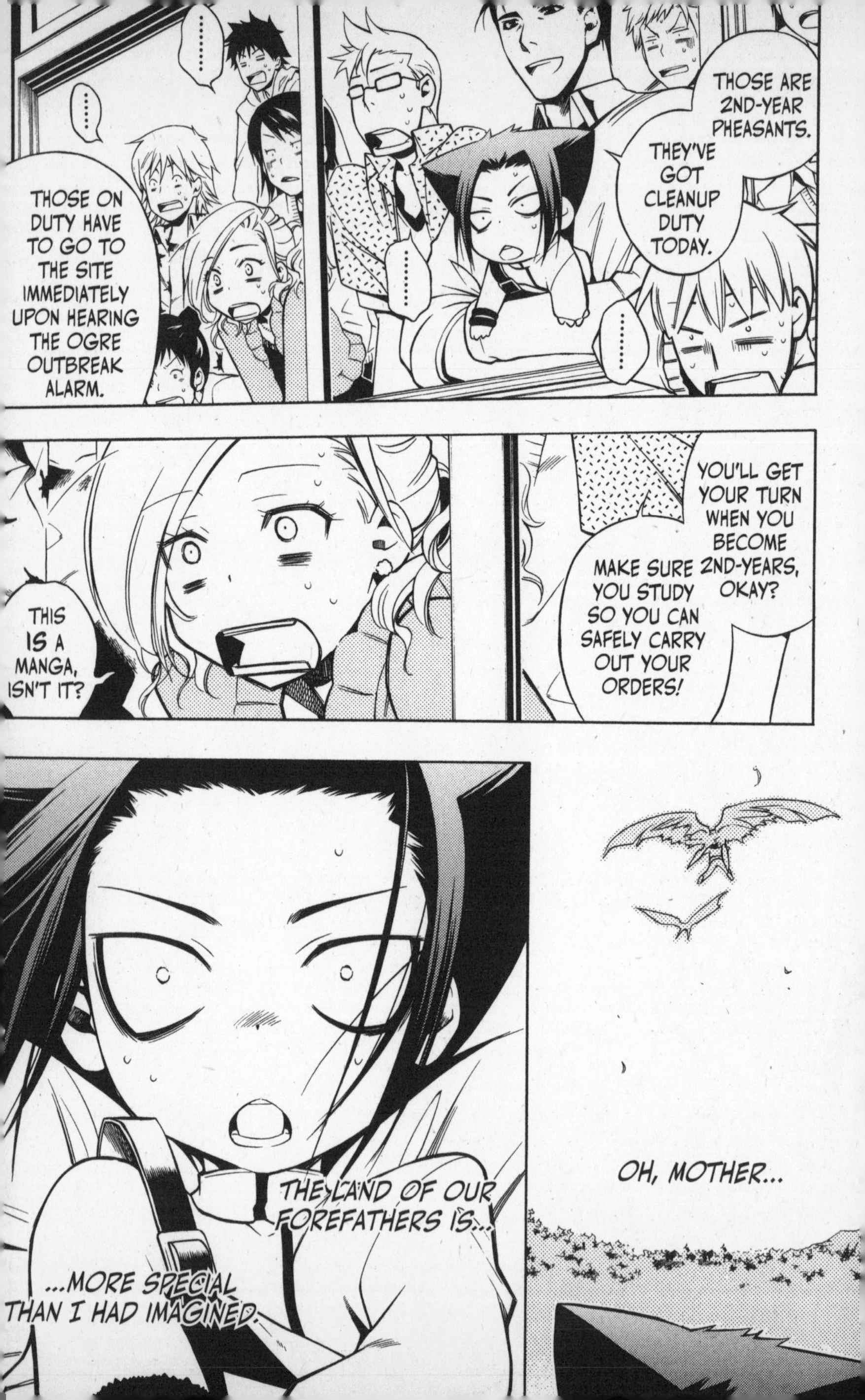
THOSE ARE 2ND-YEAR PHEASANTS.
THEY'VE GOT CLEANUP DUTY TODAY.
......
......
......
......
THOSE ON DUTY HAVE TO GO TO THE SITE IMMEDIATELY UPON HEARING THE OGRE OUTBREAK ALARM.
YOU'LL GET YOUR TURN WHEN YOU BECOME 2ND-YEARS, OKAY?
MAKE SURE YOU STUDY SO YOU CAN SAFELY CARRY OUT YOUR ORDERS!
THIS IS A MANGA, ISN'T IT?
OH, MOTHER...
THE LAND OF OUR FOREFATHERS IS...
...MORE SPECIAL THAN I HAD IMAGINED.

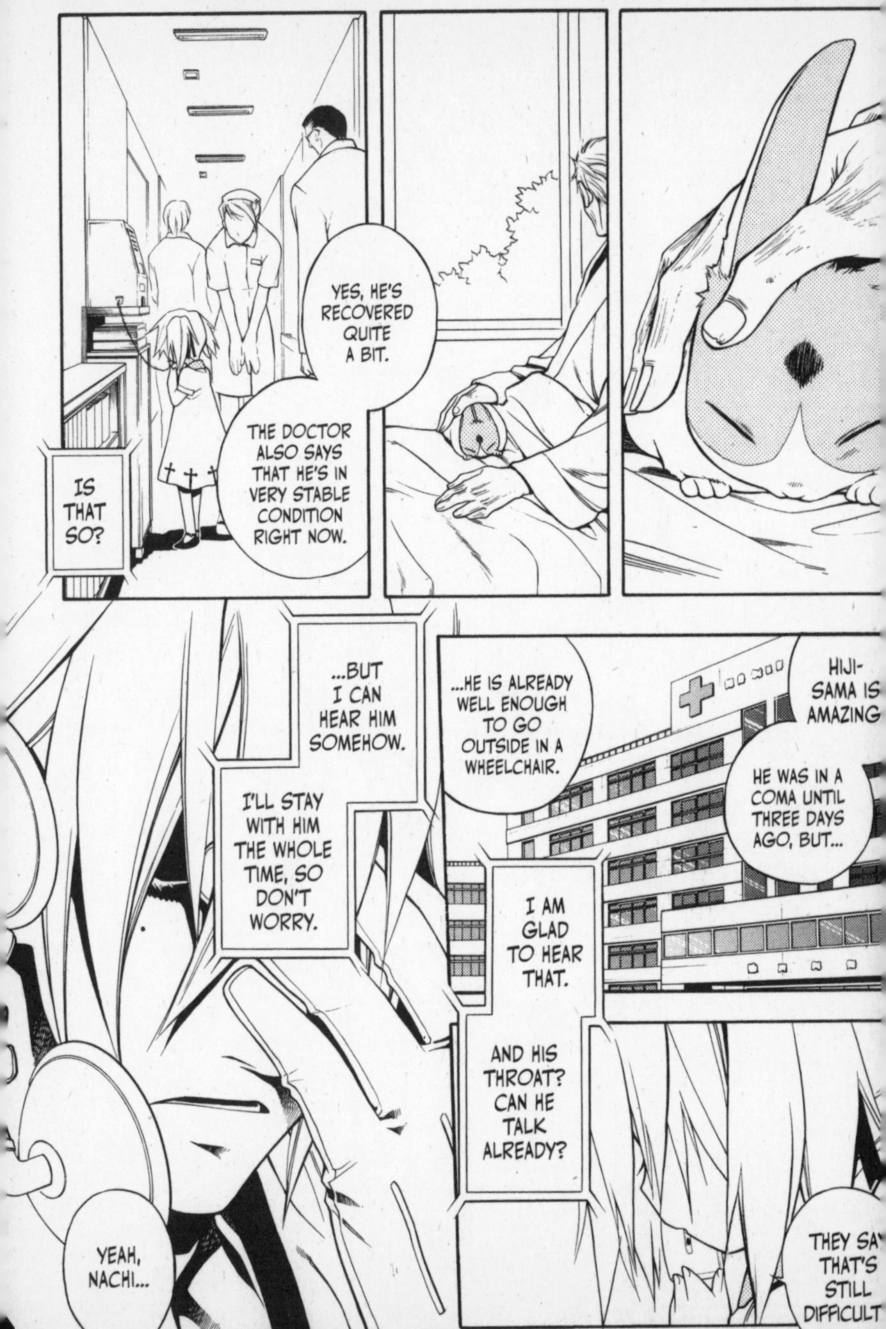
YES, HE'S RECOVERED QUITE A BIT.
THE DOCTOR ALSO SAYS THAT HE'S IN VERY STABLE CONDITION RIGHT NOW.
IS THAT SO?
HIJI-SAMA IS AMAZING
HE WAS IN A COMA UNTIL THREE DAYS AGO, BUT...
...HE IS ALREADY WELL ENOUGH TO GO OUTSIDE IN A WHEELCHAIR.
I AM GLAD TO HEAR THAT.
AND HIS THROAT? CAN HE TALK ALREADY?
THEY SAY THAT'S STILL DIFFICULT
...BUT I CAN HEAR HIM SOMEHOW.
I'LL STAY WITH HIM THE WHOLE TIME, SO DON'T WORRY.
YEAH, NACHI...

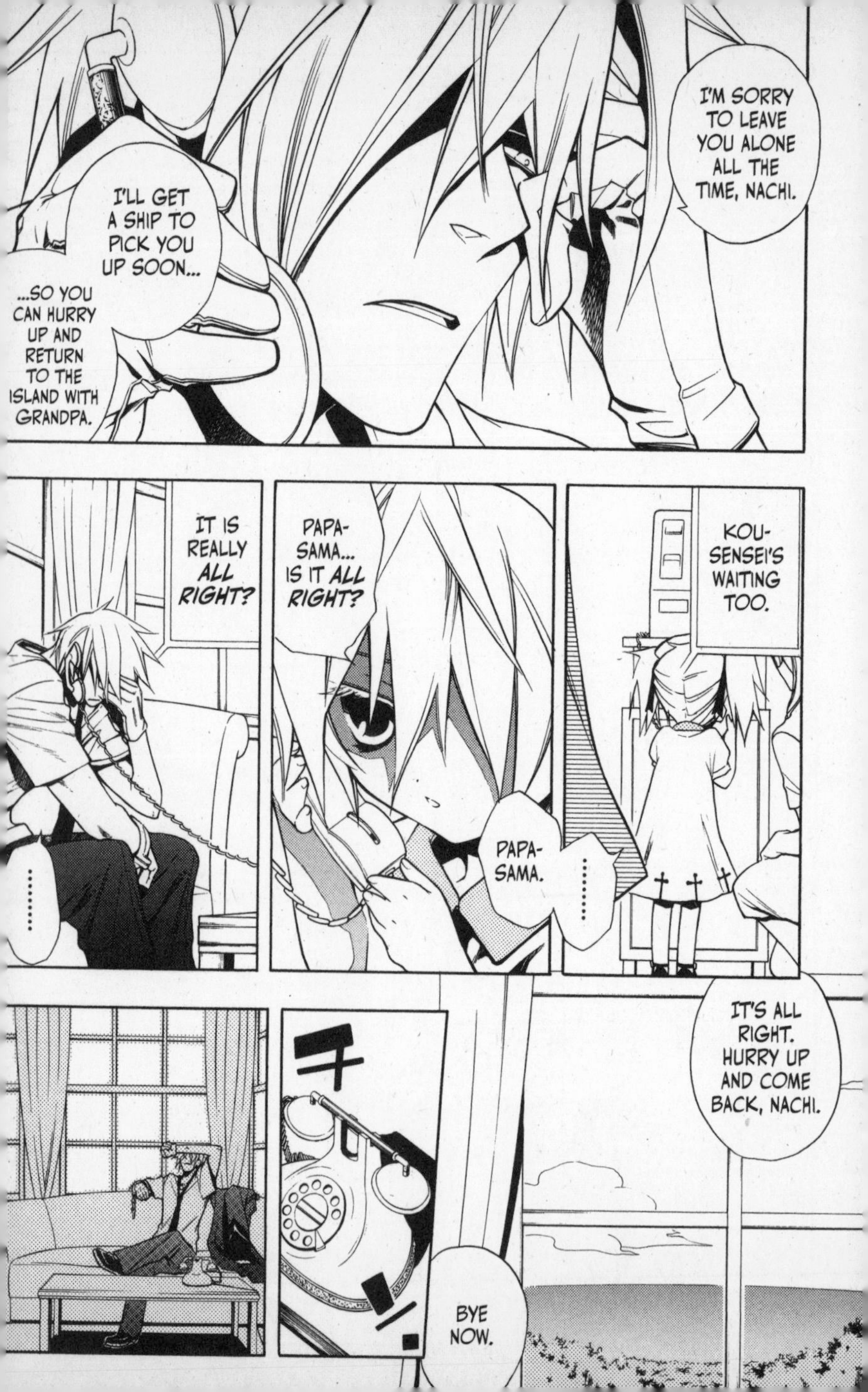
I'M SORRY TO LEAVE YOU ALONE ALL THE TIME, NACHI.
I'LL GET A SHIP TO PICK YOU UP SOON...
...SO YOU CAN HURRY UP AND RETURN TO THE ISLAND WITH GRANDPA.
KOU-SENSEI'S WAITING TOO.
......
PAPA-SAMA.
PAPA-SAMA... IS IT *ALL RIGHT?*
IT IS REALLY *ALL RIGHT?*
......
IT'S ALL RIGHT. HURRY UP AND COME BACK, NACHI.
BYE NOW.

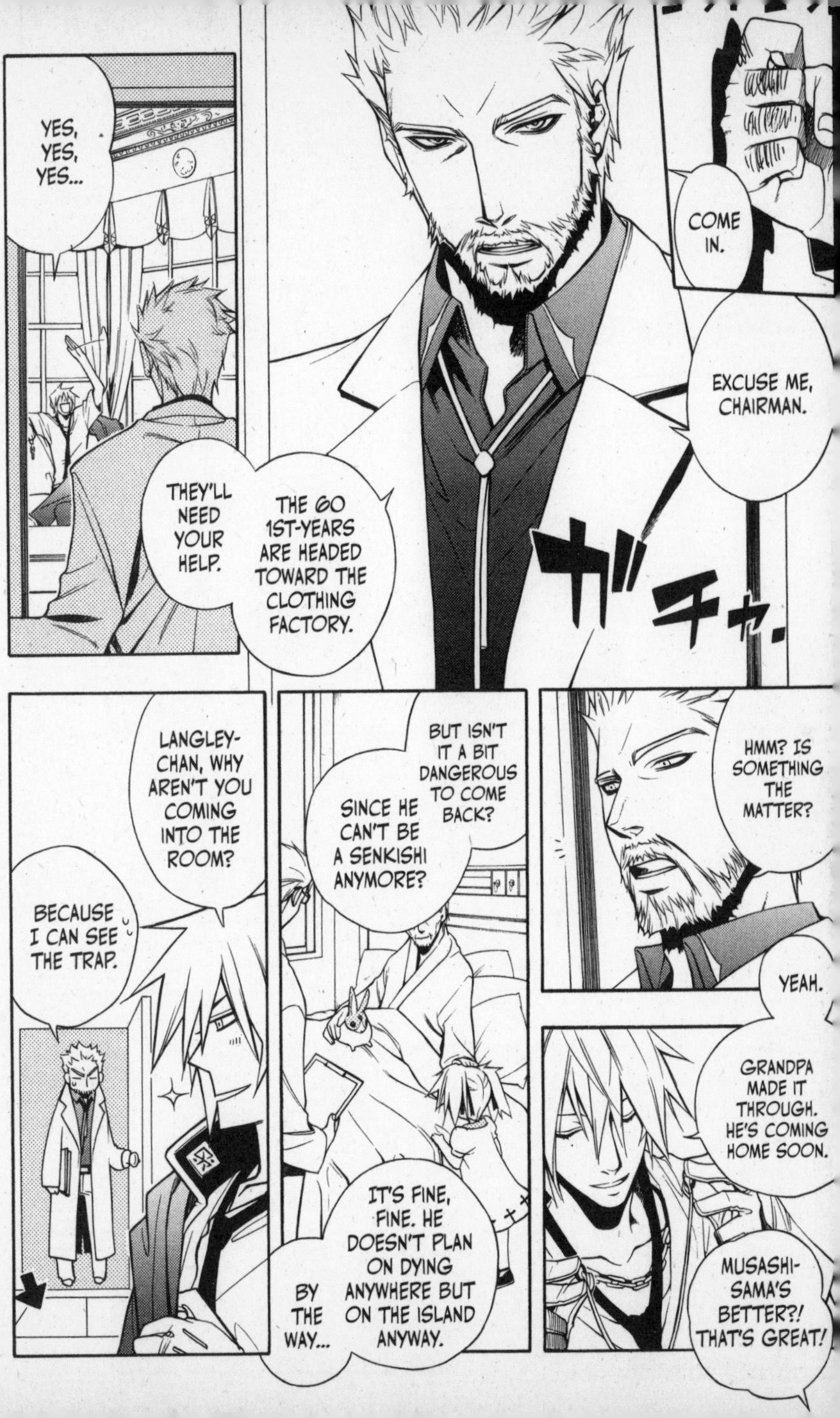
COME IN.
EXCUSE ME, CHAIRMAN.
ガチャ
THE 60 1ST-YEARS ARE HEADED TOWARD THE CLOTHING FACTORY.
THEY'LL NEED YOUR HELP.
YES, YES, YES...
HMM? IS SOMETHING THE MATTER?
YEAH.
GRANDPA MADE IT THROUGH. HE'S COMING HOME SOON.
MUSASHI-SAMA'S BETTER?! THAT'S GREAT!
BUT ISN'T IT A BIT DANGEROUS TO COME BACK?
SINCE HE CAN'T BE A SENKISHI ANYMORE?
IT'S FINE, FINE. HE DOESN'T PLAN ON DYING ANYWHERE BUT ON THE ISLAND ANYWAY.
BY THE WAY...
LANGLEY-CHAN, WHY AREN'T YOU COMING INTO THE ROOM?
BECAUSE I CAN SEE THE TRAP.

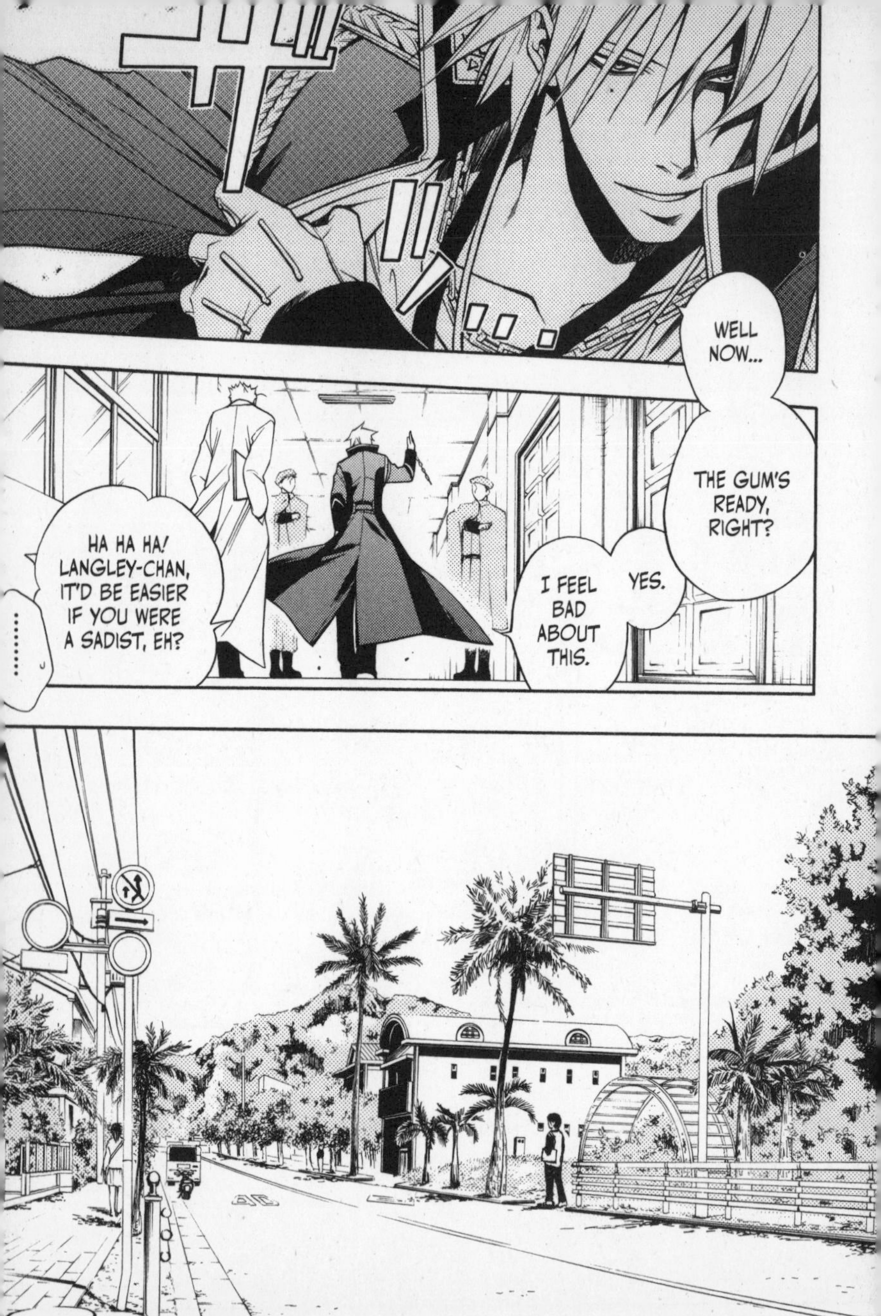
WELL NOW...
THE GUM'S READY, RIGHT?
YES.
I FEEL BAD ABOUT THIS.
HA HA HA! LANGLEY-CHAN, IT'D BE EASIER IF YOU WERE A SADIST, EH?
....

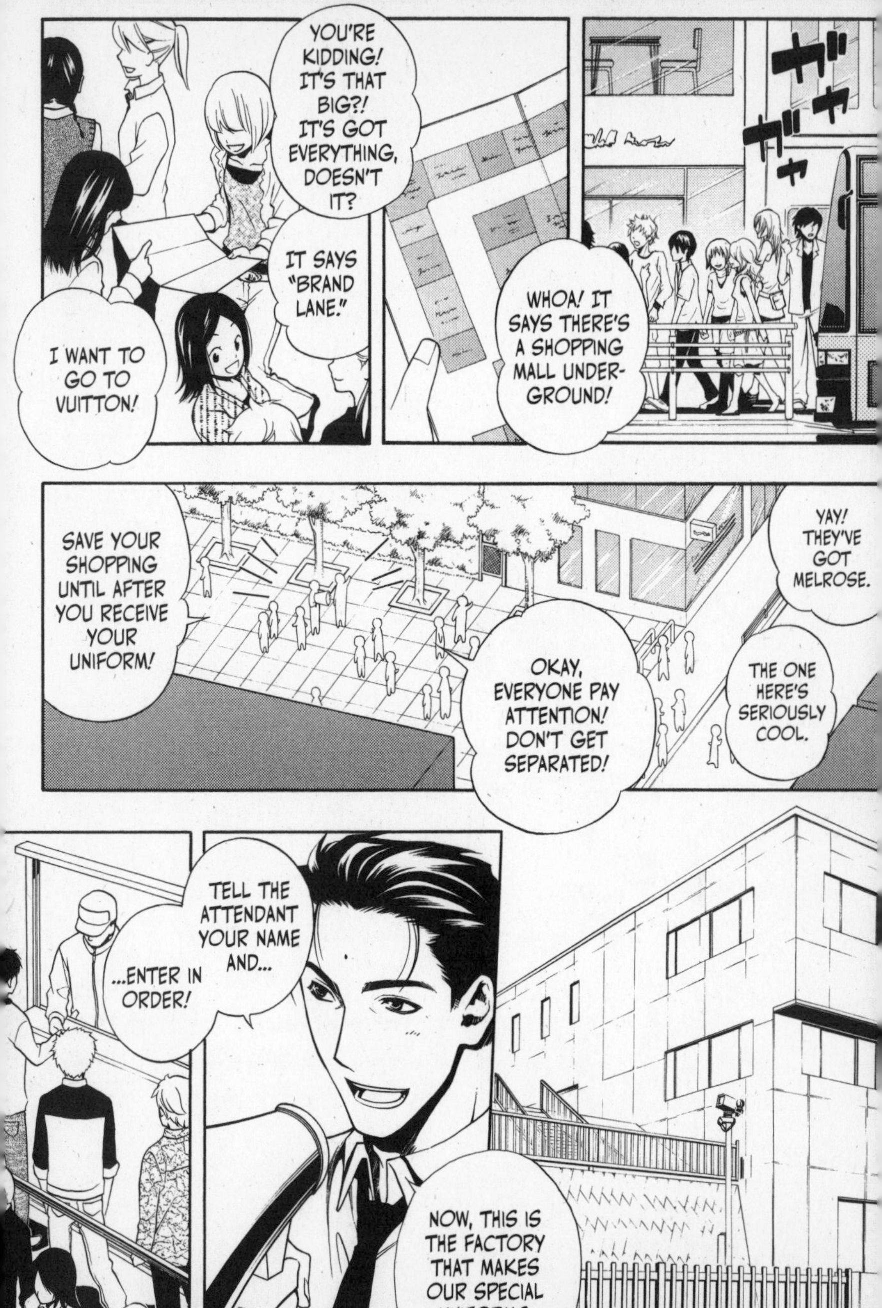
ガヤガヤ
WHOA! IT SAYS THERE'S A SHOPPING MALL UNDER-GROUND!
YOU'RE KIDDING! IT'S THAT BIG?! IT'S GOT EVERYTHING, DOESN'T IT?
IT SAYS "BRAND LANE."
I WANT TO GO TO VUITTON!
YAY! THEY'VE GOT MELROSE.
THE ONE HERE'S SERIOUSLY COOL.
OKAY, EVERYONE PAY ATTENTION! DON'T GET SEPARATED!
SAVE YOUR SHOPPING UNTIL AFTER YOU RECEIVE YOUR UNIFORM!
NOW, THIS IS THE FACTORY THAT MAKES OUR SPECIAL UNIFORMS.
TELL THE ATTENDANT YOUR NAME AND...
...ENTER IN ORDER!

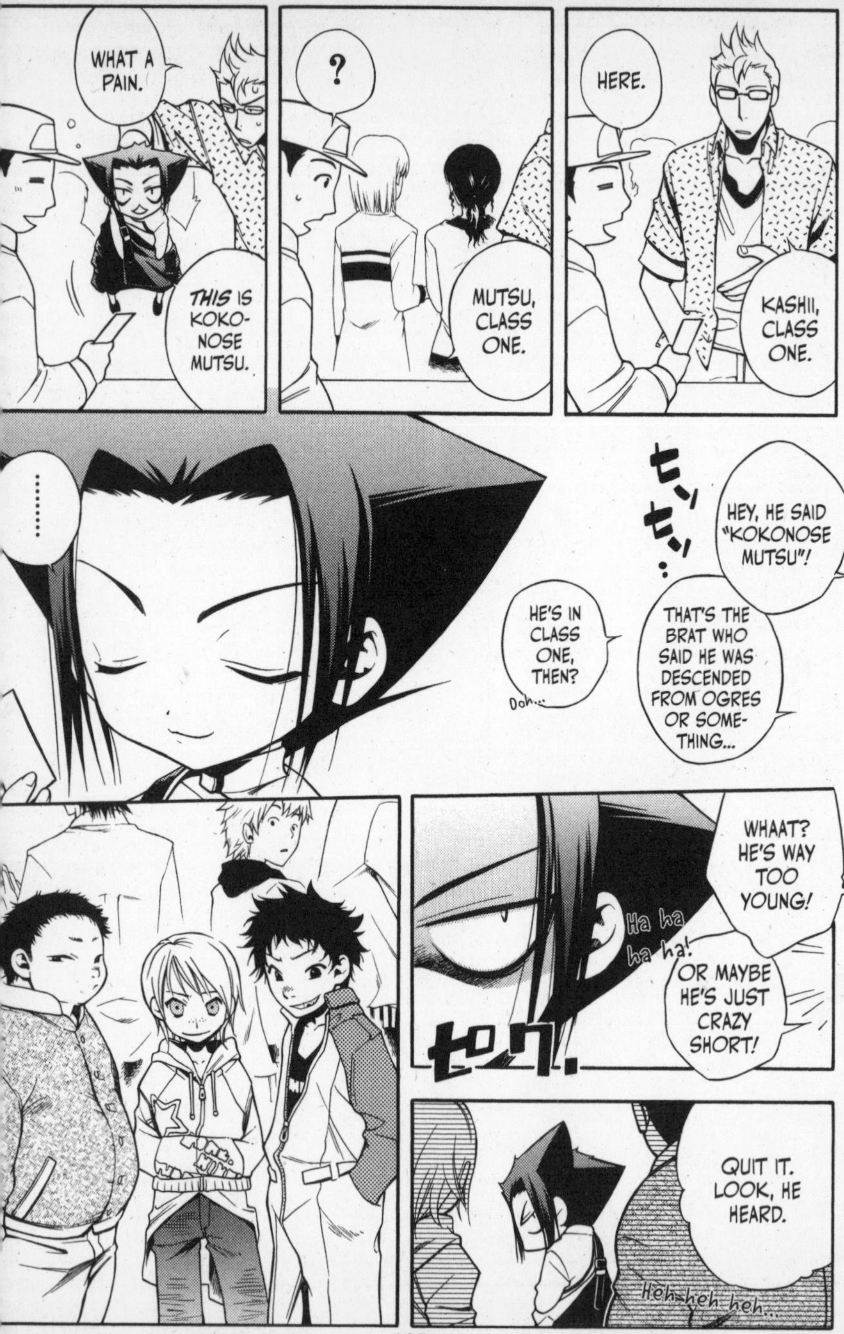
KASHII, CLASS ONE.
HERE.
?
MUTSU, CLASS ONE.
WHAT A PAIN.
THIS IS KOKONOSE MUTSU.
HEY, HE SAID "KOKONOSE MUTSU"!
THAT'S THE BRAT WHO SAID HE WAS DESCENDED FROM OGRES OR SOMETHING...
HE'S IN CLASS ONE, THEN?
Ooh...
....
WHAAT? HE'S WAY TOO YOUNG!
Ha ha ha ha!
OR MAYBE HE'S JUST CRAZY SHORT!
QUIT IT. LOOK, HE HEARD.
Heh heh heh...

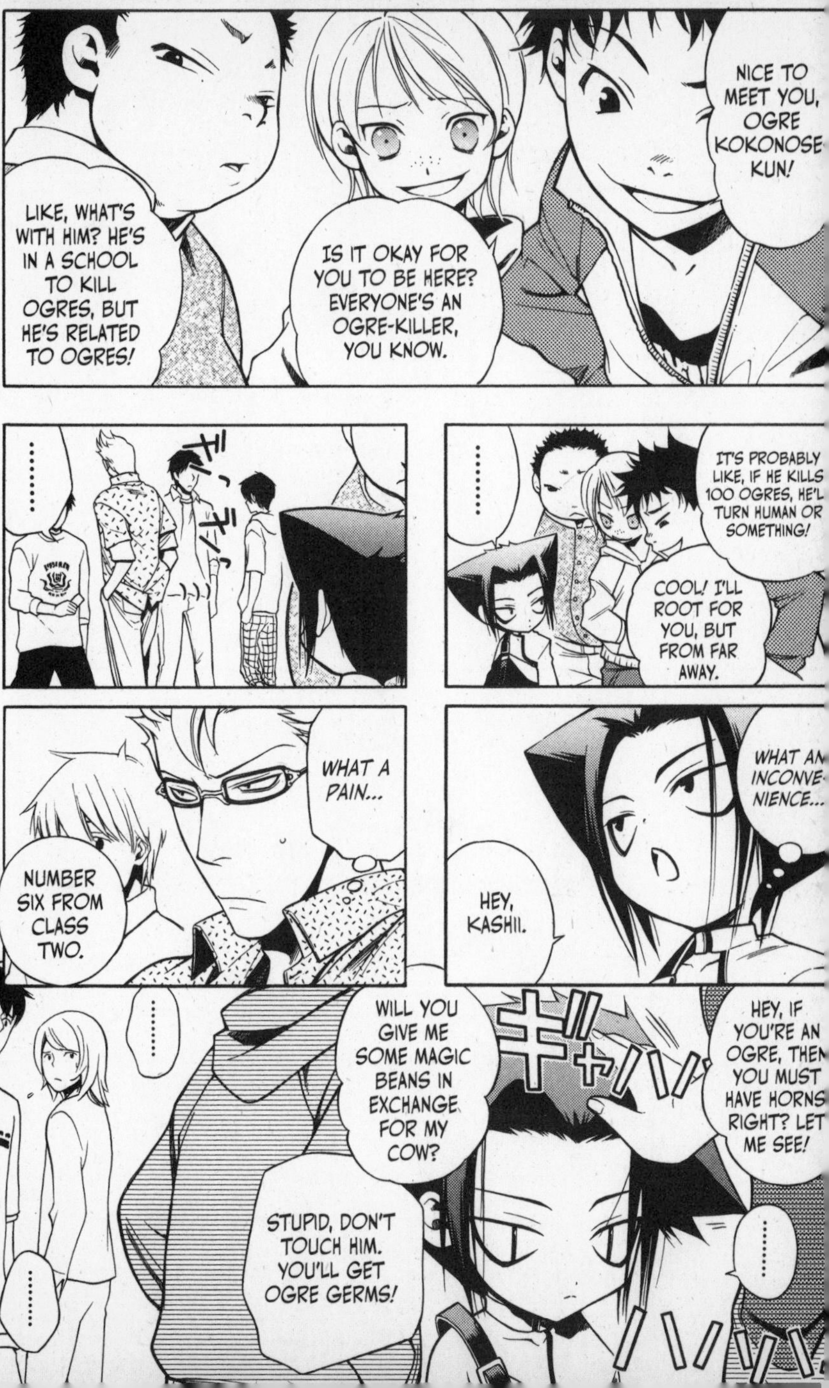
NICE TO MEET YOU, OGRE KOKONOSE KUN!
IS IT OKAY FOR YOU TO BE HERE? EVERYONE'S AN OGRE-KILLER, YOU KNOW.
LIKE, WHAT'S WITH HIM? HE'S IN A SCHOOL TO KILL OGRES, BUT HE'S RELATED TO OGRES!
IT'S PROBABLY LIKE, IF HE KILLS 100 OGRES, HE'L TURN HUMAN OR SOMETHING!
COOL! I'LL ROOT FOR YOU, BUT FROM FAR AWAY.
......
......
WHAT AN INCONVE NIENCE...
HEY, KASHII.
WHAT A PAIN...
NUMBER SIX FROM CLASS TWO.
HEY, IF YOU'RE AN OGRE, THEN YOU MUST HAVE HORNS RIGHT? LET ME SEE!
ギャハハ
WILL YOU GIVE ME SOME MAGIC BEANS IN EXCHANGE FOR MY COW?
......
......
STUPID, DON'T TOUCH HIM. YOU'LL GET OGRE GERMS!
......

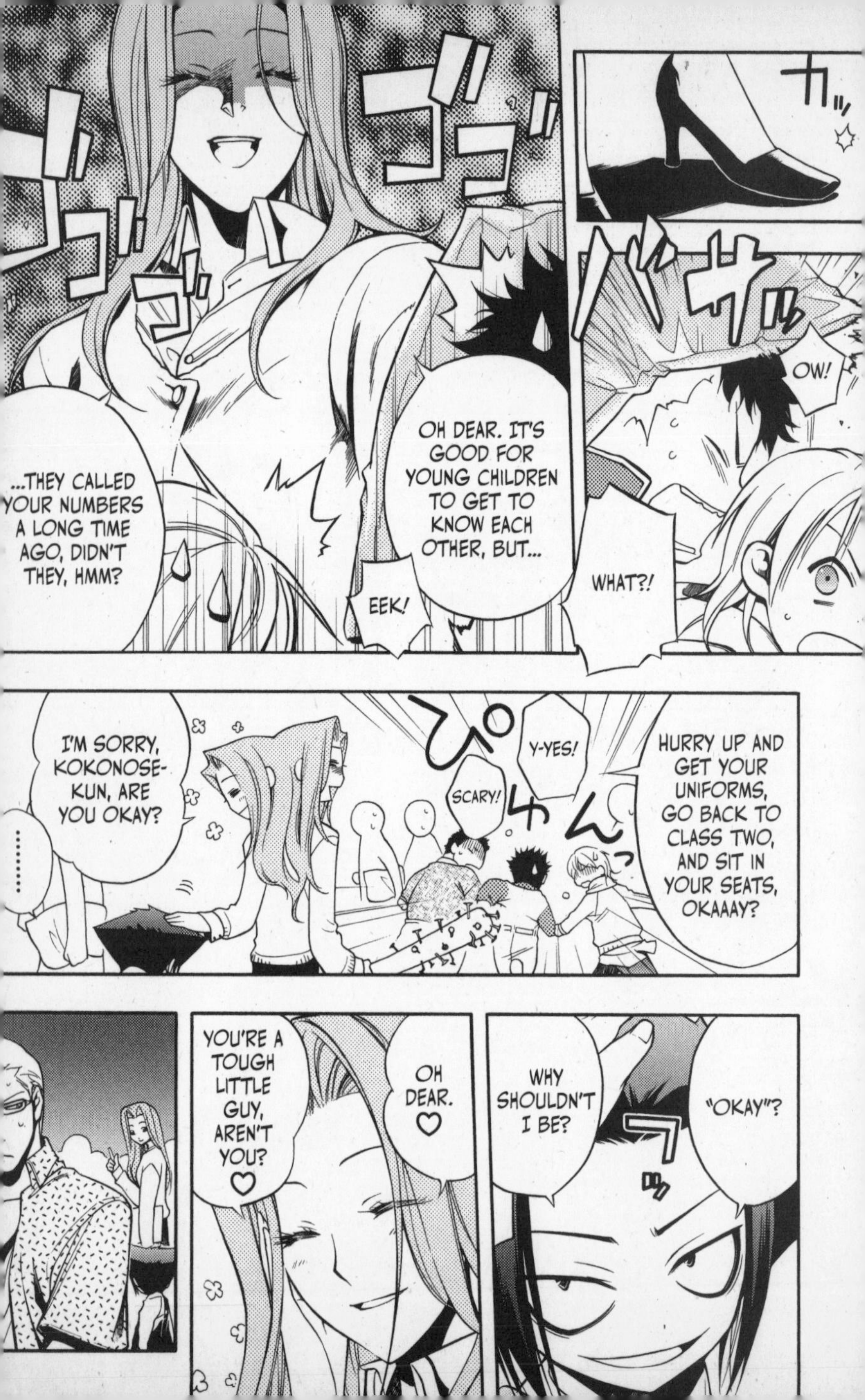
OW!
WHAT?!
OH DEAR. IT'S GOOD FOR YOUNG CHILDREN TO GET TO KNOW EACH OTHER, BUT...
EEK!
...THEY CALLED YOUR NUMBERS A LONG TIME AGO, DIDN'T THEY, HMM?
HURRY UP AND GET YOUR UNIFORMS, GO BACK TO CLASS TWO, AND SIT IN YOUR SEATS, OKAAAY?
Y-YES!
SCARY!
I'M SORRY, KOKONOSE-KUN, ARE YOU OKAY?
......
"OKAY"?
WHY SHOULDN'T I BE?
OH DEAR. ♡
YOU'RE A TOUGH LITTLE GUY, AREN'T YOU? ♡

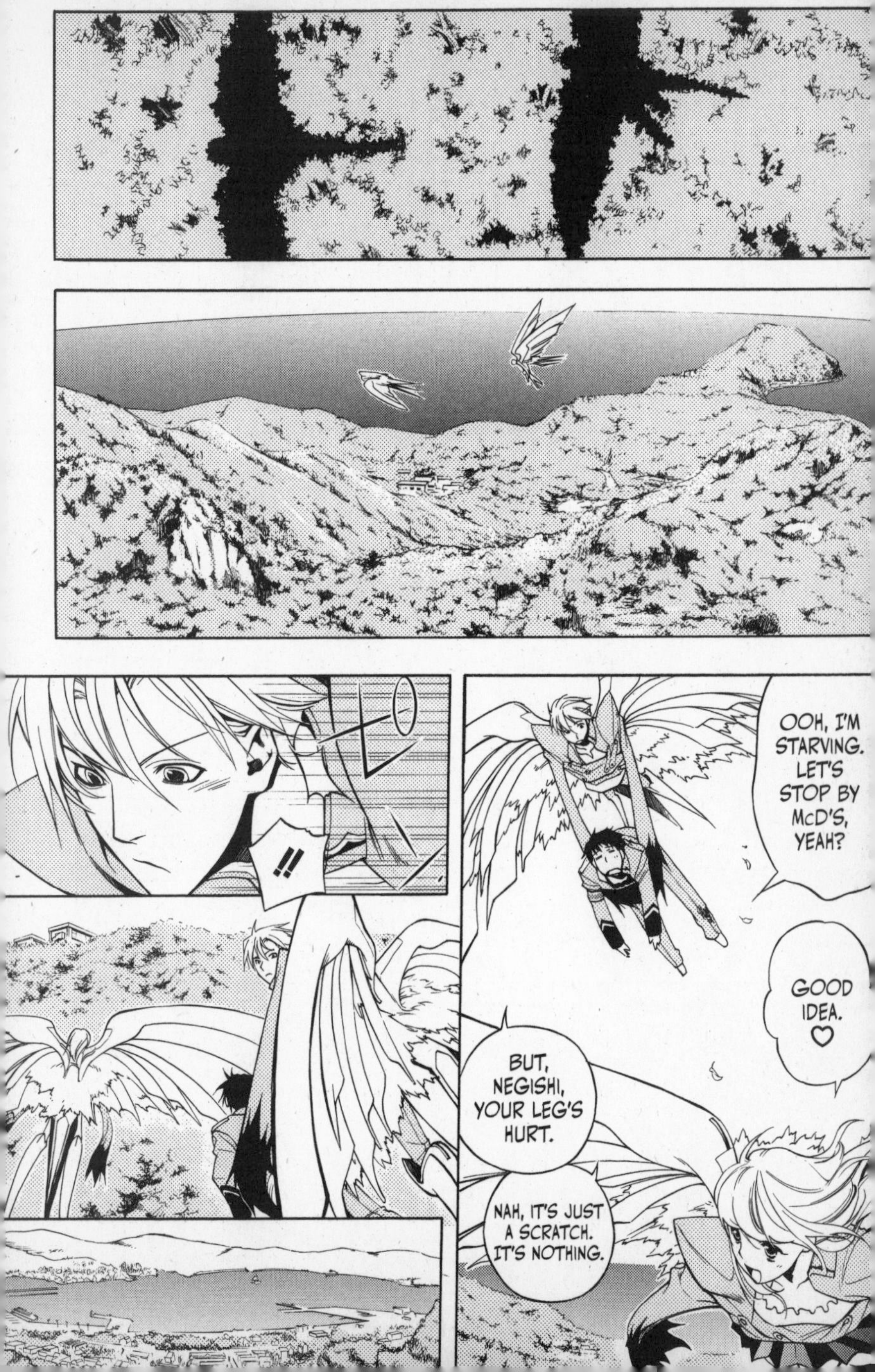
OOH, I'M STARVING. LET'S STOP BY McD'S, YEAH?
GOOD IDEA. ♡
BUT, NEGISHI, YOUR LEG'S HURT.
NAH, IT'S JUST A SCRATCH. IT'S NOTHING.
!!

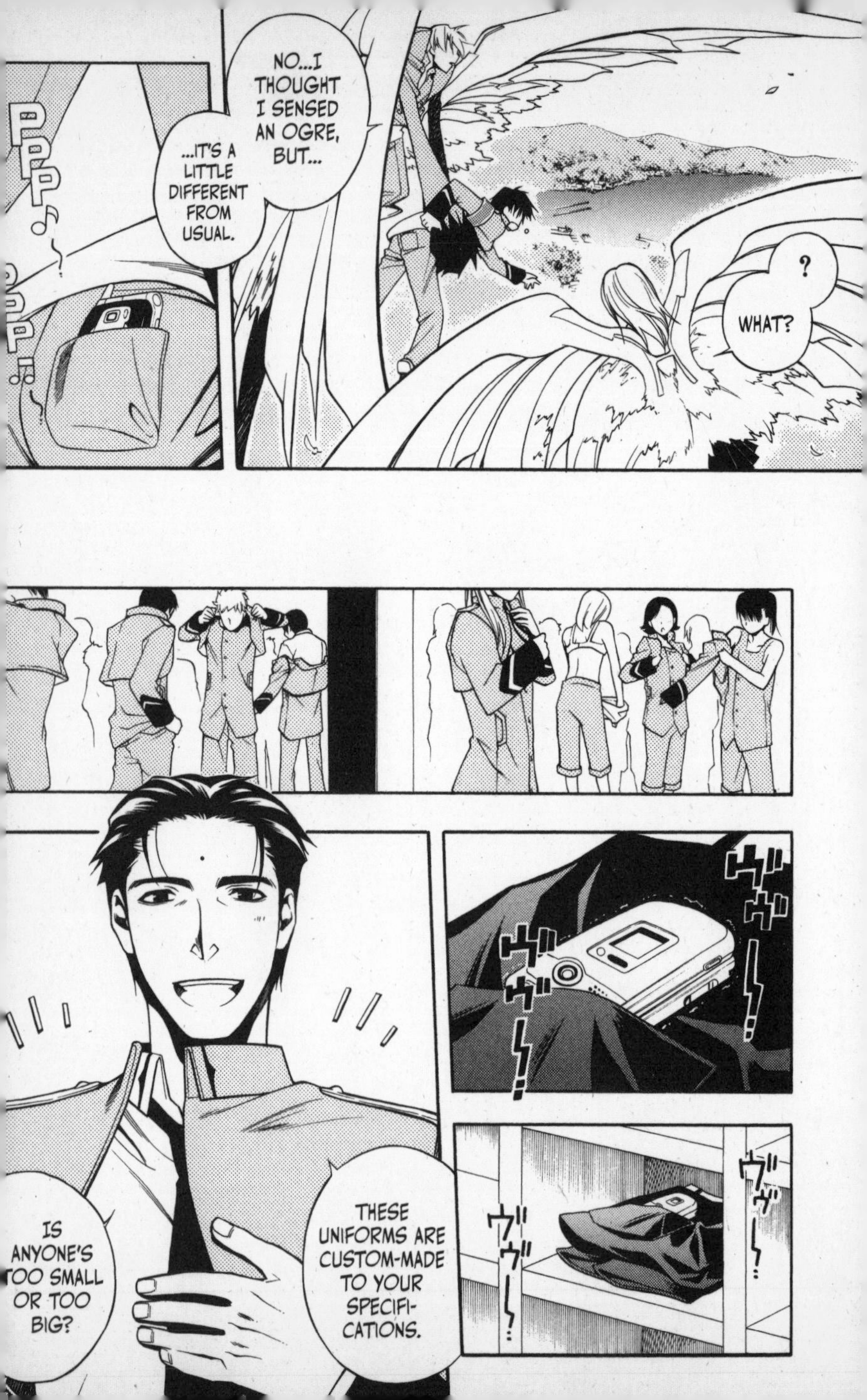
?
WHAT?
NO...I THOUGHT I SENSED AN OGRE, BUT...
...IT'S A LITTLE DIFFERENT FROM USUAL.
PPP♪
PPP♪
ヴヴー!
ヴヴー!
ヴヴー…
ヴヴー…
THESE UNIFORMS ARE CUSTOM-MADE TO YOUR SPECIFI-CATIONS.
IS ANYONE'S TOO SMALL OR TOO BIG?

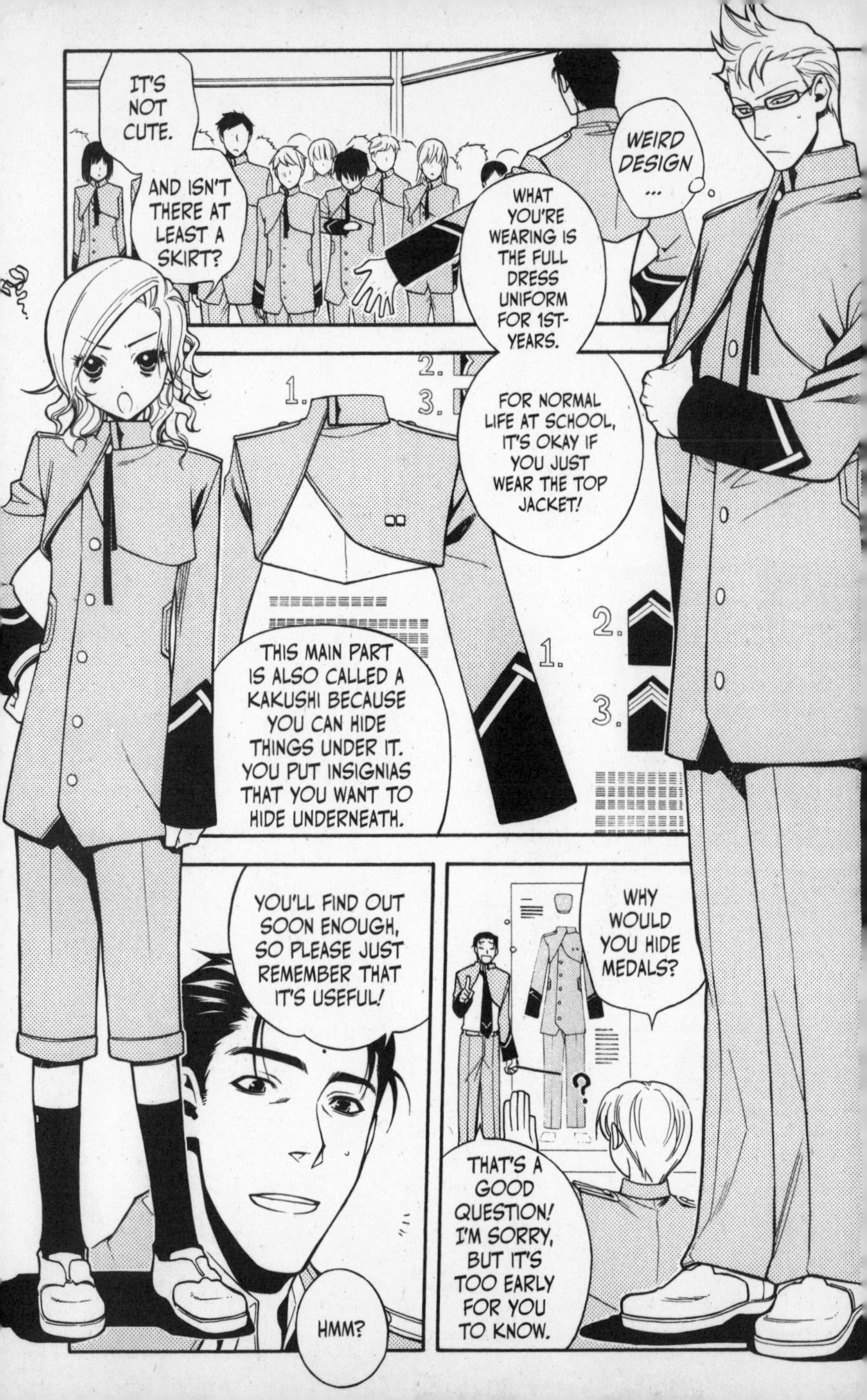
WEIRD DESIGN...
WHAT YOU'RE WEARING IS THE FULL DRESS UNIFORM FOR 1ST-YEARS.
IT'S NOT CUTE.
AND ISN'T THERE AT LEAST A SKIRT?
FOR NORMAL LIFE AT SCHOOL, IT'S OKAY IF YOU JUST WEAR THE TOP JACKET!
THIS MAIN PART IS ALSO CALLED A KAKUSHI BECAUSE YOU CAN HIDE THINGS UNDER IT. YOU PUT INSIGNIAS THAT YOU WANT TO HIDE UNDERNEATH.
WHY WOULD YOU HIDE MEDALS?
THAT'S A GOOD QUESTION! I'M SORRY, BUT IT'S TOO EARLY FOR YOU TO KNOW.
YOU'LL FIND OUT SOON ENOUGH, SO PLEASE JUST REMEMBER THAT IT'S USEFUL!
HMM?

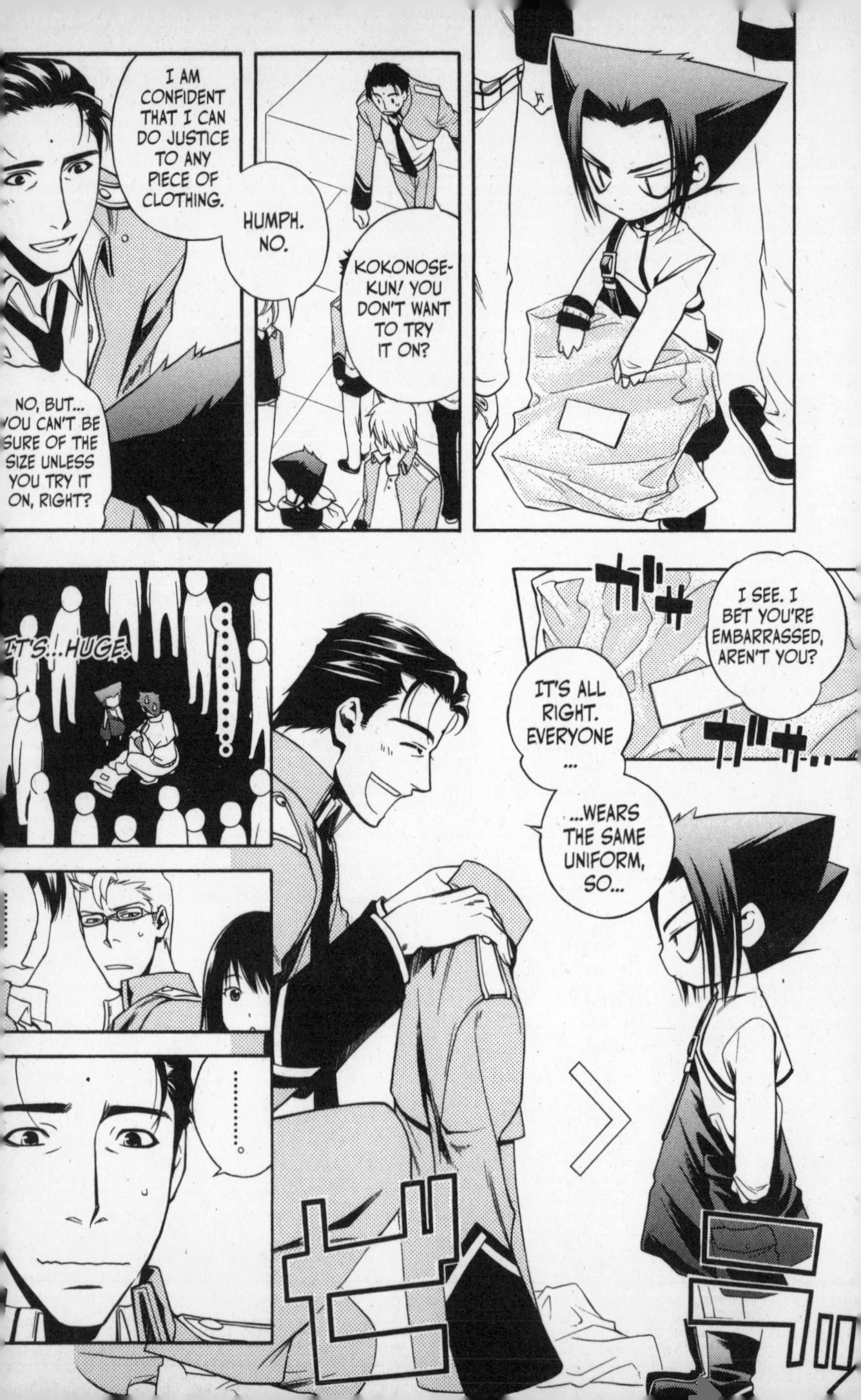
KOKONOSE-KUN! YOU DON'T WANT TO TRY IT ON?
HUMPH. NO.
I AM CONFIDENT THAT I CAN DO JUSTICE TO ANY PIECE OF CLOTHING.
NO, BUT... YOU CAN'T BE SURE OF THE SIZE UNLESS YOU TRY IT ON, RIGHT?
ガサ
I SEE. I BET YOU'RE EMBARRASSED, AREN'T YOU?
IT'S ALL RIGHT. EVERYONE ...
...WEARS THE SAME UNIFORM, SO...
ガサ..
IT'S...HUGE.
....
....

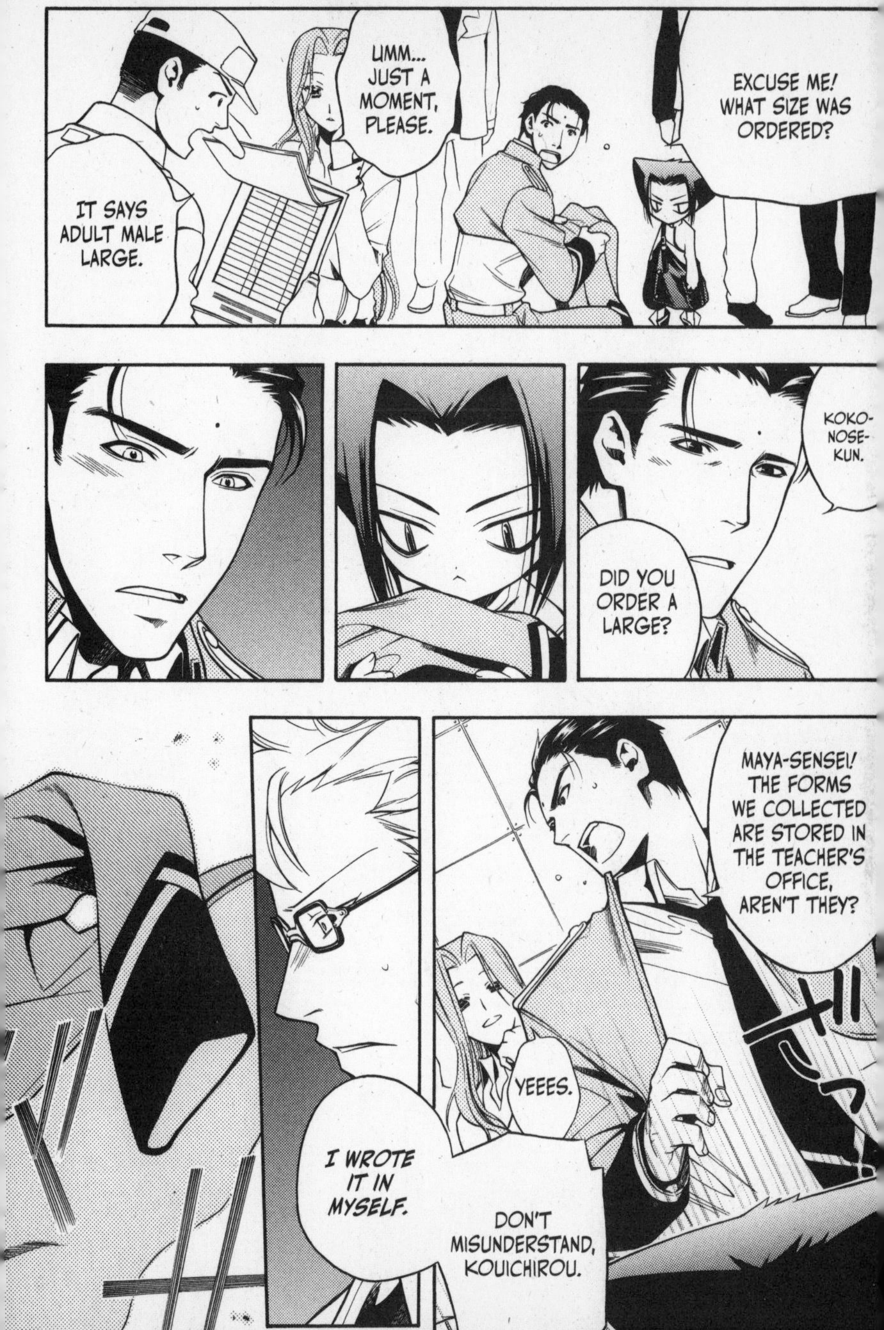
EXCUSE ME! WHAT SIZE WAS ORDERED?
UMM... JUST A MOMENT, PLEASE.
IT SAYS ADULT MALE LARGE.
KOKO-NOSE-KUN.
DID YOU ORDER A LARGE?
MAYA-SENSEI! THE FORMS WE COLLECTED ARE STORED IN THE TEACHER'S OFFICE, AREN'T THEY?
YEEES.
DON'T MISUNDERSTAND, KOUICHIROU.
I WROTE IT IN MYSELF.

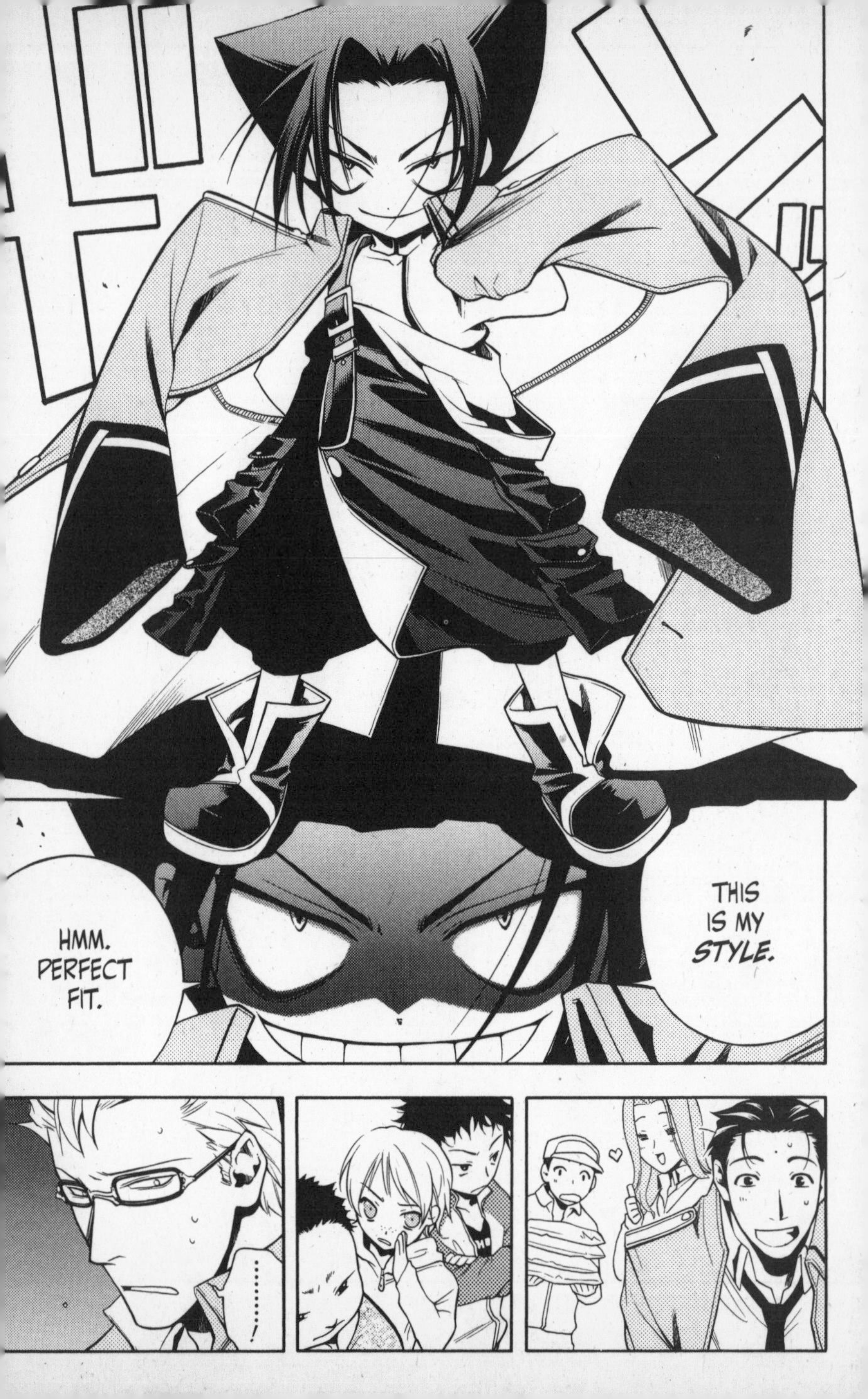
THIS IS MY *STYLE.*
HMM. PERFECT FIT.
......!

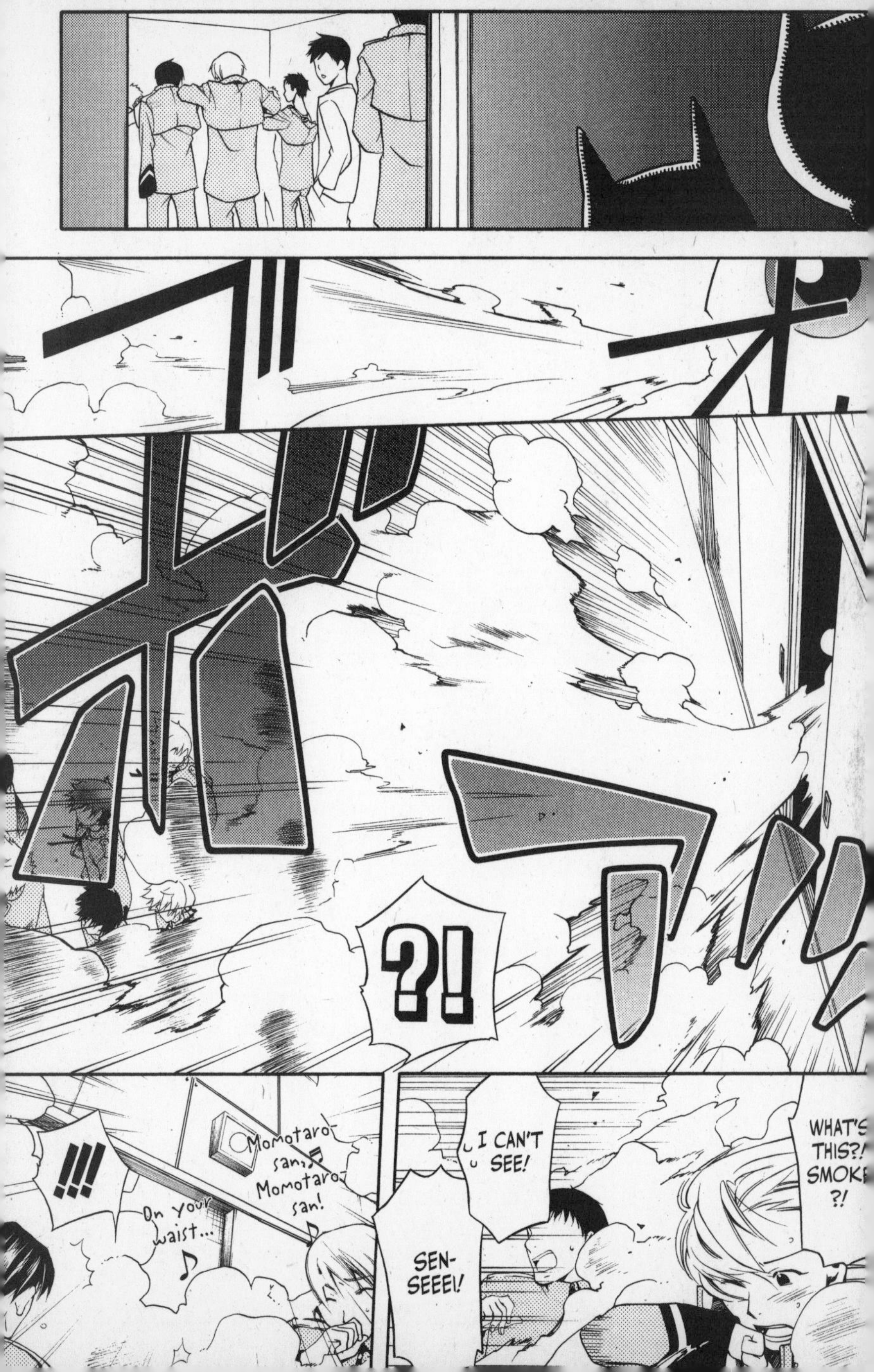
?!
WHAT'S THIS?! SMOKE?!
I CAN'T SEE!
SEN-SEEEI!
Momotaro-san, Momotaro-san!
!!!
On your waist...

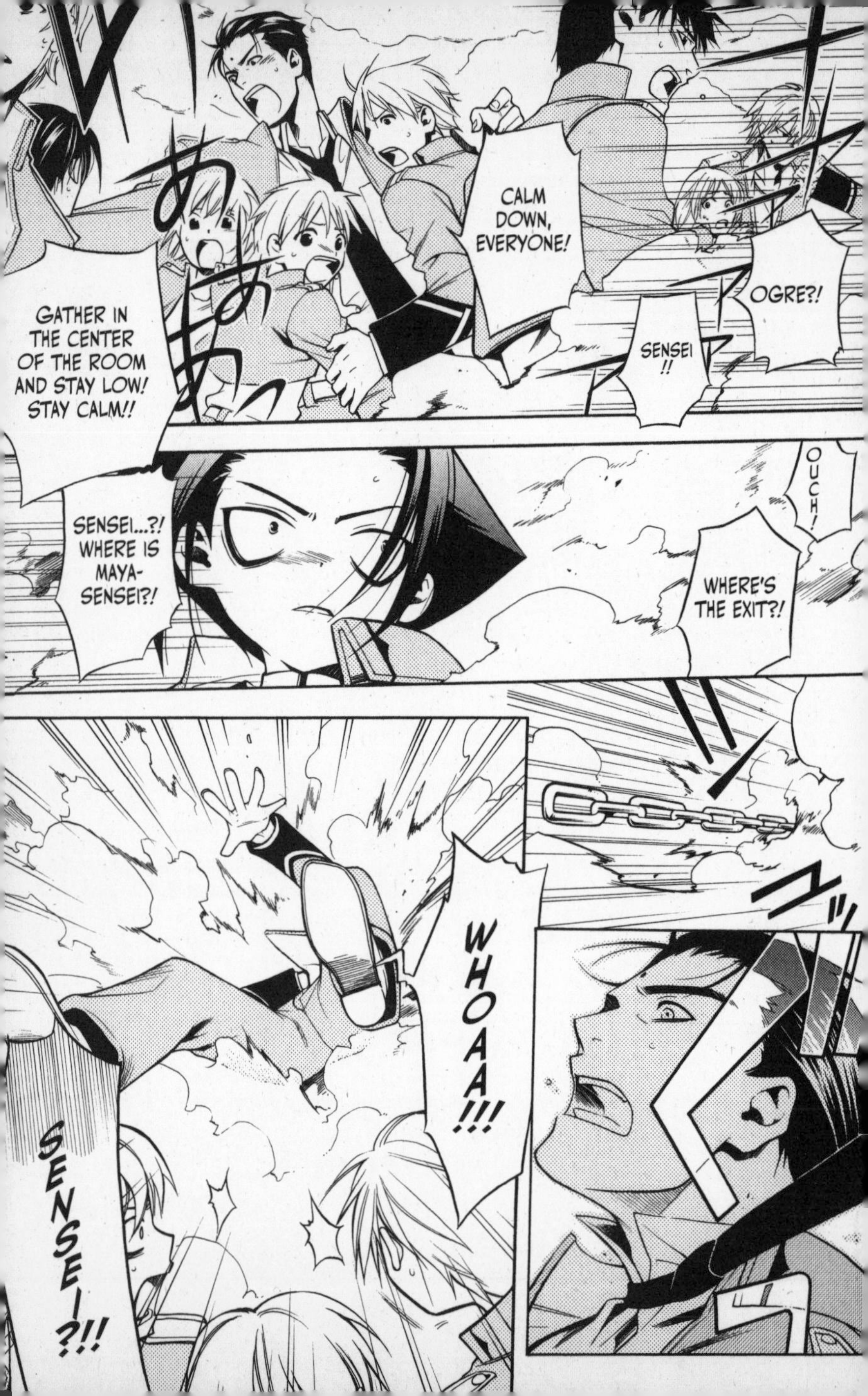
OGRE?!
SENSEI !!
CALM DOWN, EVERYONE!
GATHER IN THE CENTER OF THE ROOM AND STAY LOW! STAY CALM!!
OUCH!
WHERE'S THE EXIT?!
SENSEI...?! WHERE IS MAYA-SENSEI?!
WHOAAA!!!
SENSEI?!!

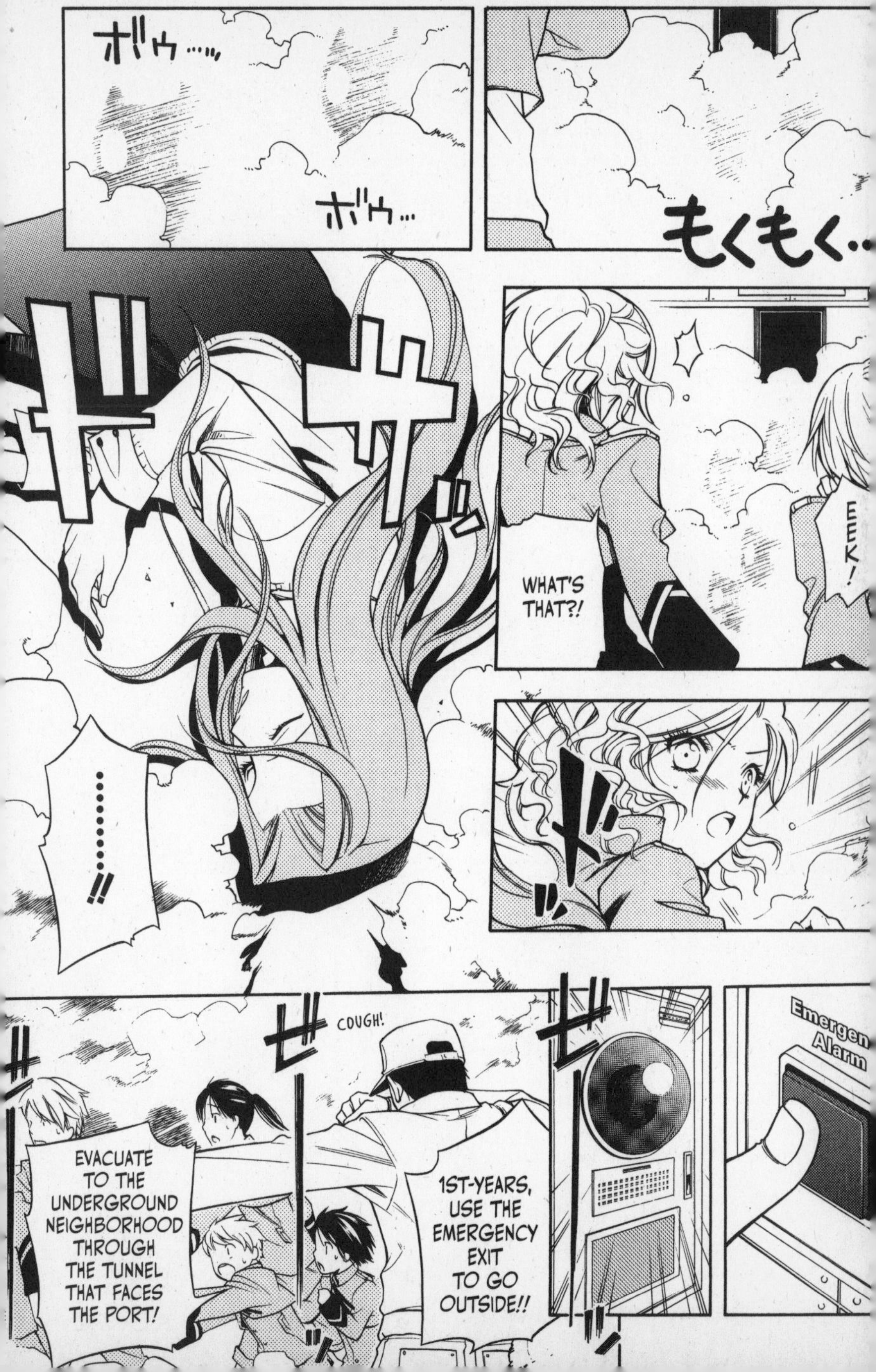
もくもく…
ボウ…ッ
ボウ…
EEK!
WHAT'S THAT?!
ドッ
ザザッ
……!!
Emergen
Alarm
ゼ
1ST-YEARS, USE THE EMERGENCY EXIT TO GO OUTSIDE!!
ゼ
COUGH!
ゼ
EVACUATE TO THE UNDERGROUND NEIGHBORHOOD THROUGH THE TUNNEL THAT FACES THE PORT!

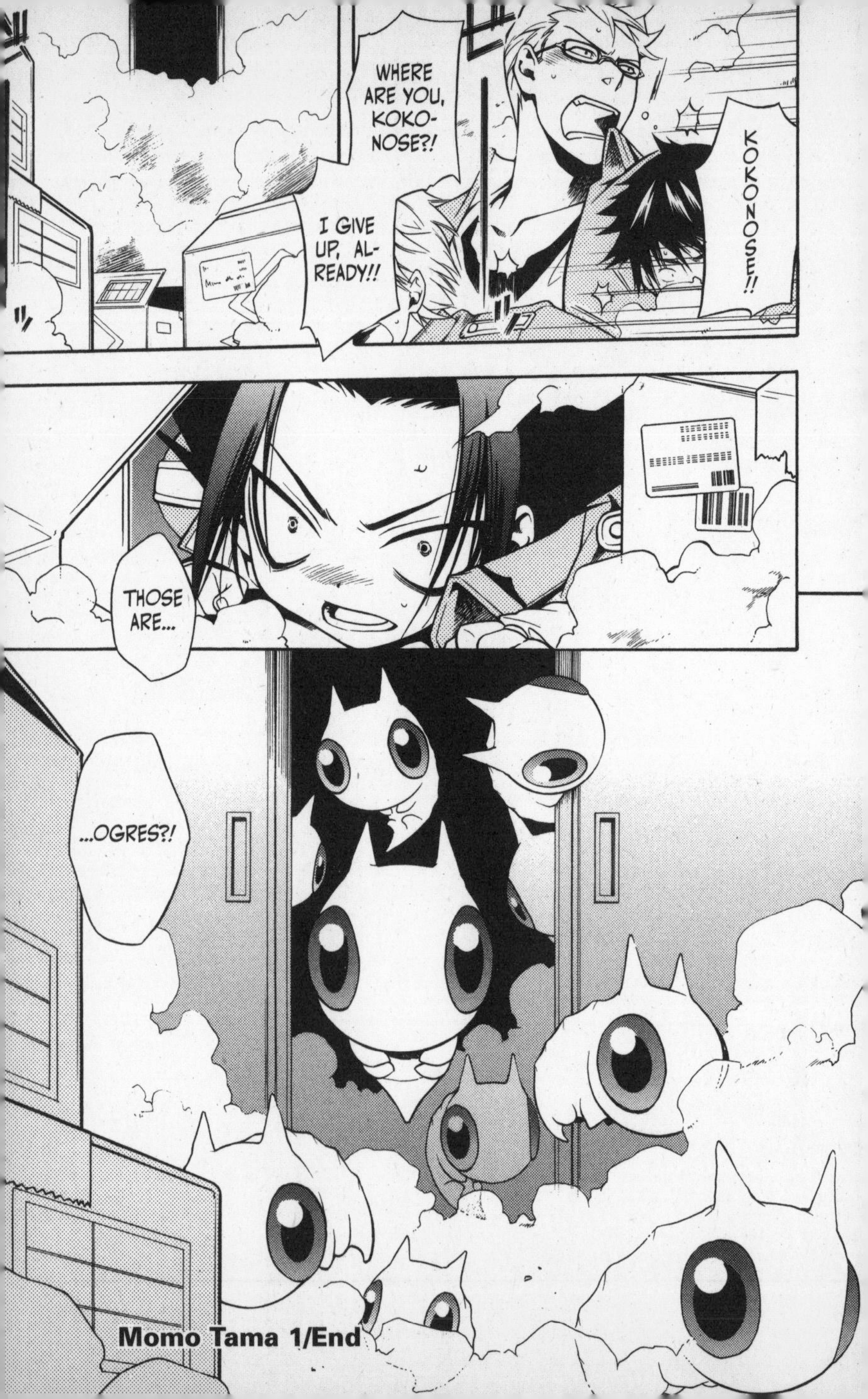
KOKONOSE!!
WHERE ARE YOU, KOKO-NOSE?!
I GIVE UP, AL-READY!!
THOSE ARE...
...OGRES?!

Momo Tama 1/End

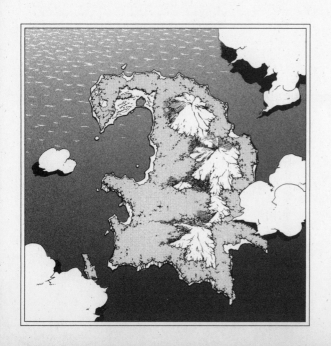

Afterword

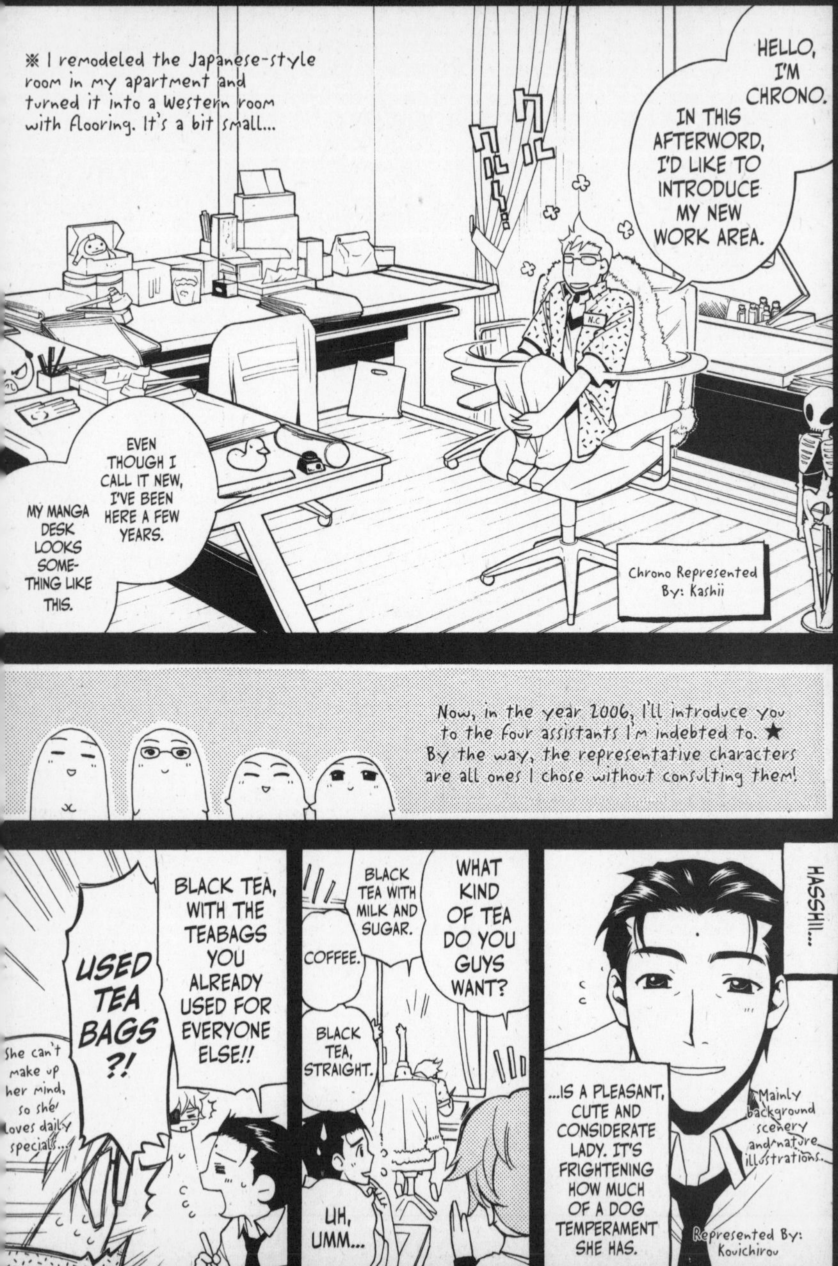
HELLO, I'M CHRONO.
IN THIS AFTERWORD, I'D LIKE TO INTRODUCE MY NEW WORK AREA.
Chrono Represented By: Kashii
※ I remodeled the Japanese-style room in my apartment and turned it into a Western room with flooring. It's a bit small...
EVEN THOUGH I CALL IT NEW, I'VE BEEN HERE A FEW YEARS.
MY MANGA DESK LOOKS SOMETHING LIKE THIS.
Now, in the year 2006, I'll introduce you to the four assistants I'm indebted to. ★ By the way, the representative characters are all ones I chose without consulting them!
HASSHII...
...IS A PLEASANT, CUTE AND CONSIDERATE LADY. IT'S FRIGHTENING HOW MUCH OF A DOG TEMPERAMENT SHE HAS.
Mainly background scenery and nature illustrations.
Represented By: Kouichirou
WHAT KIND OF TEA DO YOU GUYS WANT?
BLACK TEA WITH MILK AND SUGAR.
COFFEE.
BLACK TEA, STRAIGHT.
UH, UMM...
BLACK TEA, WITH THE TEABAGS YOU ALREADY USED FOR EVERYONE ELSE!!
USED TEA BAGS?!
She can't make up her mind, so she loves daily specials...

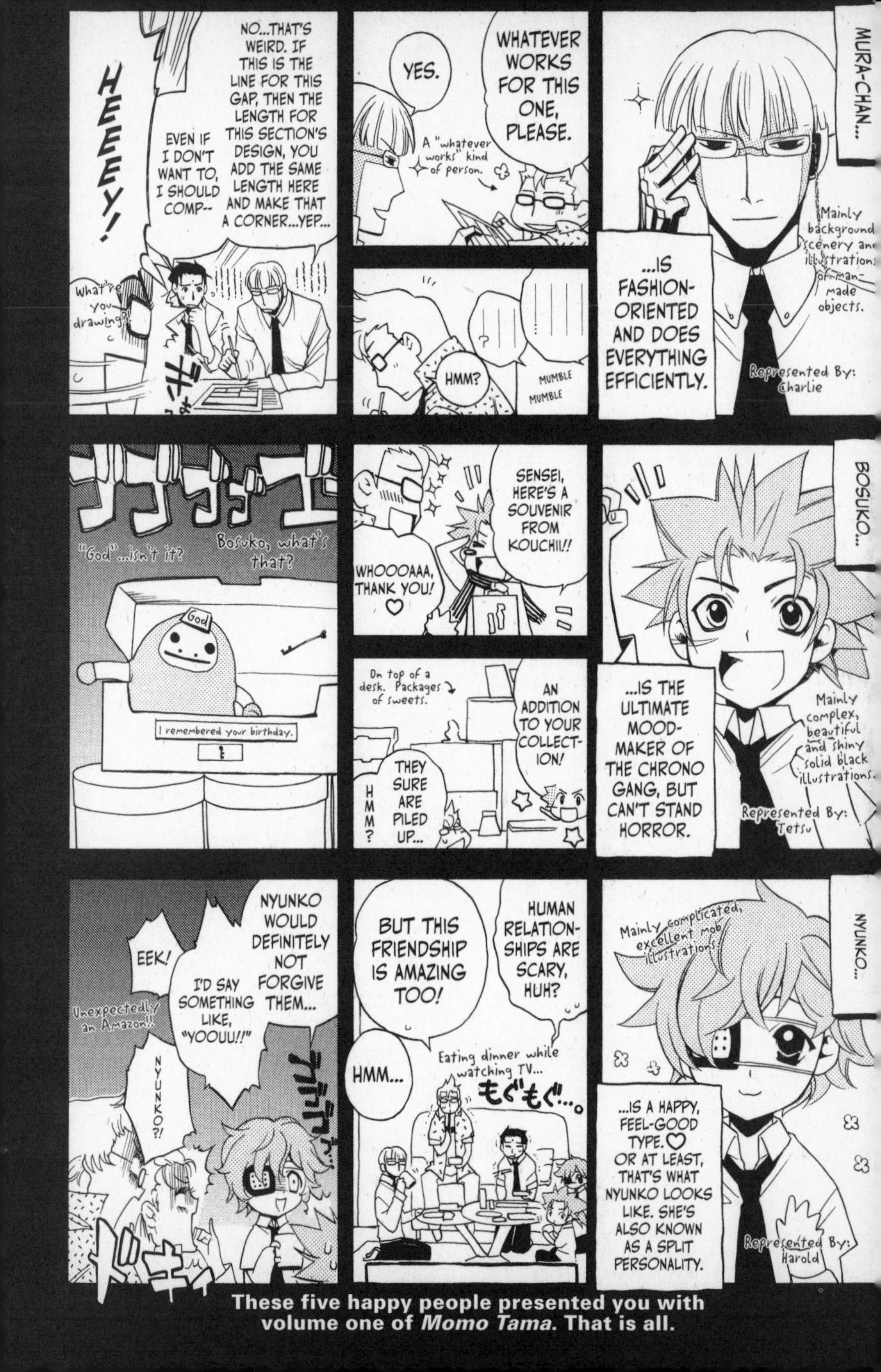
MURA-CHAN...
...IS FASHION-ORIENTED AND DOES EVERYTHING EFFICIENTLY.
Mainly background scenery an illustrations of man-made objects.
Represented By: Charlie
YES.
WHATEVER WORKS FOR THIS ONE, PLEASE.
A "whatever works" kind of person.
HMM?
MUMBLE MUMBLE
NO...THAT'S WEIRD. IF THIS IS THE LINE FOR THIS GAP, THEN THE LENGTH FOR THIS SECTION'S DESIGN, YOU ADD THE SAME LENGTH HERE AND MAKE THAT A CORNER...YEP...
EVEN IF I DON'T WANT TO, I SHOULD COMP--
HEEEEY!
What're you drawing?!
BOSUKO...
...IS THE ULTIMATE MOOD-MAKER OF THE CHRONO GANG, BUT CAN'T STAND HORROR.
Mainly complex, beautiful and shiny solid black illustrations.
Represented By: Tetsu
SENSEI, HERE'S A SOUVENIR FROM KOUCHI!!
WHOOOAAA, THANK YOU! ♡
On top of a desk. Packages of sweets.
AN ADDITION TO YOUR COLLECTION!
THEY SURE ARE PILED UP...
HMM?
Bosuko, what's that?
"God"...isn't it?
God
I remembered your birthday.
NYUNKO...
Mainly complicated, excellent mob illustrations.
...IS A HAPPY, FEEL-GOOD TYPE. ♡ OR AT LEAST, THAT'S WHAT NYUNKO LOOKS LIKE. SHE'S ALSO KNOWN AS A SPLIT PERSONALITY.
Represented By: Harold
HUMAN RELATIONSHIPS ARE SCARY, HUH?
BUT THIS FRIENDSHIP IS AMAZING TOO!
HMM...
Eating dinner while watching TV...
もぐもぐ…。
NYUNKO WOULD DEFINITELY NOT FORGIVE THEM...
I'D SAY SOMETHING LIKE, "YOOUU!!"
EEK!
Unexpectedly an Amazon!!
NYUNKO?!

These five happy people presented you with volume one of *Momo Tama*. That is all.

In the Next Volume of

THE OGRES SUCCESSFULLY INVADE THE ONCE IMPENETRABLE SCHOOL GROUNDS. FOR REASONS EVEN KOKONOSE CAN'T FATHOM, THE PUPPY-EYED, CUTE LITTLE OGRES KIDNAP THE NINTH SUCCESSOR ALONG WITH SOME OF HIS FELLOW CLASSMATES. WILL KOKONOSE UNLEASH HIS MONSTROUS POWERS AND LET THE LITTLE BUGGERS HAVE IT, RETURNING HOME A HERO WITH AN EVEN BIGGER EGO? OR WILL HE RETURN AS A PATHETIC RUNT WHO HAD TO BE RESCUED BY SENKISHI ONCE AGAIN?

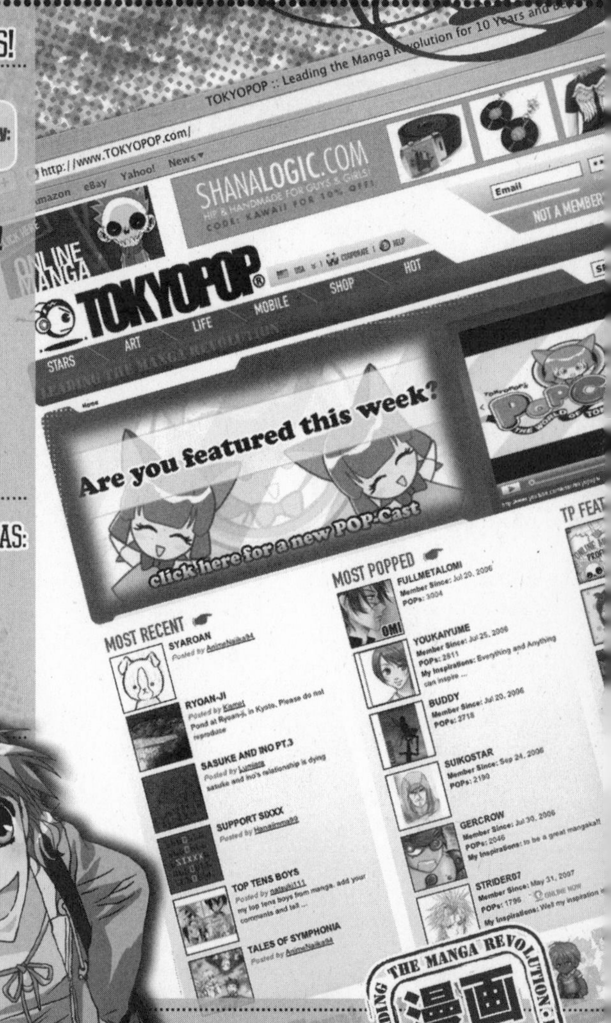

TOKYOPOP :: Leading the Manga Revolution for 10 Years and Beyond
http://www.TOKYOPOP.com/
Amazon eBay Yahoo! News
SHANALOGIC.COM
HIP & HANDMADE FOR GUYS & GIRLS!
CODE: KAWAII FOR 10% OFF!
Email
NOT A MEMBER
ONLINE MANGA
TOKYOPOP®
STARS ART LIFE MOBILE SHOP HOT
LEADING THE MANGA REVOLUTION
Are you featured this week?
click here for a new POP-Cast
MOST RECENT
SYAROAN
RYOAN-JI
SASUKE AND INO PT.3
SUPPORT SIXXX
TOP TENS BOYS
TALES OF SYMPHONIA
MOST POPPED
FULLMETALOMI
YOUKAIYUME
BUDDY
SUIKOSTAR
GERCROW
STRIDER07
TP FEATURES

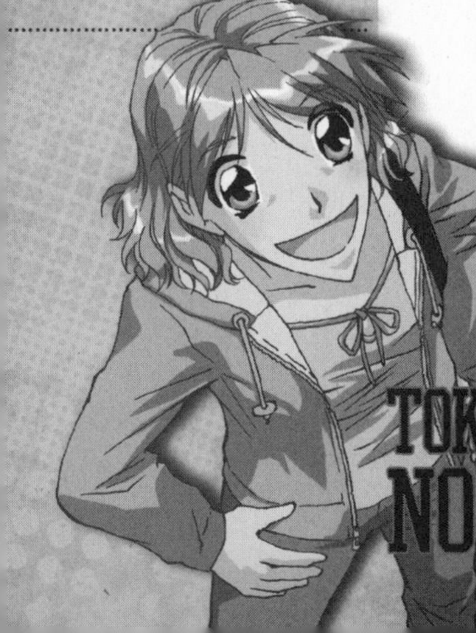

STOP!

This is the back of the book.
You wouldn't want to spoil a great ending!

This book is printed "manga-style," in the authentic Japanese right-to-left format. Since none of the artwork has been flipped or altered, readers get to experience the story just as the creator intended. You've been asking for it, so TOKYOPOP® delivered: authentic, hot-off-the-press, and far more fun!

DIRECTIONS

If this is your first time reading manga-style, here's a quick guide to help you understand how it works.

It's easy... just start in the top right panel and follow the numbers. Have fun, and look for more 100% authentic manga from TOKYOPOP®!